Locational Analysis in Human Geography

Locational Analysis in Human Geography

PETER HAGGETT

Professor of Urban and Regional Geography in the
University of Bristol

 EDWARD ARNOLD

FOR PIER

© Peter Haggett 1965
First published 1965 by
Edward Arnold (Publishers) Ltd.
41 Maddox Street, London W.1
Reprinted 1966
Reprinted 1967
Reprinted 1968
Reprinted 1969
Reprinted 1970
Reprinted 1971

ISBN 0 7131 5179 X

Printed in Great Britain by
Butler & Tanner Ltd, Frome and London

Preface

Locational studies have only recently begun to recover from the tragic loss of their most original and provocative scholar. August Lösch died in 1945 at the age of only thirty-nine and it is clear, both from the preface to the second edition of his major work and from its tantalizing footnotes, that he believed himself to be standing on the very edge of a new breakthrough. Isolated in wartime Kiel from the American data on which he relied so heavily for his empirical tests and unwilling '. . . to offer what may be attractive . . . but would not stand a rigid test' he was forced to stand with hands tied before a harvest he could see but not reap.

In the twenty years since Lösch's death the pace and quality of locational research has begun to quicken. In the United States a group of economists led by Isard and groups of geographers led by scholars like Garrison and Berry have struck out into new country, while in Sweden the Hägerstrand school has given a new impetus to temporal studies. For English geographers these developments have been both exciting and disturbing. Exciting because they promised to breathe life into traditional human geography which—with a few exceptions—remained wedded to conservative regional or commodity lines or split-up into confusing subvarieties like 'resource' geography or 'medical' geography. Disturbing because they increasingly used mathematical methods and were scattered with unfamiliar and unwelcome incognitas like Eigen values or Beta coefficients.

On returning to Cambridge in 1957 I found myself increasingly conscious of this problem—particularly as it affected undergraduate geographers. So it was that I began to develop somewhat haltingly a course of lectures which tried to set out what I thought was happening in locational research (both as regards concepts and method) and why I thought it important they should know something of it. It was one of my colleagues, Richard Chorley, who encouraged me to convert the spoken word into the written and so it was that the chapters of this book began to emerge from the much-thumbed and much-revised lecture notes used for the course. It still bears the marks of its classroom origin and I am much indebted to Mrs Marion Clegg who did much to tease out my terse phrases into something more nearly recognizable as English prose. For her hours of careful revision I am most grateful, as I am to Miss Gillian Seymour who skilfully converted my rough blackboard sketches into the many illustrations scattered throughout this book.

In the years this book has been a-writing research has continued to pour out and already some significant syntheses like those of Alonso, Bunge, and Chisholm have been published and several others, like

Garrison's symposium on quantitative geography, are promised. This volume is clearly then a report from an active battlefront rather than a well-rounded and reflective essay, and it may well be that this is a fairer picture of the present state of play: it could well be another twenty years before another major codification on the scale of Lösch's will be possible.

Throughout my studies I have been exceptionally fortunate in my teachers. Long ago my father introduced me to the landscape he loved around our Somerset home and there both family finances and petrol-rationing ensured that we followed Carl Sauer's dictum that '. . . loco-motion should be slow; the slower the better'. This small piece of country-side, like Lösch's native Swabia, seemed to illustrate most of the major locational questions and even to hint at their answers; later, larger and more rapidly traversed landscapes in southern Europe, in Brazil and in the western United States have been grafted on to this slow-grown native rootstock. It was Harold Storey who encouraged me to study geography formally at university, and to try for Cambridge. There, I was again fortunate in arriving at St Catharine's College in the same year as a newly elected Fellow, A. A. L. Caesar, and to find myself studying under him with a group of fellow undergraduates that included men as talented as Michael Chisholm, Peter Hall, Gerald Manners, and Ken Warren. Through all our later writing, including this book, run the marks of prolonged exposure in Cambridge 'supervisions' to Caesar's formidable powers of critical dissection and logical re-arrangement.

Since graduation my specific debts have gathered momentum and I cannot give any complete list of those who have helped this book on its way. My colleagues Richard Chorley and Tony Wrigley have always been ready with advice and encouragement and I might well have shelved the whole idea for some hypothetical 'future day' but for their active examples of industry and scholarship. I am likewise indebted to David Stoddart for his rare talent in digging out unexpected sources; to Christopher Board and David Harvey for reading and commenting on specific sections; to Michael Chisholm and Jay Vance for clarifying my thinking on many points; and to Brian Berry who, by encouraging me to gate-crash a Regional Science seminar at Berkeley in summer 1962, showed me how much I had still to learn on quantitative methods of analysis.

Finally to my wife, Brenda, I dedicate this book with great affection and still greater respect. The manuscript was written painfully slowly and almost entirely at home; only those who also have wives who simul-taneously cope single-handed with four very small children, deal with most of the correspondence, and create regular quiet spells for a husband in labour with his typewriter, can know the full extent of the debt I owe her.

PETER HAGGETT

Stapleford, Cambridgeshire. *Spring, 1965*

Contents*

* A detailed contents-list is given at the beginning of each of the ten chapters.

Acknowledgments

The Author and Publisher wish to express their thanks to the following for permission to reprint or modify material from copyright works:

The American Association of Petroleum Geologists for Figs., pp. 2170 & 2176, Vol. 40, 1956 (Paper by W. C. Krumbein) and Figs. 2 & 3, pp. 88–95, Vol. 44, 1960 (Paper by J. M. Forgotson), both from *Bulletin of the American Association of Petroleum Geologists*; the American Geographical Society for the following from *Geographical Review*: Fig. 5, Vol. 51, 1961 (Paper by E. N. Thomas), Figs. 3 & 5, Vol. 51, 1961 (Paper by J. R. Borchert), Figs. 1 & 5, Vol. 53, 1963 (Paper by E. N. Taaffe *et al.*), Figs. 1 & 10, Vol. 53, 1963 (Paper by B. J. L. Berry *et al.*); the American Geophysical Union and the author for Fig. 4 & Table 6, Vol. 36, 1955 from *Transactions* (Paper by W. C. Krumbein) from *Journal of Geophysical Research* (Paper by W. C. Krumbein) and Figs. 2, 3 & 4, Vol. 64, 1959; the American Zinc, Lead & Smelting Co. for Table VII–1, p. 134 and Table, p. 62 from C. H. Cotterill: *Industrial Plant Location*; the Association of American Geographers for the following from *Annals*: Fig. 1, Vol. 46, 1956 (Paper by A. H. Robinson), Table 4, Vol. 48, 1958 (Paper by L. Zobler), Table 1, Vol. 48, 1958 (Paper by B. J. L. Berry & W. Garrison), Table 2, Vol. 50, 1960 (Paper by M. F. Dacey), Table 1, Vol. 51, 1961 (Paper by L. J. King), Fig. 2 and Table, p. 214, Vol. 51, 1961 (Paper by A. H. Robinson *et al.*), Figs. 2 & 3, Vol. 52, 1962 (Paper by R. I. Wolfe), Figs. 2–15, Vol. 52, 1962 (Paper by J. H. Thompson *et al.*), Fig. 13, Vol. 52, 1962 (Paper by D. W. Meinig), Figs. 1 & 7, Vol. 53, 1963 (Paper by G. F. Jenks), Fig. 14, Vol. 53, 1963 (Paper by R. L. Morrill), Figs. 3 & 4, Vol. 53, 1963 (Paper by P. R. Gould), Table 1, Vol. 53, 1063 (Paper by H. G. Kariel), Fig. 1, Vol. 54, 1964 (Paper by R. J. Chorley), Fig. 2, Vol. 54, 1964 (Paper by J. Wolpert); the British Ecological Society for Fig. 1, Vol. 48, 1960 from *The Journal of Ecology* (Paper by W. T. Williams & J. M. Lambert); the *Bulletin of the Geological Society of America* and the authors for Fig. 7, Vol. 67, 1956 (Paper by W. C. Krumbein & W. C. Slack); C. W. K. Gleerup Publishers, Sweden, for the following from *Lund Studies in Geography, Series B, Human Geography*: Figs. 5 & 6, Paper No. 4, 1952 by T. Hägerstrand, Figs. 38, 68, 55, 65 from Paper No. 24, 1962 by T. Hägerstrand, Table 5 from Paper No. 24, 1962 by E. N. Thomas, Table 1 from Paper No. 24, 1962 by L. Curry, Fig. 7 from Paper No. 24, 1962 by M. F. Dacey, Figs. 1 & 11 from Paper No. 24, 1962 by R. L. Morrill, Fig. 2 and Table 4 from Paper No. 24, 1962 by E. L. Ullmann & M. F. Dacey, Fig. 1 from Paper No. 24, 1962 by H. E. Bracey; from *Lund Studies in Geography, Series C, Mathematical Geography*: Figs. 3.3, 5.3, 7.10, 7.14 and Table, p. 86 from the monograph by W. Bunge: *Theoretical Geography*; Cambridge University Press for Fig. 5.5 from T. J. Fletcher: *Some Lessons in Mathematics*; the Controller of Her Majesty's Stationery Office for Fig. 64, p. 301 from C. E. P. Brooks & N. Carruthers: *Handbook of Statistical Methods in Meteorology*, 1953 and Tables, pp. 66–67 from the Ministry of Transport: *Report of the Jack Committee*, 1961; D. Van Nostrand Co., Inc. for Fig. 1, p. 101 and Table 8, p. 458 from J. P. Gibbs: *Urban Research Methods*, 1961; Department of Regional Science, University of Pennsylvania for the following from *Papers & Proceedings of the Regional Science Association*: Fig. 4, Vol. 6, 1960 (Paper by W. Garrison), Fig. 2 and Table 1, Vol. 7, 1961 (Paper by J. Nystuen & M. F. Dacey), Fig. 8, Vol. 9, 1962 (Paper by B. J. L. Berry *et al.*); *Economic Geography* and the authors for the following: Figs. 1–9, Vol. 31, 1955 (Paper by H. L. Green), Figs. 4 & 8, Vol. 34, 1958 (Paper by J. W. Alexander *et al.*), Fig. 3, Vol. 39, 1963 (Paper

X   ACKNOWLEDGMENTS

by H. A. Stafford), Figs. 2*b* & 6, Vol. 39, 1963 (Paper by A. Getis), Figs. 1 & 4, Vol. 39, 1963 (Paper by J. J. Hidore); the Free Press for Fig. 11, p. 86 and Table 1, p. 35 from Duncan *et al.*: *Statistical Geography*, 1961; *Geografiska Annaler*, Sweden for Fig. 1, Vol. 42, 1960 (Paper by E. Bylund); Geographisches Institut der Universität Bonn for Fig. 3, p. 112 from *Erdkunde*, Vol. 17; Hafner Publishing Co. for a Fig. from G. F. Zipf: *Human Behaviour and the Principle of Least Effort*; Holt, Rinehart & Winston, Inc. for information from Map 6 from Hagood & Price: *Statistics for Sociologists*; Hutchinson & Co., Ltd for Fig. 9 and Table 6 from M. Chisholm: *Rural Settlement and Land Use*; the Institute of British Geographers for Table II from Paper no. 21, 1955 by W. Smith, Figs. 2 & 3 from Paper No. 20, 1954 by K. A. Sinnhuber and Fig. 4 from Paper, Dec. 1965 by R. J. Chorley & Peter Haggett, all from *Transactions*; John Wiley & Sons, Ltd for Fig. A, p. 102 from S. van Valkenburg: *Europe*; the Johns Hopkins Press and Resources for the Future for Fig. 10 and Table D-9 from M. Clawson *et al.*: *Land for the Future*; the author and the M.I.T. Press for Figs. 2 & 4, pp. 270–272 from W. Isard: *Location and the Space Economy*; the author and the M.I.T. Press for Tables 1, p. 191, 1, p. 416 and Fig. 1, p. 417 from W. Isard *et al.*: *Methods of Regional Analysis*; McGraw-Hill Book Co. for Table 21, p. 167 from W. A. Duerr: *Fundamentals of Forestry Economics* and Fig. 3.9, p. 41 from E. M. Hoover: *Location of Economic Activity*; the Macmillan Co., N.Y., for Figs. 3.4–3.8 from *Decision Making Processes in Pattern Recognition* by G. S. Sebestyen, 1962; the authors and Macmillan (Journals) Ltd for Figs. 1 & 2 and Table 1, Vol. 205, 1965 (Paper by Haggett, Chorley & Stoddart) from *Nature*; Methuen & Co., Ltd for Tables 4 & 5 and Fig. 18.2 from R. J. Chorley & P. Haggett: *Frontiers in Geographical Teaching*; the *Netherlands Journal of Economic and Social Geography* for Figs. 5 & 1, Vol. 15, 1963 (Paper by J. T. Coppock) and Figs. 2 & 4, Vol. 53, 1962 (Paper by L. J. King); Peat, Marwich, Caywood, Schiller & Co. for Fig. 1, Vol. 2, 1954 from *Operation Research* (Paper by G. Dantzig *et al.*); *Planning Outlook* for Table 3, Vol. 3, 1953 (Paper by J. W. House); *Professional Geographer* for the following: Figs. 1 & 2, Vol. 5, 1953 (Paper by J. R. Mackay), Figs. 2 & 3, Vol. 15, 1963 (Paper by M. Yeates), Fig. 1, Vol. 15, 1963 (Paper by R. J. Kopec), Fig. 1, Vol. 16, 1964 (Paper by P. Haggett & K. A. Gunawadena); Regional Science Research Inst. for Fig. 2, Vol. II, 1960 from the *Journal of Regional Science* (Paper by W. Warntz & D. Neft); the Research Centre in Economic Development and Cultural Change, Chicago, for Figs. 1–3, Vol. 9, 1960 from *Economic Development and Cultural Change* (Paper by B. J. L. Berry); the *Review of Economics and Statistics* for Table 1, p. 297, Vol. 35, 1953 (Paper by W. Isard & R. E. Kuenne); Routledge & Kegan Paul, Ltd for Tables IIB and IH from P. S. Florence: *The Logic of British and American Industry*; the Royal Geographical Society for Tables 1–4 and Figs. 2–5 from *Geographical Journal*, Vol. 130, 1964 (Paper by P. Haggett); the State University of Iowa, Dept. of Geography for Table 47, p. 109 from *Report No. 1* (McCarty *et al.*) and Fig. 4, p. 45 from *Report No. 2* (E. N. Thomas); Thomas Nelson & Sons, Ltd and the editors for a Fig. from F. H. Perring & S. M. Walters: *Atlas of British Flora*; the author and *The Times*, p. 18, Oct. 19th, 1964 for the map by T. H. Hollingsworth; the U.S. Conservation Foundation and the authors for Figs. 12 & 13 from W. B. Langbein & W. G. Hoyt: *Water Facts for the Nation's Future; U.S. Geol. Surv. Prof. Paper 500-A* for Figs. 6 & 8, 1962 (Paper by L. B. Leopold & W. B. Langbein); the U.S. Dept. of Agriculture Publications for Figs. 1 & 5, *U.S.D.A. Farm Econ. Div. Agric. Handbk. No. 237* (Report by B. J. L. Berry); the University of Chicago Press for the following from *Dept. of Geography, University of Chicago, Research Papers*: Table 3, Fig. VI-4 from Paper No. 62, chapter by B. J. L. Berry, Figs. 3, 10, 17, 30, 31 from Paper No. 84, report by K. J. Kansky, Fig. 18 from Paper No. 90, report by M. Helvig, and from the *Atlas of Economic Development* by N. Ginsburg, Tables pp. 60 & 70; the University of Liverpool for Fig. 4 from the *Liverpool & Manchester Geological Journal*, Vol. 2, 1960 (Paper by W. C. Krumbein); the University of Michigan for Figs. XII & XXI from Paper No. 5, 1965 by R. S. Yuill, and Table, p. 35 from Paper

No. 3, 1965 by W. Bunge, all from *Michigan Inter-University Community of Mathematical Geographers* (unpublished material); University of Toronto Press for Fig. p. 5 from *Canadian Geographer*, Vol. 11, 1958 (Paper by J. R. Mackay); the University of Wales Press for Fig. 23 from D. Thomas: *Agriculture in Wales During the Napoleonic Wars*; Yale University Press for Figs. 23, 27, 50 & 60 and Table 21 from A. I.ösch: *Economics of Location*, 1954.

Conventions

Although the book makes few departures from the normal format these few deserve a word of explanation. *Structure:* A detailed list of contents is given at the start of each chapter and cross-references between chapters are given in terms of this structure, e.g. Chap. 2.II(3a). For ease of reference these index numbers are given at the top of each page. *Maps:* Instead of the conventional scales, areas are referred to a new scale of magnitude, the *G*-scale. This is described in detail on pp. 5–9. Places on maps are given by Greek symbols. *References:* Sources throughout the text are given in the Harvard-System format and are gathered together at the end of the text in alphabetical order (pp. 311–26). *Terminology:* In so far as practicable, terms have been standardized with respect to established sources, e.g. for geographical terms Monkhouse's *Dictionary of geography* (1965), for statistical terms Kendall & Buckland's *Dictionary of statistical terms* (1957), for mathematical terms James & James' *Mathematics dictionary* (1959), and for behavioural terms Gould & Kolb's *Dictionary of the social sciences* (1964).

Chapter one   Assumptions

Geographical writing, like any other, inevitably reflects the assumptions and experience of the writer. Some of the inevitable bias in this treatment of human geography will be very readily apparent. It is, for example, clearly based largely on research carried out in the Western world, particularly northwest Europe and the Americas: neither the Soviet nor Afro-Asian sources have been fully tapped—the former by reason of language barriers and the latter on account of the relative scarcity of research. Although some of the emerging results from Africa and Asia (e.g. Ukwu, 1965; Gunawardena, 1964) suggest that the locational patterns of society there may not be fundamentally different from our own, the final decision must be postponed awhile. A second apparent source of bias is towards the use of quantitative rather than qualitative analysis. This too may be rationalized in terms of the fundamental need for improved definition in geographical analysis. If the historian of geography's development looks back on the 1960's as a decade of 'mathematical extravaganza' we can at least fortify ourselves with the knowledge that, without exception, all natural and social sciences went through, or are going through, such a phase (Woolf, 1961); students graduating in this decade need to be aware of both the possibilities and dangers in this trend.

    This first chapter tries to set out some of the fundamental, but less obvious, assumptions on which the nine chapters which follow are built. These are concerned with the need to look for pattern and order in geography, with the nature of geography itself, with the locational systems we study and the models we create to describe them, and with the type of explanation we use in making sense of our findings.

I. ON THE SEARCH FOR ORDER

Most of the fundamental questions in human geography have no single answer. If we ask of a given region whether its settlements are arranged in some predictable sequence, or its land-use zones are concentric, or its growth cyclical, then the answer largely depends on what we are prepared to look for and what accept as *order*. Order and chaos are not part of nature but part of the human mind: in Sigwart's words 'That there is more order in the world than appears at first sight is not discovered *till the order is looked for*' (Hanson, 1958, p. 204). Chorley (1962) has drawn attention to Postan's lively illustration of this problem as it afflicted Newton, newly struck on the head by an apple: 'Had he asked himself the obvious question: why did that particular apple choose that unrepeatable instant to fall on that unique head, he might have written the history of an apple. Instead of which he asked himself why apples fell and produced the theory of gravitation. The decision was not the apple's but Newton's' (Postan, 1948, p. 406).

The convincing psychological demonstrations (for example by Köhler's famous goblet-or-faces drawing) that order depends not on the geometry of the object we see but on the organizational framework into which we place it, has enormous significance for geography. For geography of all sciences has traditionally placed emphasis on 'seeing'. In how many field classes have we been asked to 'see' an erosion level or 'recognize' a type of settlement pattern. The 'seeing eye' beloved of the late S. W. Wooldridge, is a necessary part of our scientific equipment in that pattern and order exist in knowing what to look for, and how to look.

1. Exceptionalist traditions in geography

In this book emphasis is placed squarely on asking questions about the order, locational order, shown by the phenomena studied traditionally as *human geography*. The first half suggests some broad categories of questions concerned with movements, networks, nodes, hierarchies, and surfaces, while the second explores the way in which we may check the answers we think we find. This general approach stands a little apart from the traditional approach of human geography (e.g. Brunhes, 1925; Vidal de la Blache, 1922) which has been concerned with asking biographical questions about the phenomena we observe. Indeed, after the most searching and scholarly review of the historical development of the subject, Hartshorne finds in his classic *Nature of geography* that '. . . no universals need be evolved, other than the general law of geography that all its areas are unique' (Hartshorne, 1939, p. 468). This uniqueness concept, one shared with history, has a strong hold on much of our geographical teachings at all educational levels, building up in our students the inevitable conviction that region *A* must be different from region *B*.

Huckleberry Finn shared this conviction. In one of his escapades in a flying-boat he shouts: 'We're right over Illinois yet . . . Illinois is green, Indiana is pink . . . It ain't no lie; I've seen it on the map, and it's pink (Twain, 1896, Chap. 3). Tom Sawyer's patient explanation of the geographer's task '. . . he's got to paint them so you can tell them apart the minute you look at them, hain't he?' seems to sum up the conventional role of geographic analysis: to differentiate the earth's surface, to sort over and separate it into convenient areas of 'like' characteristics. Some of the methods of achieving this differentiation are discussed in Chapter 9.I–II.

This differentiation concept has certainly led to some of the great regional writing on which much of the present academic status of geography has been built. Classics like Paul Vidal de la Blache on *France de l'Est* (1917), Carl Sauer on the Ozarks (1920), Isaiah Bowman on the Andes of southern Peru (1916), or Robert Gradmann (1931) on southern Germany, are part of a heritage of biographical regional studies in which observational acumen and literary skill are combined. Our argument here is not that such studies were misdirected, but that their very success led geographers to overlook the equal need for comparative studies. Areal differentiation dominated geography at the expense of areal integration.

On metaphysical grounds both Schaefer (1953) and Bunge (1962) have found the 'unique' approach unsatisfactory. Both suggest, with Postan, that uniqueness is a point of view and not an inherent property of regions. Bunge (1962, pp. 7–13) goes further in arguing that there is no compromise on the issue of uniqueness. Let us consider the trivial case of two pieces of white chalk and imagine them lying on the desk in front of us. If we pick them up and examine them closely, we shall see that they are not identical in every detail. Then to describe them both as 'white chalk' is surely an error. To be accurate each piece should be given a special and unique identifying term; but in practice we assign the two objects to the same class of 'white chalk'. To do other than this is to abandon all our descriptive terms and to be reduced to saying, in Bunge's phrase, '. . . things are thus'. Such an intellectual retreat is unthinkable and both in everyday life and in scientific thinking we constantly assign unique phenomena into broad classes. The gains that come from this classification process may or may not outweigh the losses in accuracy: science is always trying to invent new, more efficient categories in a never-ending attempt to pigeon-hole reality in more and more accurate terms.

The fact that one can do little with the unique except contemplate its uniqueness, has led to the present, unsatisfactory position where systematic studies and unique regional geography work uneasily together. Bunge scorns such compromise; for him systematic geography must move into theoretical spheres and regional geography into a search for generic and not unique studies. In Schaefer's terms, regional geography must become the laboratory side of an essentially theoretical subject.

2. On scale and theory

How far the criticism of the biographical view may be sustained, depends in part on the scale factor. Clearly there are absolute limits to the size of the earth itself, i.e. the geographical 'population' (Chap. 7.I) is finite. At one extreme therefore the world-wide study must of necessity be concerned with the 'unique' since it is drawn from a population of one! However, a study of the regional system centred on a small village may draw a large

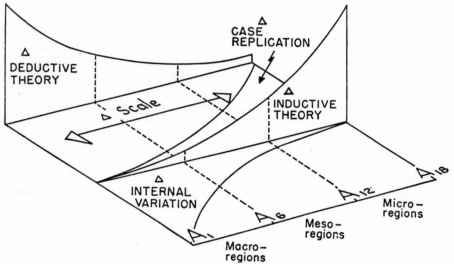

Fig. 1.1. Implications of scale for geographical analysis. Source: Haggett and Chorley. In Chorley and Haggett, 1965-A, p. 367.

number of cases from a population which is certainly in excess of one million.

Some of these implications of changes in magnitude are shown in Fig. 1.1. On the horizontal plane are shown two logical concomitants of scale change: the increase in the number of potential cases and the decrease in complexity as the regions get smaller. These lead in turn to the changes shown in the vertical plane. These are the increase in comparability, in case-replication, and therefore in the significance levels of findings as the regions get smaller, whereas, on the contrary, as regions get larger there are fewer cases to compare and explanations have to rest increasingly on external analogies.

In settlement distribution, the study of clusters at the world scale (northwest Europe, India, etc.) has been marked by rather speculative application of climatic or historical models (Spate, 1952), together with a considerable range in academic views. Conversely, the study of local urban clusters (where a large population of potential cases is available) has been marked by comparative observation and inductive settlement models (e.g. Christaller, 1933) with a smaller range of academic opinion on their significant features. Our reliance on external theory for explanation of macro-regional features may be set against the lower levels of regional magnitude where geography certainly appears to be more self-supporting, in both its physical and human aspects. The persistence of scale effects and the problem of readily converting regions of different sizes to a common yardstick, suggests that some standard form of comparison might be useful throughout (Chorley and Haggett, 1965, Chap. 18).

Geographers are concerned with subjects which range in size from continents (about 1,000,000 to 10,000,000 sq. miles) through parishes (about 1 to 10 sq. miles) to even smaller units, and although many of the more antique areal units have been dropped, the variation between the four conventional units (square miles, square kilometres, acres, and hectares) are sufficiently great to make easy comparison impossible. Although in practice we may use conventional natural standards (e.g. 1,000,000 acres is about the size of Somerset; 100,000 sq. miles about the size of the state of Colorado, and so on) or rapidly convert the various units through tables (Amiran and Schick, 1961), the method remains cumbersome and difficult.

The range of interest of geographical inquiry in absolute terms may be seen with reference to a linear diagram published by Brillouin (1964, p. 85) (Fig. 1.2-c). This consists of a logarithmic scale ranging from 10^{30} to 10^{-50} cm., and includes the largest and the smallest distances so far measured (approximately 10^{27} and 10^{-13} cm., respectively). Within this spectrum, the area with which geographers are concerned occupies a median position, ranging from $4 \cdot 01 \times 10^9$ cm. (the circumference of the earth) down to around 10^3 cm. The question arises whether any absolute units may be used to define the range of geographic interest, and to replace the arbitrary conventional units now in use. Brillouin (1964, p. 32) has suggested we might use as a base an absolute minimum linear distance (a *fentometer*) operationally defined as that distance below which no wave or other measuring device exists to be used as a standard. However appropriate this natural standard may be for the physical sciences there is a good case for regarding an equally fundamental unit—the *surface of the earth*—as the appropriate natural standard for geographic measurement.

Haggett, Chorley, and Stoddart (1965) have proposed a standard of geographical measurement based on the earth's surface area (G_a), with a scale of measurement (the *G-scale*) derived by successive subdivisions of

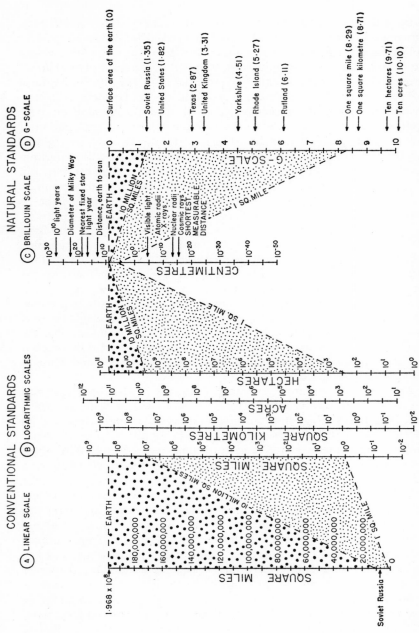

Fig. 1.2. Relation of the *G*-scale to conventional measures. Scale *C*, the Brillouin scale, is linear and is therefore not directly comparable to scales *A*, *B*, and *D*. Figures in brackets after regions indicated in scale *D* give the appropriate *G* values.

Source: Haggett, Chorley, and Stoddart, 1965, p. 845.

this standard area by the power of ten. Table 1.1 shows the general progression of G-values, while Fig. 1.2 shows the relation of the G-scale to conventional standards of areal measurement.

Table 1.1. Derivation of G-values

G-value	Subdivision of earth's surface (G_a)	Area in sq. miles
0	G_a	$1 \cdot 968 \times 10^8$
1	$G_a (10)^{-1}$	$1 \cdot 968 \times 10^7$
2	$G_a (10)^{-2}$	$1 \cdot 968 \times 10^6$
3	$G_a (10)^{-3}$	$1 \cdot 968 \times 10^5$
n	$G_a (10)^{-n}$	$1 \cdot 968 \times 10^{(8-n)}$

Source: Haggett, Chorley, and Stoddart, 1965, p. 846.

The value of G may be given by the general formula:

$$G = \log (G_a/R_a)$$

where both G_a (the earth's surface) and R_a (the area under investigation) are measured in the same areal unit (e.g. acres). In practice, it is more convenient to compute the value of G by subtracting the logarithm of the earth's surface. Table 1.2 gives constants for four common areal standards.

Table 1.2. Computation of G-values for standard areal units

Conventional areal standard	Appropriate formula for computation of G
Square miles	$8 \cdot 2941 - \log R_a$ (ml.²)
Square kilometres	$8 \cdot 7074 - \log R_a$ (km.²)
Acres	$11 \cdot 1003 - \log R_a$ (ac.)
Hectares	$10 \cdot 7074 - \log R_a$ (ha.)

Source: Haggett, Chorley, and Stoddart, 1965, p. 846.

The advantage of the G-scale as a geographical reference system stems from four characteristics. First, it uses a natural standard, the surface of the earth, rather than existing arbitrary standards. Second, through its logarithmic nature it reduces a very wide range of values to a simple scale, for example running from *zero* (the earth) through *ten* (for an area roughly the size of Trafalgar Square) to smaller units. Third, it allows ready comparison of the relative size of areas; in that regions which are different in area by a factor of ten have values *one* unit apart on the G-scale, regions which are different in area by a factor of one hundred are *two* units apart, and so on. Fourth, it simplifies the present confusion of conventional standards (Fig. 1.2-B) and substitutes a simpler scale of natural values (Fig. 1.2-D).

Application of the *G*-scale to existing geographical areas shows some interesting results (Fig. 1.2-D). Values for continents range from $G = 1·06$ to $G = 1·83$ and help to correct some of the distorted size concepts which arise both from the Mercator projection and from relative accessibility

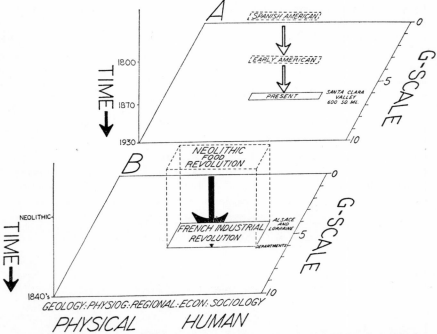

Fig. 1.3. Comparison of regional studies by Broek (1932) and Vidal de la Blache (1917) with reference to the *G*-scale, subject range and time span. Source: Haggett, Chorley, and Stoddart, 1965, p. 846.

(e.g. Hägerstrand's hypothesis that 'distant' areas are under-estimated in size, whereas we exaggerate the relative size of nearby areas). There are however more fundamental implications for the whole character of geographical research.

One of the many illustrative, and even analytical, potentialities presented by the *G*-scale is shown by a comparison of two important regional works given in Fig. 1.3. The study by Broek (1932) of the Santa Clara Valley, California, appears here (Fig. 1.3-A) as three regional time-slices, linked by short textural segments, in which physical and economic aspects of the area are knit into a regional treatment. Although some ranch-scale information is given, the areal scale of the study, at all historical periods, is fundamentally that of the 600-square-mile Santa Clara Valley ($G = 5.52$). Contrast is provided in Fig. 1.3-B by a similar representation of Vidal de la Blache's (1917) classic treatment of eastern France. Here, bounded by the two hiatuses of the Neolithic Food Revolution and the French Industrial Revolution, the region of Alsace-Lorraine is treated in the context of a time-continuum. Carrying his balanced treatment from this scale ($G = 4.12$) down to *Département* levels ($G = c.$ 6), Vidal de la Blache integrates the physical and human aspects of eastern France, carrying his emphasis more deeply into the field of sociology than did Broek.

Whether these differences in regional magnitude have any deeper significance is a matter for debate, but it is perhaps worth noting that dimensional differences are of key importance in classical physics where changes in one dimension (e.g. length) may be associated with disproportionate changes in area, mass, viscosity, and so on. These problems in 'similitude' also have crucial importance in biology where D'Arcy Thompson (1917) devotes a considerable part of his *On growth and form* to a consideration of magnitude in zoological and botanical design. As geographers draw increasingly on physical models and their biological derivatives, we shall need to be increasingly alive to the dangers of 'spatial or dimensional anachronisms' if we may call them such. Measurements of distance inputs (length), boundaries (perimeters), populations (masses) in the 'gravitational' models of economic geography (Chap. 2.II) may need to be successively re-cast at different areal levels if we are to retain their principles of similitude.

II. ON GEOGRAPHY

Geography has long been a thorn in the side of school and university administrators. It seems doubtful whether its natural home should be in the VIth Science or VIth Arts sides of a grammar school organization. Similarly at the university level it has been variously classified as an 'earth science' (at Cambridge it is part of the Faculty of Geography and Geology, which include geophysics, mineralogy, and petrology), a 'social science' (as in most universities in the United States), and less commonly as a 'geometrical science', a position it held in Greek times and which a few workers, notably members of the Michigan Inter-University Community of Mathematical Geographers, would like it to resume.

Part of the difficulty in 'placing' geography within the formal academic structure stems from (i) the natural ambivalence in the ways in which geographers have viewed their subject matter (Chap. 1.I), and at least as much from (ii) the debate over which sections of reality should be studied by geographers. Here we look at the long internal debate within geography and suggest ways in which it might be resolved.

1. Geography: the internal dialogue

Certain geographers or groups of geographers have conceived the field of geography in different terms at various stages of its evolution. The most widely held view is probably that put forward by Hartshorne as the traditional position of geography—*areal differentiation*. There are however a number of 'deviations' from this view; the view of geography as the science of the earth's surface; the view of geography as the study of the relationships between man and his natural environment; and the view of geography as the study of the location of phenomena on the earth's surface. These three major departures are termed here the *landscape* school, the *ecological* school, and the *locational* school.

    a. Areal differentiation: the traditional view. Geography has had separate and recognizable existence as an academic subject for over two thousand years. Even before its formal teaching by the Greeks, the basic curiosity of man to know what lay 'over the hill' must have led to a passing on of experience and conjecture on the form of the earth's surface. The subsequent history of geography with the widening knowledge of the Great Age of Discovery, the nineteenth century with the growth of the great exploring societies (like the Royal Geographical Society founded in London in 1833, and other parallel societies in Paris, Berlin, and New York), the present century with its emphasis on rapid and precise survey techniques; these have all been part of the basic need for organized knowledge about the earth's surface. Hartshorne has explicitly stated the historical role in the following definition: 'Geography is concerned to provide accurate, orderly, and rational description and interpretation of the variable character of the earth surface' (Hartshorne, 1959, p. 21). In order to perform this considerable task, Hartshorne argues that geographers are primarily concerned with region construction, with what he terms the *areal differentiation* of the earth's surface (Chap. 1.I(1)).

    There is little doubt that Hartshorne's definition represents one of the common denominators that runs through the greater part of geographical work from the Greeks onward. But one of the most interesting and explosive of internal debates within geography today is not over the accuracy of Hartshorne's view of the past nature of geography; but rather, whether this past should govern the nature of geography in the future. Hartshorne argued cogently that only by subjugating our personal idiosyncrasies to the great weight of geographic work over the centuries could we hope to achieve a balanced and consistent view: '. . . If we wish to keep on the track . . . we must first look back of us to see in what direction the track had led' (Hartshorne, 1939, p. 31). By careful textual criticism he was able to show both the enormous range in views of scholars over their lifetime, and the need to distinguish what geographers claimed to be doing from what they actually did.

One of the strongest dissents from this approach has come from Bunge (1962). His approach is to try logically to deduce the nature of geography from a series of assumptions. Like Lösch (1954), he is concerned with what should be, rather than what is. In his approach, the statements by the great geographers of the past are pointedly ignored because '. . . the great men of our past might now, in view of more recent events, hold opinions different from those they then held' (Bunge, 1962, p. 1). In fact neither Hartshorne nor Bunge hold the inductive or deductive approach in its pure form; each extends his work by reference to empirical example or logical argument.

b. Deviations: the landscape school. The concept of 'landscape' has long been obscured by the double meaning attached in common German usage to the apparently parallel term *Landschaft.* Much of the thinking in this 'deviationist' school has been derived from German literature and confusion has apparently arisen from the meaning of *Landschaft* as either (*a*) the landscape in the sense of the general appearance of a section of the earth's visible surface or (*b*) a restricted region of the earth's surface. In the first meaning, the terms *Landschaft* and landscape are synonyms; in the second the appropriate English synonym must be 'region'. Hartshorne (1939, pp. 149–58) has expertly exposed the confusion in the original German literature—for example the different uses of the same term by Passarge and Schlüter—and the inevitable take-over of some of this confusion into American literature, particularly through the important essay by Carl Sauer on the morphology of landscape (Sauer, 1925).

Sauer argued that it was possible to break down the landscape of an area into two separate components: the 'natural landscape' (*Urlandschaft*) and the 'cultural landscape' (*Kulturlandschaft*). He conceived as natural landscape the original landscape of the area before the entry of man; as cultural landscape, that landscape transformed by man. The most important effect of Sauer's essay was in urging that the same morphological methods so fruitful in the analysis of the physical landscape could be transferred to the study of the cultural, a message taken up by Miller (1949). Before Sauer's 1925 essay the role of man as a morphological agent had been recognized, notably by George Perkins Marsh (1864), but it was in the 'Berkeley' school (described by Clark, in James, Jones, and Wright, 1954, p. 86) that Sauer gathered together a group of scholars who like Broek (*The Santa Clara Valley,* 1932) organized their work around the theme of landscape change. *Man's role in changing the earth* (Thomas, 1956), an international symposium in which Sauer played a leading part, gives the clearest picture of the strength and vitality of this important theme in the development of human geography.

c. Deviations: the ecological school. The idea of geography as a study of the relationship between the earth and man has long held a central position in its teaching in both colleges and schools in England. Paradoxically, its origins may be thought to lie in a country where it subsequently played a very small part in the development of geographic thinking, i.e. Germany. Friedrich Ratzel's views on 'anthropogeography' appear to have had an indirect but important effect both on Vidal de la Blache in France and more particularly on Ellen Semple in the United States. Her *Influences of geographical environment* (1911) had a decisive effect in spreading the idea of the study of 'geographic influences', as a major goal in geographic study, throughout the English-speaking world.

A separate and less extreme branch of this environmental school evolved around H. H. Barrows at the University of Chicago. His view of geography was as 'human ecology' (Barrows, 1923); a study in which physical geography is largely eliminated from the field and in which geography becomes a social science concerned with the relationships of human society and its physical environment. Hartshorne (1939, p. 123) suggests that under this view geography stands in relation to the social sciences in an exactly similar location as does plant ecology to the biological sciences. Certainly the dividing line between this view of human geography and the work of sociologists like McKenzie (1933) and Hawley (1950) is very finely drawn, and recent reviews of human ecology (like that of Theodorson, 1961) contain contributions from both sociologists and geographers. The convergence of sociological and geographical lines of thought in Britain have been shown by Pahl (in Chorley and Haggett, 1965, Chap. 5) while Stoddart (1965) has traced the very wide application of biological-ecological concepts (e.g. that of *ecosystems*) throughout geography.

It is perhaps in France however that the ecological view of human geography has had the most important influence. Two of the most decisive studies of human geography yet produced, the *Géographie humaine* of Jean Brunhes (1925) and the *Principes de géographie humaine* of Vidal de la Blache (1922) show a strongly environmental approach to the 'essential facts' of man's occupation of the earth's surface; and Max Sorre in his *Fondements de la géographie humaine* (1947–52, 1961) has followed this trend. For their detailed treatment of an abundance of regional examples and for their broad philosophy of man as part of a closely knit environmental syndrome, these three scholars—Brunhes, Vidal de la Blache, Sorre—may be regarded as corner-stones on which much of the discipline of human geography has been built.

d. Deviations: the locational school. The view that geography is essentially a distributional science is a third recurrent theme. Bunge (1962, 1964) has recently emphasized the strong dependence of geography on the concepts of geometry and topological mathematics; but nearly a century ago Marthe (1877) described the field of geography as the study of 'the where

of things'. Certainly a central concern for location and distribution is a
hallmark of all geographical writing and a recurrent theme in methodological reviews (e.g. de Geer, 1923) and inaugural addresses (e.g. Watson,
1955).

The strongest development of locational 'theory' has come from one
of the social sciences, economics, rather than from within human geography. Both the early classics of locational theory, von Thünen (1875) on
agricultural location, and Weber (1909) on industrial location, were concerned essentially with economic location; and the object of both contemporary and subsequent workers, Launhardt, Predöhl, Ohlin, Palander,
Hoover, Lösch, and Isard, has been largely '. . . to improve the spatial and
regional frameworks of the social sciences, especially economics' (Isard,
1956, p. viii). Nevertheless the excellent reviews of economic-location
literature, available from both English (Hoover, 1948; Isard, 1956), German (Boustedt and Ranz, 1957), and French scholars (Ponsard, 1955),
have served as spurs to the application, development, and refinement of
spatial concepts by geographers. Bunge's *Theoretical geography* (1962)
shows how far this stimulating process has gone.

To acknowledge this fundamental role of locational concepts within
human geography, is not to dismiss its importance for every systematic
science. Works like the *Atlas of the British flora* (Perring and Walters, 1962)
or the *National atlas of disease mortality in the United Kingdom* (Howe, 1963)
show the importance of distributional studies to two systematic studies,
botany and medicine. Hettner saw clearly the dangers in over-emphasizing
location as a purely geographic concept: 'Distribution by place forms a
characteristic of the objects . . . and must therefore necessarily be included in the compass of their research and presentation' (Hettner, 1905;
cited by Hartshorne, 1939, p. 127). The simple and plausible links
between history as a study of 'when' and geography as a study of 'where',
does less than justice to both fields.

2. Towards a set-theory integration

The diversity of viewpoints within geography may well be matched by
similar diversities in other fields. In economics, the debate over the classificatory or functional view of the subject (Robbins, 1935) has engendered
similar internal heat and Vining's weary conclusion that 'economics is
what economists do' strikes a familiar chord in geography. Nevertheless
the desire to codify and integrate alternative views remains, and in this
section an attempt is made, through very elementary set-theory, to integrate at least some of the alternative geographical schools.

Let us take the statement at the beginning of Chapter 1.II that geography is variously placed within the earth sciences, the social sciences,
and, less frequently, the geometrical sciences. Then each of the three
sciences into which geography has been placed can be viewed as a *set*, and

each separate subject as an *element* within that set. Three sets can be defined: an earth sciences set (α), a social sciences set (β), and a geometrical sciences set (γ). Set α contains geography (1), geology (2), and other earth sciences and can be written as

$$\alpha = \{1, 2\}$$

Similarly we can define the other two sets:

$$\beta = \{1, 3\}$$
$$\gamma = \{1, 4\}$$

where 3 is demography together with other social sciences, and where 4 is topology together with other geometric sciences. This situation can also be shown diagrammatically by the use of Venn diagrams as in Fig. 1.4-A.

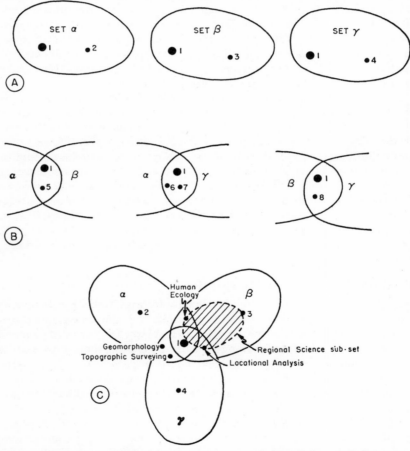

Fig. 1.4. Towards a definition of geography in terms of set theory. A Original sets. B Two-set intersections. C Three-set intersections.

We can show the relations between any two sets by overlapping the diagrams. Thus geography is by definition part of both α and β sets, and its position is shown in the shaded area of Fig. 1.4-B. Overlap of the three sets in pairs also suggests the position of the human ecology view of geography ('man in relation to his environment') (5) at the overlap of the α and β sets, of geomorphology (6) and of cartography and surveying (7) at the overlap of the α and γ sets, and of locational analysis (8) at the overlap of the β and γ sets. We can write these intersections as

$$\alpha \cap \beta = \{1, 5\}$$
$$\alpha \cap \gamma = \{1, 6, 7\}$$
$$\beta \cap \gamma = \{1, 8\}$$

More complicated relationships between the three sets are shown in Fig. 1.4-C where geography (1) is seen to occupy the central position at the intersection of all three sets, that is

$$\alpha \cap \beta \cap \gamma = \{1\}$$

with the cognate subjects, geomorphology, human ecology, cartography and surveying, and locational analysis occupying two-set intersections about it.

It is not suggested here that this type of analysis solves our problems of definition but it does suggest, if our analysis is correct, just why it is so difficult to 'locate' geography or to define it simply. To describe it as 'the study of the earth's surface', or 'man in relation to his environment' or 'the science of distribution', or 'areal differentiation' is to grasp only part of its real complexity. Geography can be defined not solely in terms of *what* it studies or of *how* it studies but by the intersection of the two. It is what Sauer (1952, p. 1) has called a 'focussed curiosity' which has created techniques, traditions, and a literature of its own.

3. Neglect of geometrical traditions in geography

Although it is now probably the weakest of the three elements in Fig. 1.4, the geometrical tradition was basic to the original Greek conception of the subject, and many of the more successful attempts at geographical models have stemmed from this type of analysis. The geometry of Christaller hexagons, of Lewis's shoreline curves, of Wooldridge's erosion surfaces, of Hägerstrand's diffusion waves, of Breisemeister's projections come vividly to mind. Indeed from one point of view, much of the new statistical work relating to regression analysis (Chap. 10.II(3)) and generalized surfaces (Chap. 9.III(4)) represent merely more-abstract geometries. Much of the most exciting geographical work in the 1960's is emerging from applications of higher-order geometries; for example, the multidimensional geometry of Dacey's settlement models (Dacey, 1964) and the graph theory and topology of Kansky's network analysis (Kansky, 1963). It is an interesting reflection on the history of geography that the increasing separation of geomorphology and human geography may have come just at the time when each has most to offer to the other. Sauer (1925) in his *Morphology of landscape* drew basic parallels between the two, but it was unfortunate, as Board (Chorley and Haggett, 1965, Chap. 10) so clearly shows, that 'landscape' was seized upon and 'morphology' neglected by those who drew inspiration from Sauer's important paper. The topographic surface is only one of the many three-dimensional surfaces that geographers analyse and there is no fundamental reason why for example the analysis of landform and population-density surfaces should not proceed along very similar lines (Chap. 6.I.(1)). Geometry not only offers a chance of welding aspects of human and physical geography into a new working partnership, but revives the central role of cartography in relation to the two.

4. Regional science and geography

The position of the emerging field of 'regional science' with its strong connections with locational studies, geography, human ecology, and social sciences (notably economics) is shown in Fig. 1.4-c by the shaded zone. Regional studies have been booming in North America since World War II. A recent survey (Perloff, 1957) reported about 140 U.S. universities had established programmes in regional studies, while two new institutions, the Regional Science Association and Resources for the Future, have polarized regional research on a new scale. In Britain, the Hayter and Parry Committees on Afro-Asian and Latin American studies have seen the founding of such new regional research centres as the South-Asian centre at Cambridge.

While such regional studies tend to deal with many features and involve several academic disciplines, the strongest lead in these studies has come from economics or, more specifically, from econometrics. Thus it is that the first major textbook on regional science, *Methods of regional analysis* (Isard, Bramhall, Carrothers, Cumberland, Moses, Price, and Schooler, 1960) is essentially concerned with *economic* regions. The paramount problem is seen as the economic 'performance' of a region (p. 413); what industries does it need to smooth out employment irregularities?; how can it optimize the use of its often niggardly resource endowment? Questions of this kind throw the weight of interest solidly towards economic development, and Fisher (1955, p. 6) has summed up this view when he describes '. . . the most helpful region . . . is what might be called the *economic development region*'.

Whether the present interests shown by economists in regions is a major departure, or whether in the future '. . . regional economics may increasingly be indistinguishable from the rest of economics', as argued by Meyer (1963, p. 48), remains to be seen. Whatever the long-run importance for economics may be, the impact on geography has been catalytic.

Both economic geographers and regional geographers have been either exposed to the literature, or drawn in to participate on interdisciplinary regional research of a rigorously high standard. As Garrison's review (1959–60) indicates, the boundary-line work has been immensely productive both of new ideas and new techniques and this is already being translated into action in the research output of a few geography schools. No one who follows through the research theses published by the University of Chicago's geography department since 1948 can be unaware of both the nature and pace of the revolution.

III. ON SYSTEMS AND MODELS

1. Human geography and general systems theory

During the last decade there has been a remarkable growth of interest in the biological and behavioural sciences in *general systems* theory (Bertalanffy, 1951). Some attempts have been made (notably by Chorley, 1962) to introduce its concepts into geomorphology and physical geography, and there seems no good reason why the concept of systems could not be further extended into human geography. In this section we explore the possibilities.

a. Nature of systems. What is a system? One loose definition, cited by Chorley, describes it as '. . . a set of objects together with relationships between the objects and their attributes' (Hall and Fagen, 1956, p. 18). In everyday plumbing parlance we speak of a 'hot-water system' in which the set of objects (stove, pipes, cylinders, etc.) are related through circulating water with inputs of energy in the form of heat. In geomorphology we may speak of an 'erosional system' in which the set of objects (watersheds, slopes, streams) are related through the circulation of water and sediment with inputs of energy in the form of rainstorms.

In human geography, our nearest equivalent is probably the nodal region (Chap. 9.I) in which the set of objects (towns, villages, farms, etc.) are related through circulating movements (money, migrants, freight, etc.) and the energy inputs come through the biological and social needs of the community. This idea is implicit in most central-place theory (Chap. 6.I(3)), though in only a few statements (notably that of Vining, 1953, and Curry, 1964-B) is the description couched in 'system' terms.

Clearly then, systems are arbitrarily demarcated sections of the real world which have some common functional connections. Von Bertalanffy (1950) distinguishes two separate frameworks: the *closed system* and the *open system*. Closed systems have definable boundaries across which no exchange of energy occurs, but since they are likely, by this definition, to be rather rare in geographical studies (except in the limiting case of a world-wide study) they are not considered here.

b. Nodal regions as open systems. The view taken in the first half of this book is that we may regard nodal regions as open systems (Philbrick, 1957; Nystuen and Dacey, 1961). Indeed the organization of the chapters (Chaps. 2–6) shows the build-up of such a system; viz., the study of *movements* (Chap. 2) leads on to a consideration of the channels along which movement occurs, the *network* (Chap. 3), to the *nodes* on that network (Chap. 4) and their organization as a *hierarchy* (Chap. 5), with a final integration of the interstitial zones viewed as *surfaces* (Chap. 6). This progression, from energy flows to recognizable landforms, may be seen more clearly from Fig. 1.5, in which more familiar geographical forms may be

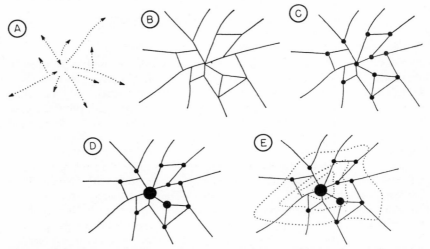

Fig. 1.5. Stages in the analysis of regional systems. *A* Movements. *B* Networks. *C* Nodes. *D* Hierarchies. *E* Surfaces.

substituted for their abstract geometrical equivalents, i.e. roads, settlements, the urban hierarchy, and land-use zones. If the sceptic still regards the nodal region as a purely mental construct, then Dickinson (1964, pp. 227–434) has provided a detailed review of city-regions within the United States and western Europe, while Caesar (1955; 1964) has shown strong nodal organization within regions as unlike in scale as the communist block in eastern Europe and northeast England.

If we wish to view nodal regions as open systems we must first look at the typical characteristics of such systems and check their existence in the regional system. Chorley (1962, pp. 3–8) suggests that open systems have some of the following six characteristics: (i) the need for an energy supply for the system's maintenance and preservation, together with, the capacity to (ii) attain a 'steady-state' in which the import and export of energy and material is met by form adjustments, (iii) regulate itself by homeostatic adjustments, (iv) maintain optimum magnitudes over periods of time; (v) maintain its organization and form over time rather than trending (as do closed systems) towards maximum entropy, and (vi) behave 'equi-finally', in the sense that different initial conditions may lead to similar end results.

In our regional systems we certainly find some of these six char-acteristics. Regional organization needs a constant movement of people, goods, money, information to maintain it; an excess of inward movements may be met by form changes (city expansion and urban sprawl) just as decreased movement may lead to contraction and ghost cities. The first two conditions are clearly met. Similarly, on the third condition the urban region follows Le Châtelier's Principle in that its hinterland may expand or contract to meet increased or decreased flows. Berry and Garrison (1958-c) would also suggest that it meets the fourth and fifth require-ments in that the form of the urban rank–size relationships (Chap. 3.II) tends to be relatively constant over both space and time. Finally, the growing convergence of the form of the major cities in different continents suggests that the urban open system is capable of behaving equifinally.

The advantages of viewing the region as an open system are that it directs our attention towards the links between process and form, and places human geography alongside other biological and social sciences that are organizing their thinking in this manner. Exchanges between students of 'ecosystems' at all scale levels should prove rewarding (e.g. Thomas, 1956, pp. 677–806).

2. Model building in human geography

In everyday language the term 'model' has at least three different usages. As a noun, model implies a representation; as an adjective, model implies ideal; as a verb, to model means to demonstrate. We are aware that when we refer to a model railway or a model husband we use the term in different senses. In scientific usage Ackoff (Ackoff, Gupta, and Minas, 1962) has suggested that we incorporate part of all three meanings; in model building we create an idealized representation of reality in order to demonstrate certain of its properties.

Models are made necessary by the complexity of reality. They are a conceptual prop to our understanding and as such provide for the teacher a simplified and apparently rational picture for the classroom, and for the researcher a source of working hypotheses to test against reality. Models convey not the whole truth but a useful and comprehensible part of it (Society for Experimental Biology, 1960).

a. Types of models. A simple three-stage breakdown has been suggested by Ackoff (Ackoff *et al.*, 1962) into *iconic, analogue,* and *symbolic* models, in which each stage represents a higher degree of abstraction than the last. Iconic models represent properties at a different scale; analogue models represent one property by another; symbolic models represent properties by symbols. A very simple analogy is with the road system of a region where air photographs might represent the first stage of abstraction (iconic); maps, with roads on the ground represented by lines of different width and colour on the map, represent the second stage of abstraction (analogue); a mathematical expression, road density, represents the third stage of abstraction (symbolic). At each stage information is lost and the model becomes more abstract but more general.

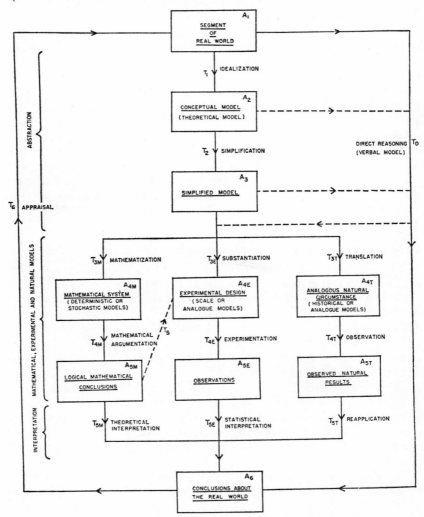

Fig. 1.6. A model for models. Source: Chorley, 1964, p. 129.

Chorley (1964) carried this classification process further and created a 'model of models' (Fig. 1.6), illustrating it with examples from both physical and human geography. His model consists of a flow diagram in which a series of *steps* (A_1 to A_6) are linked by *transformations* (T_1 to T_6). Each step contains some aspect of the real world, model, observation or conclusion; each transformation connects these by some process (idealization, mathematical argument, statistical interpretation, etc.) which advances or checks on the reasoning process.

The first section of Fig. 1.6 is concerned with the 'abstraction' process in which the complexities of the real world are so simplified that they may become more comprehensible. Chorley argues that this process is difficult largely because as huge amounts of information are lost, extraneous 'noise' is introduced; a Cézanne painting represents an abstracted model of a landscape in which the noise level (brush-marks, etc.) is high, while a Van Ruysdael is less simplified but considerably less noisy (Chorley, 1964, p. 132). Successful models are those which manage a considerable amount of simplification without introducing extraneous noise.

The second section of Fig. 1.6 breaks into the three main stems of mathematical, experimental, and natural models. *Mathematical models* might be represented in human geography by Isard's distance-inputs equations (Isard, 1956) or Beckmann's 'equation of continuity' (Beckmann, 1952) in which features of the system being studied are replaced by abstract symbols and subjected to mathematical argument. *Experimental models* might be represented by Hotelling's use of a heat-flow analogue in migration theory (Hotelling, 1921; cited by Bunge, 1962, p. 115) or Weber's weight and pulley machine in industrial location (Weber, 1909) where tangible structures are used to simulate certain aspects of reality. Finally *natural models* might be represented by the Garrison ice-cap analogy of city growth (cited by Chorley, 1964, p. 136), where some analogous natural circumstance which is believed to be simpler or more readily available is substituted for reality. The problem in each case is to translate the circumstances being studied into some analogous form in which it is either simpler, or more accessible, or more easily controlled and measured; to study it in this analogue or model form; and to reapply the results of this study to the original system. Models then represent idealized parts of systems, just as systems represent an arbitrarily separated segment of the real world.

b. Approaches to model building. In economic geography, model building has proceeded along two distinct and complementary paths. In the first, the builder has 'sneaked up' on a problem by beginning with very simple postulates and gradually introducing more complexity, all the time getting recognizably nearer to real life. This was the approach of Thünen (1875) in his model of land use in *Der Isolierte Staat* (Chap. 6.II). In this 'isolated state' he begins by assuming a single city, a flat uniform plain, a single transport media, and like simplicities and in this simple situation is able to derive simple rent gradients which yield a satisfying alternation of land-use 'rings'. But Thünen then disturbs this picture by reintroducing the very things that he originally assumed inert and brings back soil differences, alternative markets and different transport media. With their introduction, the annular symmetry of the original pattern gives way to an irregular mosaic far more like the pattern we observe in our land-use surveys. Nevertheless, Thünen's model has served its point; in Ackoff's terminology it has 'demonstrated certain properties' of the economic landscape.

The second method is to 'move down' from reality by making a series of simplifying generalizations. This is the approach of Taaffe (Taaffe, Morrill, and Gould, 1963) in his model of route development (Chap. 3.III(1)). The study begins with a detailed empirical account of the development of routes in Ghana over the period of colonial exploitation. From the Ghanaian pattern a series of successive stages is recognized. In the first, a scatter of unconnected coastal trading posts; in the last, an interconnected phase with both high-priority and general links established. This Ghanaian sequence is finally formalized as a four-stage sequence, common to other developing countries like Nigeria, East Africa, Malaya, and Brazil.

Not all such models have developed inductively from observations within geography. Some of the most successful have come from borrowing ideas from related fields, especially the field of physics. Thus Zipf (1949) attempted to extend Newton's 'divine elastic' of gravitation to social phenomena and his $P_i P_j / d_{ij}$ formula for the interaction between two cities of 'mass' P_i and P_j at a distance d_{ij} is a direct extension of Newtonian physics. When modified by Isard's refined concept of distance (Isard, 1960) and Stouffer's addition of intervening opportunity (Stouffer, 1962) it has proved a very powerful predictive tool in the study of traffic genera-tion between points (Chap. 2.II). A less widely known borrowing was used by Lösch (1954, p. 184). He has related the 'bending' of transport routes across landscapes of varying resistance and profitability to the sine formula for the refraction of light and sound (Chap. 3.I). While such borrowing may have its dangers, it is a most fruitful source of hypotheses that can be soberly tested for their relevance to the problems of economic geography. A book like D'Arcy Thompson's *On growth and form* (1917) illustrates how many subjects find common ground in the study of mor-phology; there is inspiration still to be found in his treatment of crystal structures or honeycomb formation as Bunge (1964) has illustrated. These models are treated at length in Part One of this book and in Chorley and Haggett (*in press*).

   c. *Role of models.* In his *Novum Organum*, Bacon describes scientific theory as consisting of 'anticipations, rash and premature'. Certainly we might argue that most of the models put forward in the first half of this book fit this description admirably: all are crude, all full of exceptions, all easier to refute than to defend. Why then, we must ask, do we bother to create models rather than study directly the 'facts' of human geography? The answer lies in the inevitability, the economy, and the stimulation of model building:

(i) Model building is inevitable because there is no fixed dividing line between facts and beliefs; in Skilling's terms '. . . belief in a universe of real things is merely a belief . . . a belief with high probability certainly, but a belief none the less' (1964, p. 394A). Models are theories, laws, equations, or hunches which state our beliefs about the universe we think we see.

(ii) Model building is economical because it allows us to pass on generalized information in a highly compressed form. Like rules for the plurals of French adjectives there may be exceptions but the rule is none the less an important ladder in learning the language. This use of models as teaching aids is discussed by Chorley and Haggett (1965-A, pp. 360–4).

(iii) Model building is stimulating in that, through its very over-generalizations, it makes clear those areas where improvement is necessary. The building and testing of models is as important to geography as aero-nautics; the test flight of a hypothesis, no less exciting, nor much less dangerous, than the test flight of a prototype 'Comet'. Each leads on to urther research and modifications.

In short the role of models in geography is to codify what has gone before and excite fresh inquiry. To be sure the present stock of models may be unprepossessing enough, but as Lösch asked '. . . does not the path of science include many precarious emergency bridges over which we have all been willing to pass provided they would help us forward on our road'; certainly his hope that his work on regions would open '. . . a path into a rich but almost unknown country' (Lösch, 1954, p. 100) has been richly fulfilled.

IV. ON DETERMINISTIC AND PROBABILISTIC EXPLANATION

1. The retreat from determinism in human geography

In the spirit of optimism that seized science after Newton's triumphant demonstration of the laws of gravitation there was much nonsense dreamed about scientific prediction. It was the French mathematician, Laplace, who suggested that it was conceptually possible to forecast the fate of every atom of the universe both forwards and backwards through time. Although all doubted that the technical possibility lay remotely far in the future it served as a goal towards which science might slowly progress. In geography this optimism had its expression in the ideas of *environmental determinism* in which human behaviour was seen to be predictable in terms of the physical environment. The excessive claims, the burnt fingers, the debate over 'possibilism' is part of the history of geographical development (see Hartshorne 1939, pp. 56–60) which reflects little credit on our powers of observation, let alone discrimination.

Reactions to the period of excessive environmentalism in geography were both negative and positive. On the negative side, the retreat led to an almost complete rejection of any kind of theory (see Chap. 1.I(3)), so that our literature became at once more accurate but infinitely less exciting. Description was substituted for hypothesis, repetition for debate. On the positive side, geographers approached the intricate regional systems wary of any simple cause-and-effect keys. Meinig (1962) in an analysis or the railway network of the Columbia basin in the northwestern United

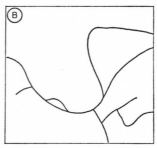

Fig. 1.7. Contrast between routes which were proposed (*A*) and actually built (*B*) by the Northern Pacific Railroad Company in a sector of the northwestern United States (*G = 3·7*). Source: Meinig, 1962, p. 413.

States is a case in point. Fig. 1.7-B shows the railways built by the Northern Pacific Railroad in the second half of the nineteenth century. Viewed in relation to present conditions they yield a satisfying logic in which terrain and cities serve as either barriers or magnets to shape the twisting geometry of the network. However as Meinig stresses, such logic is largely illusory. Most of the cities were the subsequent products of the railway, rather than its antecedent causes. As for the rigorous influence of terrain, the map of projected routes constructed from the files of the railway's consulting engineers (Fig. 1.7-A) shows a cordon of routes, *all* of which on purely technical grounds were serious contenders for the railway route. Meinig's point is that in order to 'explain' the reason why one route was chosen, another abandoned, would involve nothing short of a psychological analysis of board-room decisions. Indeed, the detailed examination of most aspects of human behaviour of interest to human geography (e.g. migration, industrial location, choice of land use) tend to '. . . leave one stranded in the thickets of the decision-making process' (Meinig, 1962, p. 413).

Meinig's view is reinforced by Morrill (1963) in a study of town location in central Sweden, where it is suggested that man is not always able to distinguish between equally good choices, nor can he always recognize optimum locations should these exist. There are, Morrill contends, basic uncertainties in the pattern of human behaviour that we simply cannot wish away. These difficulties are compounded by two further sources of indeterminacy: first, the multiplicity of equal choices, and second, the inability to take into account the myriad of very small effects from many small sources. There are far more potential town sites than towns in central Sweden, so that no unique locational significance springs from site alone; there is instead a multiplicity of factors that enter into urban growth, each factor linking with the other in a labyrinth of small-scale causal links. If Newton was right in principle that an alighting butterfly shifts the earth, it is equally true that the net effect of such infinitesimal causes may be considered random. Unless we wish to follow Aquinas in the metaphysics of the 'First Cause' we can hope only to disentangle some of the main threads in any situation, the rest we can only regard as a sort of background noise, a Brownian motion.

2. Normative and probabilistic laws

a. Impact of the uncertainty principle. One of the fundamental doubts cast on the possibility of extending cause-and-effect interpretations into the world of human behaviour came from the field of small-scale or quantum physics. Once Max Planck had discovered in 1900 that energy, like matter, is not continuous but appears in small groups or quanta, both the theoretical and empirical study of this branch of physics ran into increasing problems. It proved impossible to apply rigid mechanistic laws to these tiny particles and it was a German physicist, Heisenberg, who in 1927 put this problem into a formal principle: the *uncertainty principle*. This stated in effect that all our observations of the natural world contain some final and essential uncertainty. If we try to measure location more accurately, we must sacrifice some aspect of its precise time; in estimating its speed more accurately, we are less sure of its position.

Despite later revision of Heisenberg's physical experiments, this principle, together with the spread of the concepts of Francis Galton and Karl Pearson on statistical probability, had a dramatic effect on the metaphysical battle over determinacy. The replacement of *normative* laws (latin *norma* = a rule) by the idea of probabilistic trends allowed a totally new view of human behaviour in which both 'free will' and 'determinacy' could be accommodated. Indeed both extreme views may be based on a misunderstanding of scale, for Bronowski (1960, p. 93) would argue that '. . . a society moves under material pressure like a stream of gas; and on the average, its individuals obey the pressure; but at any instance, any individual may, like an atom of gas, be moving across or against the stream'.

This realization that physical laws were not deterministic but only statistical approximations of very high probability based on immense —but finite—populations, seeped rather slowly into the social sciences. As Kates (1962) in a study of floodplain hazards has argued, neither Freud's vision of man driven by inner and largely unknown impulses, nor the rigid principles of classical economics (with its vision of *Homo economicus* bending to every flicker in the stock market) give a satisfactory framework within which to study locational behaviour. Both views were attacked from within and look in retrospect '. . . as mistaken as the attempts of the early physicists to explain everything in terms of four elements, or of the early physicians to explain temperament in terms of four humours' (Kendall, 1960, p. 7).

Simon (1957, pp. 196–200) has drawn attention to two alternative models of individual behaviour, the *optimizer* and *satisficer* models. The optimizer concept has been tacitly introduced into human geography through the assumption of models like those of von Thünen, Weber, Christaller, and Lösch that individuals or groups would arrange themselves spatially so as to optimize the given set of resources and demands. Simon has argued, and Wolpert (1964) has demonstrated (see his findings on Swedish farming discussed in Chap. 6.III(4)), that the optimizer model is rather unsatisfactory. Optimization requires information and decision processes at the highest capacity of the individual or group, and as individuals and as groups there is plentiful evidence that we simply do not operate nor indeed can we operate (because of *time* uncertainties) at that level. Simon would replace this with a satisficer model which postulates that (i) we rank all the alternative courses of action of which we are aware along a preference scale and (ii) select from this set the course that will satisfy a set of needs. Clearly our choice is often sub-optimal, since '. . . to optimize requires processes several orders of magnitude more complex than those required to satisfice' (March and Simon, 1958, p. 140).

b. Emergence of stochastic models. Demonstration of the insufficiency of classic normative models of human behaviour, and the replacement of this with the idea of the 'bounded rationality' of man, stimulated the search for alternative kinds of behavioural models. The break-through came in economics with World War II. Here the fusion of mathematics, economics, and logistics led to the appearance of game theory in general, and in particular to a remarkable book *The theory of games and economic behaviour* (Von Neumann and Morgenstern, 1944). In this, the uncertainty principle was formally introduced into economics through the mathematical theory of games. The formalism of supply, demand, and perfect knowledge was replaced by a more robust and yet mathematically more elegant *probability* theory in which uncertainties (e.g. of market, price, and production) were the only constants. This is of course the world which as individuals we know: a world which is neither wholly rational nor wholly chaotic, but a probabilistic amalgam of choice, calculation, and chance.

In human geography, academic isolation delayed the impact of the indeterminacy principle still further. It was not until 1957 that Neyman introduced a growth theory in which chance or *stochastic* (Greek στόχος = aim, guess) processes played a major part. The theory itself (Chap. 2.IV) was abstract and as equally applicable to star galaxies (Neyman, Scott, and Shane, 1956) as to animal populations (Neyman and Scott, 1957). There is some indication that Lösch, had he survived, would have taken up these ideas with enthusiasm. He wrote in 1940: 'I doubt that the fundamental principles of zoological, botanical and economic location theory differ very greatly' (Lösch, 1954, p. 185). The spread of models, such as those of Neyman, into geographical research is tending to reduce old lines of division between subjects and to create new areas of common endeavour.

In Sweden, Hägerstrand and his associates have already begun work on the application of stochastic Monte Carlo models of migration (Hägerstrand, 1953; Morrill, 1963), while game-theory methods were being applied to both urban and rural locational problems (Stevens, 1961; Gould, 1963). Curry (1964) has gone still further in applying wholly random processes to the building up of settlement patterns with varying degrees of industrial specialization. Some of these theories are reviewed in subsequent chapters (Chaps. 2.IV(2); 4.I(3); 6.III(1b); 10.III(2)) but the number yet developed in human geography is still regrettably small and investigation of some models (e.g. Markov-chain models) has scarcely begun.

Part One: Models of Locational Structure

Bold ideas, unjustified anticipations, and speculative thoughts, are our only means of interpreting nature: our only organon, our only instrument for grasping her. And we must hazard to win our prize. Those among us who are unwilling to expose their ideas to the hazard of refutation do not take part in the scientific game. (KARL POPPER, The Logic of Scientific Discovery, 1959, p. 280.)

One of the difficulties we face in trying to analyse integrated regional
systems (Chap. 1.III(1b)) is that there is no obvious or single point of
entry. Indeed, the more integrated the system, the harder it is to crack.
Thus in the case of nodal regions, it is just as logical to begin with the
study of settlements as with the study of routes. As Isard comments:
'. . . the maze of interdependencies in reality is indeed formidable, its tale
unending, its circularity unquestionable. Yet its dissection is imperative
. . . at some point we must cut into its circumference' (Isard *et al.*, 1960,
p. 3)? We choose to make that cut with movement.

This chapter outlines the various types of movement that are important
in the build-up of other parts of the regional system and reviews some of
the models that have been evolved to describe their pattern. The idea of
movements leads on to a consideration of the natural fields that are created
by them and to the 'unnatural' territories that are set up to demarcate
between overlapping fields. Ideas of diffusion are also introduced into the
treatment at this stage as a logical extension of movement over time, and
as an attempt to link together its separate applications in succeeding
chapters.

I. MOVEMENT AND MORPHOLOGY

Movement is an aspect of regional organization that has been too lightly
stressed in human geography. Crowe (1938) took his geographical colleagues to task for their overweening concern with the static elements on
the earth's surface. Is progressive geography, he asked, to be solely concerned with the distribution of *Homo dormiens*? To be sure, the quarter

century since Crowe's strictures has seen a growing recognition of momentum and circulation patterns (Capot-Rey, 1947) in geographical research, not least in migration studies where the Lund School have put population movements at the centre of their field (Hannerberg, Hägerstrand, and Odeving, 1957). In this view, human population is regarded not as a static feature (the dot-maps of conventional geographical analysis) but as a complex of oscillating particles, with short loops connecting places of sleep, work, and recreation, and longer loops connecting old hearths and new areas of migration. Other components in the regional system may be viewed in a similar manner—agricultural zones in terms of freight movements, or city growth in terms of commuting (Kain, 1962). Each of these types of movement leaves its special mark on the face of the earth. Bunge has suggested that both physical and social processes leave comparable trails: '. . . Davis's streams move the earth material to the sea and leave the earth etched with valleys; Thünen's agricultural products are moved to the market and leave their mark on the earth with rings of agriculture; . . . agricultural innovations creep across Europe, as do glacial fronts, to yield Hägerstrand's regions of agricultural progress and terminal moraines' (Bunge, 1962, p. 196).

This dualism between physical and human geography is part of a far wider parallelism between movement and geometry. In biology, the classic work in this field is D'Arcy Thompson's *On growth and form* (1917) in which he attempted to show how mathematical concepts (e.g. magnitude and transformation) and dynamical principles (e.g. available energy) help to explain biological forms. Like another biologist, Henri Fabre, Thompson was fascinated by the regularity and mathematical perfection of a bee's cell or a dragon-fly's wing and drew them together in basic consideration of geometry and movement. A similar ability to recognize links between fields that are conventionally divided was shared by one of the greatest locational theorists, August Lösch, who saw fundamental parallels between biological and economic forms.

Lösch (1954, p. 184) drew attention to what he terms, grandiosely, the *lex parsimoniae* or 'law of minimum effort'. This concept suggests that natural events reach their goal by the shortest route. It appears first in physics in the eighteenth century with the work of Lagrange as the *principle of least action* and reappears in systems analysis as the concept of *minimum potential energy*, in operations research as *geodesics* (or optimal movement paths), and in the social sciences as the *principle of least effort* (Zipf, 1949).

We shall be resorting to 'least movement' as an explanatory model in many parts of Part One of this book where the geometry of settlement arrangements (Chap. 4.II), or industrial patterns (Chap. 5.IV) or agricultural zones (Chap. 6.II) conforms to regular and often symmetrical distribution. The symmetry discovered in these sections may well be critical for in 1883 Mach (1942) argued that 'forms of equilibrium' are often symmetrical and regular, and that in mechanical terms they correspond to a maximum or minimum of work. Fig. 2.1 shows a practical application of the minimum-work concept as modified by the probabilistic viewpoint outlined in Chapter 1.IV. If we assume a uniform plane then the least-effort path between points α and β is shown by the broken line in Fig. 2.1-A. However, we may argue (e.g. from Meinig's findings on railway routes in the northwestern United States (Chap. 1.IV)) that the actual

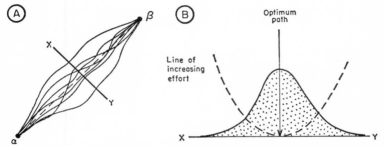

Fig. 2.1. Optimum paths between centres viewed in terms of probability theory.

paths are likely to diverge from the optimum paths (in distance terms) for a wide range of rational and irrational reasons. Examples of actual paths are shown by the bundle of lines connecting α and β. If we draw a cross-section from *X* to *Y* across the shortest route we can show that as paths diverge further from the optimum path the amount of work they have to do, in distance travelled, goes up. This is plotted as the parabolic line in Fig. 2.1-B. We may suspect that the actual paths will tend to fluctuate about the optimum in a random way to give a Gaussian distribution about the least-effort path (the shaded normal curve in Fig. 2.1-B).

II. INTERACTION—MOVEMENT AND DISTANCE

The attenuating effect of distance on movement has been recognized intuitively by societies at all levels of development; for at least eighty years, since the work of Ravenstein (1885–9) in England and Andersson (1897) in Sweden, this effect has been scientifically investigated. Ravenstein's observations on the relations between distance and the volume of migration proved so striking that a number of attempts were made to express this relationship in a general, often mathematical, form. These attempts have been discussed in detail by Hägerstrand (1957, pp. 112–54) and by Isard *et al.* (1960, pp. 493–568). Some of the more important models are briefly reviewed here together with their locational implications. Other models come more logically under a consideration of fields and territories and are reviewed in Chapter 2.III.

1. Regional studies of lapse rates

Studies of movements in relation to distance have ranged very widely in terms of both the movements studied and the range of distances involved. Fig. 2.2 draws together three typical examples of freight movements over three different scales. In the first (Fig. 2.2-c) the volume of freight moving

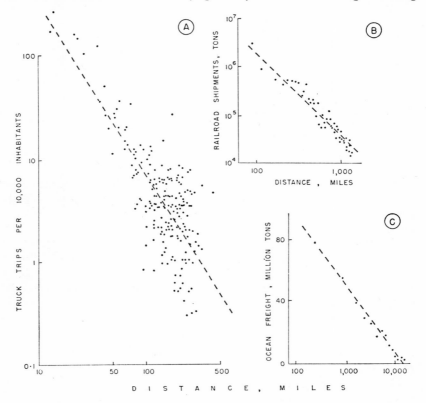

Fig. 2.2. Movement lapse rates. *A* Truck trips around Chicago, United States. *B* Class I railway shipments, United States, 1949. *C* World ocean-going freight, 1925. Sources: Helvig, 1964, p. 78; Zipf, 1949.

between twenty-five areas in ocean-going shipping in 1925 is plotted against distance. Despite the limitations of the data, the steady fall-off of movement with distance up to 13,000 miles is clearly apparent. Over a more limited area, that of the continental United States, the fall-off of the tonnage of Class I railroad shipments in 1949 with distance up to 1,500 miles is also clearly shown (Fig. 2.2-B). For a still smaller area, the Chicago region, Helvig (1964) has shown that the number of truck trips is also associated with distance in a zone extending out to around 350 miles (Fig. 2.2-A).

Studies of freight movements are paralleled by a very large number of studies of other movements. Dåhl's (1957) study of the contacts between the town of Västerås, Sweden, with the rest of that country is typical. He mapped movements of population, passenger traffic, telephone traffic, newspaper subscriptions, business contacts, retail trade contacts, and goods traffic. Despite detailed variations, as between movements based on private and business contacts and from one time period to the next, Dåhl found the general fall-off of movement with distance was strikingly confirmed. Alongside such regional studies stand a few systematic studies. Zipf (1949), in an intriguing book *Human behaviour and the principle of least effort*, brought together dozens of varied examples of movements mostly for the United States. More recently Isard (1956, pp. 55–76) prefaced his *Location and the space economy* with a review of similar distance–movement studies.

2. Elementary interaction models

The models put forward to explain the fall-off or lapse rates described above have been of two kinds—models which draw heavily on physical analogies, and models which are empirical attempts to generalize the detailed findings in a general mathematical form.

a. Deductive models: gravity and absorption analogues. One of the most productive borrowings from physical science by geographers has been in the field of gravitational theory. Reilly (1929) drew directly from Newtonian theory (Sears and Zemansky, 1964, p. 103) in suggesting that movement between two centres would be proportional to the product of their populations and inversely proportional to the square of the distance separating them. This we can formulate as

$$M_{ij} = P_i P_j (d_{ij})^{-2}$$

where M_{ij} is the interaction between centres i and j, P_i and P_j is a measure of the mass of the two centres, and d_{ij} is a measure of the distance separating them. As Carrothers (1956) has shown in a historical survey, gravity concepts were rapidly taken up in both Europe and North America. Two American social scientists, Stewart (1947) and Zipf (1949), studied interactions over a wide range of social phenomena (migration, freight traffic, exchange of information, etc.) in terms of the gravity formula, using a modification of the Reilly formula

$$M_{ij} = P_i P_j (d_{ij})^{-1}$$

The difference between the two exponents, -2 as used by Reilly and -1

as used by Stewart and Zipf, has been analysed by Hägerstrand (1957, pp. 118–19) who suggests that it may reflect real differences between Europe and North America. It may well be true that Europe, the more retarded area, has steeper movement gradients than North America.

Another analogy used in the study of lapse rates is that of absorption. Johnsson (1952) suggested that migration from a centre might be likened to the emission of a ray of light. Light is gradually absorbed by the medium in proportion to flow per unit of distance. In the same way migrating population may be thought to be gradually absorbed by the areas into which it moves. This idea may be written as a formula

$$M_x = k \ X^{-1} e^{-a_x}$$

where M_x is the percentage of in-migration to a centre from a zone at

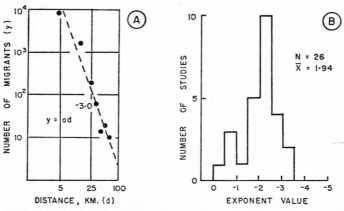

Fig. 2.3. A Outward migration from Asby, southern Sweden, 1860–1939. B Histogram of exponent values in Pareto-type formulae fitted to migration data for selected Swedish parishes. Source: Hägerstrand, 1957, pp. 114, 115.

distance X, k is a constant, and a is the absorption coefficient. Hägerstrand suggests the curve derived from the absorption equation may give a better fit to given movement data than a simple gravity model. However, the difficulties in deriving the curve and in comparing it with other findings make it far less useful than the gravity formula.

b. Inductive models: curve fitting. A somewhat different type of approach has been used in analyses of Scandinavian migration movements. Kant (1946) in a study of in-migration to the Estonian town of Tartu suggested a Pareto-type formula

$$M = aD^{-b}$$

where M is the number of migrants reduced to a standard population, D is the distance, and a and b are constants. Fig. 2.3-A shows such a formula fitted to out-migration from the town of Asby (Sweden) during the period 1860–9 with the values equal to

$$M = 2 \cdot 1 \times 10^6 (D^{-3 \cdot 0})$$

(Hägerstrand, 1957, p. 113).

In subsequent studies in Sweden a great many similar expressions have been calculated using Pareto-type formulae and particular interest has centred around the value for the exponent b. In the studies reviewed by Hägerstrand, it varied from as low as $-0 \cdot 4$ to as high as $-3 \cdot 3$. Low b values indicate a gentle gradient with a wide field of movement and are more common for studies based on twentieth-century movements, while high b values, indicating a steep gradient and limited movement field, are more characteristic of nineteenth-century migrations. While values have clearly ranged considerably from the exponent of $-2 \cdot 0$ predicted by the 'inverse square law', it may be significant that in this sample (plotted as a frequency histogram in Fig. 2.3-B) the modal class is at just this value. Significantly the mean value for all the studies was $-1 \cdot 94$. The suggestion from regional migration studies is that while the inverse-square hypothesis does not yield a unique solution it is a very useful approximation.

3. Modified interaction models

a. Difficulties of the gravity model. Although in principle gravity formulae appear to offer simple and effective guides to predicting movement between areas, in practice they meet a number of difficulties. For it is not clear how the various parts of the expression shall be defined nor how they shall be related. Here we examine the problem for each component: for mass, distance, and relations between mass and distance.

(i) *Mass* has conventionally been equated with population size in many gravity studies. Population has the prime advantage of convenience as data on the size of most population clusters in the world is readily available. On the other hand, population may conceal important differences between regions and the use of some system of weighting has been urged. Even in terms of the original physical concepts, this weighting may be justified, for as Isard argues: 'Just as the weights of molecules of different elements are unequal, so should the weights of different kinds of people be different. The average Chinese peasant does not make the same contribution . . . as the United States urban dweller' (Isard *et al.*, 1960, p. 506). Empirical weights of 0·8 for population in the Deep South, 2·0 for population in the Far West, and 1·0 for population in other areas of the United States are given by Isard as a rough indication of the range such regional 'multipliers' might show. Alternatively, multiplication of the population of each cluster by its mean *per capita* income suggests itself as a useful improvement on Isard's weighting system, though it still does not yield a unique answer. In practice, interaction studies have used indices like commodity output (Warntz, 1959) or retail sales (Dunn, 1956) as relevant measures of mass in gravity formulae.

(ii) *Distance* can also be measured in a number of ways. The conventional measure is simply that of the straight-line or cross-country distance between the two points. Although Bunge (1962, p. 52) has illustrated that distance is a much more complex function, Yeates (1963) found that cross-country distance may be a useful yardstick in rural areas with a good road network. In commuting studies, time rather than distance might be the appropriate measure, with small distances in the urban areas being equal to longer distances in the rural areas. Where different transport media are introduced, the difficulty becomes more acute. Here Harris (1954) has suggested that 100 miles by truck (at 4·0 cents per ton-mile), might be equivalent to 160 miles by rail (at 2·5 cents per ton-mile), or to 1,600 miles by ship (at 0·25 cents per ton-mile), though even these weightings are complicated by terminal costs and delivery charges at destination.

Vining (1949) and Huff (1960) have stressed that the migrant's view of remoteness and distance may not be a simple geographical one; we may regard nearby areas as strongly differentiated and remote areas as uniform, a view reinforced by the curvilinear relations of travelling costs to distance. Hägerstrand (1957) has suggested that we may generalize both the psychological and economic view of distance within a logarithmic transformation of distance. He uses an azimuthal logarithmic projection centred on the place of migration, Asby in central Sweden (α), to suggest the migrant's impression of distance. The contrast between the conventional map of Sweden (Fig. 2.4-A) with the transformed map on the azimuthal logarithmic projection (Fig. 2.4-B) shows the drastic change in spatial relationships: β and γ show the location of Stockholm and Gothenburg on both maps and δ the approximate location of the United States on the second map!

(iii) The *relations between mass and distance* pose the third difficult problem. The rather simple functions proposed in both the gravity models and the Pareto models describe a straight-line relationship on double-log graph paper. However, Isard has shown that it is equally possible to fit a quadratic rather than a linear function to a set of interaction data, and that this must modify our view of the attenuating effect of distance (Isard *et al.*, 1960, p. 510). Helvig (1964) has supported this view in a regional study of truck movements in the Chicago area. He adopts a quadratic form for the familiar mass–distance model, viz.,

$$M_{ij} = 0·42\{\sqrt{P_iP_j}/d_{ij}{}^2\}^2 + 4·9\{\sqrt{P_iP_j}/d_{ij}{}^2\} + 160$$

His justification for this new and more complex form is entirely empirical: it gives a better fit to the particular movement lapse rates he is studying.

Clearly there are a number of ways in which the gravity type of model

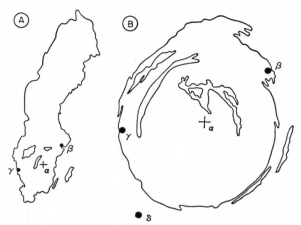

Fig. 2.4. Conventional map of Sweden ($G = 3\cdot1$) (A) 'transformed to an azimuh, logarithmic-distance map (B) based on Asby, α. Source: Hägerstrand, 1957, p.t 54

can be adapted to make it more valuable in empirical studies. There remain however a number of other doubts about its ultimate usefulness in complex situations (Beckerman, 1956).

b. Refinements of the gravity model. We are familiar in economic theory with the 'push-pull' concept of supply and demand. Ullman (in Thomas 1956, pp. 862–80) mapped the tendency for material flows to move from areas of abundance to areas of scarcity while Bunge (1962, pp. 121–2) suggests that we may recognize here a wider principle, that of 'self-repulsion' introduced from the mathematical theory of heat conduction by Hotelling (1921). Goodrich (1936) in a study of *Migration and economic opportunity* traced population movements within the United States from undesirable' to 'desirable' areas.

How important is such regional *complementarity* in modifying the gravity type of relationships? Kariel (1963) analysed by multivariate methods population growth due to net migration in the United States in the 1950–60 decade. As Table 2.1 shows, four factors were tested by Kariel: (i) *desirability* as measured by increase in manufacturing employment, by median family income, and by proportion of professional and technical workers in the population: (ii) *size* as measured by number of the employed labour force. The proportion of the variation 'explained' by the four hypotheses was measured by the coefficient of determination. This showed striking confirmation of the importance of size in determining the volume of migration: it was nearly four times as important as any of the other three factors. Even with Kariel's reminder, that in the period of study there were local short-term slumps (e.g. in the Detroit area's motor industry) which might affect the findings, this result is important in showing surprisingly strong support for the gravity type of model.

Table 2.1. Complementarity models and migration movements*

	Variance reduction
Complementarity hypothesis:	
Increase in manufacturing employment	12%
Median family income	12%
Professional and technical workers (per cent)	10%
Size hypothesis:	
Size of employed labour force	44%
Joint four-factor hypothesis:	47%
Joint four-factor hypothesis with climatic adjustment:	55%

Source: Kariel, 1963, p. 210.

* United States, 1950–60.

Isard has attempted to build in this complementarity of areas to the simple inverse-distance gravity model. This may be written as

$$M_{ij} = (P_j/d_{ij}) \cdot f(Z_i)$$

where M_{ij}, P_j, and d_{ij} are defined as in Chapter 2.II(2a) and $f(Z_i)$ is some function of Z_i where Z_i measures the attractive force of destination i (Isard *et al.*, 1960, p. 68). 'Attractive force' remains to be defined in detail and we can at this stage point only to its variability. For example in migration studies it seems clear that amenities in general and climate in particular are playing an increasing part in migration within more developed countries (Ullman, 1959). This gives point to Kariel's finding that his overall level of 'explanation' jumped by 8 per cent (Table 2.1) when results were adjusted for climatic desirability by contrasting areas to the north and south of the 45° F. mean winter isotherm.

III. 'FIELD' AND 'TERRITORY'— MOVEMENT AND AREA

1. Continuous areas of movement: the field concept

The view of interactions given in the preceding section is clearly an over-simplified one: movements do not in fact take place along a one-dimensional line but over a two-dimensional area. We are familiar with such areas in human geography in a number of guises—the 'sphere of influence' of a city, the 'hinterland' of a port, the 'migration field' of a parish. All hold in common the fact of interaction between a centre and its periphery: here we refer to them by the common term *field*.

a. Size of fields. One of the striking features of the relationships between movement and distance is that the graphs are frequently drawn on double-log paper, and thus in no case is a zero origin shown for movement. This fact underlines a fundamental characteristic of interaction fields— they are theoretically *continuous* distributions with a very rapid fall-off near their centre and a very slow, almost asymptotic, fall-off at their outer ranges. Indeed we may describe them in statistical jargon as 'strongly leptokurtic log-normal bivariate distributions', or, more graphically, compare them to the sharp peaks on the newly iced surface of a birthday cake.

Because of their continuous nature we cannot always describe the size of fields by their *absolute* limits, but we can make a useful generalization about their size if we are prepared to substitute the concept of *mean field* for that of maximum or potential field. Thus if we take any local English newspaper (e.g. the *Bridgwater Mercury*) we are likely to find that its maximum field is immense (i.e. a few copies are sent to expatriates in Argentina or New Zealand), but its mean field is very small, perhaps not more than ten miles across. For the San Francisco Bay area, Vance (1962, p. 509) has shown that while about 17 per cent of the customers of the regional shopping centres come from over ten miles away, one half the customers live within three miles of the centre. Similarly, although one per cent of the visitors to the Shenandoah national park come from over 2,000 miles, its mean field is less than 300 miles in radius (Clawson, Held, and Stoddard, 1960, p. 171).

For mean fields two generalizations appear valid: (i) The size of mean fields varies with the *transferability* of the item being moved. Ullman (in Thomas, 1956, pp. 862–80) has shown for the United States that different products move with unequal ease, and that this friction is reflected in relative freight costs. His atlas of commodity movements (Ullman, 1957) shows clearly the contrast between products. Duerr (1960, p. 167) has attempted to define Ullman's concept of transferability more rigorously, arguing that we may measure transferability as the *specific value* of a

Table 2.2. Relative transportability of three products

Lumber product:	Type I (veneer logs)	Type II (pulpwood)	Type III (mine props)
Specific value, dollars/ton	150	20	5
Maximum railroad haul, miles	400	100	25

Source: Duerr, 1960, p. 167.

product—that is, its value per unit of weight or bulk. As Table 2.2 shows, low-value products (e.g. mine props) normally move short distances, while high-value products (e.g. veneer logs) move relatively long distances.

Christaller (1933) suggested the same basic idea in his concept of the 'range of a good' (Chap. 5.III), and in a reverse sense we may regard Thünen's discussion of agricultural location (Chap. 6.II) in the same way. Products with low specific value (e.g. forest products) tend to cluster near the city in Thünen's ideal landscape.

(ii) The size of mean fields varies over *time*. Rapidly increasing mobility is one of the dominant features of movement this century. Mean fields for the movement of information, population, and goods have grown steadily larger as technical innovations have reduced the *relative* cost of distance. Chisholm (1962, pp. 171–97) has brought together a number of examples of this trend, showing for example that the real cost of ocean

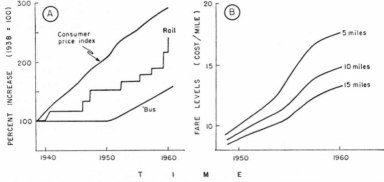

Fig. 2.5. Sample changes in movement costs over time. *A* British passenger transport. *B* Scottish omnibuses. Source: Ministry of Transport, 1961, pp. 66, 67.

shipping fell by about three-fifths between 1876 and 1955, or that railway freight costs in New Zealand fell by about one-quarter between 1884 and 1956.

For the United Kingdom, the Jack Report (Ministry of Transport, 1961) has shown the relative fall in the cost of rural bus services. Fig. 2.5-A shows the increase in rail and bus fares over the period 1938 to 1960 in relation to the general index of consumer prices. Despite recent increases, the cost of both services has lagged well behind the general price index. A second important finding of the Jack Report is shown in Fig. 2.5-B. This shows the relative increase of bus fares over the same time period for three distances (five, ten, and fifteen miles). It is interesting that the increase over the longer distances has been less than over the shorter, so that the relative cost of long-distance travel has been specially reduced.

The result of lowering in relative movement costs is seen in the widening range of interactions of all kinds. For passenger traffic, the average distance travelled in the United States in the year 1906 was 631 miles (Table 2.3). Within half a century this distance had increased eightfold to

Table 2.3. Changing patterns of movement*

Period:	1906	1956
Travel, miles *per capita*	631	5,080
Means of travel, proportion of total passenger miles:		
Airlines	—	2·6%
Automobiles	0·6%	87·0%
Inland waterways	1·5%	0·2%
Inter-city buses	—	3·0%
Local public carriers	51·0%	3·9%
Railroads	46·9%	3·3%

Source: Clawson, Held, and Stoddard, 1960, pp. 534–6.

* United States.

over 5,000 miles, although the main cause here was less the reduction in the costs of conventional media but the introduction of entirely new transport media, notably the private motor-car. Vance (1960) has mapped this growing zone of interaction for the Massachusetts town of Natick.

This growing range of interaction has made the complicated problem of field overlap and field definition still more acute. Traditionally, attempts to delimit fields have been based on a variety of measures. Theodorson (1961, pp. 511–94) brings together a collection of typical studies of field delimitation in which newspaper circulation, wholesale trade, commuting, telephone calls, banking, bus services, and the like have been tried with varying degrees of success. Little attempt has been made to test the comparative values of the various measures and no general conclusions can be drawn on optimum indices. These are likely to vary considerably over time—local bus-service areas have been widely used in field delimitation in England and Wales (e.g. Green, 1950)—but there is strong evidence that their importance is dwindling. The astounding rise in importance of automobile travel (see Table 2.3) in the United States is well documented, and in post-war Britain the motor-car 'bulge' has introduced a new and not fully understood element into the interaction patterns of this country. Certainly when many indices are plotted for interaction about the same centre, the most likely outcome is a 'garland' of intertwining lines after the manner of Fig. 2.6-A. Exact coincidence of the boundaries which are in any case arbitrary limits (as argued above), is very rare and if a single synthetic boundary to a field is needed, some inexact compromise such as the median line may serve for inexact purposes. Other types of compromise are discussed in Chapter 9.I.

b. Shape of fields. If we allow that some line, however arbitrary and subject to changes over time, may be drawn around a centre to delimit its field, then we can make some observations on the shape of that field. We

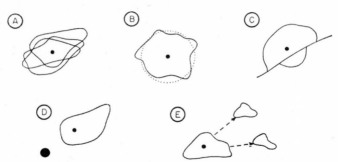

Fig. 2.6. Alternative types of movement fields. *C Truncated* field. *D Distorted* field. *E Fragmented* field.

are in fact cutting a section through our density distribution (parallel to the plane over which it is spread); and should therefore expect our fields to be circular in shape only if our original notion of interaction fields as 'conic' forms is correct. In fact, truly circular fields are not found by empirical regional study; the most common form tends to be an irregular, amoeba-like, closed figure. Davis (1926, p. 106) described them as 'roughly circular in outline' and little work has been done since then to measure their shape with more precision, or to improve on Davis's verdict. Certainly most fields approximate the circle (Fig. 2.6-b) and we might well accommodate random variations (lobes, waves, and indentations) within a theory which allowed stochastic 'blurring' of the regular form. Beckmann (1958) has shown the value of a random element in reconciling Christaller's stepped hierarchy with the log-normal distribution (Chap. 5.I(3)) and we might borrow his argument here and apply it to field shape.

There are however departures from the theoretical form which are more serious and more persistent. These demand a different type of explanation. Some fields are severely truncated, others are systematically distorted, still others are fragmented. These non-symmetric forms demand a different type of explanation and are treated separately here:

(i) A typical form for the *truncated* field is shown in Fig. 2.6-c. Perhaps the most dramatic and well-known illustration of this type comes from a study of the location of El Paso bank accounts made by Lösch (1954, p. 448). He was able to show for an American bank on the United States–Mexican border that in 1914 the radius of its field on the Mexican side was only half that of the United States side.

A similar indication of the distorting effect of political boundaries has been given by Mackay (1958). He compared the observed interactions between Montreal and surrounding cities (as measured by long-distance telephone traffic) with the 'expected' interactions using a non-linear P/d

formula. His results show that the traffic between Montreal and other cities in Quebec province (Fig. 2.7-A) was from five to ten times greater than traffic between Montreal and cities with comparable P/d values in the neighbouring Ontario province (Fig. 2.7-B). The strength of the provincial barrier in blocking the extension of the Montreal field was itself overshadowed by the blocking effect of the international boundary to the south. Traffic with comparable cities in the United States was down to one-fiftieth that of the Quebec traffic. Mackay's technique allows a rather clear measurement of the effect of boundaries on shaping fields and might usefully be extended to other areas. Truncation may not however be just a political effect. Vance (1962) has shown how the trade areas of eleven regional shopping centres in the San Francisco Bay area are modified by

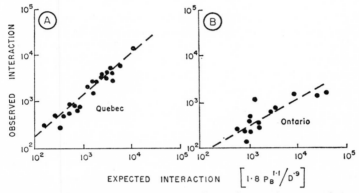

Fig. 2.7. Impact of the Quebec–Ontario border on interaction around the city of Montreal. Source: Mackay, 1958, p. 5.

the north–south trend of the Coastal Ranges and more specifically by the relatively high toll-costs in crossing the inlets of the Bay itself.

A general graphical model which relates the blocking action of both physical and political elements has been devised by Lösch (1954, p. 341). When the barrier is a political one, marked by tariff increases, the potential field of centre α is restricted by the distance x, but the actual form of the truncated field may vary. Fig. 2.8-A shows the probable form if the political boundary can be crossed at all points along its length; Fig. 2.8-B the probable form if it can be crossed only at a customs point, β. If the boundary is not a political one but a natural feature (e.g. a river) with a single crossing point at β, the field will probably conform to that of Fig. 2.8-C.

(ii) *Distorted* fields vary more widely in shape. Applebaum and Cohen (1961, p. 81) describe the shape of the trading areas of outlying shopping centres, as parabolically elongated away from the central business district. Similarly Park (1929) was able to show that the circulation fields for daily newspapers in part of the central United States (South Dakota) were asymmetrically elongated away from the areas of intense competition. Fig. 2.6-D shows a general case for these types of distorted field.

There is a strong probability that some of this asymmetry can be accommodated within the ideas of Isard and Getis (reviewed in Chapter 2.III(2c)) who argue that fields may *appear* as distortions, merely because they are the transformations of fields which are regular in terms of non-geographic space. In the special case of migration fields, Stouffer (1940), a sociologist, has argued that we should not in any case expect fields to be circular because there is no necessary deterministic relation between migration and geographical distance. His hypothesis may be stated in the form

$$M_{ij} = \{N_j/N_{ij}\}.k$$

where M_{ij} is the expected interaction between location i and location j, where N_j is the number of opportunities at location j, N_{ij} is the number of

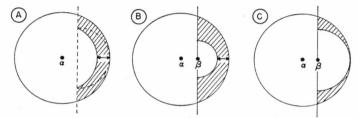

Fig. 2.8. Impact of boundaries on the size of field centred on α. Source: Lösch 1954, p. 341.

opportunities in the intervening area between i and j, and k is a constant. This model, the *intervening opportunity* model, states simply therefore that the amount of interaction over a given geographical distance is directly proportional to the opportunities at that distance, but inversely proportional to the number of intervening opportunities. The model has been used by Isbell (1944) and Folger (1953) in studies of internal migration in Sweden and the Tennessee Valley in the eastern United States. In both cases the intervening-opportunity model gave better prediction than the simple gravity-type model.

In terms of our distorted fields (Fig. 2.6-D), we may argue that Stouffer's model allows an adequate explanation both for the restriction of the field on the inner side (i.e. the intervening opportunities of the larger centre cut into its potential area) and the extension on the outer side (i.e. lack of intervening opportunity gives the centre a clear run to extend on this side). While more sophisticated models are clearly needed, some progress has been made towards accommodating our distorted fields within general interaction models.

(iii) *Fragmented* fields consist of a contiguous inner area with one cr more 'outliers' of high interaction. Fig. 2.6-E suggests the general form of such a field. Hägerstrand (1957, pp. 126–54) has drawn together a number of regional examples of this type of field in migration movements. One of the most striking examples is that of Värmland, in central Sweden, which was the main source of migrants for nearby areas and for an area 400 kilometres away but *not* for intervening areas. Other cases of similar discontinuities come from migration into Paris and Budapest at the national level, and the remarkable concentrations of German migration within specific small areas of North America at the international level (Johnson, 1941).

Hägerstrand finds three common elements in all these cases: (i) the importance of the information chain represented by individual contacts, (ii) the division of migrants into *active* and *passive* elements with the latter following the definite channels made by the former, and (iii) the random element in the initial choice of areas. While it was not possible to build a comprehensive *feedback* model to accommodate all three elements, Hägerstrand has suggested a short-term model. This is given by the expression

$$M_{ij} = (V_j I_j)/P_j.k$$

where M_{ij} is the number of migrants from location i to j, V_j are the vacancies at j, I_j is the *information level* about these vacancies existing at the source i, P_j is the population of the destination j, and k is a constant. That is the volume of migration is related to the *vacancy density* of the destination and the level of information about it. Here distance is introduced indirectly through the information level since more information is likely to be available about very near places than very distant places. Hägerstrand has tested his model on Swedish migration data using Monte Carlo methods (see Chap. 10.III) to simulate the random selection of areas and

---

Table 2.4. Comparison of intervening-opportunity and feedback models in predicting migration*

Distance zone (kilometres):	0–19	20–39	40–59	60–79	80–99
Observed migration	86	132	42	18	12
Predicted migration using model:					
Intervening-opportunity	105	89	39†	29	29
Feedback	89†	131†	41†	17†	13†

Source: Hägerstrand, 1957, pp. 125, 153.

    * Dädesjö, Sweden, 1946–50.
    † Estimates within ±10 per cent of observed migration.

their relative growth. Some indication of the considerable relative success of the feedback model is shown in Table 2.4 where its predictions are compared with a simple intervening-opportunity model.

2. Bounded areas of movement: the territory concept

While continuous fields which fluctuate over time are the dominant pattern in the organization of regional systems, they pose such severe administrative problems that human society establishes boundaries (for continuities) and discrete non-overlapping territories (for overlapping and indistinct fields). Political areas are the most readily recognizable reaction to this problem but they are by no means unique and we can argue that the clerical diocese in England, the state planning *oblast* in Soviet Russia, and the tribal area in Amerindian Brazil are all reactions to that common problem. To be sure, there are differences between parish and state but each involves the notion of property and here we refer to them by the general term *territory*. Parallel ideas of territory are common in biology (Howard, 1920; Wynne-Edwards, 1962).

a. Elementary packing theory. With discrete territories the basic problem is simply that of the efficient partitioning of areas between competing centres. We may define efficiency in two ways: *efficiency of movement* as measured by the distance from the centre to outlying parts within the territory, and *efficiency of boundaries* as measured by the length of the territory's perimeter. This second criterion, important in practical terms as fencing costs on the farm or defence costs for the state, is not pertinent in continuous fields.

Three geometrical principles are important in applying these minimum energy criteria to the division of an area (Coxeter, 1961):

(i) Regular polygons are more economical shapes than irregular polygons. If we take the familiar four-sided polygon, we can illustrate that for the regular square shape with an area of one square kilometre the furthest movement (i.e. from the centre to the furthest point within the square) is 0·707 kilometres and the perimeter is four kilometres. If we convert the regular square form to a rectangle of similar area but with two of its sides twice as long as the others, the furthest movement goes up to 1·031 kilometres and the perimeter to five kilometres. Experimentation demonstrates how the greater the contrast in the sides of the rectangle, the less economical it becomes in terms of both accessibility from the centre and length of perimeter.

(ii) Circles are the most economical of the regular polygons. If we imagine a continuum of regular polygons running from the triangle (3-gon), square (4-gon), pentagon (5-gon), and hexagon (6-gon) upwards, then at each stage we are increasing the number of sides and vertices by one. The limiting case is clearly the circle which we may regard as a regular polygon with an infinite number of sides and vertices. If we examine this sequence (Fig. 2.9-A) we see that, if the area remains constant, the accessibility from the centre as measured by the *maximum radial distance* improves and the perimeter becomes shorter. The relation of these two parameters is plotted in Fig. 2.9-B and it is important to note that though the improvement in economy is consistent, the gains are not regular: the square is about half as efficient as the circle and the 10-gon is about 90 per cent as efficient as the circle.

(iii) Hexagons are the regular polygons which allow the greatest amount of packing into an area, consistent with minimizing movement and boundary costs. The problem of packing circular fields into a hypo-thetical area is illustrated in Fig. 2.10 which shows with shading its inefficiency as measured by the unused areas lying between the circles. The problem of filling a plane with equal-area regular polygons was first

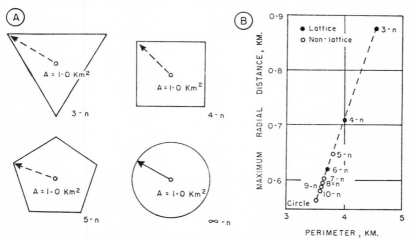

Fig. 2.9. Efficiency of alternative types of regular polygons in relation to distance from centres and perimeter length.

investigated by Kepler in the early seventeenth century, who suggested there were three solutions: the regular triangle, the regular square, and the regular hexagon. Of these three *regular tessellations* (Coxeter, 1961, pp. 61–4), the hexagon retains most of the advantages of the circle. Indeed, as Fig. 2.9-B shows, the hexagon $(6 - n)$ is about four-fifths as efficient as the circle in terms of maximum radial distance and perimeter

Hexagons have held a fascination for natural scientists and mathe-maticians since the Greeks; concepts of hexagonal symmetry played a key role in the growth of crystallography and Thompson (1961, pp. 102–25) has shown its importance throughout the biological sciences. It is not surprising therefore that the two main theoretical works on settlements and their support fields, Christaller's *Die zentralen Orte in Süddeutschland* (1933, Baskin, 1957) and Lösch's *Die raumliche Ordnung der Wirtschaft* (1940; 1954) should have used the hexagon as the modular unit in their models of settlement structure. These are discussed in Chapter 5.I.

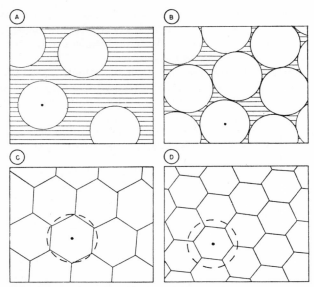

Fig. 2.10. Packing of centres in the colonization of a plain to give hexagonal territories. Source: Lösch, 1954, p. 110.

b. Regional packing studies. Despite the great theoretical importance of the hexagon, rather little interest has been shown in trying to test whether hexagonal arrangements do in fact exist. Certainly the dominant impression one receives on examining maps of territories such as counties, or parishes or states, is one of irregularity and complexity. To test whether this impression is a correct one, a sample of 100 counties was drawn by random-number methods for one country (Brazil) and its packing characteristics examined. Since this country had, in 1960, some 2,800 counties (*municipios*) and since, unlike the United States with its 'township and range' system (Chap. 4.I(1a)), it did not set out its administrative units on geometrical lines, Brazil represents a reasonably unbiased sample for such an examination.

A simple shape index, S, was used to measure the shape characteristics of the Brazilian sample. It was given as

$$S = \{1 \cdot 27A\}/l^2$$

where A is the area of the county in square kilometres, and l the long-axis of the county drawn as a straight line connecting the two most distant points within the perimeter. The multiplier ($1 \cdot 27$) adjusted the index so that a circle would have an index of $1 \cdot 00$ with values ranging down towards zero. The actual shape values recorded by this method are shown in Fig. 2.11 and range from values as low as $0 \cdot 06$ for very elongated counties to values as high as $0 \cdot 93$ for compact near-circular counties. In this measuring system the values for the three lattices is 0·42 for triangular, 0·64 for square, and 0·83 for hexagonal, and boundary lines have been interpolated on Fig. 2.11 to divide the sequence into three zones about these values. The results strongly suggest the generally elongated nature of the counties. However, the possible correspondence of the lattice boundaries with gaps in the frequency distribution may suggest that shapes tend to cluster about the three alternative tessellations proposed by Kepler.

A second characteristic associated with the regular hexagonal tessellation is the number of contacts between any one territory and adjacent territories. In a regular hexagonal system the *contact number* would clearly be six as one area would be contiguous with its six neighbours, each of

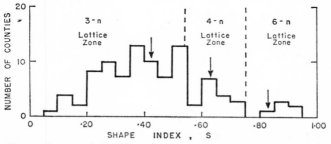

Fig. 2.11. Shape characteristics of a sample of 100 Brazilian counties in relation to lattice zones.

which would in turn have six neighbours. Since coastal counties and those on the international frontier had their fields truncated, these were eliminated from the sample; the remaining eighty-four counties were examined and their contact numbers recorded. The frequency curve of the results is shown in Fig. 2.12-A. It shows that although the number of contacts varied from two to fourteen nearly one in three counties had exactly six neighbours. The mean contact number for the sample was 5·71. This rather striking approximation to the hexagonal number proposed by Christaller and Lösch suggests that criticism of the hexagonal system as over-theoretical may have been too hasty. Preliminary counts on administrative areas in France and China suggest that the Brazilian figure is not exceptional, but further investigation is necessary before we can be sure we have isolated a regularity in territorial organization.

One recognizable trend within the sample was for high-density counties to be more closely packed and therefore to have a higher contact number than lightly populated areas. Fig. 2.12-B shows the *contact index* (contact number/area of the county) plotted against the population density of each county to give a positive relationship. This relationship has been examined over a ninety-year period for one of the Brazilian states

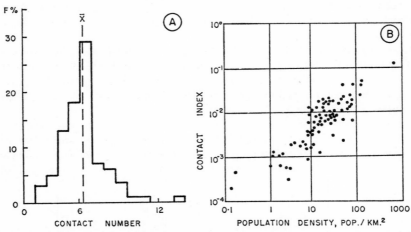

Fig. 2.12. Histogram of contact numbers of 100 Brazilian counties (*A*) and their relation to population density (*B*).

(Santa Catarina) and shows that with the build-up of population density the counties have become smaller (Fig. 2.13) while the contact numbers have increased from 3·50 in 1872 to 5·22 in 1960. The lower numbers in the latter period compared to the rest of Brazil are due to the nature of the sample: all counties (including those in coastal and state-line locations)

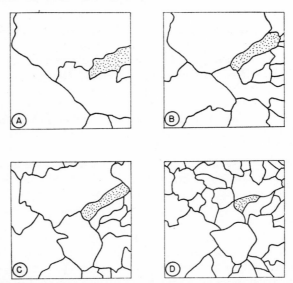

Fig. 2.13. Progressive territorial subdivision of sample quadrat (*G = 4·9*) in Santa Catarina state, Brazil. *A* 1872. *B* 1907. *C* 1930. *D* 1960. Source: Buchéle, 1958.

were examined. How far the increasing congruence with the 'minimum-energy' solution over time can be interpreted in rational terms remains to be seen.

    c. Modifications of the hexagon model. Isard (1956) has shown that the *regular* (i.e. equal-area) pattern of hexagons suggested by Christaller and Lösch are unlikely to occur in practice. Because of the high density of population at the central core postulated by Lösch, the size of the market area here is likely to be smaller, while away from the market it is likely to be larger. Isard has produced a figure (Fig. 2.14) which retains as many

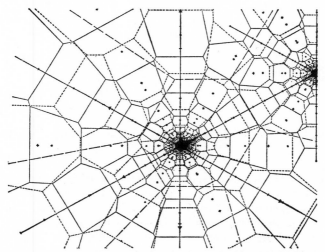

Fig. 2.14. Löschian system of hexagonal territories as modified by agglomeration. Source: Isard, 1956, p. 272.

of the assumptions of the Löschian system as possible, but introduces this concept of more closely packed centres near the overall nodal point. Extreme difficulty was found in working with the hexagonal form and, as the figure shows, it was impossible to retain both the hexagon and urbanization economies. As Isard points out, the hexagon is a pure concept much as perfect competition is a pure concept to the economist. It loses its significance as a spatial form once the inevitable agglomeration forces—which are themselves inherent in the Löschian system—are allowed to operate.

    Confirmation of the changing size of territories away from the dense urban centres is available from Brazil. By using the same sample of 100 Brazilian counties (Chap. 2.III(2)), the size of territories in relation to population density was investigated. County areas were found to be approximately log-normal in distribution with a few very large areas (like Sena Madureira in the Acre Territory of the upper Amazon with an area

c

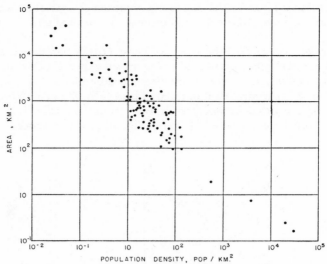

Fig. 2.15. Relationship of the size and density of a sample of 100 Brazilian counties.

of 46,000 square kilometres) extending down to areas as small as London boroughs in the Rio de Janeiro area. As Fig. 2.15 shows, size was rather strongly but inversely correlated with population density so that the large fields occurred in lightly populated areas whereas the small fields were characteristic of areas of dense population. Again, this phenomenon does not appear to be limited to Brazil: the county maps of the United States or the parish maps of Britain show a generally similar trend.

A second source of confirmation for Isard's modification has come from a study by Getis (1963) of the southeastern part of the city of Tacoma, in the United States. Getis investigated the distribution of stores within this urban area in relation to locational theory. He found that the 'normal' geographical pattern shown by the regular divisions of township-and-range on Fig. 2.16-A showed little suggestion of any regularities in store distribution throughout the area. Income values were computed for each of the forty-eight cells within this area, and a map drawn (Fig. 2.16-B) to show the size of each cell proportional to its income value; thus cell α with a high income has a large area and cell β with a low income a small area. In this map the distribution of stores appears far more regular.

It will be clear from both maps that the overall size and shape of the maps is the same and that only the internal divisions, the cells, have been changed. What Getis has achieved is a transformation of normal or geographical space into *income space*. As Tobler (1963) has urged, there are a number of such projections or transformations that might prove useful in

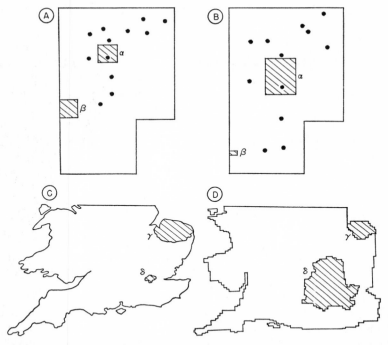

Fig. 2.16. Transformation of conventional maps into income and population space. *AB* Transformation of sample sector $(G = 7 \cdot 2)$ of Tacoma city, United States, into income-space map. *CD* Transformation of southern England $(G = 3 \cdot 8)$ into population-space map. Sources: Getis, 1963, pp. 18, 20; *The Times,* London, October 19, 1964, p. 18.

testing locational theory. One example of a *population-space* map is shown for southern Britain. Fig. 2.16-c shows the familiar geographical shape, and Fig. 2.16-D a transformation of this shape on the basis of the voting population of electoral districts in 1964. The relative change in size of the counties of Norfolk (γ) and London (δ) show the extent of the distortion. In this case contiguity between electoral districts has been preserved but otherwise distortion in the outline of the area has been allowed.

We may argue from the work of both Isard and Getis that we should not expect regular hexagonal territories to be generally visible on the earth's surface, because they are related not to geographical space but to population or income space. Hexagons may therefore be thought to be *latent* in most human organization but only through appropriate transformations of geographical space is their form likely to be made visible.

IV. DIFFUSIONS—MOVEMENT AND TIME

1. Regional studies of diffusion

Although they may often be labelled as 'historical' geography, *diffusion* studies account for a major portion of geographical research effort over the last half-century. In a review of the development of historical geography in the United States, Clark (in James, Jones, and Wright, 1954, p. 86) has traced the importance of the 'Berkeley school', led by Carl Sauer, in developing this type of analysis into American geography. Sauer himself has contributed a major diffusion study at the world scale on *Agricultural origins and dispersals* (Sauer, 1952), while his students (e.g. Stanislawski (1946), with a study of the diffusion of the grid pattern town in the Americas) have traced man and his innovations over a wide canvas of space and time.

It was in the United States that the historian, Frederick Jackson Turner, developed his great theme of the frontier in American history; a theme taken up by Webb (1927) in his classic regional study of the central grasslands of the United States, *The Great Plains*. In geometrical terms at least, Turner's frontier thesis was a simple one. He saw the tide of innovations moving remorselessly outwards from the centre: '... stand at the Cumberland Gap and watch the procession of civilization, marching single file—the buffalo following the trail to the salt springs, the Indian, the fur trader and hunter, the cattle raiser, the pioneer farmer—and the frontier has passed by. Stand at South Pass in the Rockies a century later and see the same procession with wider intervals between' (Turner, 1920, p. 12).

Gulley (1959) and Mikesell (1960) have shown how Turner's ideas spread rapidly to areas outside North America. They were applied enthusiastically, if indiscriminately, to movements as unlike as the Russian settlement of Siberia and the Roman occupation of Europe and ranged widely in time and space over human migration. Like the Davisian cycle in geomorphology, the frontier concept was weakened by its extension to explain aspects of historical growth that lay well outside its competence and in recent years it has come in for severe criticism from historians. Nevertheless it played an important part in the development of human geography in the inter-war years. Isaiah Bowman lead a vigorous school in the United States concerned with the frontiers of settlement in various parts of the world and the consequent findings, published by the American Geographical Society as *The pioneer fringe* (Bowman, 1931) and *Pioneer settlement* (Joerg, 1932), have become classics of that period. In the postwar period the strong tide of urbanization has begun to run so fiercely that interest in the extension of rural settlement has, with some notable exceptions (e.g. Parsons, 1949; Farmer, 1957), been on the wane.

A second line of approach to diffusion study has come from the field of sociology. Here the concern has been with the spread of concepts through a society, the role of leaders in starting such innovations, and the problem of resistance to change. Rogers (1962) has reviewed some hundreds of such studies, largely concerned with the innovation of new techniques through the farming communities of the United States but ranging back to include Neolithic diffusion rates (Edmondson, 1961). The link between this type of social study with its strong links with market research and sales resistance, the historical study of the Turnerian school, and the geographical studies of diffusion of the Berkeley school, was forged by a group of Swedish geographers.

2. Diffusion models

Work in Sweden is particularly important in human geography both for its empirical detail in an area with some of the longest and most accurate record of population movements in Europe, and for its theoretical content. Broadly, two sorts of model have been evolved: an inductive model which tries to organize existing information about the geographical form of diffusion waves, and a stochastic model which suggests a mechanism for explaining them.

a. Inductive models. Hägerstrand (1952) has suggested a four-stage model for the passage of what he terms 'innovation waves' (*innovations-förloppet*). From the isarithmic maps of the diffusion of various innovations in Sweden, ranging from motor-bus routes (Godlund, 1956) to agricultural methods, he has constructed a series of cross-profiles. Study of the profiles has suggested certain repeating patterns in the diffusion process. Fig. 2.17-A shows a profile in which the ordinate represents the innovation ratio, that is the proportion of the population with the introduced item, plotted on a logarithmic scale. The abscissa represents distance. Point α is the centre of innovation and points β and γ are at locations increasingly remote from that centre.

The four stages are shown by profiles I to IV in Fig. 2.17-A: Stage I, termed the *primary* stage, marks the beginning of the diffusion process with a strong contrast between the innovating centres and the remote areas; Stage II, the *diffusion* stage, marks the diffusion process proper in which there is a strong centrifugal effect with the creation of new rapidly growing centres in the distant areas and a reduction in the strong regional contrasts of Stage I; Stage III, the *condensing* stage, in which the relative increase is equal in all three locations; Stage IV, the *saturation* stage, in which there is a general but slow asymptotical increase towards the maximum under existing conditions.

As an illustration of this process, Fig. 2.17-B shows the diffusion of a recent innovation (radio receivers) along a profile from Malmö to Hässleholm in southern Sweden in the years between 1925 and 1947.

Certainly by 1945 this innovation appears to be reaching the saturation stage.

b. Stochastic models. Hägerstrand's innovation-wave model was intended largely as a descriptive synthesis of the many individual cases of diffusion movements over time that had been described in historical and sociological literature. Since 1952 he has gone on to explore diffusion waves through the use of dynamic simulation methods in which Monte Carlo methods play an important part. This feedback model has been discussed in general terms in Chapter 2.III and the basis of the Monte Carlo method illustrated in Chapter 10.III(2).

Perhaps the simplest stochastic model of diffusion has come from outside geography in the work of Neyman and Scott (1957). They suggest that

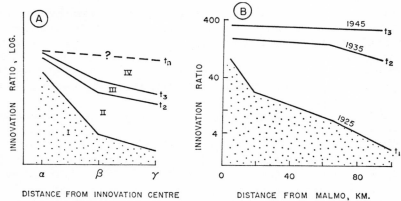

Fig. 2.17. Hypothetical (*A*) and actual (*B*) profiles of innovation waves. Source: Hägerstrand, 1952, pp. 13, 17.

the spatial distribution of a population on a basic 'habitat plane' is dependent on the interplay of four forces: (i) chance distribution of 'cluster centres' where the litters of one generation are born; (ii) chance variation in litter size; (iii) chance mechanisms of dispersal; and (iv) chance mechanism of survival up to a preassigned moment in time. In criticism of this approach Skellam has pointed out that this random process would, in the long run, lead to a normal leptokurtic distribution and that there is a need to build in some density-dependent mechanism to stop the build-up of excessive densities at the centre.

This stochastic type of approach to diffusion processes has implications of importance outside human geography. Bailey's *Mathematical theory of epidemics* (1957) uses probability theory in predicting the spread of disease, and Hägerstrand (1953, 1957) uses similar techniques in tracing the spread of ideas. Fig. 2.18 shows six stages in the diffusion of information on a random-spread model. Although the pattern is in this case a theoretical

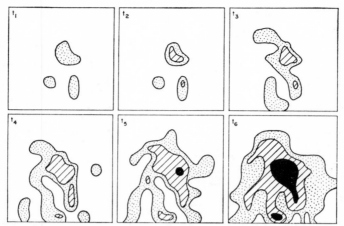

Fig. 2.18. Areal diffusion of a hypothetical innovation over successive time periods, t_1, t_2 ... t_6. Source: Hägerstrand, 1953; Bunge, 1962, p. 118.

one, it bears a strong likeness to the real historical patterns of settlement, route, and zone diffusion which are described in succeeding chapters.

One of the most interesting applications of Hägerstrand's ideas on diffusion waves has been made by Yuill (1965) using Monte Carlo simulation programmed for an IBM 7090 computer. Yuill investigated the effect of four types of barriers on the diffusion of information within a matrix of some 540 cells using a nine-cell floating grid (compare the twenty-five cell floating grid shown in Fig. 4.7). Fig. 2.19-A shows the nine-cell grid with the *barrier cells* stippled, the *transmitters* shown by dots, and the *diffusion* (i.e. transmission of information) shown by arrows. Four types of barrier cells are envisaged in decreasing order of blocking effectiveness: *Type I*, the 'super absorbing' barrier, absorbs the diffusion but destroys the transmitters; *Type II*, the 'absorbing' barrier, absorbs the diffusion but does not affect the transmitters; *Type III*, the 'reflecting' barrier, does not absorb the diffusion but allows the transmitter to transmit a new diffusion in the same generation (see arrows); and *Type IV*, the 'direct reflecting' barrier, does not absorb the diffusion but deflects it to the cell nearest available to the transmitter. Each situation was separately programmed and its results plotted from the computer output. Fig. 2.19-B shows the advance of a linear diffusion wave through an opening in a bar barrier where the 'recovery rate' (i.e. the number of generations, t_0, t_1, ... t_n) was recorded for varying types of barrier and width of gap; in the case shown, the form of the wave-front has recovered by about the eleventh generation (t_{11}). An alternative version of the bar barrier is shown in Fig. 2.19-C where the diffusion wave passes around a bar and

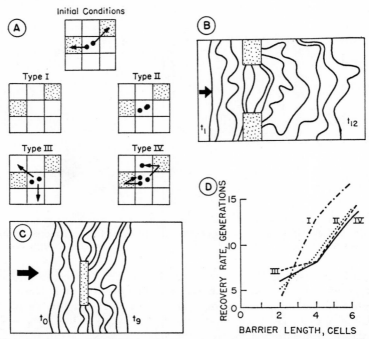

Fig. 2.19. A Four types of *barrier cells* used in the simulation model. *B* Diffusion wave passing through bar-barrier opening. *C* Diffusion waves passing around bar-barrier. *D* Recovery rates around bar barriers. Source: Yuill, 1965, pp. 19, 25, 29.

reforms after about nine generations. Here the recovery rate is directly related to both the barrier length and to the type of barrier, with the curve for the Type I super-absorbing barrier showing strong contrasts to those of the other three types (Fig. 2.19-D).

Although Yuill's results were limited by the range of postulates and the capacity of the computer, he has opened up exciting simulation possibilities of direct interest to historical geographers. The exact impact of the Appalachians, the Blue Mountains, or the Serra do Mar in holding back the inland spread of settlement from American, Australian, and Brazilian coastal base-lines has long been argued; Yuill's work suggests that more sophisticated simulation models may be evolved in which more precise answers to these questions may be possible. By using more complex environmental weightings (e.g. Chorley and Haggett, 1965-A, p. 113) series of complex simulation models adjusted to different actual or hypothetical conditions may be used in much the same way as the experimental hydrological models of estuaries and deltas developed at Wallingford and Vicksburg.

Chapter three   Networks

Although many of the movements considered in the first chapter were un-
restricted in the sense that they could flow freely in any direction, most
movements are restricted into some sort of channel. Thus even air-routes
are, as Warntz (1961) has shown for the North Atlantic, partly restricted
and most movements flow along fixed channels—roads, pipelines, telephone wires. These features themselves pose distinct locational problems
which are regarded here as part of a general class of network problems.
Network location has a literature which includes some classic early studies
(e.g. Lalanne, 1863) but is a topic which has been strangely neglected
in standard treatments of locational theory. Currently it represents one of
the most interesting growing points in both human geography and
physical geography (Haggett and Chorley, *in preparation*).

I. LOCATION OF ROUTES

Route theory is one of the least developed parts of locational theory and in
treating it here an attempt is made to piece together some of the fragments
rather than illustrate a complete structure. We begin by considering the
location of the simplest component, the single route, and then move on to
the form of the route network.

1. Location of the single route

If we assume the need to build a route between two settlements, α and β,
then the intuitive answer to the locational problem of where to build the
route is simply to join them by a straight line (Fig. 3.1-A). However, when
we observe the actual location of routes we find that with very few exceptions all routes between centres follow a more or less complex path which

deviates at least slightly from the geometrical straight-line solution. Two types of deviations have received special mention in locational theory.

a. Positive deviations. One type of deviation in which the route is lengthened in order to collect more freight, here termed *positive* deviation, has been considered in an early work by Wellington on *The economic theory of the location of railways* (1877). Wellington, a mining engineer, worked for some time in the third quarter of the nineteenth century on the planning of the railway system in Mexico, and was particularly concerned with alternative routes between the capital, Mexico City, and the gulf port, Vera Cruz (Wellington, 1886).

Here his major difficulty was to estimate the effect of connecting or ignoring smaller centres lying between them along the general line of the route. His dilemma is shown in Fig. 3.1. It consists essentially of a problem

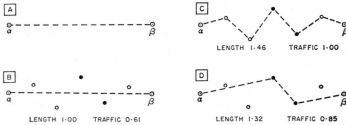

LENGTH 1·46   TRAFFIC 1·00

LENGTH 1·00   TRAFFIC 0·61

LENGTH 1·32   TRAFFIC 0·85

Fig. 3.1. Alternative paths between two points which ignore intermediate centres (*A*), minimize length (*B*), maximize traffic (*C*), and optimize length and traffic (*D*).

in optimizing the relationship between length of railroad (shorter the better) and the amount of traffic (greater the better).

From the data he was able to assemble, Wellington put forward three basic propositions: (i) that if all intermediate points were of equal generating capacity and if they were equally spaced, then traffic varied as the square of the number of points served; (ii) that if the intermediate points were 'small country towns' without a competing alternative railway, then the effect of placing the station away from the town (Fig. 3.1-B) was to reduce gross revenue by 10 per cent for every mile that the station was removed from the town centre; (iii) that if the intermediate points were 'large industrial cities' with competing railway facilities, then the loss would be still more abrupt: a reduction of 25 per cent for every mile that the station was removed from the town centre.

Extreme solutions to a hypothetical problem are to minimize length of line (Fig. 3.1-B) or to maximize traffic (Fig. 3.1-C). If we assume both the direct distance from α to β is 1·0, and the maximum traffic from the intermediate towns (open circles) and industrial cities (closed circles) is 1·0, then the first solution reduces traffic to 0·61 and the second solution increases the rail-length to 1·46. An intermediate compromise (Fig.

3.1-D) linking only the industrial centres keeps the traffic to 0·85 and increases rail-length to only 1·32.

The value of this early analysis lies not in its absolute findings so much as in its illustration of the kind of locational problems faced in route construction. The actual values used by Wellington were of doubtful accuracy even for nineteenth-century Mexico, and like Thünen's ring distances (Chap. 6.II(1b)) their use is largely illustrative. Railway location was on the other hand largely a locational problem for the middle and late nineteenth century rather than today, and we should perhaps view the rationale of railroad location over most of the world's railroad systems in this historical context.

b. Negative deviations. The second type of deviation, here termed

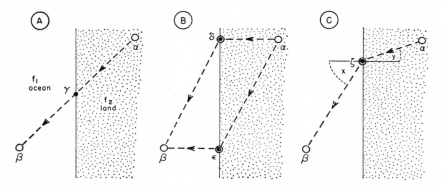

Fig. 3.2. Laws of refraction applied to route location. Source: Lösch, 1954, p. 184.

negative deviation, comes from the need to avoid certain barriers or to minimize the distance travelled through high-cost areas.

August Lösch (1954, p. 184) commented on the application to the study of route location of the 'laws of refraction'. Fig. 3.2 shows two standard applications of Snell's law (Sears and Zemansky, 1964, p. 842) in a simplified context. The problem is to find a route by which a product can be shipped as cheaply as possible from site α to site β and to locate a port along the coastline assuming the coastline is everywhere favourable for port construction. The direct route between α and β crosses the coastline at γ (Fig. 3.2-A). If we introduce a practical element of transport cost we know that the cost of the overland hauls are not the same as ocean hauls, and we assume a cheap ocean freight f_1 and a more costly land freight f_2 Lösch shows that the least-cost location of the port will be where

$$f_1 \sin x - f_2 \sin y = 0$$

where x and y are the angles that the two transport routes make to the coastline. This gives the least-cost port site, ζ (Fig. 3.2-c). The greater the cost of rail freight in relation to ocean freight the nearer will the location of the port approach δ; conversely as ocean freights rise the optimum transhipments point moves towards ε (Fig. 3.2-B).

Figure 3.3 shows a more complex case of the same refraction principle with the problem of a route between α and β which has to cross a mountain range (stippled). Again the cost per mile of the route across the plains is much smaller than the cost through the mountains, so that the direct route is not the cheapest. The higher the cost of traversing the mountain area (or the greater the 'refractive index' in Lösch's analogy) the more the least effort route will be deflected southwards (Fig. 3.3-B). Again the final compromise location (Fig. 3.3-c) will depend on the construction and running costs over the two mediums of plain and mountain.

Lest this example seems too highly theoretical Lösch reminds us of the

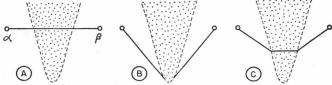

Fig. 3.3. Alternative case of route refraction. Source: Lösch, 1954, p. 186.

'deflection' of a great deal of nineteenth-century trade between the east coast of the United States and California via the Cape Horn route, a diversion which added some 9,200 miles to the direct distance overland across the United States. An equally direct parallel occurs in this century with the planning of a trans-isthmian canal across central America. Of the two major routes considered (the Nicaraguan cut and the Panama cut), the sea distance between the eastern and western United States would have been most strikingly reduced by the northern route but this saving was insignificant compared to the saving in construction costs on the shorter Panama cut. Again it is the ratio of the costs that is important. Had the cost of ocean transport been much higher, the advantages of a more northerly route might have been decisive. Since other than United States shipping used the canal, the decision was far less simple in reality but the basis of Lösch's idea remains valid. Specht (1959) has drawn attention to ferry costs and resultant route 'bending' around Lake Michigan while a small-scale example from the English countryside that makes the point as well is the orientation of bridges across railway lines. Unless a road is of very major importance the bridge spans the railway at or near a right angle, deviating from the general direction of the road on either side of the bridge. Lösch would describe this as a result of the very strong refractive or bending power of the bridge-construction costs on the alignment of the route.

Lösch finds in the obvious parallel of the economic law to the formula for the refraction of light and sound not so much evidence for human behaviour following physical principles but a general principle of least resistance (Chap. 2.I). He states: 'It runs through the history of natural science as *lex parsimoniae* the principle of simplest means or least resistance; as the hypothesis that natural events reach their goals by the shortest route' (Lösch, 1954, p. 184).

Empirical studies of individual routes, like those of Vance (1961) on the contrasting course of the Oregon Trail and the Union Pacific Railroad across the Rocky Mountains, or Monbeig (1952) on the routes across the Serra do Mar in southeastern Brazil, show that in no case was the location ever as simple as Lösch's geometry suggests. Equally in no case does its influence appear to be lacking.

2. Location of route networks

a. Minimum-distance concepts. Bunge (1962) has drawn heavily on concepts of the most basic part of geometry, topology, to illustrate the character of transport networks. He suggests that if the problem is a simple one of building a route to connect five centres, the 'shortest-distance' route cannot be so simply resolved as with the two-point problems considered above. Fig. 3.4 illustrates Bunge's contention. In this diagram six line networks have been drawn, each of which illustrates a different answer to the problem.

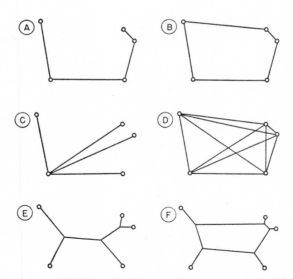

Fig. 3.4. Alternative definitions of minimum-distance networks. Source: Bunge, 1962, pp. 183–9.

The first network (Fig. 3.4-A) shows the minimum-distance network for starting at a particular point and travelling to all the others in the shortest mileage: a solution described by Bunge as a 'Paul Revere' type of network. Fig. 3.4-B shows a similar distance problem, that of the shortest distance around the five points: the 'travelling salesman' problem. The next two definitions, shown in Fig. 3.4-C and Fig. 3.4-D, are for more complete networks; the first for a hierarchy connecting *one* point to all the others, and the second for a complete network connecting *any* point to all the others. If we examine this solution it appears to be the complete answer to our network problem in that it contains all the possible lines for the three solutions that precede it. Quandt (1960) and others certainly make that assumption when they regard the optimal transport network as containing links from a completely connected network.

As Bunge points out, however, the *shortest* set of lines connecting all five points does not in fact contain any of the elements shown in the

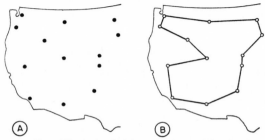

Fig. 3.5. Shortest cyclic path around thirteen major cities in the western United States ($G = 2 \cdot 1$). Source: Dantzig, Fulkerson, and Johnson, 1954, p. 219.

previous diagrams. This shortest set solution is shown in Fig. 3.4-E. It can be found analytically (or indeed by the use of mechanical or soap-bubble analogues (Miehle, 1958; Silk, 1965)) and its intersections do not include any of the original points. Finally, Fig. 3.4-F shows the general topological case for a network of lines connecting five points as presented by Beckmann (Bunge, 1962, p. 189). Examination of this final diagram shows that the two preceding cases—the completely linked network (*D*) and the shortest link network (*E*)—are but special limiting cases of Beckmann's general network.

b. Practical application of optimum network designs. Of the simple definitions of minimum-distance networks that of the 'travelling salesman' type (Fig. 3.4-B) has attracted most attention. Although the solution is trivial for only five points, with larger numbers of points the computational problems become enormous. For example in Fig. 3.5 there are 479,002,000 solutions to the problem of the shortest cyclic line connecting all thirteen cities shown for the western United States: only one of these, that shown in

Fig. 3.5-B, is the optimum solution. The general relation is given by the formula $(N - 1)!$ where N is the number of points, so that for one hundreds cities the number of possible solutions rises to the astronomical figure of $9 \cdot 3 \times 10^{158}$. The practical significance of the derivation of such solutions (usually through high-speed computers) is for undertakings such as oil companies which have to ship products regularly by road to hundreds of local depots. Intensive studies are now being made of optimal routes and networks (Flood, 1956; Garrison, 1959–60) in an attempt to find practical solutions to these route-location problems.

The Bunge–Beckmann classification also has considerable practical application in route-building practice. If we replace the abstract topological symbols of points and lines by the empirical one of cities and railroads, this relevance becomes clear. Basically, solution D in Fig. 3.4 represents the railroad pattern which is the least-cost from the point of view of the *user* (i.e. it is the shortest and most convenient to and from any of the five cities). Solution E on the other hand is least-cost from the point of view of the *builder*, i.e. it is the shortest railway length linking all five cities.

Bunge (1962, p. 187) suggests that the actual pattern of railway building depends on the ratio between these two costs: user costs and builder costs. Where large cities are clustered he suggests that the great flows of traffic generated between them will favour the least-cost-to-user pattern; a pattern which may be visible in the railroad network of the northeastern United States (Ullman, 1949). Away from the centre where cities are sparse and traffic is light the building costs become dominant and the least-cost-to-builder patterns dominate. Again the railway pattern of the western United States (admittedly strongly influenced by terrain) may be held to show this type of pattern, although detailed analyses (like those of Thomas, 1960, on the Denver and Rio Grande Railroad) suggest this is somewhat blanketed by other factors.

A further practical application of the kind of minimization problem posed by Bunge is seen in the planning of road networks in rural areas. Where new farm settlements are being planned, as in the reclaimed Dutch polders, there are at least two distances to be minimized (Chisholm, 1962, pp. 136–8): (i) internal distance from farmstead to fields, and (ii) external distance from farm to public services (roads, water supply, electricity).

If we assume that for cadastral and operating reasons the farm must be organized within rectangular boundaries, then Fig. 3.6 illustrates four possible arrangements of farmstead, roads, and farm boundaries. In the first two cases (Fig. 3.6-A and Fig. 3.6-B), the farm units are square, and the farmsteads are optimally sited (from the operator's viewpoint) in the centre of the square; but this solution has the disadvantage that it takes 2·0 miles of service road to connect all four farmsteads in the square-mile block. The second case has a marginal advantage over the first in that the farm area is less interrupted by the public road, but this is partly offset by the fact that parts of the 160-acre farms are further than a quarter mile from the nearest public service road. These less accessible areas are stippled on the diagrams.

In the third case (Fig. 3.6-c) the square farm shape is retained but farmsteads are moved from their optimum central location. Service road length is halved to 1·0 mile but overland hauls from the farmstead to the fields are increased. This trend is continued in the fourth case (Fig. 3.6-D), where the farm unit is changed to a less convenient rectangular strip, the farmsteads are eccentrically located (on the road) but the total length of

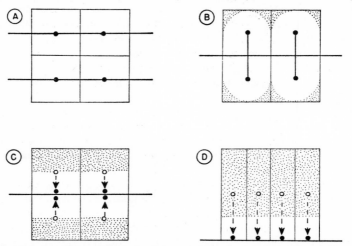

Fig. 3.6. Alternative definitions of minimum-distance rural road networks. Areas more than ¼ mile from roads are stippled. Source: Chisholm, 1962, p. 156.

service road is halved again to only 0·5 mile (assuming similar farmsteads are located on the southern flank of the road).

More complex combinations of alternative boundaries, roads, and farmsteads are possible if we introduce another factor to be maximized, size of farmstead cluster. In the first two cases single farmsteads form the settlement module but in the third and fourth cases two farmsteads cluster together. If these are moved to corner locations on their properties, this unit goes up to four. This 'social-contact' principle gives modified alternatives of Fig. 3.6-c and Fig. 3.6-D which appear to be ones adopted in practice. Empirical evidence from the Dutch polders, from West German land consolidation schemes, from *rang* settlement in Canada (Mead and Brown, 1962), and from strip settlement in Japan (Inouye, in International Geographical Union, 1964, p. 308) and southern Brazil (Monbeig, 1952), appear to conform to this modified pattern.

c. Political distortion of networks. It was C. H. Cooley in a remarkable early study of transport theory, who stressed the importance of political factors in understanding route patterns, and suggested that '. . . the political aspect increases as time goes on' (Cooley, 1894, p. 53). His theme is taken up in a recent study by Wolfe of *Transportation and politics* (1963). Certainly in railroad building, the link between the Canadian-Pacific railroad and Canada or the Trans-Siberian railroad and Russia are symbolic even though their impact may have been less decisive than once thought. Even the detailed pattern of route networks may reflect major and minor political differences. In Fig. 3.7 the 'aligning' effect of the major boundary between the United States and Canada (stippled) on railroads (Fig. 3.7-A) is paralleled by the 'blocking' effect of the minor boundary between Ontario and Quebec (stippled) on road patterns (Fig. 3.7-B).

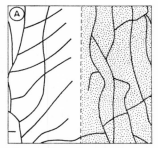 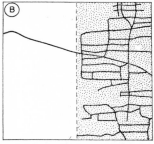

Fig. 3.7. Truncation of networks by territorial boundaries. *A* Rail network in a sample quadrat ($G = 3.9$) on the Canada–United States border. *B* Road network in a sample quadrat ($G = 5.3$) on the Ontario–Quebec border, Canada. Source: Wolfe, 1962, pp. 184, 185.

Meinig (1962) has examined the historical geography of two railnets: (i) a wholly state-directed enterprise in South Australia and (ii) one built and operated by several private companies in the northwestern United States. They were chosen for comparative study since they were built and developed at roughly the same time, were both in wheat-growing regions, and were both designed largely to move export grain from the farming districts to tidewater ports.

Meinig finds a number of common features in the railway net developed in the two areas. Both extended at about the same pace, the one in response to political pressure and concepts of public service and the other to profit possibilities. Both were complicated by changes in the general orientation of trade to different ports and both were affected by the influence of local communities on routing. In both too, the number of alternative possible routes always outweighed the routes that could be built and were decided in an intimate context (see Fig. 1.7).

Differences between the state and private networks are found, however, to be the more striking. Meinig places first the contrast in (*a*) duplicate routes and (*b*) duplicate services. In the Columbia basin the links between inland exporting centres and tidewater ports are commonly duplicated and the exporter is faced with a choice of competitive services to different tidewater ports. There is complete absence of such alternatives in South Australia. Moreover, the hinterlands of individual lines in South Australia remain stable in contrast to the constant piracy and 'invasion' of territories in the Columbia basin. Such fluidity in the privately owned network is suggested by Meinig as a cause of the rapid conversion and subsequent development of the Columbia basin system on a uniform gauge while the South Australian system retained its relatively watertight hinterlands each served by its own gauge. With the growth of government regulation in the United States the original contrasts in the patterns are now fading slightly.

3. Impact of network geometry

Knowledge of the relationship of network geometry to the development of regional resources has been greatly extended by recent research by Garrison (1960) and Kansky (1963). They devised a series of measures of network form based on a branch of mathematics (*graph theory*) which allow accurate comparisons between the 'connectivity' and 'shape' of networks. These measures are discussed at length in Chapter 8.II(3b).

Two illustrations of Kansky's findings are given in Fig. 3.8 where the railway networks of twenty-five selected countries are related to their

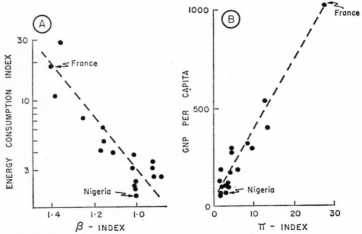

Fig. 3.8. Relation of topological measures of the connectivity (*A*) and shape (*B*) of railway networks to indices of economic development. Source: Kansky, 1963, p. 42.

general level of economic development. In the first graph (Fig. 3.8-A) energy consumption (*y*-axis) is plotted against a measure of connectivity, the *Beta* index (*x*-axis). Highly developed countries like France have high connectivity indices for their railway system while underdeveloped countries like Nigeria have low connectivity indices. In the second graph (Fig. 3.8-B) another measure of development, gross national product per capita (*y*-axis) is plotted against a measure of network shape, the π index (*x*-axis). Again, France with its high shape values (approximating to a circle) stands in sharp contrast to Nigeria with its elongated system. In both graphs there is a high and consistent trend which is significant statistically and strongly suggests that the geometry of some route networks

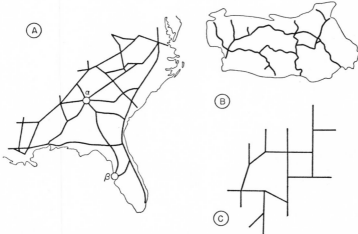

Fig. 3.9. A Interstate highway network in the southeastern United States ($G = 2 \cdot 7$). *BC* Graphic simplification of the railway network of Sardinia ($G = 4 \cdot 3$). Sources: Garrison, 1960, p. 132; Kansky, 1963, p. 8.

may be very closely related to the general development of regional re-sources. Should this be so, we must slightly modify Cooley's views on the importance of purely political factors; we suggest that while they may have a dramatic effect on individual routes the major pattern suggests the importance of more purely economic factors.

Network analysis using graph theory has also proved useful for the analysis of the position of particular places on a route system. Using one measure of accessibility, the Shimbel–Katz index, Garrison (1960, pp. 131–5) was able to analyse the relative accessibility of forty-five places in the southeastern part of the United States which were linked together by Interstate Highway System (Fig. 3.9-A). The places were defined partly on urban size criteria and partly on their topological position (e.g. at the end of a route). While the location of low-accessibility places is perhaps

predictable, the Shimbel–Katz index reveals an interesting and unexpected pattern of high-accessibility places: Atlanta (α), the most accessible
point on the network, looks more reasonable than St Petersburg (β),
among the least accessible places on the network. Part of the reason for
this contrast lies in the fact that graph theory concentrates on the topological property of the network, its connectivity, rather than on its
dimensions (Chap. 8.II(3b)). Kansky (1963) has reminded us that from
the topological view the railways of Sardinia look not like Fig. 3.9-B, but

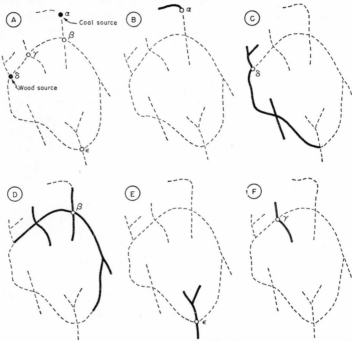

Fig. 3.10. Impact of network geometry on the location of manufacturing plants.
The heavy line indicates the parts of the network best served from each of the five
potential processing points (a, β, . . . ε). Source: Hoover, 1948, p. 41.

more like Fig. 3.9-C. The advantages that this more abstract model confers
from the viewpoint of analysis must of course be weighed against the loss
of other significant detail.

Hoover (1948, pp. 301–2) has demonstrated that the simple tug of war
between source and destination in industrial location (discussed in Chapter
5.IV) may be strongly affected by route layouts. Fig. 3.10-A shows a
hypothetical transfer system, with a series of towns along the routes. Two
of the towns, α and δ, are sources of raw materials, coal and wood respectively, in a finished industrial product. Hoover assumes that the

relative transfer costs per mile (ignoring long-haul economies in transfer) stand in the ratio 2 : 3 : 4 for wood, coal, and the finished product. He goes on to demonstrate that in these conditions the question of the 'least-cost' location is not appropriate for '. . . under these conditions there is no unique optimum plant location nor even a unique type of orientation. A number of possible orientations can occur, depending on the sequence of the material sources and market on the route system' (Hoover, 1948, p. 301).

This indeterminacy is illustrated by Figs. 3.10-B to 3.10-F where production is assumed to be carried out at five points on the system. In the first two cases, production is assumed to be at the source of coal (Fig. 3.10-B) and the source of wood (Fig. 3.10-C) and in the last three at nodes on the system. No point is optimum for the whole system and the best, in the sense of serving the largest route, is that of the junction (β) in Fig. 3.10-D. In practice location at such junction points is favoured when both the sources of materials and destinations of products are scattered (a common occurrence) and by the 'in-transit' type of freight rates which give a single through-rate for products which are processed at some point along a route and would otherwise have two shorter but higher rates charged (Alexander, 1963, p. 476).

II. DENSITY PATTERN OF ROUTE NETWORKS

If we stand further back from the route network, its individual characteristics blur and we observe a simple density pattern in which some areas have a very dense route network while in others the network is very sparse. In approaching this problem we proceed from the local scale of the city street and subdivision network (1) up through regional differences within a state (2) to the world scale (3).

1. Local level

Examination of the large-scale maps or plans for any urban or rural areas usually reveals rather strong differences in route density. Villages stand out with their denser pattern from the surrounding countryside, downtown urban areas (even in geometrically planned American cities) stand out by their denser street pattern from the more open network of the suburbs.

Qualitative observations of this kind have recently been supported strongly by a detailed study by Borchert (1961) of the road pattern in the 'twin-cities' area of Minneapolis–St Paul in the north central United States. Instead of measuring road density by length of road per unit, he evolved a simple measure of counting all the road junctions on the map. The density of junctions was found to be so highly correlated with road length (coefficient of correlation of $+0.99$) that it could usefully be substituted for conventional and slower length measure. Borchert's findings

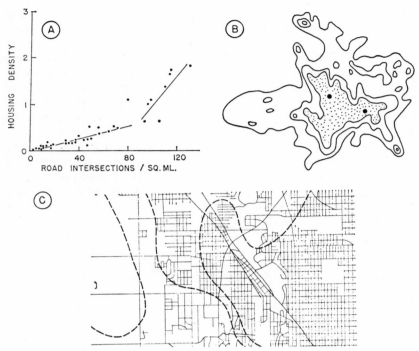

Fig. *3.11*. Density of road networks in and around Minneapolis–St Paul, United States. *A* Relationship of network to housing density. *B* Concentric zones of network density $(G = 5.1)$. *C* Sample quadrat $(G = 7.0)$ of network with density contours. Source: Borchert, 1961, pp. 50–6.

are summarized in Fig. 3.11-A which shows for the Minneapolis–St Paul area the very strong association between population density, as measured by number of single family dwellings (*y*-axis), and the network density, as measured by intersections (*x*-axis). The strongly concentric pattern of the network density zones about the two city centres is shown in Fig. 3.11-B.

2. Regional level

At the regional level a very thorough investigation of the distribution of road densities in Ghana and Nigeria has been made by Taaffe (Taaffe, Morrill, and Gould, 1963). Route density for each of Ghana's thirty and Nigeria's fifty sub-regions was measured for first- and second-class roads and related in the first instance to the population and the area of each unit. Using regression analysis, population was found to explain about 50 per cent of the variation in road density in both Ghana and Nigeria. When area was included with population in multiple regression, the level of explanation rose to 75 and 81 per cent respectively.

Taaffe went on to suggest four other less important variables that might help to solve the 'unexplained' differences between the actual densities and the expected densities on the regression analysis. These four variables were identified as: (i) hostile environment; (ii) rail-road competition; (iii) intermediate location; and (iv) commercialization and relation to the development sequence.

Hostile environment, a familiar and basic geographical theme, was illustrated in Ghana by the very low route densities in the swampy lands of the Volta river district and where the Mampong escarpment sharply restricts the development of feeder routes. Railroad competition was found to be a more complex factor in that one could argue either that railroads would curtail the need for roads by providing an alternative form of transport, or that railroads would stimulate road building by its gingering effects on production for inter-regional trade. The second argument appeared the stronger in Ghana and Nigeria.

Units with an intermediate location, between two important high-population areas, were found to have densities well above those expected on the basis of population and area alone. Road density was positively associated with the degree of commercial activity; the more productive areas having a heavier road pattern than more backward areas. One anomaly noted from this pattern was the mining areas, relying largely on rail movements, which did not follow the resource development–road density relationship.

3. International level

Difficulties in comparing network densities at the world level between countries raise acute problems of differences in operational definition of routes (Chap. 7.I(3)). Not only are definition problems multiplied (i.e. differences between single- and multiple-track railways or farm roads and eight-lane freeways), but similar information is recorded and classified in very different ways. Ginsburg has attempted to standardize these conflicting figures in his *Atlas of economic development* (1961) and his findings will be used here as a basis for argument.

Two critical maps in the Ginsburg atlas are of railway density (Map XXIV) and road density (Map XXIX). Both maps show density as length of road per 100 square kilometres, though it is emphasized that there are a number of other and equally valid ways of showing density (e.g. in relation to population or population and distance). For our purposes the density per unit area provides the more basic parameter in that it describes the actual existence on the ground of specialized routes whether those routes be intensively or lightly used.

Table 3.1. Distribution of route density*

Route media:	Roads	Railways
Number of countries compared	126	134
World mean density, km./100 km.^{2}	10·3	0·95
Maximum density, km./100 km.^{2}	302·0	17·90
Minimum density, km./100 km.^{2}	0·0	0·00
Countries below world mean, per cent	64%	67%

Source: Ginsburg, 1961, pp. 60, 70.
* World data, 1956–7.

The basic characteristics of the world distribution pattern are shown in summary form in Table 3.1. Road density, an index compiled from a variety of sources and with rather unstandardized figures, gives a world average of around 10 kilometres/100 square kilometres or about ten times as great a density as that for railways. The gap between the maximum values and the means is, however, considerably greater for roads; Belgium, reported with the highest road density, was about thirty times as dense a network as the world mean, while Luxembourg with the highest railway network was only about twenty times as dense as the world mean. At the other end of the distribution, one country (Greenland) is reported with zero road density and twenty-seven countries have no railways. The distribution is then a very skewed one with a few countries with very dense networks and many countries with very sparse networks. Nearly two-thirds of the countries have densities below the world mean.

Transport networks are demonstrably part of the development 'infrastructure' and the distribution of countries with high and low densities may be reasonably linked to their general level of economic development. This hypothesis may usefully be explored by adopting the economic–demographic development scale developed by Berry (1960-B) based on the values in the Ginsburg atlas (Ginsburg, 1961, pp. 110–19). The construction of this scale is taken up in a later discussion of components analysis (Chap. 8.I(3d)), but we may briefly state here that it represents a scale derived from forty-three separate indices of economic development which plots countries on a demographic scale along the shorter x-axis and a technological scale along the longer y-axis. Some ninety-five countries are distributed along this scale (Fig. 3.12) with highly developed countries on the upper left of the scale and poorer countries on the lower right.

On this continuum countries with high and low road and rail densities

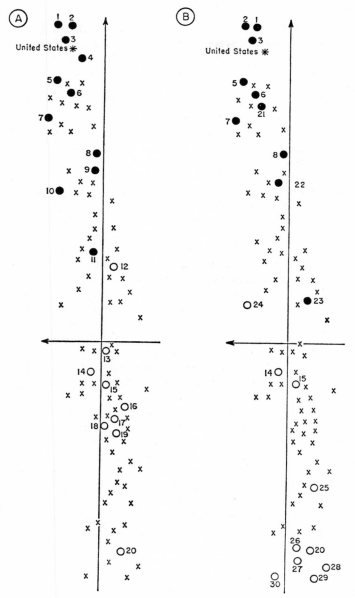

Fig. 3.12. Relationship of countries with high and low road (*A*) and railway (*B*) density to Berry's development spectrum. Source: Berry, 1960, p. 91.

77

have been superimposed: the first ten countries with high densities are shown with large solid circles and the last ten countries with the lowest densities are shown by large open circles. The location of the United States on this continuum has been marked with an asterisk (*) for reference.

The road density pattern (Fig. 3.12-A) shows a cluster of high-ranking countries at the developed end of the spectrum. Nine of these ten are European countries; United Kingdom (1), West Germany (2), Belgium (3), France (4), Switzerland (5), Netherlands (6), Denmark (7), Poland (8), and Ireland (10). Only one other country, Hong Kong (11) lies outside this pattern. Indeed the only highly developed countries with relatively modest road densities are the United States, Canada, and Sweden. The pattern for railway density (Fig. 3.12-B) follows in general the same pattern with European countries in leading positions. Seven of the countries reoccur with two eastern European countries, Czechoslovakia (21) and Hungary (22), and the far eastern state of Taiwan (23) coming into the picture. The apparently anomalous position of Taiwan reflects the relatively high-ranking position the railway density map of a number of southeast Asian countries like India and Burma developed under the railroad-building British colonial administration or Japan and Taiwan (a former Japanese colony) in which transport was deliberately developed about the railroad net.

At the other end of the extreme the position of low-ranking countries is complicated by the absence from Berry's economic–demographic development scale of most of the very underdeveloped countries. Not enough data was available to place them accurately on the scale and the 'ten lowest density countries' are drawn from the more restricted population of the ninety-five countries on the continuum. Nevertheless the pattern shown is an interesting one. In terms of railway density (Fig. 3.12-B) the low-ranking countries cluster strikingly at the bottom of the development ladder. Six of the seven countries at this base are African states, Sudan (25), Ethiopia (28), Libya (30), Liberia (20), Gambia (27), and French Equatorial Africa (26), together with Afghanistan (29). More developed colonial countries with low-density railroad nets were Surinam (14) and British Guiana (15), both with excellent river transport, and the only major anomaly, Iceland (24).

For road density (Fig. 3.12-A) the pattern of the low-ranking countries was not so clear. Relatively developed countries with very large land areas, U.S.S.R. (9) and Brazil (12), stand out as major anomalies, while at the lower extreme only Liberia represents the African cluster noted on the railway density map. Surinam and British Guiana here form the centre for a cluster of non-African tropical states in the lower-middle range of development with Costa Rica (13), Ecuador (16), Bolivia (18) from the Americas, and Iran (19) and British Borneo (17) from Asia. In general the road density pattern is less easy to interpret and reflects in part the wide range in definition of 'roads'. The lack of correspondence between the lows on the two media suggests that railways have served as substitutes for roads, and in other cases, like British Guiana, river and coastal shipping has served as a substitute for both.

III. MODELS OF NETWORK CHANGE

The growth of roads, railways, canals, and the like is inextricably woven with the whole process of economic growth and regional development. Here we look at some rather simplified models of network change that have been developed and examine the kind of changes associated with such changes.

1. Route development in underdeveloped areas

a. Statement of the model. One of the few attempts to bring together the broad regularities in the diffusion of internal transport lines has been by Taaffe (Taaffe, *et al.*, 1963). On the basis of specific study of the growth of transport in Ghana and Nigeria with less intensive study of Brazil, British East Africa, and Malaya they propose a four-phase sequence of development (Fig. 3.13).

Phase One consists of a scatter of small ports and trading posts along the coast of the hypothetical region being developed (Fig. 3.13-A). Each small port has a small inland trading field but there is little contact along the coast except through occasional fishing boats and irregular traders. This phase they identify in Nigeria and Ghana as running from the fifteenth century to the end of the nineteenth century with groups of indigenous peoples around a European trading station.

Phase Two consists of the emergence of a few major lines of penetration, the growth of inland trading centres at the terminals, and the differential growth of coastal ports with inland connections (Fig. 3.13-B). With the growth of the coastal ports the local hinterland also expands and diagonal routes begin to focus on the growing ports. Again the phase is identified in Ghana and Nigeria with the growth of inland trunk routes. These appear to have been built inland for three major reasons: (i) to connect a coastal administrative centre politically and militarily with its sphere of authority up-country, e.g. in Ghana the desire to reach Kumasi, capital of the rebellious Ashanti; (ii) to tap exploitable mineral resources, such as the Enugu coalfields in Nigeria; and (iii) to tap areas of potential agricultural export production, such as the cocoa areas north of Accra. Although each motive has played its part, the role of mineral exploitation has been a critical one in African railway building and examples from Uganda (Kasese copper line), the Cameroons (Garoua manganese line), and

Mauritania (Fort Gourard iron-ore line) suggest this phase has not yet ended.

Phase Three consists of the growth of feeder routes and the beginnings of lateral interconnection (Fig. 3.13-C). The feeder-routes growth is accompanied by continued growth of the main seacoast terminals in a spiral of trade-capture and expansion. Intermediate centres grow up between the coastal and interior terminals. Taaffe (Taaffe *et al.*, 1963, pp. 511–14) shows a series of maps of road development in Ghana and Nigeria in the

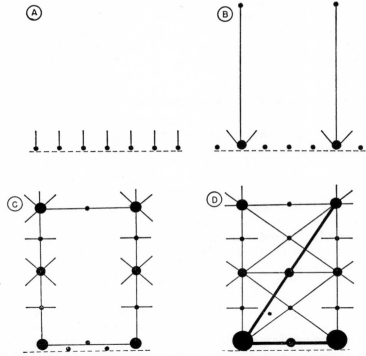

Fig. 3.13. Four-stage diachronic model of network development in an underdeveloped country. Source: Taaffe, Morrill, and Gould, 1963, p. 504.

period since 1920 to suggest the lateral connections of earlier disconnected lines of penetration and exploitation.

Phase Four repeats the process of linkage and concentration and shows the emergence of 'high-priority linkages' between the most important centres (indicated by a broader line in Fig. 3.13-D). The best paved roads, the heaviest rail schedules and airline connections will follow these 'main street' links between the three major centres. The heavy traffic in the 'triangle' of southern Ghana suggests such a development here.

b. Validity of the model. There is little doubt that the Taaffe model provides a very useful summary of certain regularities in the growth of internal route systems in colonial seaboard areas. The fact that Gould's careful historical analysis of the development of transportation in Ghana (Gould, 1960) was used as an empirical basis for the model ensured a strong realistic basis.

Two questions we must bear in mind in using the model are: (i) how far is it applicable outside West Africa in particular and colonial areas in general, and (ii) how far is the division into separate stages justified? Comparison with the growth of selected routes, like the railway route system focused on the cities of São Paulo (α) and Rio de Janeiro (β) in

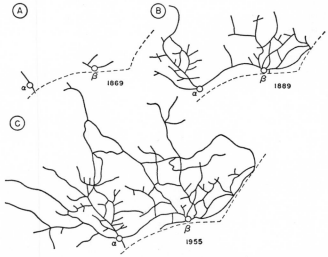

Fig. 3.14. Stages in the growth of the railway network in southeastern Brazil
$(G = 2 \cdot 8)$.

southeast Brazil are suggestive. The maps show the state of the rail system in 1869 (Fig. 3.14-A), in 1889 (Fig. 3.14-B), and in 1955 (Fig. 3.14-C), and one can readily see the characteristics of extension and branching mentioned in the Taaffe model. Similar maps from ex-colonial areas like the western United States show a rather similar pattern.

Indeed the implication of the pattern is to suggest a diffusion wave on the lines of Hägerstrand's *innovationsförloppet* (Hägerstrand, 1953) rather than a stage-by-stage process. Like Rostow's *Stages of economic growth* (Rostow, 1960), this four-stage sequence gains its greatest value in stimulating the study of growth and there is likely to be a good deal of academic discussion over how many stages we should recognize and where the significant breaks, if any, occur.

2. Route substitution in developed areas

a. Search for a model. While the foregoing model may have wider application than was originally intended, there remains the problem of a comprehensive model of route development in developed areas. Here, we may assume, an existing route system already functions and we are concerned with the way in which networks are adjusted to technical changes in transport and widening circles of interaction with rising economic-social levels.

Some of the problems in the changing route needs of road traffic have been raised in the Buchanan Report (Ministry of Transport, 1963, pp. 71–136), which stresses that 'desire lines' (i.e. lines linking the origin and destination of movements) are lengthening and are being strongly constricted by routes developed to meet earlier shorter-range desire lines.

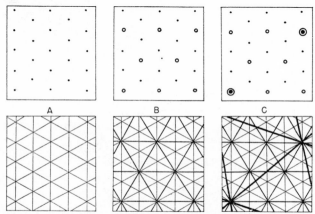

Fig. 3.15. Network development by route substitution between successively higher-order centres in a Löschian landscape.

Slowly the old pattern is changing as new roads, motorways, freeways and 'by-passes' are built around settlements.

An attempt to fuse this sequence with a theoretical Löschian landscape (Lösch, 1954, p. 127) is shown in Fig. 3.15. We begin with an idealized Löschian landscape in which desire lines connect each settlement with the next in a network of intersecting pathways, the type of pattern still discernible on maps of rural areas in tropical Africa. In the second stage (Fig. 3.15-B) the economic level has been raised to give a longer interaction-distance and to halve the number of major centres and leave a series of by-passed smaller centres connected by smaller routes. In the third stage (Fig. 3.15-C) the interaction has been raised still further with a new set of optimum routes, a new and smaller set of major centres, and a larger set of by-passed centres.

The major difference of this Löschian model from that of Buchanan is that this assumes that new routes *will* be created to meet new demands between emerging centres. The evidence of Buchanan is that this long-distance traffic is forced along existing small-scale arteries with resulting slow movement, confused desire lines, high accident rates, etc. The eventual emergence of higher-order routes in Britain is seen both in the new motorway pattern and in the revised network of railway services foreshadowed in the Beeching Report (British Railways Board, 1963).

b. Impact of substitution. Although the exact manner in which substitution occurs between routes in developed areas is not clear, the impact of such changes is vital. A number of studies known under the general title of 'highway impact' studies have been carried out in the United States by geographers.

One of the most important of these studies, *Highway development and geographic change* (Garrison, Berry, Marble, Nystuen, and Morrill, 1959), has investigated the effect of such route changes on the urban hierarchy. A typical example is the effect of a new by-pass on the trade and function

Fig. 3.16. By-passing of Marysville. Source: Garrison, Berry, Marble, Nystuen, and Morrill, 1959, p. 102.

of two small American towns Everett (α) and Marysville (β), which lie some thirty miles north of Seattle, Washington state, on the highway (U.S. 99) running north to the Canadian border. Fig. 3.16-A shows the situation prior to October 1954, with the main road running through Marysville, and Fig. 3.16-B the situation after this date with traffic diverted around the town on to a four-lane limited-access highway.

The effects of this new route on traffic was clear and expected. In the year following the by-pass the traffic through downtown Marysville (had fallen to about a third of its previous flow (about 5,400 as against 14,000 vehicles a day). Less obvious were the effects on the functions of the town. Here Garrison found that the fall in through-traffic had made Marysville so much more attractive as a local trade centre that sales of 'first- and second-order functions' increased to 121 per cent of pre-by-pass volumes. On the other hand, since it was now easier to get to Everett (a larger town) from the rural areas around Marysville, the higher 'third-order' functions of Marysville had dropped to 83 per cent of pre-by-pass levels (while the corresponding level in Everett went up). Against this, Marysville, minus its heavy through-traffic became a pleasanter place to live, rents of undeveloped sites went up and a residential boom appeared likely. Garrison's study illustrates clearly the effect of changes on route structure in reorientation and realignment of demands and supplies. People travelled further along the new highway for their higher-order needs at Everett, but Marysville had become a better local centre. Throughout the changes the urban system appeared to reorganize itself to the strains and stresses placed upon it in the way suggested as typical of open-system behaviour (Chap. 1.III(1)).

Although comparable studies are less common in England there have been some interesting attempts to forecast the impact of route shortening by bridge-building across estuaries. Woodward (1963) has shown the probable effects on extending the urban sphere of influence of Plymouth into the adjacent areas of southeast Cornwall by the building of the Tamar Road Bridge. One particularly dramatic effect envisaged in the plans for the area is on the town lying immediately across the river from the major city, Saltash, which with a 1960 population of about 7,500 has had a slowly growing population. As Table 3.2 suggests, this picture is planned to

Table 3.2. Impact of improved connectivity on urban expansion*

Time period:	Before connection (1939–59)	After connection (1959–71)
Population estimated at the end of each period	7,450	12,000
Mean annual population change:		
By natural increase	9	17
By migration	34	363

Source: Woodward, 1963, p. 23.

* Changes in the Saltash area following the building of the Tamar Road Bridge, Plymouth, southwest England.

change dramatically in the next dozen years as the smaller town begins to expand its dormitory function for the larger city. Similar striking histories of urban expansion after bridge-building have occurred around the San Francisco bay in the western United States.

Although the case for the importance of route substitution and development at the local and regional level is unanswerable, some controversy has developed over its importance at the national level. The classical view of the importance of railroads in economic growth has recently been restated by Rostow (1960, p. 55), when he suggests that *take-off* (one of his critical 'stages' in economic growth) in the United States was sparkplugged by the rapid growth of the railway system in the period 1850–90. Rostow sees railroads as a *leading sector* setting off secondary growth in other sectors like coal, iron, and engineering. This view has been challenged in a very detailed econometric study by Fogel (1964) which shows that the interregional savings from railroads in 1890 (as opposed to possible extension of the waterways–wagon road system) were surprisingly small—only 0·60 per cent of the gross national product of the United States. Fogel argues that the gains from railroads were far smaller than traditionally believed, that many were premature and uneconomic, and that the railroads were part of, and not a pre-condition for, the American industrial revolution.

3. Route development and diffusion models

We have already seen in Chapter 2.IV(2) something of the general concept of innovation waves and diffusion models. Since routes are demonstrably part of the development syndrome we might reasonably expect that they might also be explicable as a special case of general diffusion models.

On the local scale, Borchert (1961) has traced the pattern of high-, medium-, and low-density routes as they have developed about the Minneapolis–St Paul cities for the years 1900, 1940, and 1956. The position of each density frontier is mapped and a projected position for 1980 is

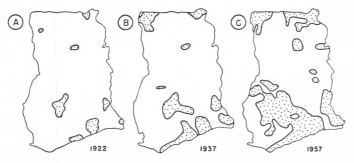

Fig. 3.17. Diffusion of zone of high-density road network in Ghana ($G = 3\cdot3$).
Source: Taaffe, Morrill, and Gould, 1963, p. 512.

added. Borchert predicted the 1980 boundary on the rate of previous expansion in a given direction together with population estimates for the urban areas. It was assumed that expansion at any time period would proceed at right angles to the density boundary and vectors were drawn forward on that basis. Where the irregular outline of the density boundary caused a boundary to be projected into the same section of land or into an impossible type of terrain the 'surplus' area was reallocated to a section of the periphery better suited by reason of access and terrain.

Taaffe (Taaffe *et al.*, 1963, pp. 511–13) has traced the sequence of road development in Ghana at three dates, 1922 (Fig. 3.17-A), after a fifteen-year gap in 1937 (Fig. 3.17-B), and after a further twenty years in 1957 (Fig. 3.17-C). In each map areas of high road density, (over 16 miles/100 square miles) are shaded. The regularity of the spread of the highway density patterns suggests that short-term prediction on the same grounds

D

as Borchert would be possible. The probability of an increase in route density appears on this basis to be greater between two nodes than for a comparable area elsewhere in Ghana, a finding in line with the suggestions of interaction models reviewed in Chapter 2.II. Godlund (1956 pp. 22–6) has mapped comparable diffusion patterns for bus-service densities in Sweden.

The findings on route development, whether stated in terms of networks or density frontiers, suggest that this may be usefully treated by the application of simulation models using the Monte Carlo technique. Morrill (1963) has built in simulated transport routes in his study of population and town growth in southern Sweden, and Kansky (1963) has attempted to predict the railway pattern of Sicily using simulation techniques and graph-theory indices. The basis for these predictive simulation models is discussed in Chapter 10.III(2).

In the same way that a study of movements leads on to a consideration of networks, so the study of networks leads to a consideration of the nodes on those networks. 'Node' is used here to describe the junctions or vertices on the network and as such it serves as a collective term which includes others—cities, central places, hamlets, population clusters—all of which are so heavily loaded with other and wider implications. Nodes can be identified at all levels of regional organization, from the macro-region with its nodal metropolitan area to the micro-region with its nodal farmstead.

In this chapter we look at the distribution of nodal centres over both size and space dimensions; in the next chapter, which is closely linked to this, at their organization into hierarchical structures.

I. MORPHOLOGY OF SETTLEMENT PATTERNS

Looking at the distribution of human population over the earth's surface is like looking up at the night sky. We can at once distinguish great galaxies and constellations, made up of clusters of population of vastly different sizes (Chap. 4.II). The few great centres of metropolitan population stand out clearly, while at the other extreme, the myriad of small rural communities lies at the extreme limit of our powers of statistical discrimination.

In discussing the basic arrangement of nodal clusters, it is convenient

Table 4.1. Alternative types of settlement classification

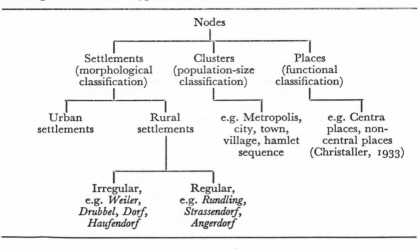

to use as a substitute their morphological expression, the settlement pattern (Table 4.1). Despite the fact that this represents, as Hägerstrand (1957, p. 27) has argued, only the 'centroid' or gravity centre of continuous population movements, settlements are a concrete expression of human occupation of the earth's surface. As such, they form an essential element of landscape and have had a central part in the syllabus of human geography. In both early statements, like that of Jean Brunhes (1925), and contemporary reviews, like that of Emrys Jones (1964), settlement patterns hold a dominant place.

1. Settlements as regular lattices

In an earlier discussion of movements (Chap. 2.III(2a)), it was argued that the hexagon provides the most economical geometrical form for the equal division of an area between a number of points. By the same argument we can show that the centres of those hexagons, the nodal points, must form a regular triangular lattice to conform with the same minimum energy requirements (Fig. 4.1-A).

The notion of settlements arranged in this regular triangular fashion was used by Christaller (1933) in his original development of central-place theory, and by Lösch (1938, 1954) in his subsequent development of the Christaller model (Chap. 5.1). We might therefore expect, on theoretical grounds, that settlements would be found to be arranged in the form of a triangular lattice. However, Lösch (1954, p. 133) has pointed out practical difficulties in adopting this arrangement, and has suggested that the square lattice might be adopted where new areas of settlement are being planned. Squares are (as Fig. 2.9-B shows) only moderately less efficient than the hexagon and form a very useful substitute.

   a. Observed regularities: qualitative evidence. Inspection of settlement patterns described by European geographers, shows little immediate indication of a regular lattice. Indeed attention has been focused on the shape of individual settlements rather than their general pattern. Thus while a complex typology of village forms has been evolved (e.g. Meitzen, 1895; summarized by Pfeifer, in Thomas, 1956, pp. 240–77), particularly in the German literature (Table 4.1), the description of pattern has not moved much beyond a simple dispersed–nucleated dichotomy. There are, of course, certain regular geometric forms which are clearly recognizable. The Roman *centuriation* pattern or the arrangement of new villages on the reclaimed virgin land of Dutch polders are small examples of regular lattices in Europe, but the major examples lie overseas in areas of European colonization.

   In the most spectacular case, the 'township and range' system of the

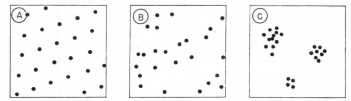

Fig. 4.1. Typical regular (*A*), random (*B*), and clustered (*C*) distributions.
Source: Greig-Smith, 1964, p 12.

United States, a regular system of square subdivisions was laid out over an area of some two million square miles—the greater part of the central and western sections of the country. Pattison (1957) has traced the various solutions that were put forward from 1785 onwards to the problem of dividing the unoccupied lands of the Western Territories. The difficulty of meridional convergence created surveying problems and it was not until the nineteenth century that a relatively uniform scheme was adopted. The rectilinear system, with its nested divisions into square townships (thirty-six square miles in area), sections (one square mile in area), and quarter-sections (160 acres in area) provided the common mould into which the complex society that settled the West was poured. Through the Homestead Act of 1862, the quarter-section became the module of farm organization at a critical time in land occupation, and despite subsequent revision, its pattern has been firmly struck on landscapes as unlike as Oklahoma and Alaska. Mead and Brown (1962) give some excellent examples of the relation of the township and range system to roads, settlement, and land use in various parts of the United States.

   In the century since its imposition, the rigid geometrical lines of the township and range system have been somewhat blurred. Johnson (1957) in a study of Whitewater basin, Minnesota state, has shown how the original quarter-section claims of 1853–4 were themselves made up of contiguous but irregular combinations of forty-acre units in an attempt to align the farm boundaries with the basic soil and terrain characteristics of the area. Since then the forces of abandonment, re-sale, and combination have further adjusted the pattern. As was shown in Chapter 3.I(2b), access to highways played a major part in the location of the farmstead within the quarter-section (Fig. 3.6) and a linear settlement pattern along the roads has developed over large areas. Kollmorgen and Jenks (1951) have confirmed this trend for another quarter-section area, western Kansas. Here farm size was found to have increased fivefold since 1890 with the new farms being arranged along the east–west highways (the main direction of traffic movement) in a linear manner.

b. Observed regularities: quantitative evidence. Dacey (1962) has analysed the distribution of hamlets, villages, and towns in an area of the United States settled under the township and range system. He selected an area of southwestern Wisconsin, previously studied by Brush (1953), which contained some 235 settlements divided into three strata: hamlets (61 per cent of the total settlements), villages (31 per cent), and towns (8 per cent). Dacey uses a technique of *nearest-neighbour analysis* (Chap. 8.II(2a)) to compare the observed pattern with three expected distributions: (i) the hexagonal distribution, (ii) the random distribution, and (iii) the clustered distribution (Fig. 4.1). Table 4.2 shows the relationship between the

Table 4.2. Actual and theoretical settlement arrangements*

Class of settlement:	Hamlets	Villages	Towns
Difference between observed and expected distribution (*D*-values):			
Regular (hexagonal) distribution	5·41	6·31	5·81
Random distribution	1·79	1·57	2·73
Clustered distribution	13·39	15·21	15·52

Source: Dacey, 1962, p. 71.

* Southwestern Wisconsin, United States.

observed and expected patterns by means of *D*-values which measure the difference between the two: high *D*-values indicate strong differences, and vice versa. Comparison of the three columns shows clearly that the pattern of settlements in this area approximates a random (rather than a regular or clustered) distribution. However, there is some variation between the three levels of the settlement strata—hamlets show the greatest degree of regularity in their relations to the higher strata of settlement. Dacey's work suggests therefore that even in an area of planned land-division the dominant pattern of settlement appears to be random, but that the smallest settlements (the hamlets) show more vestiges of regular arrangement than do the higher-order settlements.

Nearest-neighbour analysis has also been used by King (1962) in a comparative analysis of twenty sample areas within the United States (Fig. 4.2-A). Within each area all urban places were plotted and a series of straight-line measurements taken between each place and its nearest neighbour (regardless of size). The number of towns varied from 177

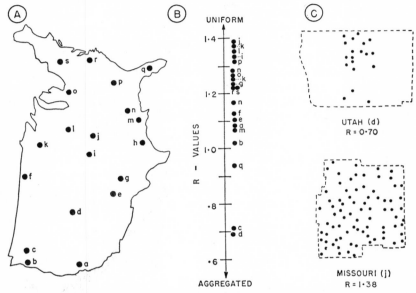

Fig. 4.2. A Sample study areas within the United States $(G = 1.8)$. *B* Scale of *R*-values. *C* Clustered settlements in the Utah sample area $(G = 4.7)$ contrasted to regular settlements in the Missouri sample area $(G = 4.8)$. Source: King, 1962, pp. 3–4.

towns in the Pennsylvania sample area down to twenty-three towns in the New Mexico sample area. By comparing the observed spacing with the expected spacing in a random distribution the nearest-neighbour statistic, R_n was derived. Values for R_n range from zero when all points are clustered in one location, through 1·00 which represents a random distribution, up to 2·15 for a uniform triangular lattice. Values for R_n are plotted for the twenty sample areas in Fig. 4.2-B. They show a small range from 0·70 in the case of the Utah sample area with its relatively clustered distribution, to 1·38 for Missouri sample area with its rather regular pattern. The actual distribution for both these two areas is shown in Fig. 4.2-C. Thus the main conclusion from King's work is to support the view that the settlement pattern of the United States is not regular, but approximates a random distribution.

2. Settlement patterns and distorted lattices

The failure of the regular lattice as a model for actual settlement arrangements is hardly surprising. The triangular lattice, like the hexagon, is a pure theoretical concept and in practice we would expect it to be distorted by other relevant considerations.

a. Distortion by agglomeration. One of the most serious defects in the Löschian system of regular hexagons is its failure to allow for inevitable variations in hexagon size. Lösch postulated a high density of population around the core of his market area, but failed to adjust his hexagonal network (Fig. 5.8) to accommodate it. Although a detailed formulation still waits to be made, a graphical modification has been attempted by Isard (1956, p. 272) in which hexagons get steadily smaller in size, the nearer their location to the central core (Fig. 2.14). The implications for the settlement pattern are clear. We should expect settlements to be more closely packed around major urban centres than in the remoter parts of a region.

One of the most interesting confirmations of this trend comes from a study by Bogue (1949), *The structure of the metropolitan community,* in which he analysed the distribution of population around sixty-seven of the major cities of the United States. Bogue has drawn up his results in the form of generalized cross-sections running from the city out to the rural peripheries, up to 300 miles away from the cities. These cross-sections suggest four general conclusions:

(i) Urban population declines with distance from the central city in a logarithmic fashion. In all the graphs in Fig. 4.3 urban population density is plotted as a broken line on the y-axis against distance from the nearest metropolis on the x-axis, and both axes are transformed to logarithmic scales. At twenty-five miles from the city the density is over 200 people per square mile; at 250 miles out it has fallen to about four per square mile.

(ii) Density and rate of decline varies with the size of the central city. For the fourteen metropolitan communities with populations of over 500,000 inhabitants, the urban population density was found to be about eight times higher than for the fifty-three cities below this level at twenty-five miles out from the centre, but the difference diminishes at greater distances from the metropolis.

(iii) Density and rate of decline varies with the region of the United States. The contrast between the Northeast (Fig. 4.3-A), the South (Fig. 4.3-B), and the West (Fig. 4.3-C) comes out very strongly: the Northeast with its high overall density and steep lapse rate, the South with its lower density and irregular lapse rate, and the West with its precipitous lapse rate, stand in marked regional contrast.

(iv) Density and rate of decline vary with direction from the city. Bogue divides the hinterlands around his sixty-seven cities into three types of sector: the *route* sector, the *subdominant* sector, and the *local* sector. Twelve

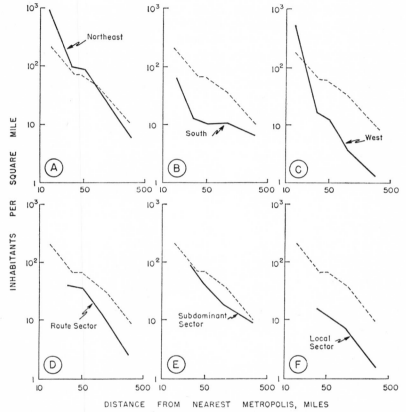

Fig. 4.3. Variations in urban population densities by region (*ABC*) and by sector (*DEF*) in the United States. Source: Bogue, 1949, pp. 47, 58.

thirty-degree sectors were demarcated on a transparent mask which was rotated about the city centre until it made the 'best fit' with the main highways leading from the city to other major metropolitan areas (Fig. 4.4-B). Sectors which contained a major highway were classed as route sectors, those that contained at least one city of 25,000 or more inhabitants were termed the subdominant sectors, and the remaining sectors were termed the local sectors. In each case, urban population was measured for counties and these were assigned to one or more of the sectors. Convergence of sector boundaries eliminated this process near the city and sector differences were only recorded for areas more than twenty-five miles out from the centre. Fig. 4.4 shows the stages in sector delimitation for one of the cities, Memphis (Tennessee): route sectors are unshaded, subdominant sectors are in black, local sectors are stippled.

Examination of the trends in density for the three sectors (Figs. 4.3-D, E, F) show that urban population is most dense in the subdominant sector. The effect of route sectors in spilling urban settlement out along the major intermetropolitan highways is less strong than might be expected: local sectors are well below the levels of the other two.

b. Distortion by resource localization. It is implicit in the assumptions of a

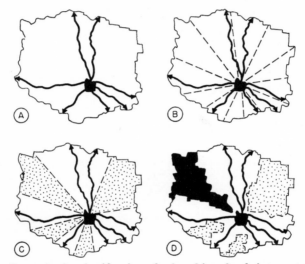

Fig. 4.4. Stages in the classification of urban hinterlands into sector types.
Source: Bogue, 1949, p. 25.

triangular lattice of settlements, that the resources needed by each settlement are everywhere available. If, however, we take a fairly simple settlement unit, the village, and list its traditional requirements—agricultural land, water, building materials, fuel, etc.—it is clear that in reality these resources are localized. The full analysis of the minimum energy location when resources are localized must wait until the next chapter (5.III) but it is clear that (i) the different requirements will exert varying 'pulls' on the location of the settlement, and (ii) the regular lattice will be correspondingly distorted. Some indication of this distortion is given in Fig. 4.5. In the first case, seven settlements are distributed regularly over areas of *uniform* resources (Fig. 4.5-A). In the second, a *zonal* resource (stippled) is introduced (Fig. 4.5-B). On the assumption that all settlements must have access to this resource, but that they will move as short a distance as possible from their lattice positions, a set of new locations is assumed (with appropriate changes in their territories determined by Thiessen analysis (Chap. 9.I(3a)). In the third, a *linear* resource (e.g. a stream or routeway) is assumed and an appropriate change in the location of the settlements calculated (Fig. 4.5-C). In the final case, a *point* resource is assumed (e.g. single well or defensive site), and the appropriate moves made (Fig. 4.5-D).

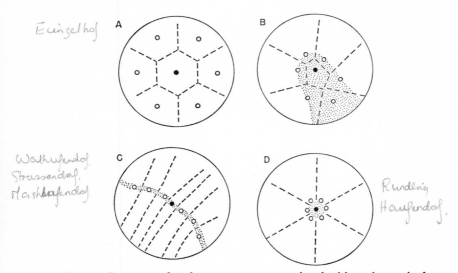

Fig. 4.5. Sequence of settlement patterns associated with an increasingly localized resource.

Clearly the four cases described are hypothetical and we should not expect such clear-cut distortions to occur in practice. Nevertheless, if we compare them with the scheme of settlement types recognized by European scholars (Jones, 1964, pp. 123–7) there are a number of apparent similarities. We may see in Fig. 4.5-A some characteristics of the scattered farmsteads, the *Einzelhof*; in Fig. 4.5-C, traces of the *Waldhufendorf*, the *Strassendorf*, or the *Marschhufendorf*, all string-like villages of differing degrees of organization and environment; in Fig. 4.5-D, the *Rundling* with its radial fields, or the *Haufendorf* with its irregular open-field pattern. Clearly the actual development of regional settlement patterns is a multivariate product in which social conventions play as big a part as environment. Nevertheless, basic geometrical considerations, even though severely modified, still play a part in that syndrome.

3. Distortion due to time lags

a. Models of settlement evolution over time. One of the problems of the Christaller and Lösch models of settlement is that they are essentially static, whereas we know in reality that the central-place hierarchy is complicated by time. Thus in an area like the eastern United States or eastern Brazil, the settlement hierarchy is heavily weighted towards the areas of earliest settlement: in the later areas, the hierarchy is still in a very active phase of evolution. Two major lines of theory are examined

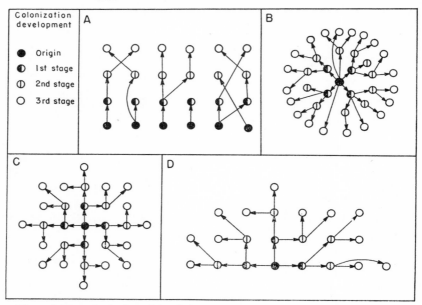

Fig. 4.6. Hypothetical models of settlement diffusion. Source: Bylund, 1960, p. 226.

here in which the time element is made explicit: (i) deterministic models, and (ii) probabilistic models.

(i) One of the few attempts to place settlement expansion within a deterministic framework has come from Bylund (1960). A historical study of colonization in the central Lappland area of Sweden before 1867, led him to consider the way in which 'waves' of settlements moved within this area, and he produced four simple models (Fig. 4.6) of development. In each of them the basic assumptions are (i) that the physical conditions of the land are equal in all areas (settled or unsettled) and (ii) that further areas will not be settled until those close to the 'mother settlements' have been occupied. The only major difference between the four models is in the number and the location of the mother settlements; clearly the first and last cases assume spread from a coastal location, the second and third cases assume spread from an inland location.

Like Thünen (Chap. 6.II), Bylund attempts to reintroduce reality into his model by varying the physical conditions of the land, access to roads, and variations in the number of migrant farmers moving out in each generation to found new farmsteads. Comparison between much more refined model and the historical records for Arvidsjaur parish between 1775 and 1867 shows sufficient agreement to suggest further research on this type of Thünen-like growth model to settlements might be rewarding.

(ii) An alternative approach to the evolution of settlement patterns is through the framework of stochastic theory. In this, growth is simulated by random processes (the so-called Monte Carlo technique discussed in Chapter 10.III) which are in turn restricted by the operation of certain 'rules' based on empirical observations of settlement behaviour.

A typical example of this simulation approach to settlement evolution is provided by Morrill (1962). He begins with an initial settlement, the founding settlement, and observes the build-up of a settlement hierarchy around it as governed by a sequence of *random numbers*. These numbers may be generated by dice, by a computer, or from tables in sources such as Fisher and Yates, *Statistical tables* (1957, pp. 126–31). The three basic rules followed by Morrill are: (i) for each time period or generation $(T_0, T_1, T_2 \ldots T_n)$ every place generates at least one migrant in the order of its origin, with the total number of migrants from each place proportional to its size; (ii) any place may be settled more than once and enlarged in size, provided it does not clash with the 'distance-compatibility rule' which restricts the size of a place according to its distance from the larger places (e.g. a settlement five cells from the origin, may increase to five and then remain stagnant); (iii) the distance and direction of each migrant's move is governed by the numbers in the probability matrix shown in Fig. 4.7-A, a matrix based on empirical studies of local population movements in Scandinavia by Kulldorff (1955) and Hägerstrand (1957).

Fig. 4.7-B shows a simple example from Morrill of the growth of a six-settlement hierarchy $(A, B \ldots F)$. The sequence begins with the single settlement, A, in a seaboard location. The numbers in brackets refer to random numbers. *First generation:* (10)—impossible (in the ocean), (22)—locate new settlement, B; A grows to size 'two'. *Second generation:* (24)—impossible (B cannot grow beyond size 'one' as it is only one cell from A), (42)—locate new settlement, C; A grows to size 'three'. *Third generation:* (37)—locate new settlement, D; A grows to size 'four', but B and C are too close to it to grow further. *Fourth generation:* (96)—locate new settlement, E, (77)—locate new settlement, F (n.b. matrix is centred on D, the parent centre for this operation); A grows to size 'five', D grows to size 'two'. At the end of this sequence, using seven random numbers (10, 22, 24, 42, 37,

1	2–3	4–7	8–9	10
11–12	13–18	19–28	29–34	35–36
37–40	41–50		51–60	61–64
65–66	67–72	73–82	83–88	89–90
91	92–93	94–97	98–99	100

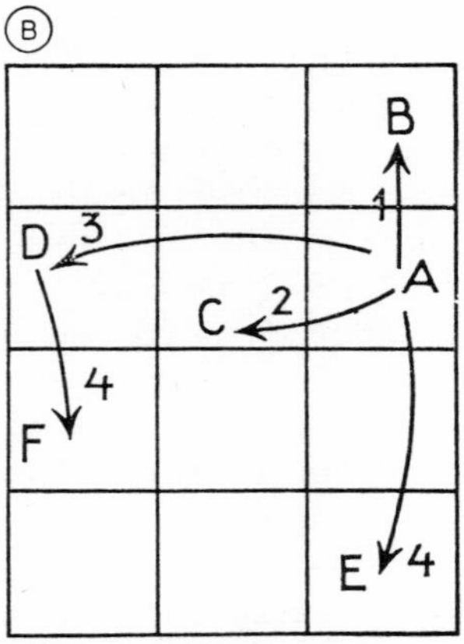

Fig. 4.7. A Distance and direction probability matrix. *B* Sample simulation sequence using Monte Carlo methods. Source: Morrill, 1962, p. 112.

96, and 77) and the probability matrix in Fig. 4.7-A, a hierarchy of six settlements has been formed with one large settlement (*A* at size 'five'), one medium settlement (*D* at size 'two'), and four smaller settlements (*B*, *C*, *E*, and *F*, each at size 'one'.)

By following these rules and re-centring the matrix over the settlement from which migrants are originating, a hierarchy can be slowly built up which simulates a general pattern of settlement (though not its exact location) (Fig. 4.8). Hierarchies and rank-size rules are built up even though they are (as in reality), imperfect and asymmetric.

Fig. 4.8. Simulated settlement pattern generated by Monte Carlo methods. Source: Morrill, 1962, p. 119.

b. Observed diffusion patterns. The tracing of the complex patterns of actual diffusion processes is a problem in historical detection which demands a wide range of evidence. Mitchell (1954) in her scholarly reconstruction of the evolution of settlement in East Anglia has pieced together fragments of information as unlike as place-names, church architecture, and air photographs. Sandner (1961), in an outstanding survey of the spread of Spanish colonization in Costa Rica, relies more heavily on archival documents and, for the more recent phases, census records. Both studies, and others like them, have tended to recognize distinct phases in the settlement process, e.g. Mitchell distinguishes *primary* settlement in the river valleys from *secondary* settlement on the till-covered interfluves, and Sandner describes the process in which 'mother settlements' serve as bases for later offsprings.

Chisholm (1962) has suggested that the diffusion of new and smaller settlements around older and larger settlements may be linked to four major changes: (i) socio-economic changes in the land-holding system, (ii) removal of the need for defensive agglomeration, (iii) elimination of such factors as disease, which inhibit earlier land settlement, and (iv) technical improvements in water supply. Of these, perhaps the most important in industrialized areas has been in the changes in systems of land holding. Hoskins (1955, p. 157) in his *Makings of the English landscape* has discussed the impact of the Parliamentary enclosure of great tracts of land in England between 1750 and 1850. Isolated farmsteads with consolidated holdings were substituted for nucleated villages with communal strip-holdings, i.e. in terms of Fig. 4.5, the fourth type reverted to the first type. For Japan, Inouye has traced the slow breakdown of linear villages (the third type in Fig. 4.5) into a more dispersed form. For one village, Kamitome near Tokyo, a continuous record of farmsteads and holdings enabled the evolution to be traced in detail from the late seventeenth century: with successive population increases the width of the strip farms was progressively narrowed as new farms crowded along the roadside in the traditional manner until a point was reached when the roadside location was saturated. Further narrowing of the strips was then impractical and new farmsteads were then set up away from the road.

New patterns of farm distribution in southern Italy, and the new colonization schemes in the Dry Zone of Ceylon (Farmer, 1957), suggest examples for Chisholm's second and third dispersal-factors. Technical change, the fourth dispersal-factor, has of course worked in both directions. For while barbed-wire and steel windmills may have allowed the dispersion of farm settlement over the Great Plains (Webb, 1927), further technical changes, notably the automobile and the combine-harvester allowed the growth of absentee farming—the 'sidewalk' and 'suitcase farming described in Chapter 6.I(3).

Chisholm (1957) has provided data on one such aspect of concentration economics. He computed for England and Wales in 1956 the costs of milk collection from farms to the local milk depot for bulking for cityward consignment. The cost of collecting varied very closely with the number of gallons collected per mile travelled by the lorry. For low-density jour-neys (five gallons of milk per vehicle mile) the cost of collection was as high as 3·8 pence per gallon, while for high-density journeys (forty gallons of milk per vehicle mile) the cost was only 0·6 pence per gallon. Low-density journeys reflect a combination of small widely scattered farms with low production of milk per farm, and it is clear that collecting from these areas is about six times as expensive as collecting from high-density areas. Similar arguments apply to the provision of most services for widely scattered sparse settlements. Electricity supplies, water and sewerage, telephone and postal services, roads and transport services, all cost more in such areas.

II. POPULATION CLUSTERS: THE SIZE CONTINUUM

Although it is very convenient to regard the world's population as dis-tributed in a series of discrete and isolated *clusters*, we must recognize at the outset that this is a somewhat artificial concept. Our definition of a cluster depends largely upon how we draw our boundaries and how we define the term 'isolated'. Thus Inouye (International Geographical Union, 1964) defines an isolated unit of settlement as one which is at least 150 metres away from the next unit. Clearly we have to adopt some such artificial standard, but must be prepared to modify this with larger settlements. The problem of the operational definition of 'cities' is a com-plex one and is discussed in detail in Chapter 7.I(3). In this chapter we make extensive use of the excellent survey by the International Urban Research Unit of the University of California at Berkeley, which has attempted to standardize the definition of metropolitan areas throughout the world (International Urban Research, 1959).

Examination of the available information on the larger, city-size clusters suggests a remarkable regularity. Like the regular branching of a drainage network (Leopold, Wolman and Miller, 1964), each cluster appears to occupy some definite place in the urban hierarchy, the whole system appearing as '. . . a chain, almost a feudal chain of vassalage, wherein one city may stand tributary to a bigger centre and yet be a metropolis of a sizeable region of its own' (Careless, 1954, p. 17). As Table 4.3 shows, there are relatively few large cities, many medium-sized cities, and a host of smaller cities, whether we take our measurements at the world scale, for a single nation (e.g. United States), or for a single region within that nation (e.g. Texas): the number of clusters is clearly

Table 4.3. Distribution of cities by size*

Region:	Texas	United States	World†
Size group by number of inhabitants:			
100,000– 250,000	6	65	565
250,000– 500,000	3	23	163
500,000–1,000,000	1	13	86
Over 1,000,000	1	5	53

Source: International Urban Research, 1959, and Berry, 1961-A, p. 588.
* Data for early 1950's.   † Forty countries.

directly proportional to size at all three scales. Evidence of this kind, pointing to rather regular relationships, has led to a number of attempts to define the number–size ratio in precise terms.

1. Detailed relationships between rank and size

Regular relationships between the size of towns and their rank was noted over half a century ago by Auerbach (1913). We may state this relationship formally as the *rank-size rule*, given by the formula

$$P_n = P_1(n)^{-1}$$

where P_n is the population of the nth town in the series 1, 2, 3 ... n in which all towns in a region are arranged in descending order by population, and P_1 is the population of the largest town (the *primate* town). We should therefore expect the fifth largest town to have a population exactly one-fifth that of the largest town, if the rank-size rule were an accurate description of the relationship. In the United States in 1940, Isard (1956, p. 58) has shown that with a P_1 of 11,690,000 (New York), the value of P_5 should be 2,338,000. In fact, Boston, the fifth-ranking city, had a population of 2,351,000.

Stewart (1958) has emphasized that the rank-size rule is basically an empirical finding, not a theoretical or logical proposition. Both Christaller and Lösch were concerned with functional rather than size-categories in their theoretical models (Chap. 5.I), although Beckmann (1958) has shown how, with the addition of a random element, the discrete steps of Christaller's hierarchy can be blurred into a rank-size distribution.

None the less we should gauge the usefulness of this 'rule' by the degree to which it helps us to generalize observations on population distribution. Data for the higher levels of the urban hierarchy are more readily available and, not surprisingly, attention has been concentrated on the application of the rule for large cities. Stewart (1958) examined the relationship between the primate city (P_1) and the second largest city (P_2) in a cross-section of seventy-two countries. He found that the ratios did not cluster around 0·50 as expected under the rank-size rule, but that for the whole sample the median relationship was 0·31 (i.e. the second city was characteristically one-third the size of the first). Ratios ranged from countries like Canada with values as high as 0·65 to Uruguay with only 0·06. Stewart found few regularities in the distribution of these ratios, other than the fact that the larger countries tended to have high ratios. For six of these countries (Australia, Brazil, Canada, India, United States, and U.S.S.R.) the ratios were also calculated for the cities in their various internal subdivisions (states, provinces, etc.). These ranged from median ratios of 0·43 for the United States to the remarkably low ratio of 0·07 for Australia, where five of its six states are strongly dominated by large urban centres. Again, the results suggest that ratios at the provincial level are lower than the rank-size rule would predict.

Results based on the two leading cities might be expected to be highly variable because of the small size of the sample. A number of writers (Zipf, 1949; Stewart, 1958; Gibbs, 1961, pp. 438–51) have followed these relationships further down the urban spectrum. Fig. 4.9-A shows the ratios for the five largest cities in a number of contrasting countries. The United States shows a reasonably close correspondence with the expected sequence (i.e. 1, 0·50, 0·33, 0·25, and 0·20), while Australia shows strong divergence. When the rank-size relationship is extended over the full

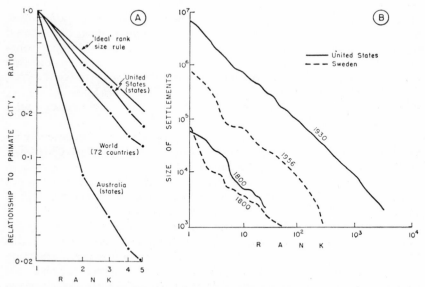

Fig. 4.9. A Median size of cities as a fraction of the largest city. *B* Changes in the size distribution of cities in Sweden and the United States. Source: Stewart, 1958, pp. 228, 231; Zipf, 1949.

range of towns for which data are available, curves like those in Fig. 4.9-B are generated. The curves show two contrasting cases: the United States (unbroken line) in which the lines are relatively straight and in which the general form of the rank-size rule is confirmed, and Sweden (broken lines) which follows an S-shaped curve. Comparison of the two curves shows an increasing linearity over time with the United States, but growing irregularity over time with Sweden. Again, both cases suggest some range in the behaviour of the city-size distribution over time as well as space.

2. General relationships: log-normal distributions

a. Form of the distribution. The fact that the rank-size rule appears as a straight line on double-log paper (e.g. Fig. 4.9-B) suggests that we may view it simply as part of a truncated logarithmic distribution. This is the approach taken by Berry (1961-A), who studied the city-size distributions in thirty-eight countries drawn with fair representation from all parts of the world, except Africa (which was under-represented). The sample countries ranged in size from Soviet Russia to El Salvador, and population data for the early 1950's were used. The statistical population studied consisted of 4,187 cities with over 20,000 inhabitants although for some countries, notably France, data for the lower size classes were not available.

Berry plotted for each country the number of cities as a cumulative percentage on the *y*-axis, and the size of cities on the *x*-axis. By transforming the first axis to the normal probability scale and the second to a logarithmic scale, the log-normal distribution should appear simply as a straight line. Using this type of graph two main types of size distribution with an intermediate class are recognized. Thirteen of the thirty-eight countries were classed as *log-normal* (or rank-size) in distribution: this included both highly developed countries like the United States (*a*) and underdeveloped countries like Korea (*b*), both large countries like China (*c*) and small countries like El Salvador (*d*) (Fig. 4.10-A). Fifteen countries were classed as *primate* distributions with a marked gap between the leading city (or cities) and the smaller city distribution. All the countries in this group are small, but the characteristics of their curves vary considerably: Thailand (*a*) lacks any signs of the log-normal curve, whereas Denmark (*b*) has signs of the log-normal distribution reasserting itself in the lower size range, while Japan shows only a small break or step in the log-normal pattern (Fig. 4.10-B).

Between these two classes, Berry recognizes an *intermediate* distribution with nine countries. This includes countries like England and Wales (*a*), which has '. . . primate cities grafted on top of a complete lower log-normal distribution' (Berry, 1961-A, p. 576), or Australia (*b*), in which smaller cities are missing from the log-normal curve, or Portugal (*c*) with its curiously 'bevelled' distribution with a log-normal middle section (Fig. 4.10-C). Superimposition of all the curves for the thirty-eight countries (Fig. 4.10-D) shows the general nature of the curves with a marked tendency towards a log-normal pattern for the world as a whole.

b. Interpretation of size-number forms. What do the variations between the various forms of the city-size distribution mean? Two groups of hypotheses are suggested by Berry.

(i) The first group of hypotheses contain ideas which seem logical in the abstract, but were not confirmed by empirical observation. We might suggest for example an *urbanization hypothesis* in which the city-size type is

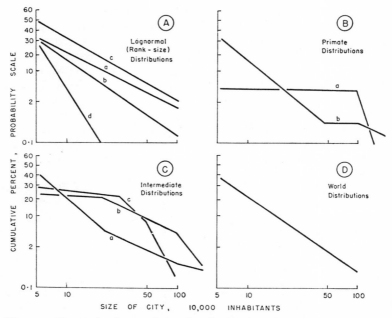

Fig. 4.10. Alternative forms of city-size distributions. Source: Berry, 1961-A, pp. 575–8.

related to the degree of urbanization. When, however, degree of urbanization, as measured by the proportion of a country's total population in cities of 20,000 or more people, was plotted against the city-size distribution, no cross-relationship was found. The primate pattern, for example, was found for both highly urbanized countries (like the Netherlands and Japan) and for largely rural areas (like Mexico and Thailand). For log-normal patterns, the same was true.

A second hypothesis, the *economic development hypothesis*, was also tested and found to be ineffective. Here pattern was related to the degree of economic development as measured on a scale derived by Berry (1960-B) from forty-three proposed indices of economic development. The scale has been used in an earlier discussion (Chap. 3.II(3)), and its construction is discussed in detail in Chapter 8.I(3d). If economic development and city-size pattern are related, we would expect to find all the primate countries at one end of the spectrum and all the log-normal at the other. In fact, as Fig. 4.11 shows, the pattern is essentially random. The primate countries (shown by open circles) and the log-normal countries (shown by closed circles) are irregularly arranged with no preferential grouping at any point in the development spectrum. We conclude therefore that the economic development hypothesis cannot be maintained.

(ii) The second group of hypotheses contain ideas which, though they seem less logical and certainly less clear in the abstract, are supported by the evidence available. A general *stochastic hypothesis* has been suggested by

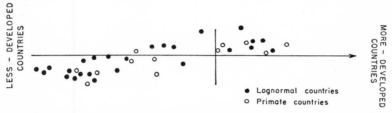

Fig. 4.11. Distribution of countries with *log-normal* and *primate* city-size distributions on Berry's development spectrum. Source: Berry, 1961-A, p. 586.

Simon (1955), and its implications for the log-normal and primate distributions are important. Simon approached the city-size distribution from the broad viewpoint of general systems theory (Chap. 1.III(1)), arguing that the stability of the rank-size relationship over space and time suggested it might be viewed as a steady-state phenomenon, i.e. a condition of entropy in which the distribution is affected by a myriad of small random forces. Simon approximated the rank-size rule to a probability formulation used by Yule in 1924 to explain the distribution of biological genera in which the log-normal distribution is produced as a limiting case of stochastic growth processes. Berry and Garrison (1958-c) have tested the Simon model for the distribution of city sizes in the state of Washington, United States, and as Table 4.4 shows, the approximation obtained was reasonably good.

In terms of the two country patterns, log-normal and primate, Berry (1961-A) has argued that the Simon model implies two sets of sub-hypotheses. First, that log-normal patterns are the product of urbanization in countries which are (a) larger than average, (b) have a long history of urbanization, and (c) are economically and politically complex. Of the thirteen countries in this group, the United States and Brazil qualify on the first sub-hypothesis, India and China and the six European countries on the second, and, possibly, South Africa on the third. Clearly some

Table 4.4. Expected and observed distribution of city sizes on Simon model*

Size of cities, inhabitants ($\times 10^4$):	*0·5*	*1·5*	*2·5*	*3·5*
Number of cities:				
Observed	36	12	7	5
Expected (on Simon model)	36	14	9	6

Source: Berry and Garrison, 1958-c, p. 89.

* Washington, United States, 1950.

qualify on all three grounds, while two in the log-normal group (Korea and El Salvador) appear to qualify on none.

Second, we may argue that primate patterns are the products of city development in countries which are (*a*) smaller than average, (*b*) have a short history of urbanization, and (*c*) are economically or politically simple. Certainly the fifteen countries in this group are small to medium in size, and in some, the impact of a few strong forces is clearly seen. Thus Portugal, Spain, Austria, and the Netherlands have capital cities which were developed to serve empires rather than the local city hierarchy: e.g. Vienna's size is logical in terms of the Austro-Hungarian empire rather than contemporary Austria. Other countries have either a commercial export sector superimposed on a peasant agricultural system (e.g. the 'dual economy' of Ceylon), or a strong primary export system (e.g. Uruguay) or a single 'Westernized' city (e.g. Thailand).

3. 'Lower-limb' relationships: an unsolved problem

One of the difficulties of both the rank-size and truncated log-normal views of the settlement-size continuum is that they fail to apply to the lower ends of the distribution. Under both rules the number of settlements should continue to expand as size decreases, so that we should not only expect more villages than towns, but more hamlets than villages, more isolated farms than hamlets. The same assumptions are made in the Christaller–Lösch ideas of the functional hierarchy (Chap. 5.I(3)). But we know that this relationship may not hold universally: isolated farmsteads may not be more numerous than hamlets.

Gunawardena (1964) studied the settlement pattern in southern Ceylon and, from detailed headmen's lists, was able to break down settlements into discrete population clusters at the sub-village level. The size distribution of settlements, when plotted on double-log paper (Fig. 4.12), shows a characteristic curve for both the Wet Zone and Dry Zone, suggesting that we may regard this as a log-normal distribution. These results suggest that the studies so far conducted on larger population clusters have, in fact, been describing only one limb (the upper or urban limb) of the population continuum. Indeed, when the data from Table 4.3 are plotted on Gunawardena's graph they roughly parallel the upper limb of the Dry and Wet Zone continua. There may therefore be a need to examine the lower part of the limb, the 'sub-village' limb, to see whether

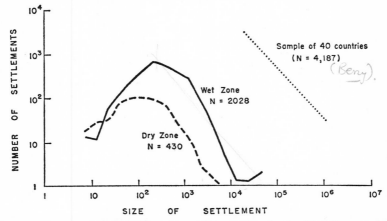

Fig. 4.12. Frequency distributions for settlement sizes in the Wet Zone and Dry Zone of southern Ceylon. Source: Gunawardena, 1964, p. 167.

the rank-size rule may be reversed in this small-settlement zone, somewhat in the way that Hjülström found relationships between size of particles and erodibility reversed in the lower zones, by aggregation of very small particles (Scheidegger, 1961, p. 135). Data difficulties at this level pose special problems and it seems probable that field survey, rather than secondary census records, are needed to clarify the intriguing relations between number and size of clusters in this rather unexplored zone.

III. SIZE AND SPACING OF CLUSTERS

1. Spacing of discrete groups

If the rank-size rule, uncomplicated by Gunawardena's findings (Chap. 4.II(3)), were to operate, then we should expect the spacing of settlements to be largely governed by their size. Large settlements would be widely spaced, small settlements closely spaced. Both Christaller (1933) and Lösch (1954) put forward evidence for discrete types of settlements to show that this proposition may be valid, at least for specified areas. For south Germany, Christaller examined in detail the hierarchy of small towns and villages around the five great regional capitals (Frankfurt, Munich, Nuremberg, Strasbourg, and Stuttgart) and showed that while these were 178 kilometres apart, the smaller provincial capitals were only 108 kilometres apart, the county seats twenty-one kilometres apart, and the villages seven kilometres apart. Lösch's evidence for Iowa, in the mid-western United States, is shown in Fig. 4.13. It suggests both the close connection between size and spacing for three classes, cities with 300–1,000 inhabitants (Fig. 4.13-A), cities with 1,000–4,000 inhabitants, (Fig. 4.13-B), and cities with 4,000–20,000 inhabitants (Fig. 4.13-C), and also the greater variability in spacing with increasing size.

Since the 1930's these findings have been supplemented by work like

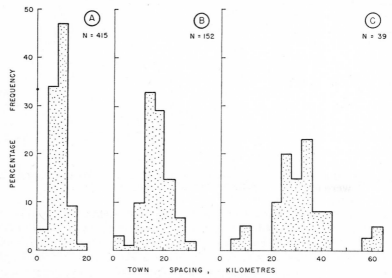

Fig. 4.13. Histograms of overland distances separating small towns (*A*), intermediate towns (*B*), and large towns (*C*) in Iowa, 1930. Source: Lösch, 1954, p. 391.

that of Brush and Bracey (1955) who compared rural central places in southwestern Wisconsin (United States) and southern England. They found that despite the strong differences in population density, economic functions, and social and political history between the two areas, *both* showed two distinct tiers of central places: a tier of higher-order centres spaced at twenty-one-mile distances and a tier of lower-order centres spaced at eight- to ten-mile intervals.

Somewhat different relations have been discovered by House (1953) in a study of medium-sized towns in these same two industrial societies. House defined a medium-sized town as one with a population between 20,000 and 100,000, and studied their distribution in England and Wales and the western part of the United States manufacturing belt (the five states of Illinois, Indiana, Michigan, Ohio, and Pennsylvania). As Table

Table 4.5. Town spacing in two industrial regions

Region:	England and Wales (1951)	United States (1950)
Population, millions of inhabitants	43·8	37·5
Density, inhabitants/sq. mile	134	63
Number of medium-sized towns	316	123
Mean spacing of medium-sized towns, miles:		
20,000– 30,000 inhabitants	6·1	14·6
40,000– 50,000 inhabitants	7·9	28·3
75,000–100,000 inhabitants	10·0	38·0

Source: House, 1953, p. 63.

4.5 shows, both areas had roughly comparable populations, but the American area was only half as densely populated and had only about one-third as many medium-sized towns as England and Wales. In both cases there is a general increase in the distance separating towns with increase in town size, but these distances are far less than Christaller's values. For south Germany, Christaller suggested that towns of 30,000 population would be spaced at intervals of about thirty-eight miles; in England and Wales the corresponding figure is about seven miles and in the United States about twenty-five miles. Much of the difference in these findings springs from the industrial character of the latter areas. Although exact definitions are made difficult by contrasts in census classifications, House's figures suggest that about half of the British towns are mining and manufacturing towns, many of which are still clustered in characteristic huddles around their original coalfield locations. In the United States, towns are both less specialized and, developing at a later phase, are less tied to early coalfield concentrations. Both the degree and the timing of industrialization appear to distort the spacing characteristics in a fundamental way.

2. Spacing as a continuous function

a. Definition of spacing. Alongside studies which have examined the average characteristics of groups of settlements are those in which spacing has been regarded as a continuous function. With these the method of study hinges on the definition of spacing adopted, in most cases measured as the overland distance between a sample settlement and its 'nearest neighbours of the same size'. However, as Thomas (1961) points out, this does not necessarily mean that the population of the sample city and the neighbour city are *exactly* the same size: rather that they are *approximately* the same size. Thomas introduces a probability concept which greatly sharpens the choice of what is meant by 'approximately the same size'. He shows from a sample approximating to a log-log-normal curve, and tha by adopting a given confidence level (e.g. 95 per cent) we can define the range that we expect a nearest-neighbour town of the 'same population' to have. The general form may be written as

$$S_i - xE_i < N_i < S_i + xE_i$$

where S_i is the population of the sample town, N_i is the population of the nearest neighbour, E_i is a random error value and x is the standard abscissa of the normal curve associated with a desired confidence level (Thomas, 1961, p. 405). To translate this into practical terms: If the sample town has a population of 105 persons, we can define the 'same population' for the nearest neighbour as lying between 72 and 159 inhabitants. Any difference in population within these limits may be regarded as due to chance and disregarded. The fact that the limits are asymmetric about 105 is due to the characteristic log-log curve of the population of Iowan towns.

 b. *Spacing and cluster size.* Using this definition, Thomas (1961) investi-gates the relationships between population and spacing for eighty-nine

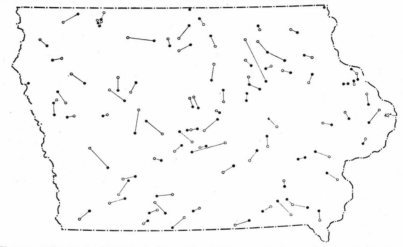

Fig. 4.14. Nearest neighbours of sample settlements in Iowa ($G = 3.5$). Links to settlements outside the state are not shown. Source: Thomas, 1961, p. 408.

sample towns in Iowa (Fig. 4.14). Statistical investigation shows, as expected, a positive association between the logarithms of distance and population size, although the proportion of distance variation 'explained' by size was only about one third ($R^2 = 0.35$). In a follow-up study (Thomas, 1962) he was able to test his findings on the 1950 population against the five earlier census records for this century. He finds a surprising degree of stability in the distance–size relationship. Only for the 1900 census did the degree of correlation differ markedly from that found in the

1950 survey, and even here the relationship shows up as statistically significant at the 95 per cent confidence level. Distance separating the sample cities from their neighbours of the 'same size' (*Hypothesis I*) was also compared with distances separating sample cities from their neighbours of the 'same or greater size' (*Hypothesis II*).

Fig. 4.15-A shows correlation values obtained on the first test against those obtained on the second. While for both sets of values the coefficients are statistically significant (95 per cent confidence level), the closer relationship is always obtained for the second test. It is clear for Iowa that town size is closely associated with spacing, and that this relationship holds in a hierarchical sense, since the sample towns are even more closely

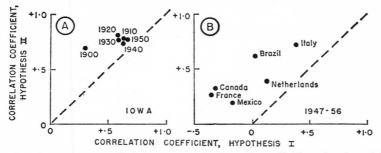

Fig. 4.15. Correlations between alternative hypotheses linking city size with spacing. Sources: Thomas, 1962, p. 27; Gibbs, 1961, p. 458.

associated with their larger neighbours. Whether the closing gap shown by the two sets of relationships represents a trend to a more highly integrated relationship between the settlements remains to be seen.

Gibbs (1961, pp. 451–9) has confirmed Thomas's hypothesis for the spacing of the major cities in six countries (Brazil, Canada, France, Italy, Mexico, and the Netherlands). As Fig. 4.15-B indicates, a higher correlation coefficient was found between the size of metropolitan area and the distance to the nearest larger metropolitan area, than between size and the distance to the nearest metropolitan area. Despite variations in the values of the coefficient, the consistently higher values for the second relationship are striking.

c. Spacing as a complex function. In one of the few studies in which spacing has been treated in a wider context, King (1961) carried out a multiple regression analysis of several alternative hypotheses. Spacing was seen as a function of the size of a town, its occupational structure, and the characteristics of the zone in which it was located. A sample of 200 towns was drawn at random from the 1950 United States census giving a range in town size from five inhabitants (Slaughter Beach, Delaware) up to Seattle, Washington, with nearly half a million inhabitants. The 'nearest neighbour' was defined for each of the sample towns using Thomas's probability definition (Chap. 4.III(2a)) and a correlation analysis of spacing as a function carried out. Table 4.6 shows that the association

Table 4.6. Relationship between settlement spacing and other variables*

Hypotheses:	Single hypothesis (Size of settlement)	Multiple hypothesis (Six-factors)
Coefficients of determination (R^2):		
National results	0·02†	0·25†
Centre classification:		
Central places	0·09†	0·26†
Non-central places	0·01	0·42†
Regional agricultural classification:		
Grazing and wheat zone	0·42†	0·67†
Specialized farming zone	0·01	0·20†
General farming zone	0·07	0·67†
Feed grain and livestock zone	0·22†	0·34†
Dairying zone	0·04†	0·36†

Source: King, 1961, pp. 227–31.

* United States, 1950.   † Significant at the 95 per cent confidence level.

discovered, though statistically significant, explained only about 2 per cent of the variations in spacing. Division of the sample into central places (162 towns) and non-central places showed that the spacing of the first group was much more predictable than that of the second. Similarly, a breakdown of the towns into five major farming zones brought out important variations between the regions of the United States. In the Great Plains and the Far West the level of explanation rose sharply to over 40 per cent and in the Corn Belt to over 20 per cent, suggesting that the regularities described by Lösch (1954, pp. 389–93) might be less typical of the whole United States than often supposed.

With the exception of specific regions, the predictive performance of population as a guide to spacing was poor and King went on to test five other hypotheses related to the characteristics of the region in which the town was located and to its occupational structure. He argued that towns of a given size were likely to be more widely spaced where (i) rural population density is low, (ii) farming is extensive, (iii) agricultural production is low, (iv) where the overall population density is low, and (v) where the town itself has a low proportion of workers in manufacturing. Regression analysis showed that while all five were slightly more valuable than town size in predicting spacing, only one, overall population density, could explain more than 10 per cent of the variation. Indeed all six hypotheses working together could only explain one quarter of the variation in spacing, though here again performance improved with certain agricultural zones (shown in the final column in Table 4.6). Clearly there is a very considerable problem in building accurate predictive models for spacing for an area as large as the United States where differences in the historical development of settlements in the various regions are so unlike. Future research using multivariate techniques but building historical factors into the model may uncover consistent explanations for the wide variation in the spacing characteristics of urban settlements.

One of the most intriguing questions about the nodal distribution of population was not answered in the last chapter. This is the question of the hierarchical organization of settlement. Some of the most prolific and important of locational theorists—the Germans, Christaller and Lösch—were intrigued with this problem and evolved some fairly complex models to explain and illustrate their own concepts of locational hierarchies. These models are examined here together with the empirical evidence for and against this type of structure. The second half of the chapter concerns the difficult and apparently aberrant cases of industrial centres which 'distort' the regular hierarchy. In suggesting that this distortion is less fundamental than is sometimes urged, an attempt is made to place the industrial location models, notably that of Weber, within the general framework of settlement location.

I. FUNCTIONAL HIERARCHIES OF SETTLEMENTS

1. Cluster size and cluster function

When a recent paper reported that a small general store near Zürich stocked only one kind of champagne, while the Bahnhofstrasse in the city centre displayed over twenty kinds, it was confirming for centres within the urban area what had been well established in central-place literature for decades, and in everyday experience since time was, i.e. the fact that large centres of population have a much wider range of goods, services, and functions than smaller centres. Despite this general accordance, interest in the size–function relationship has not decreased. Rather it has turned to the study of aberrant cases where the rule appears to break down and to a consideration of the exact *form* of the size–function relationship.

    a. Continuous relationships between size and function. A number of studies have tried to trace the precise form of the relationship between the population size of a settlement and its functional range. Fig. 5.1 illustrates two

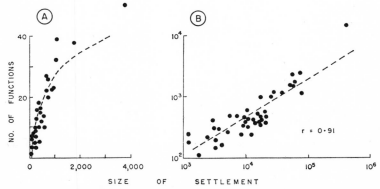

Fig. 5.1. Relationship of functional range to settlement size in southern Illinois, United States (*A*), and southern Ceylon (*B*). In the first graph the *y*-axis is arithmetic and in the second graph is logarithmic. Sources: Stafford, 1963, p. 170; Gunawardena, 1964.

sets of findings from areas of Western and non-Western society. First, those of Stafford (1963) who examined the functions of a small sample of towns in southern Illinois, and found a positive correlation of 0·89 (correlation coefficient, *r*) between population and functional range (Fig. 5.1-A). Rather similar findings with positively high relationships are found from other Western areas: King (1962) found values of 0·82 in the Canterbury district of New Zealand, and Berry and Garrison (1958) found slightly lower values (0·75) for Snohomish county, Washington, in the north-western United States.

    For non-Western society, Gunawardena (1964) has found a similar curvilinear and positive relationship for the southern part of Ceylon. Fig. 5.1-B shows the results obtained for the number of service establishments plotted against size of settlements (*r* = 0·91). Similar coefficients were obtained, for the relationship with shop numbers (0·89) and retail establishments (0·87). Although both sets of findings were drawn from mainly rural areas, Ullman and Dacey (1962) have suggested that they may be reasonably extended to larger towns and cities.

The high positive correlations suggest that (i) larger centres have a far greater range of service functions than smaller centres, but that (ii) the relationship between size and functional range is curvilinear—as settlements become larger they add fewer new functions for each new increment in population size.

b. Discontinuous relationships: the threshold problem. On theoretical grounds (Chap. 5.I(2)), the relationship between size and function might be

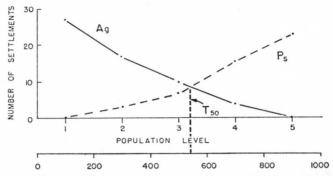

Fig. 5.2. Graphical determination of population thresholds (T_{50}) for settlement functions by the Reed-Muench method (1938). Source: Haggett and Gunawardena, 1964, p. 8.

expected to be recognizably 'stepped' in character, rather than continuous. While the evidence available is not conclusive, a number of studies of both thresholds and discontinuities throw some light on this hypothesis. Haggett and Gunawardena (1964) suggest that we may view the *threshold* of any function as the middle point of its 'entry zone'. For a given function (F_i), there is a lower population level at which no settlements of this size have F_i; conversely there is an upper population level at which all settlements of that size have F_i. By modifying a standard bioassay technique, the Reed–Muench method, the middle point of this entry zone can be measured to give the *median population threshold* or T_{50}. Fig. 5.2 shows how T_{50} may be determined in practice. The number of settlements with and without the function, F_i, are plotted on the y-axis against the population size of the settlement transformed to a category scale on the x-axis. The point where the two curves cross gives the appropriate T_{50} value in terms of the population scale. Using this technique, thresholds were determined by Gunawardena (1964) for a number of settlement functions in the southern part of Ceylon. Table 5.1 shows for some sample functions, the range in T_{50} values. Higher-order functions

Table 5.1. Median thresholds for range of functions*

Environmental zone:	Wet zone	Dry zone	Ratio
Service functions:			
Primary schools	515	260	0·50
Post offices	1,590	565	0·36
Markets and fairs	2,870	1,300	0·45
Secondary schools	3,400	1,190	0·35
Hospitals	5,250	1,260	0·24
Magistrates' courts	9,200	2,370	0·26

Source: Gunawardena, 1964, p. 180.
* Southern Ceylon.

[handwritten margin note: NB different types of area can diff[erent] pop[ulation] thresholds for the same function.]

(e.g. magistrates' courts) have median thresholds nearly twenty times as high as that for some lower-order functions (e.g. primary schools), while the two main climatic zones (Wet Zone and Dry Zone) are strongly contrasted.

Gunawardena's findings are important because they confirm for a non-Western area the type of threshold hierarchy which earlier work by Berry and Garrison (1958-A, B) had established for the United States. Moreover, Bunge (1962, p. 146) had criticized American evidence of thresholds on the grounds that (i) it referred to thresholds in the population of the settlement rather than the population of the hinterland, and (ii) it ignored highway users who contributed a large part of the true threshold population of settlements in the United States. For southern Ceylon, Gunawardena was able to show that the population of the central settlement was significantly correlated with the total hinterland population for all the functions studied. Also southern Ceylon is an area of such low mobility, at least relative to the United States, that the proportion of the threshold population that is contributed by 'through-traffic' is very small indeed.

Our knowledge of *discontinuities* in the settlement continuum is being greatly extended by a series of carefully controlled field studies by Berry (*in press*). For one of his five sample areas, southwestern Iowa (a classic laboratory area used earlier by Lösch), preliminary results have already been published (Berry, Barnum, and Tennant, 1962). These suggest that discrete hierarchies can in fact be recognized in an area of which Lösch himself wrote: 'I do not see how one could eliminate size-number effects to disclose possible hidden agglomerations' (Lösch, 1954, p. 433). Berry 'discloses' discontinuities for the twenty settlements in his area by direct questionnaire survey and by using factor analysis on the results (Chap. 8.I(3d)). Settlements were grouped by factor analysis into three distinct classes: *cities* with more than fifty-five functions, *towns* with from twenty-eight to fifty functions, and *villages* with between ten and twenty-five functions. Although *hamlets* were not included in the factor analysis,

E

Fig. 5.3-A shows that they occupied a distinct segment of the functional hierarchy. In this graph the number of functional establishments (shops, garages, etc.) are plotted on the *y*-axis, against the range of functions on the *x*-axis. For the three higher-order settlements (Fig. 5.3-B) the distinctive locations of villages, towns, and cities is shown in relation to the

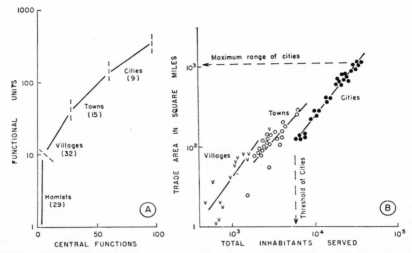

Fig. 5.3. Settlement hierarchy in southwestern Iowa, United States, for four classes of central places. Source: Berry, Barnum, and Tennant, 1962, pp. 79, 80.

trade area and the total population served (with both *x*- and *y*-axes transformed to logarithmic scales). The advantage of this graph is that both the *threshold* and the *maximum range* can be readily determined for a specific order of the settlement hierarchy: the arrows on Fig. 5.3-B indicate these values for cities.

From the theoretical viewpoint, the advantages of the type of study carried out by Berry in southwest Iowa, or by Mayfield (1962) in northern India, is that small breaks in the population size distribution can be evaluated in terms of a functional hierarchy. Whether such studies, by their mathematical rigidity, lose something of the regional character of more traditional studies (Smailes, 1946) is an open question. Certainly they build on an impressive literature of earlier study of the settlement hierarchy, and classics like Bracey's study of an English county, *Social provision in rural Wiltshire* (1952), show something of the power and flexibility of a less theoretical approach.

2. Lattices and *k*-functions

In an earlier discussion (Chap. 4.I(1)) it was argued that settlements arranged in a triangular lattice, with a separate hexagonal field about each centre, represent the optimum spatial division of an undifferentiated landscape. If we now wish to introduce the notion of a hierarchy of settlements in which some settlements provide specialized functions for others we must disturb this simple pattern.

Figure 5.4 shows some of the ways in which hexagonal fields may be

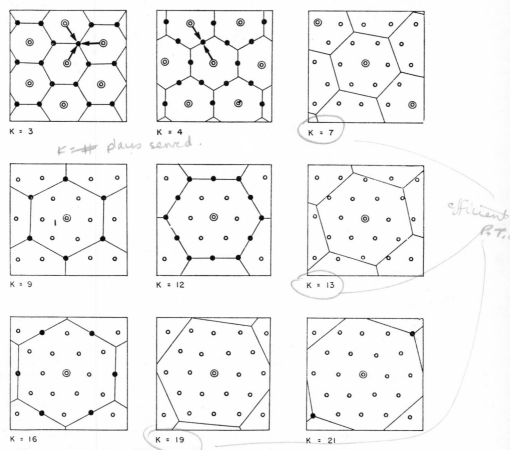

Fig. 5.4. Nine smallest hexagonal territories in a Löschian landscape. Source: Lösch, 1954, p. 118.

rearranged by the simple process of changing (i) the orientation of the hexagonal net and (ii) the size of each hexagonal cell. In these nine diagrams the *central* places that are performing specialist functions are shown by a double circle, the *dependent* places are shown by open circles if they lie within the field of a central place and by closed circles if they lie on the perimeter of such a field.

In this system the total number of settlements served by each central place is termed its k-value, following Christaller (1933). In the first diagram of Fig. 5.4 the k-value of each central place is three. This is made up of the central place itself plus a one-third share in the six border settlements: this one-third proportion is because each dependent place is shared between three central places (see arrows). In the following diagram, the hexagonal net is turned through ninety degrees so that border settlements are shared by only two central places and the value of k rises to four. When this process of net orientation and enlargement is continued nine smallest fields are found to yield a discontinuous series of k-values:

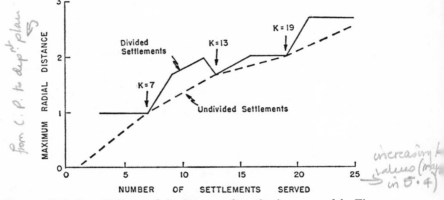

Fig. 5.5. Relative efficiency of the hexagonal territories mapped in Fig. 5.4.

i.e. three, four, seven, nine, twelve, thirteen, sixteen, nineteen, and twenty-one.

While there are a number of solutions to hexagonal hierarchies, each with its appropriate k-values, both Christaller and Lösch have argued that not all possible solutions were equally likely. When the number of settlements served is plotted on the x-axis against the maximum distance (i.e. from the central place to the furthest dependent place) on the y-axis then irregularities are revealed (Fig. 5.5). If we judge the efficiency (i.e. settlements served/distance travelled) of each solution by this graph then clearly the fifth solution ($k = 12$) is extremely inefficient, while the third solution ($k = 7$), the sixth solution ($k = 13$), and the eighth solution ($k = 19$) are very efficient. These three cases also have the advantage of consisting entirely of undivided dependent places (none of the satellite centres are shared with any other central place), which Lösch (1954, p. 120, footnote 16) suggests is both politically and economically stable and is therefore a solution likely to occur in practice.

Using arguments of this kind we can see that a regular lattice of settlements leads to (i) a discontinuous number of central-place solutions and

(ii) irregularities in the relative efficiencies of these solutions. It is on these basic numbers, the *k*-values, of the hexagonal system that the central-place hierarchies of Christaller and Lösch have been built.

3. Central-place hierarchies

Although we shall be concerned in this section with the central-place models of Christaller (1933) and Lösch (1940, 1954), our treatment is restricted to the locational geometry of the models and the implications this holds for settlement structure. Critical reviews of the economic assumptions of the models are given for Christaller by Baskin (1957) and Berry and Pred (1961, pp. 3–18), and for Lösch by Valvanis (1955) and Beckmann (1955).

a. Christaller: the fixed-k hierarchy. Christaller (1933) developed a series of central-place hierarchies on the assumption that the *k*-values in any region, once adopted, would be fixed. That is, they applied equally to the relationships between farms and villages, villages and towns, towns and cities, and so on, through all the *tiers* of the central-place hierarchy. Fig. 5.6-A shows a very simple three-tier hierarchy based on the *k* = 4 assumption: with a lower stratum of dependent villages on which is built a stratum of central towns on which is built the higher stratum of central cities. The complete hierarchy for the *k* = 4 successions, follows a regular geometrical progression (one, four, sixteen, sixty-four . . .), while that for the next solution, *k* = 7, follows a similar progression (one, seven, forty-nine, three hundred and forty-three) (Fig. 5.6-B). The general relationship

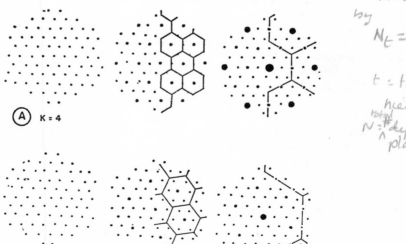

(A) K = 4

(B) K = 7

Fig. 5.6. Three-stage hierarchies in two regular fixed-*k* systems.

between the number of places for each tier in the fixed-k hierarchy is given by the formula $N_t = K^t$ where N is the number of dependent places and t the tier on the hierarchy. Using this formula we should expect that in a $k = 7$ hierarchy, a central place would dominate 2,401 dependent places on the fourth tier of that hierarchy.

Although Christaller saw the advantages of undivided centres, he suggested that this might be achieved by 'nesting' of centres rather than by adopting optimum hexagonal boundaries shown in Fig. 5.4. Three cases were envisaged: (i) Where the supply of goods from central places is to be as near as possible to the dependent places (Christaller's *marketing principle*) a $k = 3$ hierarchy is indicated since this maximizes the number of central places. To overcome the difficulty of shared dependent places, Christaller suggests connections will be made with only two of the six nearest dependent places (Fig. 5.7-A), and that this will give rise to a symmetrical

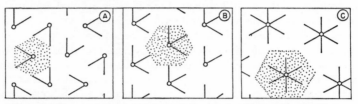

Fig. 5.7. Alternative nesting principles in the Christaller landscape.

nested hierarchy. (ii) Where the cost of transport networks is important (Christaller's *traffic principle*) a $k = 4$ hierarchy is indicated since '. . . as many important places as possible lie on one traffic route between larger towns, the route being established as cheaply as possible' (Berry and Pred, 1961, p. 16). Connections will be made with only three of the six nearest dependent places (Fig. 5.7-B) to give a different pattern of nesting. (iii) Where clear-cut administrative control is important (Christaller's *administrative principle*) a $k = 7$ hierarchy is indicated with connections between a central place and all six of the nearest dependent places (Fig. 5.7-C). Results from an Iowan study (Berry, Barnum, and Tennant, 1962, pp. 105–6) have suggested that, although nesting may occur in practice, it may be more irregular than Christaller's model suggests.

b. Lösch: variable-k hierarchies. Lösch (1954) used a similar hexagonal unit for his theoretical landscapes, but he improved and extended on the Christaller form. The major difference between the two approaches is that Lösch regarded the fixed-k assumption as a special limiting case and used *all* the various hexagonal solutions, both the nine shown in Fig. 5.4 and further extensions on the same lines. By superimposing all the various sizes of hexagons on a single point he rotated all the nets about that point to get six sectors with many and six sectors with few production sites (Fig. 5.8). With this arrangement 'all nets have a centre in common . . .

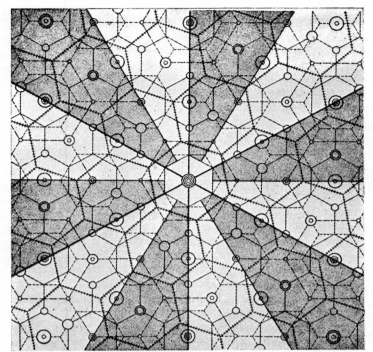

Fig. 5.8. Simplified Löschian landscape with systems of hexagonal nets.
Source: Isard, 1956, p. 270.

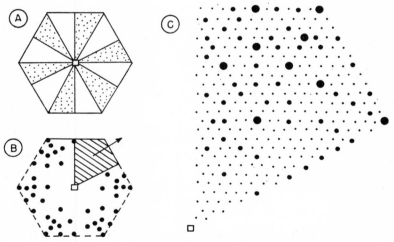

Fig. 5.9. Löschian landscape with alternating city-rich and city-poor sectors (*A*),
distribution of large cities (*B*), and distribution of all centres within one sector (*C*).
Source: Lösch, 1954, p. 127.

the greatest number of locations coincide . . . the sum of the minimum distances between industrial locations is least, and in consequence not only shipments but transport lines are reduced to a minimum' (Lösch, 1954, p. 124). As Fig. 5.9 shows, the rotation produces a strong pattern of variation, both between sectors and with distance from the metropolis. Here the metropolitan centre is the centre of 150 separate fields. Those with centres of over four and over eight coincident fields are shown by the two larger classes of dots in Fig. 5.9-c.

Although Lösch used the same basic hexagonal unit and the same k concept as Christaller, the hierarchy he evolved is markedly different. Christaller's hierarchy consists of a number of definite steps or tiers in which (i) all places in a particular tier are the same size and have the same function, and (ii) all higher-order places contain all the functions of the smaller central places. In contrast to this, the Löschian hierarchy is far less rigid. It consists of a nearly continuous sequence of centres rather than distinct tiers, so that (i) settlements of the same size need not have the same function (e.g. a centre serving seven settlements may be either a $k = 7$ central place or merely the coincident centre for both the $k = 3$ and the $k = 4$ network), and (ii) larger places need not necessarily have all the functions of the same smaller central places.

In many ways, the Löschian system—at least when it is adjusted for concentration and resource irregularities (Chap. 4.I(2a))—yields a pattern more in accord with reality than that of Christaller. Lösch's variable-k model gives a more continuous distribution with rather small deviations from the logarithmic distribution. Vining (1955) has attacked the Christaller fixed-k concept on the grounds in that it leads to a 'stepped' size distribution of cities, rather than the continuous distribution actually observed (Chap. 4.II), while Beckmann (1958) has defended the Christaller model, as both simpler and theoretically more satisfying. He argues that it may not be inconsistent with observed city-size distributions if we allow the addition of a random element. This element may be sufficient to blur the rigid steps of the hierarchy into a continuous rank-size sequence.

c. k-values: empirical evidence. One of the by-products of work on thresholds (reviewed in Chapter 5.I(1b)) has been to examine the concept of (i) *tiers* in the hierarchy, and (ii) the relations between them as shown by k-values. There has certainly been no lack of studies in which tiers were recognized. Indeed, since Christaller (1933, 1950) recognized his seven-tier hierarchy ranging from the hamlet to the world-city, there have been perhaps as many tiers recognized in human geography as erosion-surfaces in physical geography. The basic difficulty both such studies face is their definition of 'breaks' in the sequence whether of function or of terrain. In practice, more or less arbitrary divisions have to be made. Thus Bracey (1962) in a study of central villages in Somerset, England, recognizes first-order, second-order, and third-order villages (Fig. 5.10) but bases this classification on a continuum (number of shops) with breaks at five, ten, and twenty shops. Improved techniques for recognizing significant breaks (e.g. the use of factor analysis by Berry, Barnum, and Tennant

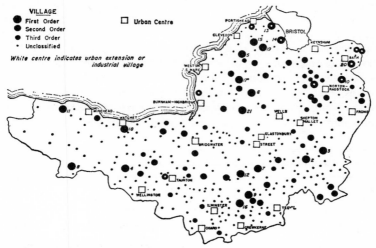

Fig. 5.10. Hierarchy of central villages in Somerset ($G = 5 \cdot 1$), southwestern England. Source: Bracey, 1962, p. 176.

(1962)) may help to overcome this problem by providing objective tests for their recognition.

Where uniform methods of classification are used, regional variations in the relationships between the various tiers can be followed. Thus Gunawardena (1964), who recognized four functional-tiers in the settlement hierarchy in southern Ceylon, was able to show that k-values ranged from $1 \cdot 6$ to $11 \cdot 0$ between the various provinces. This variation may be more important and characteristic than her other finding, i.e., that the modal class was $k = 3$, exactly accordant with Christaller's 'marketing principle'.

II. SPECIALIZED CENTRES WITHIN THE HIERARCHY

1. Concepts of specialization

Despite the evidence for regular arrangements of settlements in rather fixed hierarchies, discussed in the preceding section (Chap. 5.I), we are aware of many cases which seem to contradict these rules. The clusters of coalfield cities in northern England, or of the cotton towns of the Appalachian piedmont, seem to belong to a less-regular order, which is grafted on to the 'normal' system of central places. Thomas Hardy sensed this difference when he wrote of Casterbridge '. . . the pole, focus or nerve-knot of the surrounding country life; differing from the many manu-facturing towns, which are as foreign bodies set down, like boulders on a plain, in a green world with which they have nothing in common' (Hardy, 1886, p. 73).

Contemporary statistics allow some precision to be given to this dis-tinction. Alexandersson (1956) studied a group of United States cities and measured their occupational structure in terms of the 1950 census. For the 864 cities, each with a population of at least 10,000 inhabitants, it was found that some functions were present in all cities (*ubiquitous* types), while others occurred in very few (*sporadic* types). Table 5.2 shows a tentative

Table 5.2. Classification of urban industry*

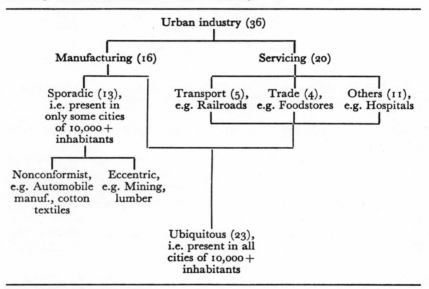

Source: Alexandersson, 1955.

* United States, 1950.

breakdown of the thirty-six groups on this presence–absence basis with a further subdivision into conventional divisions—manufacturing and ser-vice groups. Although three of the manufacturing groups (construction, printing and publishing, and food-processing) are ubiquitous, the great majority of manufacturing groups are to some degree sporadic, i.e. they occur unevenly throughout the urban system.

An extreme case of a sporadic manufacturing industry is the motor industry, which is absent from over half the towns but is dominant in a very few, e.g. Flint, Michigan, home of the Buick Motor Corporation. This characteristic distribution is shown by the curve in Fig. 5.11-A in which number of towns (*x*-axis) is plotted against the share of the total workforce (*y*-axis). A completely different sort of curve is shown by a typical ubiquitous-type, retail trade (Fig. 5.11-B), which was present in all towns: no town had either less than 5 per cent or more than 21 per cent of its workforce in this group.

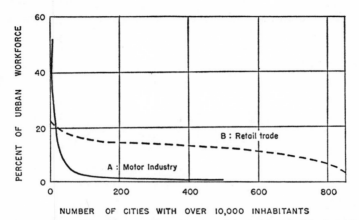

NUMBER OF CITIES WITH OVER 10,000 INHABITANTS

Fig. 5.11. Cumulative distribution of workers in two industries in relation to United States urban structure in 1950. Source: Alexandersson, 1956, pp. 49, 106.

Although Alexandersson's findings apply to one country at one particular point in time, it is significant that the sporadic activity (manufacturing) is a recessive element in urban structure—even in a highly industrial country. In two out of three of the towns in this sample, manufacturing employed less than half the workforce: in no town, however specialized, did it ever account for more than four-fifths of the workforce and this appears to be an extreme limit.

2. Evidence of accordance

On the evidence of Alexandersson's work we should expect that manufacturing, a sporadic activity, would show the greatest divergence from the regularities of city distribution. There is, however, some evidence to suggest that manufacturing shows rather close accordance with the general distribution of urban population.

a. Accordance over space. Manufacturing was selected by Bogue (1949) as one of the major 'sustenance activities' of the urban population arranged around sixty-seven United States cities (Chap. 4.I(2a)). Change in the importance of manufacturing with distance from cities is shown by a number of indices derived from the Census of Manufactures, 1940. The absolute distribution is shown in Fig. 5.12-A through one index (value added in manufacture (a)) while the relative distribution is shown in Fig. 5.12-B through three indices (value added in manufacture per person (c), employees per thousand population (d), and establishments per thousand population (e)). In both graphs, values of the indices (y-axis) and distances (x-axis) are plotted on logarithmic scales.

The fall-off with distance from the city is clear for all four measures of manufacturing, e.g. the first curve shows a rapid decline considerably steeper than that of population density (b) (Fig. 5.12-A). There is a steep

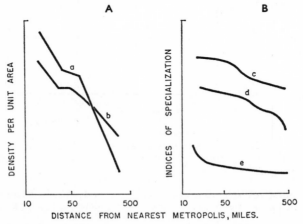

Fig. 5.12. Specialization in manufacturing with distance from the metropolis. United States, 1940. Source: Bogue, 1949, pp. 32, 184.

section to about thirty miles from the metropolis, and a similar steep curve beyond about sixty-five miles. Between these two points there is a shelf where large hinterland cities with very strong specialization tend to concentrate.

The *per capita* curves show not only that manufacturing declines in sympathy with population but that it 'thins out' amongst the population in remoter areas. Comparison of the plant numbers curve with the employees curve shows that on average the size of plant gets smaller away from the metropolis: a trend discussed in Chapter 5.III.

Bogue finds that although central cities themselves are not highly specialized, the size of the central city can have a great effect on the degree of specialization in the hinterland. Larger cities (over 500,000 in 1940) were found to be rather more specialized than the smaller cities and their hinterlands had a higher level of manufacturing throughout.

In terms of Bogue's threefold classification into route, subdominant, and local sectors (defined in Chap. 4.I(2a)), the indices of manufacturing are

Table 5.3. Specialization in manufacturing by sector*

Type of sector:	Route sector	Subdominant sector	Local sector
Indices of manufacturing intensity:			
Value added per person, dollars	164	171	107
Employees/thousand inhabitants	55	65	41
Establishments/thousand inhabitants	1·08	1·12	0·96

Source: Bogue, 1949, p. 186.

* United States, 1940.

clearly lower in the local sectors than in the other two (Table 5.3). However, one significant deviation shows on all indices where the subdominant sector is slightly higher than the route sectors. Manufacturing, unlike the other three 'sustenance activities', clusters strongly in the subdominant sectors. At the outer reaches of the metropolis, about 250 miles from the nearest city, the level of manufacturing in the local sector appears to be higher than that in the route sector. The reversal of the general trend at this extreme distance seems to indicate that the metropolis is sufficiently remote and inaccessible to allow local pockets of manufacturing to exist.

    b. Accordance over time. Instability and eccentricity are more eye-catching than stability and uniformity. Thus it is that the rapid rise of highly specialized centres (e.g. 'boom' mining towns) attracts attention and produces some of the most dynamic studies in historical geography, e.g. McCaskill's study (1962, pp. 143–169) of gold rush centres in the South Island of New Zealand or Goldthwaite's (1927) study of a declining New England town.

    Not all specialist centres show such a cycle of activity. More frequently settlements 'mature' as the original source of employment creates other and locationally less-specialized occupations. In one of the earliest of *multiplier* studies, Barford (1938) studied the impact of a new match factory on a small Danish community and suggested ways in which the employment chain-reaction it set off could be traced. In multiplier studies (Isard *et al.*, 1960, pp. 189–205), attempts are made to measure the stimulus that the establishment of one type of new employment gives to other sectors of the local economy, in terms of jobs, business, etc. Thus Isard and Kuenne (1953) set out to estimate the effect on the New York–Philadelphia region of a projected integrated steel plant being located at Trenton, New Jersey. Using input–output techniques they were able to follow the chain of ramifications (steel, steel-using industries, service industries, population) and measure their effects in terms of jobs. For example, expansion in the tin can industry was estimated at one-tenth (an expansion of 923 more workers). This expansion, in its turn, made demands on housing, retail trade, etc. Isard and Kuenne's overall findings, traced through six cycles of expansion, are shown in Table 5.4. This shows

Table 5.4. Direct and indirect repercussions of new steel plant*

Estimated repercussions:	New employees	Multiplier effect
Sectors affected:		
Primary (iron and steel plant)	11,666	1·0
Secondary (other parts of steel fabricating		
industry)	77,014	6·6
Tertiary (other sectors)	70,089	6·0
Total effects	158,769	12·6

Source: Isard and Kuenne, 1953, p. 297.

* New York–Philadelphia industrial region, United States.

that the original steel plant with its 12,000 production workers was expected to give rise to a total increase in employment of about 159,000; i.e. about thirteen times as many.

Estimates of such multiplier effects are likely to be affected by related chain-effects on other regions (e.g. regions outside the New York–Philadelphia area) and the problem of such 'inter-regional feedback' poses more computational difficulties. From the strictly locational viewpoint we would like to know more about (i) the size of the regional multipliers appropriate to particular types of activities, and (ii) the levels at which a town or region passes the critical 'take-off' threshold. Economic studies into problems of take-off have been carried out for national units (Rostow, 1960, 1963) and might well be applied to more restricted geographical areas.

3. Problems of discordance

Discordance, the existence of centres outside the hierarchy, raises both theoretical and practical problems.

a. Centre specialization: theoretical problems. With the evidence for the accordance of specialized activities with the settlement hierarchy, presented in Chapter 5.II(2), we may reasonably query the need for centres outside that hierarchy. It seems arguable that if the large urban centre may contain all the central functions for the demands of the surrounding territory, then there seems no place, within the framework of existing central-place theory, in which the specialized manufacturing centre may fit. Curry (1962) has shown, however, that the time element, studied in terms of *queuing theory*, may play some part in holding the largest central place some distance below the theoretical maximum, i.e. the largest centre may not in fact possess the full range of functions that the dependent territory demands.

In using Curry's model here, we are extending it considerably beyond its original application (which was restricted to service centres within towns), and suggesting a more general application than its originator might claim. The theory depends on four basic assumptions: (i) There exists an *order of goods* depending on the size of the population that is required for a market. First-order goods require the whole population of the given territory as a market, second-order goods require half this population, third-order goods one-third of this population, and so on. (ii) Corresponding to this order of goods is an *order of centres*. This order, running from large first-order centres to small tenth-order centres, forms the *x*-axis of the graphs in Fig. 5.13. (iii) There exists a *range of stock* for

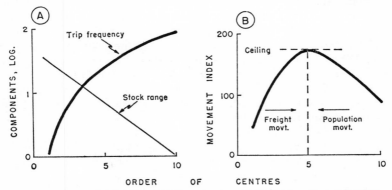

Fig. 5.13. Hypothetical model of movement optimization in central-place structure. Source: Curry, 1962, p. 41.

the order of centres, so that each lower grade of centre supplies one-third less than the next highest order of centre. Curry justifies this assumption by mathematical arguments on sections chosen at random from a continuum: it is, as he readily admits, a very rough approximation to reality. The form of the stock-range curve is shown in Fig. 5.13-A. The relative number of procurement trips in a given time period, the *trip frequency*, is the square of a centre's order. This roughly accords with known movement-behaviour (e.g. the weekly grocery trip, the monthly theatre trip, the occasional furniture-buying trip), but the exact form of the curve (Fig. 5.13-A) is probably more complex. (iv) By multiplying the stock-range by the trip frequency, a *movement index* is produced (Fig. 5.13-B).

The importance of the movement index is shown by the 'humped' nature of the curve in Fig. 5.13-B. It begins with the lowest point of the curve over the first-order centre and reaches its maximum over the fifth-order centre before declining slowly towards the tenth-order centre. We may argue that the maximum point on the curve represents the *ceiling* for the development of the central-place hierarchy in a given territory. Above that point it is not worth holding stock since the demand (as measured by trip frequency) is too low, and specialized goods (i.e. first- to fourth-order goods) will be produced in a few centres and shipped to the several fifth-order centres as the occasional demand occurs. Below that point, the central-place hierarchy extends in an unbroken sequence with sufficient volume of local demand to support it.

It is yet too early to say how applicable this model is likely to be. Certainly many of the assumptions on which it is based are shaky, but they appear to give reasonable approximations of observed traits in social and economic behaviour. The implications of the theory, that a single large centre is unlikely to emerge as the first-order central place, but that its functions may be fulfilled by lower-order centres drawing on a few specialized (i.e. non-hierarchic) centres is important. It suggests that, even in a theoretical landscape with a regular central-place hierarchy, specialized centres are likely to emerge outside the regular central-place system. Whether these specialized functions would be located in small specialist centres or would be shared between the five fifth-order centres is uncertain. Burton (1963, p. 285) has drawn attention to the *dispersed city*, a group of cities which '. . . although separated by tracts of agricultural land, function together economically as a single urban unit', and traced their existence in parts of the United States (southern Illinois and the lower Rio Grande), in southern Ontario, Canada, in the Salzgitter area of West Germany, and in the Derby–Chesterfield–Nottingham area of midland England. How far these dispersed cities point to a truncation in the central-place hierarchy in these areas and a replacement by a group of lower-level cities with complementary specialist activities, is uncertain. They may equally well be due to entirely local variations in settlement evolution.

b. Centre specialization: definition problems. The theoretical case for specialized centres, discussed above, highlights the need for working definitions of the 'specialist' centre. What do we mean by this term and how do we define it? Moser and Scott's *British Towns* (1961) illustrates the very wide range of characteristics that make up the character of a centre, and the way in which, through factor analysis (discussed in Chapter 8.I(3d)), they may be broken down into a few manageable dimensions. Where we are concerned with centre specialization, in the sense of 'discordance' with the central-place hierarchy, the problem is somewhat simpler. Two main attempts may be traced to define centres in this way, the first using local data, the second using comparisons between local and regional data.

(i) The first group of studies of centre classification have been based on the idea that the function of a centre can be broken down into two distinct components: (a) the part serving the inhabitants, and (b) the part serving external populations. The first part has been variously termed the city-serving', 'self-production', 'secondary', or 'non-basic' element; and the second, the 'city-forming', 'exchange-production', 'primary', or 'basic' element. A useful review of these *basic–non-basic* studies has been given by Isard (Isard *et al.*, 1960, pp. 189–205).

To determine how the population of a centre should be apportioned between the basic and non-basic elements presents severe technical problems and full basic–non-basic studies have been confined to a handful of individual town studies rather than nationwide comparisons. An example of such a local study is given in Table 5.5 for the town of Wichita in

Table 5.5. Computation of basic–non-basic ratios*

Employment group:	Total employment	Mining employment	Printing employment
Market served:			
Basic (national, regional, and world)	29,250	900	514
Non-basic (local)	59,325	71	1,200
Basic–non-basic ratios	2·02	0·08	2·34
Employment multiplier	3·02	1·08	3·34

Source: Isard *et al.*, 1960, p. 191.

* Wichita, United States, 1950.

Kansas. The columns show that mining was strongly basic in character, providing mainly for needs outside the town, whereas printing was non-basic, largely serving local needs. Despite the considerable work that has gone into such studies there remain doubts that many 'mixed' industries can usefully be separated in this way.

(ii) The second group of studies have been based on comparisons of the data for a single town against some national or regional benchmark. Alexandersson (1956, p. 16) has reviewed a number of Swedish and American attempts. One typical example is the index of specialization (S), given by the formula

$$S_i = (N_i - N_j)/N_j$$

where S_i is the index of specialization for the ith city in industry N, N_i is the percentage of that industry in the workforce of the ith city, and N_j in the nation as a whole. Thus Detroit with 28·0 per cent of its workforce in the motor industry, compared to a national average of only 1·5 per cent, has a specialization index of 17·6 for that industry. Unfortunately, this approach is very sensitive to changes in the definition of the benchmark area, i.e. whether a national, regional, or state comparison is made.

This difficulty has led to more refined studies in which the size of a centre has been taken into account in describing its specialization. This derivative of the basic–non-basic approach was developed by Klaasen, Torman, and Koyck (1949) for a Netherlands study, and taken up by Ullman and Dacey (1962) in the United States. By comparing the workforces of sets of cities in the same size range the lowest proportion found for an industry in any of the towns can be judged to represent the *minimum requirements*, i.e. the lowest level for that industry that a city of a given size must support.

Fourteen industries were analysed in this way for six sizes of American cities by Ullman and Dacey. For the fourteen cities over one million, Washington, D.C. with 2·3 per cent of its employment in durable manufacturing formed the 'low' for this box in the table. The minimum require-

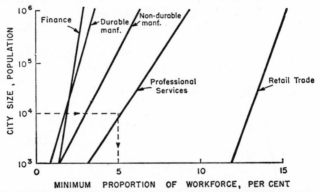

Fig. 5.14. Regression lines for minimum-requirements approach to centre classification. United States, 1950. Source: Ullmann and Dacey, 1962, p. 129.

ment for a city of over one million was therefore assumed to be 2·3 per cent Similar lows were derived for each industry and each population size of city, the two parameters plotted against each other, and regression lines derived to show the average relationships. As Fig. 5.14 shows, the minimum requirements varied with different industries (cf. retail trade, with manufacturing) but each industry showed a consistent increase in minima with the size of the city. In some cases the relationship was sharply marked, as with professional services, and in others less significant, as with finance.

The regression lines for the various industry groups are used to compute the 'expected' minimum for a city of a given size; and thus the San Francisco Bay area with a population of 2·68 millions in 1950 may be expected to have at least 3·6 per cent of its workforce in durable manufacturing: in fact (as Table 5.6 shows) it had 9·6 per cent. The deviations between the expected and observed values for each industry may be combined to give a single index of specialization, S, where

$$S = \Sigma_i \{(P_i - M_i)^2/M_i\}/\{(\Sigma_i P_i - \Sigma_i M_i)^2/\Sigma_i M_i\}$$

Table 5.6. Estimates of minimum components

Activity:	Durable manufacturing	Non-durable manufacturing
Employment parameters:		
San Francisco Bay region (observed)	9·6%	10·0%
Minimum requirements for region of this size (expected)	3·6%	5·5%
Excess above minimum requirements	+6·0%	+4·4%

Source: Ullman and Dacey, 1962, p. 131.

i refers to each of the fourteen industrial sectors, P_i the percentage of the workforce employed in each of the i sectors, and M_i the minimum percentage expected for the size of the city (Ullman and Dacey, 1962, p. 137). Their general findings suggest that there is a strong relationship between size of city and specialization. The sum of all the minima for the fourteen industries range from 24 per cent for towns of 2,500 to 3,000 inhabitants to 49 per cent for cities of 300,000 to 800,000 inhabitants. The larger the city the larger the number of specialities it can support in the 'ecological niches' of its population structure and thus the more self-contained the city can be. This finding is logically consistent in that at the lowest extreme the family can sell virtually nothing to itself while at the upper extreme the total world population (about three billions) can only sell to itself.

For the fifty-six cities of over 300,000 population in the United States in 1950 the index varied from a high of 15·2 to a low of 1·4. Cities with high values were highly specialized centres like the steel town of Youngstown (8·5), while more balanced trade centres like Dallas and Denver had low values (around 1·5). The practical importance of these values in terms of the industrial stability of the towns has been supported by work by Rodgers (1952).

III. DISTORTION DUE TO AGGLOMERATION

Despite the evidence for the accordance of industry with the urban pattern we must nevertheless recognize that patterns of specialization remain outside these regularities. These are termed here 'nonconformist' centres (Table 5.2). We view their problem in a reverse way to that of the German locational theorist, Weber, who in his *Über den Standort der Industrien* (1909; Friedrich, 1928) assumed that specialized industrial activities would be located near their *input sources* (i.e. they would show 'material orientation') unless other forces caused deviations. Here we take the opposite starting point, that industrial activities will be located near their *output destinations* (i.e. 'market orientation') unless other forces cause deviations. Agglomeration is discussed at length by Isard (1956, pp. 172–87; Isard *et al.*, pp. 400–9), and Hoover (1948, pp. 116–21).

1. Agglomeration within individual plants

Although the general importance of scale economies in industrial production is well established in theory for industry as a whole, the detailed differences between the various industrial activities is more tentative. Fig. 5.15 is based on the findings of an exceptional empirical study of

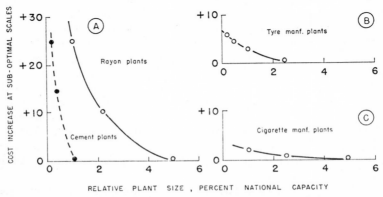

Fig. 5.15. Relation of production costs to plant size. Source: Bain, 1954, p. 25.

American industry by Bain (1954) and attempts to illustrate the varying importance of scale economies for four different types of industrial activity. In these graphs the relative increase in cost above an estimated minimum, zero on the *y*-axis, is plotted against a standard measure of plant size, share of national capacity in an industry (*x*-axis). The curves for the sample industries show that while for an industry like rayon small plants operate at a very severe cost handicap (production costs a quarter higher if smaller than 1 per cent of national capacity), an industry like cigarette manufacturing is rather lightly affected by plant-scale variations.

Isard and Schooler (1955) have shown for a chemical process industry, the petrochemical industry, the overriding importance of scale economies. For two alternative locations, Monroe on the Gulf Coast and Cincinnati in the Industrial Belt of the United States, they compute the cost of three important components—transport, labour costs, and power costs—in the production of a petrochemical product (ethylene glycol) (Table 5.7). The largest of these three items, transport costs by rail, is some five times as

Table 5.7. Regional cost differentials on petrochemical production*

	Cost differential (cents/100 lb.)†
Transport:	
Barge shipments	0·13
Rail shipments	0·60
Labour costs, maximum differential	0·12
Power costs, maximum differential	0·06
Scale economies, large vs. small plants	3·98

Source: Isard and Schooler, 1955, pp. 19, 22–4.

* Between Monroe (Louisiana) and Cincinnati (Ohio), United States.

† Ethylene glycol.

great as the maximum labour cost differential and ten times the maximum power differential. However, all three components are dwarfed to insignificance by the enormous difference in production costs between large and small plants, which are over six times as great as the largest other differential. In this situation regional differences in plant size become the dominant factor and '. . . completely overshadow any other individual or combined regional cost differential' (Isard et al., 1960, p. 240).

We may argue that, at its simplest, plant size affects location because the potential number of sites or communities that can accept a very large plant are fewer than those that can accept a small one. Certainly the evidence for the distribution of plant size suggests that large plants are less common and less widely spread than smaller plants. Fig. 5.16 shows an empirical case based on the 1950 industrial census of Portugal which suggests that size and geographical range are not unrelated.

Florence (1953) has found a strong connection between the 'prevailing size of plant' in an industry and the degree of dispersion such that industries with small plants tend to be dispersed. Table 5.8 shows the trend of three sizes of plant (small, medium, and large) against degree of localization as measured by the coefficient of localization for British and American industries in the late 1930's. The conclusion that it is the industries with small plants that are less localized is inescapable. Such industries are dispersed for a number of reasons, but mainly they follow the dispersion over the land of the population itself. The outstanding examples are industries where contact between the factory and customer must be direct and the job may pass back and forth a number of times: printing is a classic case. Other industries, such as building, demand personal contact and are correspondingly widely spread in small undertakings.

From the viewpoint of industry rather than the potential location, Bain

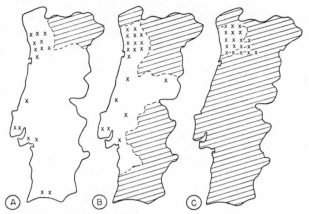

Fig. 5.16. Distribution of plants with over 100 workers (*A*), over 400 workers (*B*), and over 1,600 workers (*C*) in Portugal ($G = 3·8$), 1950. Crosses indicate location of 5 per cent of plants in each category; shading indicates districts without such plants.

Table 5.8. Plant size and localization*

Degree of localization:	*Low*	*Moderate*	*High*
Prevailing size of plant:			
Large plants	9%	10%	13%
Medium plants	6%	4%	11%
Small plants	29%	8%	10%

Source: Florence, 1953, p. 71.

* United Kingdom, 1935; United States, 1939.

(1954) has shown that the distribution of large plants was restricted in two ways: (i) by the absolute cost of the smallest economic plant, and (ii) by the relative share of the market such a plant represented. Here the 'smallest economic plant' was estimated from the data on which Fig. 5.14 was based. Table 5.9 shows his findings with industries classified into four groups on a logarithmic basis, so that plants in the first category need an investment some hundreds of times greater than those in the third, and so on. The largest investment needed was in steel production $6·7 \times 10^9$ dollars, compared to shoe production with only $2·0 \times 10^6$ dollars.

When capital supply is severely limited, as in most underdeveloped countries, then this absolute 'threshold' cost may limit the diffusion of high-cost plants and will tend to restrict them to a single specialist centre within the urban system of the country. The slow spread of the integrated steel-producing plant (Pounds, 1959) with its large initial thresholds is a

Table 5.9. Estimated minimum size of single efficient plant* †

Total capital required for single efficient plant $\times 10^6$ dollars):	1–10	10–100	100–1,000
Proportion of national capacity contained in one efficient plant:			
0·1–0·5%	Flour milling (3·5) Shoes (2) Canning (3)		
0·5–1%		Cement (25)	
1–5%		Tyres (30)	Petroleum refining (225) Steel (665)
5–10%			Rayon (135) Automobiles (500)
10–50%		Typewriters (?)	Tractors (125)

Source: Bain, 1954, p. 36.

  * Sample of United States industries, *c.* 1951.
  † Figures in brackets give the upper estimate in millions of dollars for capital required for single efficient plant.

typical example of this restriction, though national prestige reasons have somewhat distorted the expected pattern.

  If a single economic plant represents a very small share of the total industrial capacity, then we may argue that its chances of diffusion are greater than one which represents a very large part. We know from Bain's work that the share of national capacity varies greatly from industry to industry. The implications of Table 5.9 are that it needs only three or four really efficient typewriter plants to serve the whole United States market, but that it needs about 500 meat-packing plants to serve the same country. There are of course vastly more plants than these economic minima but this is largely due to historical legacy and the 'squeezing out' process is most acute in just those industries where the efficient plant can serve a very large part of the total market.

  It follows from this situation that in certain industries a new plant can be set up only if it can expect to 'capture' a large part of the existing market, and indeed that it must 'go in big' if it is not to produce at costs vastly above its existing competitors. Attempts to enter well-established markets may be met by a series of price-fixing moves by established producers—a process which Rodgers (1952) has traced for the steel industry. By contrast the industries in which small plants are efficient and need only a small share of the market may show very rapid diffusion as new local population demands build up. Clearly the locational effect of plant size, whether measured in absolute or relative terms, is either to restrict or to scatter specialist activities through the urban spectrum.

While the chemical process industries studied by Isard and Schooler (1955) may represent an extreme case, there is good empirical evidence to suggest that the average size of production unit throughout the whole of industry is increasing. Chisholm (1962, p. 192) has shown that in the period 1924–54 the mean size of manufacturing plant in the United Kingdom employing more than ten workers rose by about one-half from 87 to 134; while Florence (1953) in a comparative study of British and American industry showed an even stronger trend for American industry over a comparable period. The significance of the change is somewhat obscured by employment figures, for with automation a much higher relative production is coming from the very few larger plants. The trend to larger size is not only true of industries in which employment is increasing (automobiles and aircraft manufacture), but also in industries (like flour milling) where the total employment is contracting.

2. Agglomeration of groups of plants: regional 'swarming'

Cutting across the size-localization trend in Table 5.8 is a second trend. The industries with the *highest* localization are not, as expected, those with large plants but with medium-scale plants. Certainly the large-scale plants are more localized than the small-scale, but the outstanding cases of high localization—cotton textiles, woollen textiles, motor-car manufacture— are characterized in general by medium-scale plants (Table 5.10). This

Table 5.10. Grouping of industries by their locational pattern

Coefficient of localization	Concentration pattern	Locational pattern	Industry example
High	Localized	Swarming	Cotton textile industry
Moderate	Moderate localization	Rooted to localized extraction	Iron and steel industry
Variable	Variable	(1) Linked	Textile machinery industry
		(2) Footloose	Electric machinery industry
Low	Dispersed	(1) Rooted to scattered extraction	Brick industry
		(2) Residentiary	Baking industry

Source: Florence, 1953, p. 40.

high localization in one industry may well be due to the fact that the plants between themselves form a single large localized producing unit. The difference is that whereas in the large single plant the economies are internal, in the localized 'swarm' of plants the economies are external.

Birmingham and the Black Country conurbation, in central England, provide object lessons in what Florence has described as 'industrial swarming'. Of the seventeen main manufacturing industries localized in the area, twelve were metal industries with a high degree of linkage. Florence (1948) has recognized four types of integration between these metal industries: (i) *vertical integration* (e.g. links between refining of non-ferrous metals and production of non-ferrous hardware products); (ii) *convergent integration* (e.g. manufacture of bolts, car bodies, tyres, etc., feeding convergently into the motor-assembly industry); (iii) *diagonal integration* (e.g. foundries and tool manufactures serving a number of local industries); and (iv) *indirect integration* (e.g. food industries which with their strong preponderance of female workers tend to balance the preponderance of male employment in the metal industries).

Within this general concatenation still more strongly localized complexes of integrated small plants may be discerned. Wise (1951) has described in detail the evolution of the jewellery and gun quarters in the city of Birmingham. Here one street may contain a couple of dozen jewellery 'plants' with half as many again integrated plants working in bullion, stone merchants, and so on.

The rationale of this extreme localization does not lie in the present distribution of resources. The natural resources of coal and iron are virtually worked out and the water links are confined to a few constricted canals. As Florence argues, this is a case of localization for the sake of localization for: '. . . the whole of the Birmingham and Black Country complex of linked industries could probably flourish anywhere else, so long as the place was not too far from the centre of the country' (Florence, 1953, p. 88). All the industries hang together like a cluster of swarming bees to form a concatenation or syndrome with little reference to natures

Similar findings have been suggested for the United States by McCarty, Hook, and Knox (1956). In a study of the machinery industry they tested three alternative hypotheses by regression analysis and found that an aggregation hypothesis gave the most significant results. They conclude that '. . . birds of a feather flock together' might be an appropriate summary of the locational behaviour of industry.

3. Random nuclei: the problem of 'nonconformist' centres

Scale economies, whether the internal economies of the plant or the external economies of the regional 'swarm' may sometimes explain the *relative* location of specialist activities: they certainly do not explain the *absolute* location of such activities. Here we come to the essence of the unsolved set of problems that we may characterize as the 'Morris-Oxford', 'Ford-Detroit', or 'Carnegie-Pittsburgh' problem, i.e. the problem of why one rather than a set of apparently similar cities proved a successful launching pad for a great industrial venture. The answer probably lies outside the field of human geography and in the study of individualism and industrial opportunism, although only a few of our textbooks, notably Paterson (1960) in an excellent survey of American industry, hint at the problems. To be sure, we can argue that there are well-trodden limits within which industrial birth-rates are likely to be high (Beesley, 1955), but we are unlikely to be able to circumscribe the location much further. The problem of the random nuclei around which so much of our industrial enterprise within developed countries has grown remains an intriguing by-way in locational research which offers as much to the historical geographer as to the locational theorist.

Significant as they are, the net effect of these scale agglomerations is to distort but not destroy the urban hierarchy. Even highly industrial countries like the United Kingdom which have strong clusters of non-conformist centres, still display a rank-size distribution which, as Berry (1961-A) has shown, is not strongly different from that of countries where the population is both more rural and the towns more in accord with the ideal central-place hierarchy.

IV. DISTORTION DUE TO RESOURCE LOCALIZATION

If we allow that a general urban concentration of industry is the rule, and that random or scale-origin variations in city specialization may caues variations within the hierarchy, problems still remain. We are left with certain stubborn specialized centres that persist in apparently 'eccentric' locations outside the general distributions of urban population. In this section we consider some of the models put forward to explain the location of these deviant cases (Isard, 1956, pp. 91–119; Isard *et al.*, 1960, pp. 375–412; Hoover, 1948, pp. 10–89).

1. Movement minimization: Weberian analysis

One of the classic locational models available for tackling the problem of eccentric locations is that of Alfred Weber. In his *Über den Standort der Industrien* (1909; Friedrich, 1929) he put forward a consistent theory of industrial location which, though it has a number of theoretical and practical drawbacks, provides a useful starting point. It is illustrated here with empirical data drawn from an industry which Weber might have regarded as a classic example of the utility of his system: the zinc-smelting industry (Cotterill, 1950).

The central argument in Weber's theory of industrial location was that sites would be selected *ceteris paribus* so as to minimize unnecessary movement, i.e. that sites would represent minimum-energy positions. We may conceive movement as being made up of three separate components, the *distance* to be moved, the *weight* of the material inputs or outputs to be moved, and the *effort* or cost of moving given materials over unit distance (cf. Isard, 1956, pp. 81–90). We may combine the first two components, distance and weight, to give a *gross movement input* which we can measure conventionally in *ton-miles*; and we may combine this index with effort to give a *net movement input* which we can measure in dollar-ton-miles. For convenience this final index of movement will be referred to as Q.

Table 5.11. Derivation of net distance inputs*

Parameters:	Location	Distance, miles	Weight, tons	Freight rate, dollars/ton-mile	Net distance inputs, Q
Outputs:					
Slab zinc	ε	1·00	0·54	2·10	1·14
Inputs:					
Zinc concentrate	α	1·00	1·00	1·00	1·00
Reduction coal	β	1·00	0·37	1·10	0·41
Heating coal	γ	1·00	1·08	1·10	1·19
Fireclay	δ	1·00	0·10	0·50	0·05
Total inputs	—		2·55	—	2·65

Source: Cotterill, 1950, pp. 62, 78, 87, 110.
* Example of zinc-smelting industry.

Table 5.11 shows the calculation of net movement inputs for our case industry, and we can see how first tonnage and then freight costs modify the amount of movement over standard distances for the four major inputs and major output of a smelter. The most striking contrast is between heating coal, which, when hauled over the same standard distance as fireclay, represents a net movement input some twenty-four times greater; a contrast explicable in terms of its greater importance in the industrial process and its higher freight rates. Clearly this is an over-simplification: in practice, as Fig. 6.10 suggests, freight rates tend to be convex and stepped with distance (Alexander, Brown, and Dahlberg, 1958; Alexander, 1963, pp. 473–5) but the net movement input provides a rough guide to the relative movement that we are trying to minimize.

a. Movement minimization in a two-point case. The concept of net movement inputs may be used very simply in a two-point case by relating the movements towards the plant or assembly movements, Q_a, to the movements away from the plant after processing of finished products or distribution movements, Q_b, to give an orientation index (V). Here V is given as $V = Q_a/Q_b$. When the value of V is greater than 1·0 the orientation of the plant is towards its material sources, and when less than 1·0 to its product destinations.

In our empirical case (Table 5.11) the sum of the four assembly

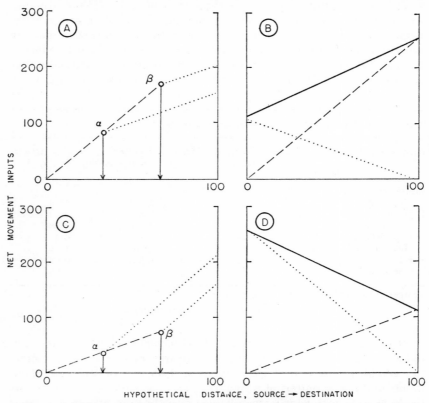

Fig. 5.17. Weberian weight-loss analysis of market or destination orientation (*AB*) and material or origin orientation (*CD*).

movements (2·65) and the sum of the single distribution movement (1·14) give an orientation index of 2·32, suggesting that the basic orientation of the industry is towards its sources. The position may be shown very clearly by plotting values of the net movement inputs for the industry over a hypothetical distance of 100 miles. In Fig. 5.17-A it will be seen that the total movement increases as the location is shifted from location α near the material source to location β near the destination. The general relation of the net movement index is shown in Fig. 5.17-B where the solid line represents the sum of both inward assembly movements and outward distribution movements. This shows clearly that location at the source is in this case the minimum energy position.

Were the ratios exactly reversed, i.e. the orientation index V is 0·43, then the locational position would be likewise reversed. Fig. 5.17-C and Fig. 5.17-D show the solutions for this reversed situation with in this case location β being more logical and the most effective minimal location being at the destination.

Weber (1909) used a simple weight relationship to derive his own orientation index, a weight coefficient, given by the division of the weight as the assembled material inputs (including coal) by the weight of the distributed material outputs. This 'material index' which gave typical values to various industries (e.g. 4·0 to blast furnaces and 1·3 to tube mills in the steel industry) enabled him to divide industries into material- and market-orientated locations and formed the basis for the convenient, if vague, distinction between 'heavy industry' and 'light industry'. This index is discussed at length in Friedrich (1929, pp. 48–75).

Smith (1955) has tested the efficiency of Weber's index with respect to sixty-five British industries. He found that while the material index discriminated reasonably well those industries located at the materials (e.g. sugar-beet processing in the mainly arable areas of England) from those industries that were patently not located at materials the correlation was by no means a perfect one. The results were clearer when the weight of coal was excluded from the calculations (Table 5.12), but Smith, un-

---

Table 5.12. Weber's material index and characteristic locational patterns*

Material index:†	Less than 1·0	1·0–2·0	Greater than 2·0
Number of industries:			
Located at materials	2	17	3
Not located at materials	16	14	1

Source: Smith, 1955, p. 8.

* Great Britain, 1948.   † Excluding coal.

---

satisfied with the results of the material index, went on to examine other indices that might separate industrial locations in a helpful way. Three of these indices (Smith, 1953, Appendix C) were at least as discriminating as Weber's index: (i) the weight of material per operative (e.g. blast furnaces had values some hundreds of times greater than in vehicle manufacture), (ii) the amount of electric power used *per capita*, and (iii) the percentage of male labour in the total workforce. Where values for these indices were very high, strong material orientation in location was observed.

Other workers like Duerr (1960) have suggested alternatives such as specific value (value of a product divided by its weight) to enable locational classification of industrial activities. But, like the Weber and Smith indices, they have proved most valid for outer extremes of the locational behaviour rather than for cases intermediate between source and destination. McCarty (McCarty *et al.*, 1956, pp. 81–121) has traced the relationship between the location of the machinery industry in the United States and the location of related metal-using industries. As Fig. 5.18 shows, this industry is not strongly associated with either (i) the early stage of metal manufacture (e.g. blast furnaces) nor (ii) with late-stage manufacture (as

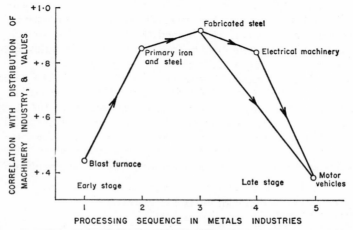

Fig. 5.18. Linkage hypothesis applied to the location of the United States machinery industry. Source: McCarty, Hook, and Knos, 1956, p. 109.

represented by the motor-assembly industry. Between these two extremes it is highly correlated with the middle stages of the metal-using chain of industries, with the closest tie ($r = +0.910$) with the 'fabricated steel' industry.

b. Movement minimization in an N-point case. Multiple sources and multiple destinations are the rule rather than the exception and the two-point cases considered above are useful only in illustrating Weber's concepts. The difficulty of solving more realistic problems is very great. Consider for example the five-point problem posed by the smelting industry (see Table 5.11). A random location for the five positions, α (zinc concentrate source), β (reduction-coal source), γ (heating-coal source), δ (fireclay source), and ε (slab-zinc destination) is assumed in Fig. 5.19-A and the problem is to find the point which minimizes the net movement input in (i) bringing these five items together for processing and in (ii) shipping the finished product to its destination.

In Fig. 5.19-B a trial location point, T_1, is chosen within the bounding polygon formed by the lines connecting the five points; in Weberian terms it is within the 'locational force-table'. Distances from this trial point to the five points are measured and weighted by the values for weight and cost to give a series of *vectors* radiating from T_1 (Fig. 5.19-c). The length of each vector is proportional to the net movement input (Q), so that the line drawn towards the heating-coal source (γ) is very long in comparison to that towards the fireclay source (δ).

Solution of the force diagram shown by the vectors in Fig. 5.19-c can

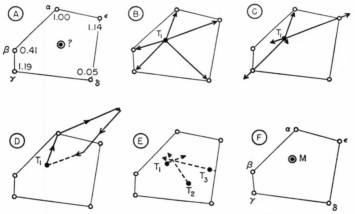

Fig. 5.19. Stages in the vector analysis of mean location, M, from a set of sources and destinations ($\alpha, \beta \ldots \varepsilon$).

be made by joining the vectors cumulatively to give a composite vector-traverse from which the *resultant* can be determined (Sears and Zemansky, 1964, pp. 9–16). The minimum-movement point lies along the line joining the end of the vector-traverse and the trial point T_1. Its exact location can be found by repeating the analysis from a second point, T_2, and checking the position from a third trial point, T_3. Although the intersection point M is a mean solution minimizing the sum of the *squared* deviations it fails to provide the optimal solution which involves minimizing the sum of the *absolute* deviations. To obtain the latter demands the use of more complex algorithms (e.g. the Kuhn–Kuenne method or Seymour's grid method) using high speed digital computers.

c. Criticism of the movement-minimization approach. A number of technical arguments can be raised against Weberian arguments on purely economic grounds: these are reviewed by Isard (1956) and by Greenhut (1956, pp. 8–16) but even from the geometric viewpoint we can see the clumsiness of this method with many *changing* sources and destinations.

Of equal importance are the technical changes which undermine the importance of transfer costs in locational analysis. These may be summarized as: (i) the progressive cheapening of transport costs relative to total production costs; (ii) the progressive reduction in the weight of material needed for a given product through improved technology so that less has to be moved; (iii) the sharper decline in costs of moving bulk goods than of finished goods. The net effect of factors (i), (ii), and (iii) is to reduce the need for eccentric locations, and to throw manufacturing still more strongly into the line with the urban hierarchy. This trend is reinforced by two further changes: (iv) the relatively greater expansion in the late-stage manufacture (which tends to be market orientated) compared to early-stage manufacture; and (v) the rise of non-economic grounds for locational decision-making, through government social or defence policies in particular).

Probably the best way to place movement-models in an appropriate balance against the other factors affecting industrial patterns is through the many studies of individual industries that have been published in the last decade. Alexander (1963, pp. 288–463) provides an up-to-date review of six major manufacturing groups with very full bibliographies on the major sources, while Lindbergh (1953) has examined Weber's thesis for a single industry—the Swedish paper industry.

2. Variations in the locational plane

In our analysis of movement costs we assumed that local production costs (labour, power, water are conventional examples) were everywhere the same. Weber was acutely aware that this concept of a uniform locational plane was unrealistic and he attempted, through his 'labour coefficient', to introduce the effect of these irregularities.

The concept of regional and local variations in our cost surface can be welded on to our earlier discussion of two-point movement problems. If we add to our earlier diagrams (Figs. 5.17-A and 5.17-B) a variable cost surface (stippled) we can see how the regular changes in the movement inputs is distorted by the local variations. These variations are sufficient in Fig. 5.20-A to reverse the locational advantages of sites α and β and to warp the minimum-effort surface in Fig. 5.20-B so that the optimum location is shifted from the origin to point a.

Clearly the importance of variations in the locational plane will vary with (i) the range of the variations in the local cost surface and (ii) the relative importance of these local cost differentials in the total cost structure of the industry. Local variations in processing costs have been

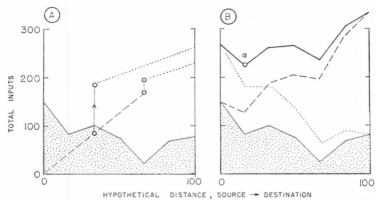

Fig. 5.20. Impact of variations in the local-resource surface on the market-orientation case plotted in Fig. 5.17-AB.

extensively reviewed by Greenhut (1956, pp. 123–39) and by Isard (1956, pp. 126–42).

3. Local substitution between inputs

In reading the standard studies of 'industrial location' it is difficult to avoid thinking in terms of common behaviour within an industry. An 'industry' is, however, as Florence (1953, pp. 15–21) has pointed out, nothing more than a convenient group-term for plants which may vary very greatly in their type of product or may produce similar products by different processes. For example, in the petrochemical industrial complexes, locations with cheap natural gas will commonly use greater amounts of this rather than crude oil; conversely at locations where crude oil is cheap relative to natural gas, the former may be substituted for the latter. Each separate location may have a local structure of factor-loadings, and these may represent a considerable economy over the fixed combinations assumed in an 'industry' analysis (Luttrell, 1962).

a. Theoretical example of substitution. A useful theoretical case of substitution has been provided by Isard (Isard *et al.*, 1960, pp. 415–19). He envisages a location in which two industrial activities, I and II, are profitable alternatives. Each activity has a different combination of four basic resource-inputs (water, land, labour, and capital) and these resources are in restricted supply. The resource requirements needed and the total resources available are, for each of the two activities, as shown in Table 5.13.

The basic substitution problem here is between the two activities. Should the location use all its resources in Activity I, or all in Activity II, or in some combination of I and II? In this simplified situation Isard suggests the problem can be solved most simply through *linear programming*.

F

Table 5.13. Hypothetical resources requirements for solution by simple linear programme

Resource units required:	For Activity I	For Activity II	Total units available at given location
Resources:			
Water (*a*)	0·5	0·6	6·0
Land (*b*)	0·2	0·15	1·8
Labour (*c*)	0·4	0·2	3·0
Capital (*d*)	3·0	2·0	24·0

Source: Isard, Bramhall, Carrothers, Cumberland, Moses, Price, and Schooler, 1960, p. 416.

A graphical solution is shown in Fig. 5.21 in which, in all graphs, Activity I (*y*-axis) is plotted against Activity II (*x*-axis).

The first four graphs show the graphic solution for single resources. For

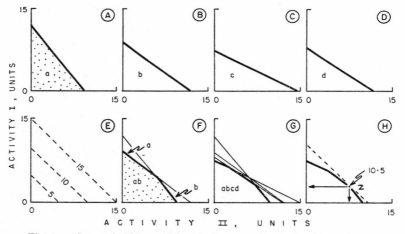

Fig. 5.21. Stages in the graphic solution to a simple four-factor linear programme. Source: Isard *et al.*, 1960, p. 417.

the water resource, the available six units can be devoted entirely to Activity I to give twelve input units on the *y*-axis (i.e. 6 divided by 0·5) or devoted entirely to Activity II to give ten input units on the *x*-axis (i.e. 6 divided by 0·6). These points are plotted on Fig. 5.21-A. The line joining them shows all the possible combinations of I and II which just exhaust the available six units of water. All combinations below the line (stippled area) are technically possible since there is enough water, but inefficient since they do not use *all* the water. Conversely combinations outside the line are technically impossible in this location because they demand more water than is locally available. Each of the other three resources has its appropriate graph pattern and these are plotted in Figs. 5.21-B, C, and D.

It is clear that to solve our problem we must take all four resources jointly into consideration. To do this the individual resource graphs can be simply superimposed. Fig. 5.21-F shows the superimposed lines for water (*a*) and land resources (*b*). Here the stippled area (*ab*) represents the feasible combinations when *both* resources are considered and the heavy line the most efficient combinations. Areas *a* and *b* on the graph show combinations which are feasible from the point of view of water resources but not of land resources; the converse is true of area *b*.

The combination process is continued in Fig. 5.21-G for all resources to give a convex polygon, the 'convex hull' of the mathematicians (Isard *et al.*, 1960, p. 418), on which all efficient solutions lie. Within the hull lie the feasible but inefficient points (area *abcd*), while outside it lie the impossible solutions. We know, however, that all efficient solutions lie somewhere on the convex segmented hull and the final problem is to determine the most efficient solution.

Equal-income lines are plotted as diagonals on Fig. 5.21-E with values increasing away from the origin. The most efficient point on the hull is that which cuts the highest equal-income line, point *z*, on the 10·5 income diagonal (Fig. 5.21-H). Point *z* is clearly a combination of the two activities and we can read off its co-ordinates on the *y*-axis as 3·00 and on the *x*-axis as 7·5. In other words, the most efficient course for our location with its particular resource suite, is to concentrate on Activity II (7·3 units or 71 per cent) but continue some production in Activity I (3 units or 29 per cent).

Clearly the case taken by Isard was a simple one and a much more complex series of resources and activities would need to be solved in practice (Vajda, 1961). Nevertheless, the principle remains that since locations are likely to differ in the local resources of site and situation, each location is likely to adopt (either scientifically or by trial and error) that 'mix' of activities that enable it to make free use of readily available resources and sparing use of scarce resources.

b. Empirical example of substitution. Cotterill (1950) has contrasted the factor-mixes used by two plants in the smelting industry in different locations—one in the 'Gas Belt' of Texas and one in the Illinois coalfield region near Chicago. Both smelters produce substantially the same product but have different cost patterns. Table 5.14 summarizes the main cost components of the two smelters.

With these two cases the evidence points to a very considerable cost advantage in favour of the more distant Gas Belt smelter on all four cost elements. Two-thirds of this cost advantage stems from its cheaper raw

Table 5.14. Production costs in two smelting areas*

Producing regions:	Illinois	Gas Belt	Source of Gas Belt advantage (% total advantage)
Cost element, relative cost:†			
Raw materials costs	1·70	0·59	70·0%
Labour costs	1·43	0·70	22·3%
Fuel and power costs	1·72	0·58	7·5%
Transport costs	1·02	0·98	0·2%

Source: Cotterill, 1950, p. 134.
    * Central United States, 1948.
    † Equal costs would give both regions a value of 1·0.

materials and a further quarter from the advantage in labour costs of the more remote location. Since the overall locational advantage of the Gas Belt smelter against the Illinois smelter is of the order of 4 : 3 we may legitimately ask what keeps the latter in production?

Cotterill's study suggests the answer lies in the sale of by-products, notably sulphuric acid, by the Illinois plant. This by-product is locationally denied to the Gas Belt plant. Sulphuric acid production entails a three-times weight gain in water, it cannot be dumped because of its corrosive characteristics, and it is a low value-to-weight product that is very sensitive to distance. On all these counts it is a strongly market-oriented product that can only be economically produced in or near a large industrial region. Through this sale of local by-products the net deficit of the Illinois smelter is turned into a profit which allows it to retain its locational equilibrium near the market. Clearly the *same* product may be produced with a *varying* resource input so that simple correlations between the location of product *x* and a standard series of resource inputs is an oversimplification.

Chapter six   Surfaces

In the preceding chapters we have been concerned with the skeleton of the regional system (the network of routes and hierarchy of nodal centres) and with the movements that hold it together. However, the greater part of the earth's surface consists of the interstitial zones around and between the skeleton and are conventionally studied from the viewpoint of land use. In this chapter we view these zones not as a mosaic of distinct land-use complexes but as density surfaces. In this more abstract form it is possible to weld together a number of apparently different phenomena and different concepts, e.g. population density lapse-rates around towns and the Thünen model of ring formation.

I. SURFACES AND GRADIENTS

1. Nature of surfaces

Whether we regard population as a series of discrete clusters of different sizes, or whether we generalize this as a continuous population density surface, is largely a matter of scale. Like height contours on a topographic map we can regard lines of equal population density as demographic contours: indeed we could produce three-dimensional models of demographic distributions in much the same way as terrain models. This surface may be thought of statistically as a response surface, in which height (i.e. population density) varies as a response to controlling factors. Ways of depicting geographical distributions depend as much on cartographic convention as on the inherent nature of the phenomena being shown. Thus we may readily convert the land-use pattern shown on Fig. 6.1-A, the distribution of cork-oak forests in central Portugal (Haggett, 1961-B), into the density surface shown in Fig. 6.1-B or into the still more generalized surface shown in Fig. 6.1-c, simply by adopting different cartographic techniques. The techniques adopted in these maps are discussed in detail in Chapter 9.III(4a).

From the analytical viewpoint, it is easier to work with a two-dimensional cross-section cut into the surface than with the three-dimensional surface itself. Thus we can imagine sections cut diagonally across the first two figures on Fig. 6.1 with the first showing a discontinuous sequence of

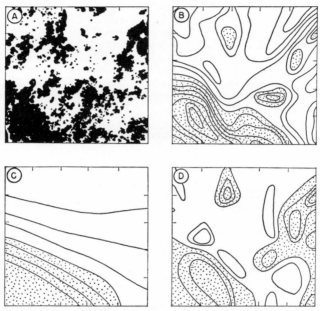

Fig. 6.1. Conversion of a discontinuous land-use distribution (*A*) into a continuous isarithmic surface (*B*) with regional trends (*C*) and local residuals (*D*). Sample quadrat (*G = 4·7*) of *sobreiro* woodland in the Tagus–Sado basin, central Portugal, with contours at five-degree intervals and areas above the mean shaded. Source: Haggett, 1961-B, p. 20.

areas with or without a particular type of forest cover, and the second a continuous but varying slope. In our discussion we refer to the first type as a *stepped* distribution with the height of the steps varying with the characteristics (intensity) of the type of land use, and the second type as a density distribution in which distinct *slopes* can be recognized and studied

2. Slopes: density gradients

a. Slopes in urban areas. Although the study of the form of density gradients around cities has been a subject of interest since Thünen's treatment in 1826 (Thünen, 1875), attention has been redirected to these phenomena by a recent controversial paper by Clark (1951). Clark studied the population density gradients around a group of thirty-six cities ranging in time from 1801 to 1950 and in space from Los Angeles to Budapest and argued that within them, urban population densities declined in a negative exponential manner and that this generalization appeared to hold in both the time and space dimensions. We can express this generalization as

$$P_d = P_0\, e^{-bd}$$

where P_d is the population density at a given distance (d) from the centre, b is the density gradient, and P_0 is the extrapolated central density. Two points about this formula should be noted: (a) that densities are for *residential* densities and (b) that the central density is extrapolated from the slopes derived from the outer areas. The fact that, like a volcanic cone, the city has a low residential (i.e. night-time) population at the centre is overcome by this convention.

Discussion has ranged around both variations in the level of the central density (i.e. the height of the extrapolated cone) and variations in the density gradients (i.e. the form of the flanking slopes):

(i) Direct studies of *central densities* (P_0) have been very few, largely because central density has proved so difficult to define. Winsborough (1961) has overcome this difficulty obliquely by demonstrating that the central density (P_0) is a function of the total population density of the whole city (P), regardless of the density gradient, b. The implication of this finding is that we may approach central density through a study of overall city density. For overall density Winsborough found that P was positively and significantly associated with age (as measured by the proportion of old dwellings), the size of the city, and the proportion of the population in manufacturing. Thus we should expect large, old, industrial cities to have rather high overall population densities.

Both the first two items in the relationship have been partly substantiated by other studies. Berry, Simmons, and Tennant (1963, p. 397) have incorporated age into a functional analysis of central densities,

$$P_0 = 0{\cdot}53 + 0{\cdot}63A - 3{\cdot}50b^{-1}$$

where A is age and b is the gradient. Both age (measured as years since the city reached a population of 50,000) and gradient were statistically significant at the 99 per cent confidence level. The two factors together explained some 61 per cent of the variance in central population density, P_0.

Size has also been investigated by Clawson (Clawson, Held, and Stoddard, 1960, p. 84) who suggest that there is an orderly increase in density as the size of the city increases. They observe that the largest cities of the United States (over 250,000) have 40 per cent of the urban population but only 19 per cent of the urban land. Fig. 6.2 shows the density of all urbanized areas in the United States in 1950, and shows the rather consistent relationship between density (*y*-axis) and city size (measured on a logarithmic scale on the *x*-axis). This relationship is maintained regardless of whether the density is based on the total urban area, or on that part of the urban area that is actually developed. The points on the graph are well scattered about the regression line showing the influence of 'disturbing' factors such as function and age on the size-density relationship, e.g. the New England 'towns' have characteristically lower densities owing to their enlarged boundaries which contain areas of farm and forest land (Chap. 7.I(3)).

(ii) Studies of the form of the gradient (*b*) are more abundant. Berry

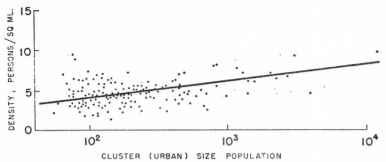

Fig. 6.2. Relation of population density (× 1,000) of cities to their size. United States, 1950. Source: Clawson, Held, and Stoddard, 1960, p. 83.

(Berry *et al.*, 1963) reviews a score of studies based on nearly one hundred cases drawn from all parts of the world and based on records of up to 159 years duration. Although the degree of fit varies, no evidence has yet been produced to counter Clark's claim that a negative exponential model would neatly describe the density 'lapse rate' around cities. Despite differences in absolute density and distance figures, the graphs for Hyderabad in India (Fig. 6.3-A) and Chicago in the United States (Fig. 6.3-B), show parallel trends.

Interest has therefore shifted in gradient study to the rationale behind variations in the gradient. Muth (1962) carried out for the United States a regression study of density gradient against eleven possible controlling variables of which only two—size of the Standard Metropolitan Area and the proportion of manufacturing outside the central city—bore significant relationships to the gradient *b*. Berry (Berry *et al*, 1963, pp. 398–9) followed this with a regression study of the gradients of forty-six United States cities against three variables: size of city (*M*), shape distortion (*S*), and spatial pattern of manufacturing (*I*). The resulting equation

$$\log b = 3 \cdot 08 - 0 \cdot 31 \log M - 1 \cdot 0 \log S + 0 \cdot 41 \log I$$

showed that only size was statistically significant (at the 95 per cent confidence level) and only 40 per cent of the variation in gradients was explained.

The measure of shape distortion was suggested by the simple geometric observation that *ceteris paribus* we should expect the density gradient to flatten as irregularity increased 'because areas that would normally be occupied by certain densities are now no longer available, and uses that

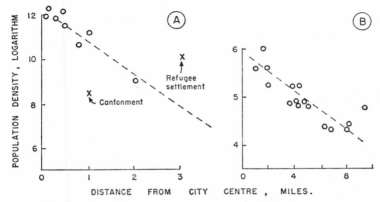

Fig. 6.3. Density–distance relationships for Hyderabad, India (*A*) and Chicago, United States (*B*). Source: Berry, Simmons, and Tennant, 1963, pp. 392, 394.

prefer these densities must move outward to the nearest available site' (Berry *et al.*, 1963, p. 398). The major distortions in shape were recorded for cities with tidewater or lakeshore locations; terrain effects on distortion were less marked.

b. Slopes in rural areas. We have already noted the results of the massive survey by Bogue (1949) based on a study of gradients around sixty-five United States cities (Chap. 4.I(2a)). The general form of these outer slopes follows the same negative exponential decline suggested by Clark (1951) for the inner zones, but extend out to distances of more than 300 miles from the city. Since the trends for urban population (Fig. 4.3) and for industrial population (Fig. 5.12) have already been treated, attention is drawn here only to the density of *rural-farm population,* an element which we might expect to show the least relationship to city-centred organization.

The general form of the rural-farm population gradient is more convex than that of population density as a whole. For the first 100 miles the density is around twenty people to the square mile with a rather gentle decline; from 100 to around 300 miles the gradient drops more steeply to around four to the square mile. The gradient is very little altered by the size of the central city (an important factor in urban and manufacturing gradients) and to a lesser extent by the sector. Here the subdominant sector containing the large secondary centres has a higher than average level while the route and local sectors (as defined in Fig. 4.4) are correspondingly reduced.

Perhaps the most striking variation in the density gradient is the variation between the major regions of the United States. The gentle

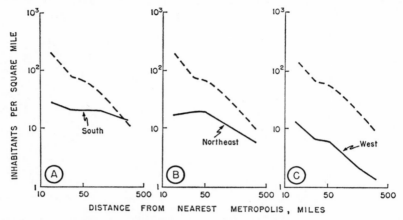

Fig. 6.4. Density–distance relationships for rural farm population in the United States, 1940, by regional divisions. Source: Bogue, 1949, p. 58.

gradients of the South (Fig. 6.4-A), the sharper fall of the Northeast with its characteristic depression of farm population densities in the near city areas (Fig. 6.4-B), and the very steep slope of the gradients in the West (Fig. 6.4-C) underline the basic differences in the agricultural resources of the three areas (Paterson, 1960).

3. Steps: land-use zones

Although the classification of the earth's surface into zones of distinct land use is a traditional geographical pursuit, none of the several schemes developed since 1892 (reviewed by Fox, 1956) has achieved the *ratio* level of measurement (Chap. 8.I). Despite the moves of the 1949 Lisbon conference of the International Geographical Union for a world-wide classification system, slow progress has been made in this direction. The most successful and significant works tend to remain the regional monograph on the land use of a limited area, e.g. Board's study of the South African Border region (1962).

The fact that land-use data are available in classes (e.g. woodland, arable land) rather than in precise ratios, means that we must view changes from one class to another as a 'break' or 'step', rather than a gradient. Chisholm (1962) has drawn together a remarkable collection of empirical studies, in which these land-use steps are directly related to continuous ratios (e.g.

distance from a settlement). The examples range in scale from the farm to
the world-city, in time from the medieval to the contemporary scene, and
in space from British Guiana to Soviet Russia.

One of the most interesting examples cited by Chisholm (1962,
pp. 61–4) is at the intermediate level for land-use zones around the
Sicilian village of Canicatti. Figs. 6.5-A to c graph the curve of land
occupied against distance from the village centre for three important

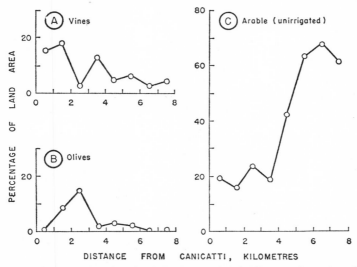

Fig. 6.5. Land use in Canicatti, Sicily, in relation to distance from the village
centre. Source: Chisholm, 1962, p. 63.

types; vineyards, olive-groves, and unirrigated arable land. Vines occupy
about 6 per cent of the area studied and are strongly concentrated in the
inner zone (less than four kilometres out from the centre) while olives are
more strongly represented in the middle zone (two to six kilometres out).
Unirrigated wheat dominates the landscape of the outer zone but, since it
makes up just over half the land area, it is strongly represented in all
zones and it occupies half the area of even the inner 'urban zone' within
one kilometre of the centre. Other crops which show sensitive reaction
to distance are pasture, waste and coppice wood, all characteristic
of the outer fringes, and citrus fruit, a characteristic type in the inner
zones.

To explain this observed pattern Chisholm has turned to estimates of
the annual labour requirements per hectare of the various crops available
from the Instituto Nazionale di Economia Agraria in Rome. Table 6.1
summarizes the figures in man-days for the three crops graphed in Fig. 6.5.
It is clear that those products which are less demanding are located further

Table 6.1. Land use, labour inputs, and distance from settlement*

Type of land use:	Vineyards	Olive-groves	Unirrigated arable
Average labour input, man-days/hectare	90	45	35
Modal distance from Canicatti, kilometres	1·5	2·5	6·5

Source: Chisholm, 1962, p. 63.

* Canicatti, Sicily.

from the centre; the fallowed wheat fields with their low labour requirements give precedence to the carefully tended and watered vineyards. Even within an individual crop there is some evidence that methods of cultivation become less intense with more distant crops.

At the smaller scale, land use varies with distance from the farmstead and Chisholm cites regularities from Sweden, Finland, the Netherlands, and India to suggest the wide occurrence of this phenomenon. Lapse rates away from the farm suggest falling inputs of both labour and fertilizers with a generally critical level at about one kilometre. An interesting extension of the farm-fields concept comes in the midwestern United States, where Kollmorgen and Jenks (1958) have drawn attention to the phenomenon of 'suitcase' farmers: defined as operators who live more than thirty miles outside the border of the county in which the farmland is located. The fact that these farmers, some of whom are recorded as living as far away as Los Angeles, have to be mobile and travel long distances in their farming has decisive effects on farming practice and through this on the land-use pattern. As Table 6.2 suggests, the distant 'suitcase' farms

Table 6.2. Land use in relation to the location of farm operator*

Locational classification of farmer:	Local	Non-local
Average size of farm, acres	1,280	730
Proportion of farm area, per cent:		
Cash crops	14	**60**
Feed crops	25	21
Pasture	**56**	11

Source: Kollmorgen and Jenks, 1958, p. 34.

* Sully County, South Dakota, United States, 1950.

devoted almost half their smaller acreages to cash crops, particularly wheat. The farms of the suitcase operators stand out as areas of high wheat production in counties in which the established local practice is dominantly a diversified crop and livestock pattern with two-thirds of the land area in pasture and feed crops.

Studies in rural areas are paralleled by land-use surveys within urban areas. Dickinson (1964, pp. 125–225) has summarized a number of significant studies of both the general structure of land-use zones throughout the city and of 'natural regions' within specific parts of the city. Despite the large number of definitive studies that have now been published on individual cities, e.g. Jones (1960) on Belfast or Azevedo (1958) on São Paulo, there remains a dearth of comparative studies. Bartholomew's *Land uses in American cities* (1955) remains one of the few analyses in which a sample of cities (in this case, fifty-three 'central' cities and thirty-three 'satellite' cities) is made available for direct comparison. Until more comparative land-use information is analysed for cities, we are unlikely to be able to check or extend the various growth models so far put forward (Chap. 6.III(3b)).

II. MINIMUM-MOVEMENT MODELS

1. Movement minimization: Thünian analysis

Paralleling the contribution of Weber in the study of industrial location is the earlier contribution of another German, Thünen, to agricultural location. In his major work, *Der Isolierte Staat in Beziehung auf Landwirtschaft* (Thünen, 1875) which first appeared in 1826, he put forward a consistent theory of agricultural location which has proved not only the starting point for more refined modern analysis, e.g. Dunn's *Location of agricultural production* (1954), but directly stimulated Weber's work in industrial location. Indeed Thünian and Weberian analyses have much in common in that both are concerned with movement minimization; they differ fundamentally in that while Weber's problem was to locate *points* in space, Thünen's problem was to locate *areas* in space (Hoover, 1948, pp. 90–102; Isard, 1956, pp. 188–206; Chisholm, 1962, pp. 21–35).

a. Basic geometrical relationships. Concern with the location of areas raises simple yet fundamental concern with plane geometry to which Bunge (1964, pp. 8–11) has drawn attention. If we are concerned with the simple problem of locating finite areas as near as possible to fixed points, then Fig. 6.6 suggests some of the alternative patterns that can emerge. In each case the total area (A) is the same and D is the maximum distance from the fixed point or line to the furthest part of the area.

The first case considered is that of arranging area nearest to a single point (Fig. 6.6-A), the classic problem in Thünen's 'isolated state' with its single market centre, which gives rise to a circular solution. In the succeeding cases two points are substituted for one (Fig. 6.6-B), a central line substituted for the two points (Fig. 6.6-C), and finally a central ring for the line (Fig. 6.6-D). In each case the bleak geometric pattern assumes a more familiar geographic aspect when we submerge half the figure with sea (shaded); now we may find parallels between the first two diagrams and agricultural zones around coastal ports; between the third and a zone about a railroad penetrating inland; and between the fourth and population clusters around the continental littorals of a central ocean.

The point we are making here is merely that the Thünen case of ring development represents only one extreme case in a set of problems in

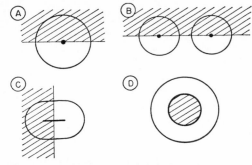

Fig. 6.6. Geometrical variants on the traditional Thünen ring structure.

which areas are grouped as near as possible to a point or line. Ring development is discussed in the following sections because it is graphically simple and clearly linked to the urban hierarchy, not because it is unique or exclusive.

b. Ring formation. If we assume a simple case of a land-use area to be placed as near as possible to a single point, then a circular form *ceteris paribus* is the minimum movement solution, and the maximum radial distance from the centre to the periphery of the area is given by the expression $(A/\pi)^{1/2}$. This trivial problem becomes more interesting when alternative types of land use are postulated.

Table 6.3. Derivation of net movement inputs*

Parameters:	Weight, tons/km.²	Cost of movement, units/ton	Movement resistance R_m	Area required, km.²	Maximum, radius, km., D	Net movement inputs at radius, Q
Land-use activities:						
Type *a*	3	1·0	3·0	100	5·64	16·9
Type *b*	2	0·5	1·0	200	8·01	8·0
Type *c*	1	2·0	2·0	300	9·76	19·5
All types	—	—	—	600	13·82	—

* Theoretical case for three land-use types.

Table 6.3 provides a set of hypothetical data to illustrate the solution of this type of problem. Three types of activity are assumed (a, b, c) and arbitrary production values in tons/km.^{2} and arbitrary movement costs in units/ton are made so that estimates of movement resistance (R_m) may be made. Values of R_m range from three for type a, down to two for type c and one for type b. Since the areas for each type are assumed to be 100, 200, and 300 square kilometres respectively, we can estimate the maximum radial distance for each type from the centre (D) and, combining this with resistance, derive our movement inputs (Q). In Figs. 6.7-A to C movement

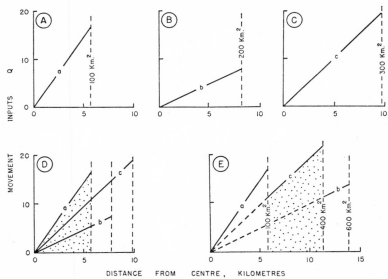

Fig. 6.7. Stages in the analysis of hypothetical movement inputs for land use.
Source: Table 6.4.

inputs are plotted for the three types on the y-axis against distance from the centre on the x-axis.

Since each type has fixed areal demands we cannot simply superimpose these three demands as in Fig. 6.7-D. We can, however, sum the demands and maximum radial distance for the combined area for the three types from the general formula

$$D_c = \left\{ \sum_{i=1}^{n} A_i / \pi \right\}^{1/2}$$

where A is the area of the ith type: with a total 600 square kilometres. We may assume that the area will be circular with a maximum radial distance of 13·82 km. What we have yet to determine is: (i) if the three types of land use will form distinct rings or annules about the centre; and (ii) what the sequence of zones will be. For our three types, the zonal sequence could be one of the following six: *abc, acb, bac, bca, cab, cba*. For *n* zones the number of possible sequences is $n(!)$ so that for Thünen's seven zones (Table 6.4) there are 5,040 possible sequences.

Examination of Fig. 6.7-D shows that in the innermost zone of 100 square kilometres (stippled) the movement inputs for type *a* are higher than the other two; while in the next 300 square kilometres zone (Fig. 6.7-E) (stippled) the movement inputs for type *c* are higher than that for type *b*. The suggestion is clearly that type *a* has the greatest locational need to be near the centre if movements are to be minimized. Since we have assumed a homogeneous type of agricultural activity there are no grounds at this stage for assuming that the location of any part of it further from the centre would bring advantages and we should expect a homogeneous zone in a circular-shaped area of 100 square kilometres immediately adjacent to the centre. For the other two types similar arguments apply, so that the sequence *acb* appears the most logical of the six possible arrangements.

We may readily compare the advantages of the sequence selected, *acb*, over other arrangements by plotting the cumulative movement inputs, Q (*cum.*), against distance (Fig. 6.8-A). The concave segmented line for *acb* is lower than any of the other five combinations; while the gap between this sequence and the most wasteful sequence (*bca*) is shown by the stippled area on Fig. 6.8-A. The ring-structure of both patterns is shown in Fig. 6.8-B.

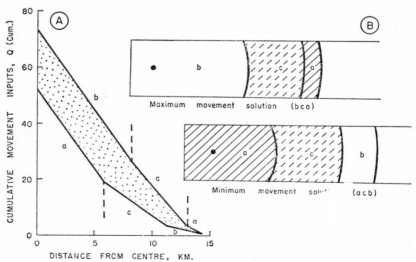

Fig. 6.8. Impact of movement inputs on the sequence of land-use rings.

The concepts we have used here are parallel to those of Thünen. We may set our movement inputs against his concept of locational rent (*Bodenrente*) which he derived from the expression

$$L = E(p - a) - Efk$$

where L is the locational rent per unit of land (the dependent variable), k is distance (the independent variable), and E, p, and a are constants: E the yield per unit of land, p the market price per unit of commodity, a the production cost per unit of commodity, and f the transport rate per unit of distance (Dunn, 1954, p. 7). Our concept of movement inputs is perhaps simpler in that it avoids specific consideration of market and production value constants, p and a, and substitutes for them assumptions about the demand for products in terms of area (A).

c. *Thünen's Isolierte Staat*. Diagram's of the concentric rings of land use in Thünen's hypothetical isolated state are among the most common textbook illustrations of locational theory for geographers. The main

Table 6.4. Der Isolierte Staat (1826): Thünen's land-use 'rings'

Zone	Area per cent of state area	Relative distance from central city	Land-use type	Major marketed product	Production system
0	Less than 0·1	−0·1	Urban-industrial	Manufactured goods	Urban trade centre of state; near iron and coal mines
1	1	0·1–0·6	Intensive agriculture	Milk; vegetables	Intensive dairying and trucking; heavy manuring; no fallow
2	3	0·6–3·5	Forest	Firewood; timber	Sustained-yield forestry
3a	3	3·6–4·6		Rye; potatoes	Six-year rotation: rye (2), potatoes (1), clover (1), barley (1), vetch (1); no fallow; cattle stall-fed in winter
3b	30	4·7–34	Extensive agriculture	Rye	Seven-year rotation system; pasture (3), rye (1), barley (1), oats (1), fallow (1)
3c	25	34–44		Rye: animal products	Three-field system: rye, etc. (1), pasture (1), fallow (1)
4	38	45–100	Ranching	Animal products	Mainly stock-raising some rye for on-farm consumption
5	—	Beyond 100	Waste	None	None

characteristics of its zones have been summarized by Grotewald (1959) and Chisholm (1962, pp. 21–35) and are reproduced in Table 6.4. It will be seen that the land-use pattern is one of concentric shells ranging from very narrow inner rings of intensive farming (**1**) and forest (**2**), through to a broad band of increasingly extensive agriculture (**3**) and ranching (**4**) to the waste beyond (**5**).

In appreciating this remarkable early statement we should recall its two somewhat paradoxical limitations: (i) its simplifying assumptions and (ii) its high empirical content.

(i) The assumptions made by Thünen may be summarized under six heads: *one*, the existence of an 'isolated state' which was cut off from the rest of the world and surrounded by waste on all sides; *two*, the domination of the state by a single large city which served as the single urban market; *three*, the setting of the city in the centre of a broad featureless plain which was assumed to be equal in fertility and trafficability so that production costs and transport costs were assumed to be everywhere the same; *four*, the supplying of the city by farmers who shipped agricultural goods to the city in return for industrial produce; *five*, the transporting of farm produce by the farmer himself who hauled his own produce to market along a dense trail of converging roads of equal standard with costs exactly proportional to distance; *six*, the maximizing of profit by all farmers with automatic adjustment of crops to the needs of the central market.

Lösch (1954, pp. 38–48) has pointed out that even with these simplifying assumptions, ring formations were not inevitable. He argued that for two crops i and j there were seventeen possible combinations in which one or other crop predominated, or both were grown side by side, and only ten in which rings were formed. To achieve rings in the order ij about the centre the following conditions had to obtain

$$1 < \{[E(p - a)_i]/[E(p - a)_j]\} < [E_i/E_j]$$

where E, p, and a are as defined by Dunn (1954) in the preceding section 6.II(1b).

(ii) The high empirical content of Thünen's theory can only be understood in terms of his background. Johnson (1962) has described the early years of Thünen's life and its influence on his locational ideas. In 1810 Johann Heinrich von Thünen, at the age of twenty-seven, acquired his own agricultural estate, Tellow, near the town of Rostock in Mecklenburg on the Baltic coast of Germany. For the next forty years till his death in 1850, Thünen farmed this estate and over this period assembled a mass of minutely documented data on the costs and revenue of its operation. His *Der Isolierte Staat* (1826) drew heavily on his farming and estate accounting and many of the assumptions and all of the empirical constants he used were based on this localized experience.

Many of the needs of nineteenth-century Mecklenburg now seem quaint or obsolete. Apparently the most serious change in demand affects the location of his second zone, timber and firewood production (Table 6.4), a type of land-use activity which is no longer able to bid for high accessibility sites near urban centres in Western countries. In the humid tropics, however, rotational timber for firewood and charcoal may still be located in about the position Thünen suggested and Waibel (1958) has drawn attention to this arrangement in southeastern Brazil. Even in highly urbanized areas the demand for 'recreational' wooded areas may well lead to its persistence in areas of high accessibility. Gottmann (1961) has illustrated this trend with rising leisure demands in the highly urbanized seaboard areas of the eastern United States.

2. Criticisms of movement models

a. Changes in movement costs. Although direct comparisons are difficult, there is little doubt that the long-term trend of real transport costs has been downwards. A succession of technical inventions, the advent of cheap fuels, and the scale economies of ever larger volumes in circulation has generally reduced the relative costs of transport in overall production costs. Chisholm (1962, pp. 185–6) has followed the course of freight rates for one transport medium, ocean shipping, and finds that when allowances are made for world-wide inflation, the real cost of ocean shipping over the years between 1876 and 1955 has fallen by almost three-fifths.

As the general level of transport costs falls the relative mobility of products increases and we should expect to find Thünen's rings growing wider. Lösch (1954, p. 51) pointed out that with the growth of a number of closely packed centres the location of rings around each centre will be distorted outwards. There may simply not be enough room for all the rings, and the outer may be displaced toward the periphery of the state, This means that for the inner rings the individual town remains the marketing centre, but for the outer rings it is the agglomeration of towns that jointly forms the market centre (Fig. 6.9-A). This point has been illustrated by Jonasson who regards northwestern Europe as 'one vast conurbation . . . one geographic centre' (Jonasson, 1925, p. 290). Maps of average decline of yield of eight crops show a remarkable decline with distance from this combined centre (Fig. 6.9-B).

This movement does not of course stop at the edge of the state, still less the continent. Backe (1942) has shown that the movement of low rent yielding land-use systems outside Europe since about 1850 (notably sheep rearing and wheat growing) might be interpreted in Thünian terms. Movements of goods at this international scale is clearly part of the same interactions continuum that we noted in Chapter 2.I; Ohlin (1933) in his classic trade study, *Interregional and international trade*, places these movements within a general framework of locational theory. At this scale it would appear then that the effect of reducing transport costs has been to alter the scale of operation of Thünen's rings, rather than their intrinsic value.

At the other extreme, empirical evidence suggests that at the small scale of field and farm and farm and village the ring-effect remains (Chisholm, 1962, pp. 47–75, 124–53). Here the movement continues to be measured in terms of time and man-days rather than in freight costs so that as labour costs rise we might expect such movement costs to become relatively more important unless offset by more rapid improvements in internal transport (tractors, jeeps, etc.).

   b. Changes in distance–movement relations. In the study of movement

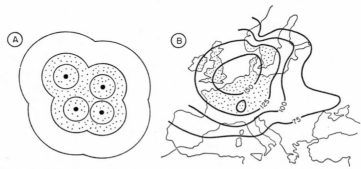

Fig. 6.9. A Fusing of ring structure around clusters of centres. *B* Contours of agricultural intensity in Europe (*G = 1·8*). Source: Valkenburg and Held, 1952, p. 102.

inputs, the cost of moving over distance was assumed to be linear. We know in fact that movement costs are in general: (i) curvilinear (convex) in form; (ii) stepped rather than continuous; and (iii) differentiated by commodity, amount, distance, direction, shipper, season, and related individual variables (Troxel, 1955). While the detailed discussion of this most complex problem remains outside our immediate field it is worth illustrating the general form of the costs–distance relationship. For Milwaukee (α) in Wisconsin, United States, Alexander (1963, p. 475) has illustrated the stepped nature of railroad freight rates (Fig. 6.10-A) and the distortion of the cost surface with directional variations from the city (Fig. 6.10-B).

   Variations in movement costs on different commodities is demonstrated by earlier work by Alexander in Illinois (Alexander, 1944). He illustrated the pattern of railway freight rates for grain moved to Chicago, β (Fig. 6.10-C), when compared to livestock rates to Chicago (Fig. 6.10-D). In both maps contours are at intervals of two cents per 100 pounds with areas over thirteen cents stippled in Fig. 6.10-C and over eighteen cents stippled in Fig. 6.10-D to emphasize the high-cost areas. If we compare the location of two points, γ and δ, west and southwest of Chicago we find

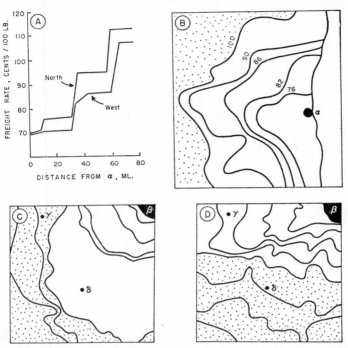

Fig. 6.10. Directional variations in railway freight costs in sample quadrats. *AB* West of Milwaukee, United States ($G = 4·3$). *CD* Southwest of Chicago, United States ($G = 3·9$). Sources: Alexander, Brown, and Dahlberg, 1958, p. 9; Alexander, 1944, pp. 26–8.

that although both are equidistant from the city (about 110 miles away) the first has a marked locational advantage in livestock production and the second in grain production.

These cases emphasize the dramatic shift from the idyllic picture of Thünen's state where each farmer took his own product to market by horse and wagon and was therefore directly concerned to minimize his own movements. The shift of transport to independent companies has undermined the logic of this minimization assumption in that we could argue, *ceteris paribus*, that the object of a transport company is to maximize rather than minimize total movement. Troxel (1955) examines some of the restraints that both competition and government place on this maximization urge. We can argue none the less that the movement of transport out of the hands of the producer has meant that the economy of the overall movement system rather than that of the individual producer becomes dominant.

III. DISTORTION OF REGULAR GRADIENTS

1. Distortion due to resource localization

a. Variation in resources. As a practical farmer, Thünen knew that, in practice, the land-use pattern was modified not only by movement costs but local availability of good soils, growing seasons, management ability, and so on. He produced a modified diagram in which the original rings (Fig. 6.11-A) were altered not only by competing centres (Fig. 6.11-B) and cheaper transport routes (Fig. 6.11-C), but also by different land qualities (Fig. 6.11-D).

Empirical support of the very close link between physical resources and

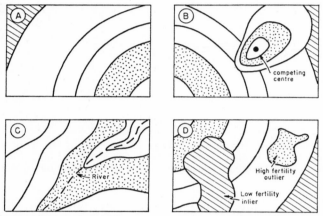

Fig. 6.11. Distortion of the regular annular structure of Thünen landscape (*A*) by a second competing centre (*B*), alternative transfer routes (*C*), and areas of different productivity (*D*).

agriculture has come from work by Hidore (1963) who investigated the relationship between: (i) flat land, defined as slopes of less than 3°; (ii) cash grain farms (Fig. 6.12). For the sample of 730 counties in the north-central United States, the correlation coefficient was statistically significant at +0·652, while for one state, Illinois, it rose to +0·690. The only major deviant state was Minnesota where its high percentage of flat land was offset by unsuitable soil conditions, the southern edge of the Laurentian Shield.

Studies like that of Hidore are part of a long tradition of environmental studies which have formed a major part of geographical literature, (Chap. 1.II(1c)). The fact that, at the world scale at least, bioclimatic factors played a major part in shaping the distribution of population clusters (Table 6.5) has led to over-concentration on this theme at the expense of others. For while the contrasts in zone densities are very marked, comparison of the same zones north and south of the equator on Table 6.5

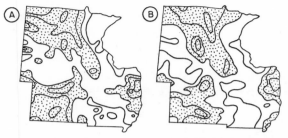

Fig. 6.12. Relations between flat land (*A*) and crop land (*B*) in the north-central United States ($G = 2.7$). Source: Hidore, 1963, pp. 85, 87.

Table 6.5. Distribution of population densities by bioclimatic zones*

Density parameters:	Inhabitants (10^6)	Area (10^6 sq. km.)	Density (inhab./sq. km.)
Bioclimatic zone:			
N. Polar zone	0·2	5·2	0·04
N. Temperate zone	850	50·2	16·8
N. Subtropical zone	555	11·8	47·0
Tropical zone	726	47·7	15·2
S. Subtropical zone	42	14·4	2·9
S. Temperate zone	3	1·5	2·0
S. Polar zone	—	16·0	—

Source: Vahl and Humlum, 1949, pp. 59–65.
* World, 1940.

suggests that both the origin of agriculture (Sauer, 1952) and the subsequent diffusion of population have strongly distorted the simple environmental pattern. Nevertheless the strength of resource variations and their direct and indirect effect on regional systems must be acknowledged at all scales of organization: from that of the farm to the city-region. Indeed with increasing mechanization and ease of transport, there are some grounds for believing, with Baker (1921), that latent physical differences might play an increasingly important part in determining utilization of land. Alexander (1964) and Dickinson (1964) contain excellent surveys of the impact of environmental complexes on the main branches of economic activity and on city-organization respectively.

    b. Substitution between resource inputs. As with industrial location (Chap. 5.IV(3)), substitution modifies any simple relationship between resources and zone location. Gottmann (1961, p. 286) has provided a useful practical illustration of substitution in the dairy industry in the United States. He compares important dairy-farming areas, the Atlantic Coast zone near the Boston–New York–Washington market, and the Wisconsin–Minnesota zone in the midwestern United States. In terms of Thünen's system the first zone would be in the intensive inner ring and the second in the extensive outer ring. Although both areas have farm units of about the same size (150 acres) and about the same yield per animal, there are striking contrasts in almost all other inputs in favour of the Atlantic Coast area. Stock per acre and investment in machinery are 40 per cent more, returns are 60 per cent more, per unit output of milk, and investment in lands and buildings is 80 per cent more. Contrasts in land use are slightly less striking, with 30 per cent more hay being grown in the inner zone and with a corresponding decrease in small grains.

The contrast in output in the two areas partly reflects the returns for liquid milk as opposed to processed milk (butter, cheese, etc.) to which Thünen drew attention in his Isolated State. A number of studies in both the United States and the British Isles have drawn attention to the characteristic locational zoning of milk, butter, and cheese production with increasing distance away from the urban-industrial market (Chisholm, 1962).

Thünen himself used substitution in his analysis of the distribution of one of his crops, rye, in the Isolated State. Table 6.4 shows that rye was grown throughout the outer agricultural zone (3–4) but was shipped to market only within zone 3. Rye was therefore shipped to market town over a very wide distance from 3·6 to 44 miles. Despite a common market price for rye and common movement costs per ton, rye from the outer zone (3) was able to compete successfully with rye grown about one-tenth this distance from the market in the inner zone (3a).

Thünen argues that the outer zone can compete with the inner only by substituting a less efficient total-production system (*Betriebssystem*), i.e. the outer zone can compete only because it has lower production costs for rye but these lower costs for this crop are bought at the expense of a wasteful total system in which one-third of the land lies fallow each year. Indeed if we compare the rotational systems in 3a, 3b, and 3c, we find that the proportion of fallow land rises in the sequence zero, one-seventh, one-third with distance from the market (see Table 6.4).

The inner zone remains the most efficient in terms of its overall production, for as Lösch has emphasized 'total profits are decisive; there is no additional criterion for individual crops' (Lösch, 1954, p. 61). As with our findings for the zinc industry (Chap. 5.III(3b)) we must conclude that rye will be grown in a variety of locations where substitutions between local resources makes its inclusion in the total crop mix profitable.

The problem of 'mixing' crops in an appropriate combination at a given location has been approached by Gould (1963) using *game-theory* analysis. He selects Jantilla, a small village in western Ghana, as typical of the problem of crop mixture in the middle zone of the country with its very variable rainfall. Here the 'environmental strategy' in game-theory parlance is twofold: it can either be wet or, under Harmattan conditions, dry. To meet this the 'villagers' strategy' is fivefold: they can grow one or all of five basic crops. However, the yield will vary considerably depending on the particular crop grown and the season (Table 6.6). For example, yams are a speculative crop with high wet-year yield but a poor dry-year yield (only one-eighth as large). By contrast, millet is a very reliable crop which differs rather little between its dry- and wet-year returns. We can see something of the villagers' dilemma: (i) should they hope for a wet season

Table 6.6. Crop yields under alternative environmental strategies*

Environmental strategies:	Wet year	Dry year
Crop yields per unit of area:		
Yams	82	11
Maize	61	49
Cassava	12	38
Millet	43	32
Hill-rice	30	71

Source: Gould, 1963, p. 292.

* Jantilla, central Ghana.

and plant high-yielding (but high-risk) crops; or (ii) play safe with moderate-yielding crops; or (iii) adopt some intermediate strategy?

Given the simple 2 × 5 assumptions, Gould shows how the optimum solution may be derived. In Fig. 6.13 yield is plotted on separate vertical axes for the wet year (w) and dry year (d) and the points joined by a diagonal line. The steeper this line, the greater are the contrasts in yield between the two years, and vice versa. Fig. 6.13-A shows the diagonal for the first crop, yams. In Fig. 6.13-B the diagonal for the second crop, maize, is superimposed, and in Fig. 6.13-c diagonals for the remaining three crops are added. The intersecting diagonals show the highest yields—yams, maize, and hill-rice—and these are marked as a segmented concave line in Fig. 6.13-c. On this line the lowest point (or saddle point), S, represents the optimum combination of crops: i.e. those crops which will yield on average the highest returns in a run of good and bad years. This is, in game-theory terms, the *minimax* solution.

Computation of the relative share of each crop in the minimax solution is shown in Table 6.7. The difference in yield between wet and dry

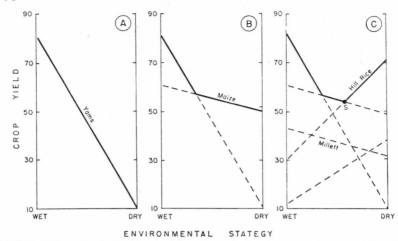

ENVIRONMENTAL   STRATEGY

Fig. 6.13. Stages in the determination of the optimum crop mix for a Ghanaian village by game-theory analysis. Source: Gould, 1963, p. 292.

years is calculated for both crops and compared; for each crop the observed difference is transferred to the other; this transferred difference divided by the comparative difference gives indices (1·4 and 0·4) which represent the share of each crop and from which percentages may be derived.

Table 6.7. Computation of optimum counter-strategy*

Alternative crops:	*Maize*	*Hill-rice*
Yield under alternative environmental strategy:		
Wet year	61	30
Dry year	49	71
Difference in yield	12	41
Proportional difference	$\left\| \frac{41}{12-41} \right\| = 1 \cdot 4$	$\left\| \frac{12}{12-41} \right\| = 0 \cdot 4$
Optimum counter-strategy	77%	23%

Source: Gould, 1963, p. 293.

* Jantilla, central Ghana.

The resulting proportions of 77 : 23 could be interpreted in the long run as planting all the village land in maize for seventy-seven years and all in hill-rice for the remaining twenty-three years of each century! In practice the short-run solution, planting three-quarters of the area to maize and a quarter to hill-rice each year, would clearly be adopted. Gould finds that the proportions derived by this method are in rough accord with the actual land-use patterns in the Jantilla area suggesting that the solution has been reached there by the rugged path of trial and error. Since error in this case must be translated in human terms into starvation, the practical importance of game-theory approaches to substitution problems are clear. A useful introduction to the simpler aspects of this type of analysis is given by Vajda (1961); more complex problems demand computer solutions.

2. Distortion due to concentration

While scale economies have not yet affected agriculture to the same extent as industry (Chap. 4.III) there are signs, in Western countries at least, that scale economies are becoming very important. If this trend continues, agricultural and industrial location theories are likely to fuse yet more closely as agriculture increasingly adopts the structure of high inputs and low land area demands typical of industry. Broiler-houses in the English landscape are a sign of the developing industrial–agricultural convergence.

Differences in land-use intensities between units of different scales are already apparent. To take one case Mead (1953) in a review of Finnish farming finds two important correlates of increasing farm-size: (i) a decline in the amount of cultivated land; and (ii) increasing specialization in 'export' crops. A survey of farms in the Helsinki area in 1944 showed that about one-third of the area of small family farms (less than thirty-six hectares) was cultivated, while on larger 250-hectare farms only one-quarter was cultivated. The remainder of the farm area was generally in woodland. On the second correlate, Mead shows that for small units a large proportion of bread grains was consumed on the farm (90 per cent on farms of less than ten hectares) but the proportion decreased sharply with size: for farms of over fifty hectares it had fallen to about 5 per cent. In tropical areas the association between the large operating unit and specialization in export crops is a well-established one. For Ceylon, Farmer (1957) has described the 'dual economy' of the plantation and peasant sectors, and Waibel (1958) has suggested a similar dichotomy in Brazil.

Local scale economies are paralleled by regional advantages. Somewhat akin to Florence's idea of industrial 'swarming' (Florence, 1953) is the growth of specialist farm producers who gain economies from common marketing arrangements. California provides a classic case in which an area with marked climatic advantages established itself as the major supplier of citrus fruit to the northeastern United States. The scale of shipment and the standardized product enabled favourable rates to be bargained with the railway companies: so that California was able to undercut nearer but smaller producing areas like Florida. The advent of road transport has enabled Florida to break back into the market as economies of scale appear less important with this form of transport (Chisholm, 1962, p. 191).

Standardized marketing is increasing in Western countries and should allow further scale concentrations of the California type to emerge. Indeed some of the curious concentrations in agricultural production in England —like that of the rhubarb cultivation in the West Riding of Yorkshire— may be as well explained as scale concentrations around a random nucleus as by the particular environment of that area.

3. Distortion due to time lags

a. Slope development over time. The debate over the nature of the gradients in population density around and within cities, has extended to the ways in which these gradients evolve over time. Two main generalizations may be made from Clark's studies of his lapse rates around cities when these were viewed progressively over time (Clark, 1951). First he found that the growth of cities was accompanied by a steady decrease in density gradient,

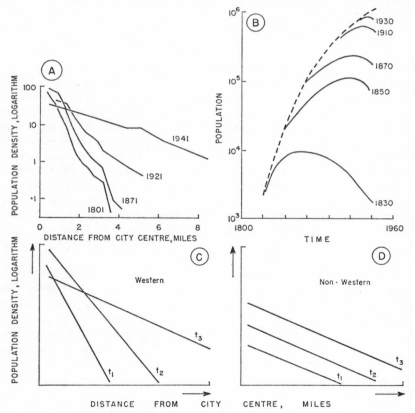

Fig. 6.14. A Density–distance relationships for London, 1801–1941. B Population–time relationships for the city of Cleveland, United States. *CD* Temporal comparisons of Western and non-Western cities. Sources: Berry, Simmons, and Tennant, 1963, pp. 400, 403; McKenzie, 1933.

a 'decompaction' trend. Fig. 6.14-A reproduces his findings for London
for the period 1801–1941; findings which were paralleled for Paris, Berlin,
Chicago, New York, and Brisbane. Secondly, he found the density of
central areas increased and then decreased. Fig. 6.14-B illustrates this
trend for Cleveland (Ohio, United States) based on a study by McKenzie
(1933; Clawson et al., 1960, p. 504). It shows: (i) the overall continuing
increase in the total population of Cleveland as shown by the continuous
outer line (from a little under 2,000 in 1830 to near a million by 1930);
(ii) continuing expansion of the legal boundaries of the city as it has spread
outwards from its centre; (iii) characteristic rise and fall in the population
of the inner section (for Cleveland, the city as defined in 1830 reaches its
peak in population by 1870 and thereafter declines, and by 1930 its
population has fallen back to about the same level that it was a century
before).

Berry (Berry et al., 1963) corroborated Clark's findings for Western
cities but suggests that they may not be applicable for non-Western cities.
From a study of Calcutta from 1881 to 1951 he suggests that the density
gradient remained more or less constant (i.e. there was no 'decompaction'
trend) and the central density continued to rise. This lack of suburbaniza-
tion and continued city-crowding may represent short-term differences in
living standards and in transit facilities, or more permanent differences
in urban morphology. Certainly they are not confined to Calcutta, but
appear to be common to southeast Asian cities in general. Whether Berry's
attempt to generalize Western (Fig. 6.14-C) and non-Western growth
gradients (Fig. 6.14-D) over time periods $(t_1, t_2 \ldots t_n)$ is fully justified, is
still at issue.

b. Step developments over time. It is a curious paradox that, though the
Thünen model of land-use steps (a static model) was developed primarily
for rural zones, the major dynamic models of step development through
time were developed for urban zones. In the same way that Thünen is
applicable to both urban and rural areas, the dynamic models can be
likewise extended. Three of the simplest models are reviewed here:

(i) The concentric-zone model (Fig. 6.15-A) was put forward by Burgess
(1927) and is based largely on his studies of urban growth in the Chicago
area (Dickinson, 1964, pp. 131–44). The theory suggests that a city expands
radially from its centre so as to form a series of concentric zones or annules.
For Chicago the five annules were, in order from the centre outwards: (a)
an inner central business district; (b) a transition zone surrounding the
central business district with residential areas being 'invaded' by business
and industry from the inner core; (c) a working-class residential district;
(d) a zone of better residences with single-family dwellings; and (e) an
outer zone of commuting with suburban areas and satellite cities. Although
Burgess acknowledged that this simple annular pattern would be inevitably modified by terrain, by routes, and so on, he nevertheless considered

that each inner zone extended by colonization of the next outer zone and that therefore radial expansion along a broad front was the dominant process in shaping the pattern of the city area.

Although the arguments over the Burgess model have largely been confined to urban areas, there is no *a priori* reason why it should not be equally applicable to rural areas. Waibel (1958) has identified a series of semi-concentric zones developing around the areas of early German colonization in southern Brazil, while the history of the colonization of the Argentine Pampas is one in which high-value land use (e.g. wheat

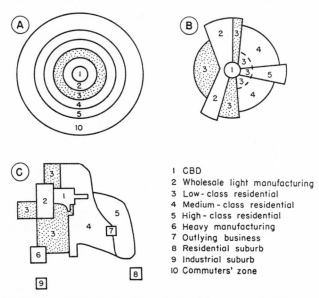

1 CBD
2 Wholesale light manufacturing
3 Low-class residential
4 Medium-class residential
5 High-class residential
6 Heavy manufacturing
7 Outlying business
8 Residential suburb
9 Industrial suburb
10 Commuters' zone

Fig. 6.15. Density–area relationships under the concentric (*A*), sector (*B*), and poly-nuclear (*D*) models of urban expansion. Source: Pred, 1964, p. 167.

farming) progressively pushed lower-value uses (e.g. sheep raising) to the outer margins of the area (James, 1959, pp. 324–55). Fusion of the static Thünen model with the dynamic Burgess model, might weld a useful descriptive tool for comparison of European overseas settlement (Thomas, 1956, pp. 721–62).

(ii) An alternative approach to urban growth patterns was put forward by Hoyt (1939) as the *sector* model (Fig. 6.15-B). Studies of rent levels in American cities led him to argue that the different types of residential areas tend to grow outwards along distinct radii, with new growth on the outer arc of a sector tending to reproduce the character of earlier growth in that sector. Hoyt's model is clearly an improvement on the earlier Burgess model in that both distance and direction from the city-centre are taken into consideration, thereby meeting some of the criticism of the annular model, e.g. on the grounds that cities like Paris (Dickinson, 1964, pp. 144–52) were more star-shaped than circular in their pattern of growth.

Again, the sector model is equally applicable to rural growth processes. Fig. 6.16 shows the successive periods in the expansion of the 'coffee frontier' in southeastern Brazil (Monbeig, 1952; Stein, 1957),

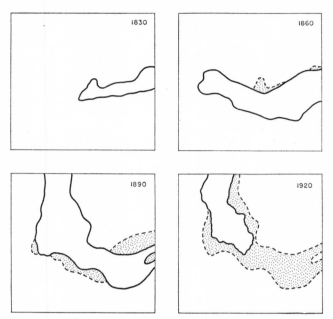

Fig. 6.16. Sequence of thirty-year stages in the growth and abandonment (*shaded*) of coffee-planting zone in a sample quadrat ($G = 4\cdot5$) of São Paulo state, Brazil.

showing the channelling of the coffee-growing area along the valley of the Paraíba river. The sequential regularity of growth, boom, and abandonment led to the development of a variant of the sector hypothesis, the *hollow-frontier* hypothesis, which has bemused so much of the thinking on Brazilian settlement expansion (Haggett, 1961-A, p. 50). Sector growth from a base-line, rather than a centre, has been used by Sauer in an interpretation of the development of the major agricultural zones in the eastern United States; here the character of the settlers on the Atlantic base-line (e.g. German settlers in Pennsylvania) was progressively transferred westwards with the 'frontier movement' into the trans-Appalachian areas.

(iii) A *multiple-nuclei* model (Fig. 6.15-c) was put forward by Harris and

Ullman (1945) in a modification of the two foregoing models. They suggest that the pattern of growth is centred on not one, but a series of distinct urban centres. The number of such growth-centres is a function both of the historical development and of the locational forces which aggregate some functions but scatter others. The problem of why some areas become active diffusion centres while others lie dormant has been pursued more actively for rural zones than for urban. Thus Sauer (1952) devoted his Bowman Lectures to the problem of agricultural *hearths* in both the New World and the Old and his findings, controversial though they may be, have stirred up interest and debate in this topic. Spencer and Horvath (1963) have also inquired into the origins of three modern but distinctive agricultural zones, the North American 'Corn Belt', the Philippine 'Coconut Zone', and the Malayan 'Rubber Zone'. It is an interesting but unanswered question whether the stochastic diffusion-models which are

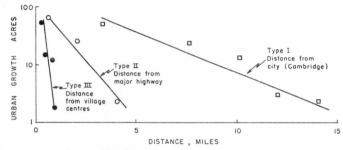

Fig. 6.17. Growth–distance relationships in urban conversion of land in southern Cambridgeshire, England. Source: Field survey by D. E. Keeble and P. Haggett, 1964.

already being applied to city growth, e.g. by Morrill and Bunge (in International Geographical Union, 1964, p. 329) to the spread of the Negro ghettoes within American cities, might be reversed so as to give some clue to the probable location of the nuclei from which growth springs. Cain (1944) has outlined for plant geography some of the indicators by which such nuclear zones might be traced.

The three models—the concentric-zone, sector, and multiple-nuclei models—are not of course mutually exclusive. We might expect zone development, whether in rural or urban areas, to show traces of all three. Thus Garrison (Garrison *et al.*, 1958, p. 144) has suggested a fused growth model in which growth proceeds radially both from the centre and from other sub-nuclei, but is intersected by axial growth pushing outwards along the transport lines from the main centre. Progressive 'sorting' of industry and residences into distinct social, economic, and technical zones is also assimilated within this general model. Evidence from the area south of Cambridge, England (Fig. 6.17), suggests Garrison's view may be correct. Here the spread of housing since World War II shows three distinct gradients: (i) a gentle gradient about the main city, in line with the concentric-zone model; (ii) a steeper gradient about the major highways, in line with the sector model; and (iii) a very steep gradient about the outlying villages, in line with the multiple-nuclei model. Clearly all three models, rather than any one, are useful in explaining the growth of this land-use zone; suggesting that eclectic rather than selective use of locational models may be the better policy in analysing geographical distributions, e.g. Chapin and Weiss (1962, pp. 425–58) used some thirteen variables, including accessibility measures, in a multiple-regression study (Chap. 10.II(3)) of urban growth around a cluster of cities in the Carolina piedmont of the southeastern United States.

4. Distortion due to 'sub-optimal' behaviour

Attention has already been drawn (Chap. 1.IV(2a)) to contrasts between the optimizer and the satisficer models of human behaviour. Wolpert (1964) has studied the distribution of farm labour productivity over a sample of farms in the Swedish Mellansverige in which he shows that the surface of actual labour productivity (Fig. 6.18-A) is substantially less than the optimum productivity surface (Fig. 6.18-B). Optimum values were

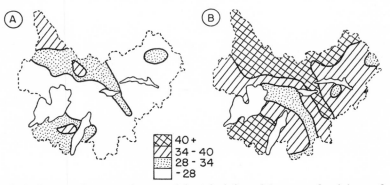

40 +
34 - 40
28 - 34
- 28

Fig. 6.18. Contrast between the actual (*satisficer*) farm-labour productivity surface (*A*) and the potential (*optimizer*) surface (*B*) for the Swedish Mellansverige (*G* = 4·0). Source: Wolpert, 1964, pp. 540, 541.

determined by linear programming for seventeen representative farms and interpolated through regression analysis for the remaining five hundred farms in the sample; although this may cast doubts on the exact values obtained the width of the gap separating the two surfaces was too great and too consistent to be explained away. Less than half the area had performances more than 70 per cent of the optimum, and in some pockets productivity was down to as low as 40 per cent. Wolpert traces the regional incidence of the gap in some detail and concludes that major factors controlling its extent were: (i) the simple fact that Swedish farmers were not aiming at optimum productivity but merely at a satisfactory (but sub-optimal) level; (ii) regional variations in the 'knowledge situation' linked to time lags in the diffusion of information (e.g. of recommended farm practices) from centres like Stockholm and Uppsala; and (iii) uncertainty as to which crop and livestock mixes were likely to prove profitable. These uncertainties were related not only to expected fluctuations of weather or disease but personal uncertainties (e.g. of health or finance) and economic uncertainties about market prices. As Wolpert wryly observes, farmers with *ex post* information would have got far closer to the theoretical optimum than with their inevitable *ex ante* information.

The spectre of sub-optimal behaviour dogs all discussion of the classic normative models discussed in the preceding pages (Chaps. 2–6) and it provides a convenient point to revive the caveat that was entered at the end of Chapter 1. We clearly need more locational models to be based on satisficer rather than optimizer principles and much research work in hand is aiming at closing the gap between the expected and the observed world. Most of our existing models have admittedly been with us too long; but they need replacing by improved and more sophisticated counterparts, not by the anarchy of regional empiricism. To ask for facts and nothing but the facts is, as Wittgenstein saw, to ask the impossible; regional geography is as sorely in need of models as systematic geography, and only by fusion of the two in model-based regions (see Chorley and Haggett, 1965-A, Chap. 18) is rapid progress in both likely.

Part Two : Methods in Locational Analysis

Only when a regularity has already been recognized or suspected can the planning of an experiment begin: until that time the mere multiplication of experiments is comparatively fruitless . . . and the accumulation of observations in large numbers will be as much a waste of energy in physics as in cartography. (STEPHEN TOULMIN, The Philosophy of Science, 1953, pp. 111–12.)

Chapter seven
Collecting

Further development of the locational models outlined in Chapters 2–6 depends largely on our ability to test them against existing geographical patterns. More theoretical models can and will be developed on deductive bases, but we are unlikely ever to know how useful these are unless an adequate feedback of information in the form of empirical data can be ensured. The last four chapters of this book are concerned with the ways in which geographical information can be gathered, measured, classified, and described; not simply to add to the present jumble of regional literature that we already have to hand, but in order that our existing concepts may be critically examined. It is all too easy to collect informa-tion in human geography, all too hard to collect information which is significant and relevant to specific locational questions. To this extent the organization of Part Two of the book follows the well-established paths of experimental design, moving from the collecting of evidence through to the testing of hypotheses.

I. GEOGRAPHICAL POPULATIONS

1. Sources of geographical information

One of the difficulties that has beset the collection of locational data in the past is the heavy dependence on secondary sources. Of the categories shown in Table 7.1, none is more important than that labelled 'archival sources' which includes both information recorded directly on an areal framework (e.g. maps and air photographs) as well as information which could be transferred to an areal framework (e.g. census records). It is difficult to make precise estimates, but a rapid check of locational research

Table 7.1. Sources of locational information in human geography

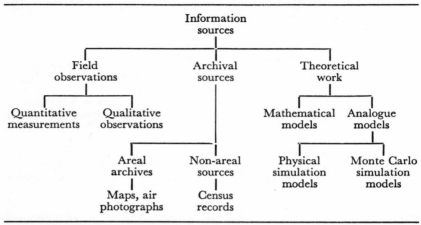

Source: Adapted from Chorley. In Dury, 1965, p. 276.

published in geographical periodicals over the last five years suggests that this source still accounts for over 95 per cent of our work.

The implications of this dependence are threefold: (i) locational data are collected primarily for non-geographical purposes, and is invariably oblique in varying degree to the direct research needs of geographers, as Gregor (1962) has shown for California and Coppock (1955) for parish data in Britain; (ii) we are dependent on the original accuracy of the survey, an accuracy which both Thatcher (1949, pp. 22–35) and Morgenstern (1963) have shown may be surprisingly low, and which is in any case outside our direct control; (iii) data are released in 'bundles' (i.e. administrative areas) which are inconvenient and anachronistic and pose extremely acute problems in mapping and interpretation (Duncan, Cuzzort, and Duncan, 1961). Although there are ways of outflanking some of these problems (Chap. 7.III) and we shall continue to make use of by-product sources for the foreseeable future, there is considerable need to explore the alternative sources of geographical information.

Much of this chapter is concerned with the possibilities of using sampling methods to collect significant information according to our particular research needs. In so far as this implies field collection, this represents a return to a tradition which was a hallmark of nineteenth-century geography and persisted strongly in the Land Utilization Survey in Britain in the 1930's (Board, in Chorley and Haggett, 1965, Chap. X). Less traditional is the possibility of information from theoretical work in which locational conditions are simulated either by mathematical models, by physical models, or by Markovian sequences (Chap. 10.III). Of the two alternative sources, that of fieldwork offers the best immediate solution in that it promises to give, at least when linked to rigorous experimental designs, directly relevant information on the applicability of existing locational models. At the same time it provides data which can be tested, extended, and manipulated in theoretical work.

The whole problem of information in geography is a complex one which has been somewhat clouded by traditional attitudes (e.g. prejudice towards 'complete' rather than sample data) and a tendency to view the problems as being uniquely geographic. Development of information theory over the last twenty years suggests that many of our difficulties are common to most sciences, and we are likely to gain in perspective by viewing them in a more eclectic framework (Abramson, 1963).

2. Definition of geographical populations

A *population* (also sometimes called a *universe*) may be defined as any finite or infinite collection of individual objects (Kendall and Buckland, 1957, p. 222). A geographical population is therefore a collection of objects with some geographical characteristic in common. Thus we might conceive the counties of the coterminous United States as a geographical population, in which there are a finite number (3,074) of individuals. Although the definition of *individuals* in this population gives difficulty (discussed in Chapter 7.I(3)), the definition of populations is an *ad hoc* process which is governed by the research objectives. As Krumbein (1960, p. 349) has argued, once the objects of the study have been defined, the population has been defined.

The vital distinction in most geographical research is between (i) the *target population* which is the conceptual or ultimate total population, and (ii) the *sampled population* which is the actual population from which samples may be drawn (Cochran, Mosteller, and Tukey, 1954). If we wish to test the validity of a locational concept, say the rank-size distribution of cities (Chap. 3.II), our target population about which we wish to generalize or predict may be the world. However, the population that we are in fact able to study is less than this, since for reasons of census shortcomings or political caution, not all countries in the world release appropriate data. Thus Ginsburg (1961), in his *Atlas of economic development*, defined a target population of 140 'countries or equivalent administrative units'. However, for most of his forty-seven indices, the sampled population was only about one hundred countries. Even for population density, the most widely available index, the sampled population (139 countries) fell just short of the target population.

In relatively few research problems are the target and sampled population synonymous. Our knowledge of diffusion waves is as strongly biased by our experience of 'Western' society, as was W. M. Davis's concept of arid cycles of erosion biased by his experience in the southwestern United

States. We must often face the fact that we are dealing with the accessible sub-population only, and '. . . it becomes a matter of [geological] judgement whether the sampled and target populations are nearly enough identical that inferences about the sampled population can be applied without qualification to the target population' (Krumbein, 1960, p. 353).

3. Operational definitions

Definition of the individuals which make up a geographical population poses very complex, but essentially local, difficulties which must be solved by adopting operational definitions. An *operational definition* is a set of arbitrary rules or criteria by which individuals that belong to a population can be clearly recognized. Although general discussions of the problem exist (e.g. Morgenstern, 1963), it may be more helpful to illustrate a specific case. Urban settlements form a typical problem case.

    a. Nature of the problem. Alexander (1963, p. 528) has shown that the concept of an 'urban settlement' varies considerably from country to country: Denmark counts as urban all settlements with 250 or more inhabitants, while Spain and Switzerland count as urban only those with 10,000 or more. For the United States, the Bureau of the Census publish data for four different types of 'urban-like areas'. These are, in rough order of size: (i) the *urban place* which includes all places of 2,500 inhabitants or more; (ii) the *incorporated city* or city of 2,500 inhabitants or more which has a separate political entity; (iii) the *urbanized area* which is centred on one city of 50,000 or more inhabitants and includes the urban fringe around each city; and (iv) the *standard metropolitan area*: this is based on a group of counties containing at least one city of 50,000 or more inhabitants with most of its area non-urban in character.

    These four kinds of areas overlap greatly and are not mutually exclusive. Each gives a different picture of urban land in the United States and each has special value in special circumstances. Indeed, since the historical record for each varies, this frequently determines which type will in fact be used. Data for incorporated cities are in the main available since 1900, while data for standard metropolitan areas was organized after World War II, and urbanized areas only after 1950. For Britain, the problem of city definitions is equally acute and Dickinson (1963, p. 68) has shown, for example, that Liverpool may be either larger or smaller than Manchester depending on how each city is demarcated.

    Davis and his group (International Urban Research, 1959, pp. 6–7) have suggested that there are a number of ways in which the 'natural' city (i.e. the urbanized area) may be misrepresented by the census records; these are shown diagrammatically in Fig. 7.1 in which the 'natural' city is shaded and the statistical units of the census are marked with a solid line.

    The first of these three types is described as the 'underbounded' city in which the statistical boundary is smaller than the urban area, which, in consequence, may be either left without any demarcation between it and surrounding rural districts or divided up among other statistical cities (Fig. 7.1-B). Such underbounded types are common in Australia where large urban areas are commonly divided into municipalities, shires, councils, etc. Thus Sydney proper had a population of only 193,100 in 1955 while the whole Sydney urban area had a population of 1,869,000.

The second type, the 'overbounded' city, is one in which the statistical boundary is larger than the urban area and may contain more than one

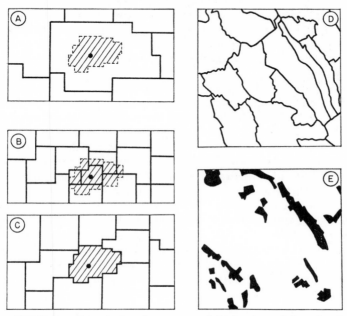

Fig. 7.1. ABC Alternative relations between statistical units and the urbanized area of a city. *D* Civil-parish boundaries in a sample quadrat ($G = 6.6$) of the central Chilterns, southern England. *E* Farmland misclassified by using the boundaries shown in *D*. Source: Coppock, 1960, p. 318.

urban area (Fig. 7.1-A). In the Philippines the political-statistical boundaries of most 'cities' include both huge areas of rural land and towns of various sizes. The third possibility, the 'truebounded' city, where the political and geographical boundaries coincide, is ideal but rare (Fig. 7.1-C). Pakistani cities appear to approach this ideal most nearly.

b. Attempted solutions. The problem of standardizing definitions of cities has not been solved. Among the partial solutions put forward, one of the most complex is that used by the United States Census Bureau in its definitions of Standard Metropolitan Areas (SMA). These they define in terms of (i) density, (ii) function, and (iii) integration (Office of Statistical

Standards, 1958). SMAs must contain at least one city of 50,000 or more inhabitants as a core. To this are added adjacent counties which are 'metropolitan' in character (i.e. they contain 10,000 non-agricultural workers, or 10 per cent of the non-agricultural works of the SMA, or have at least 50 per cent of its population residing in civil divisions with a population density of 150 or more per square mile and contiguous to the central city). In addition, non-agricultural workers must constitute at least two-thirds of the total employed population of the county. To these stringent rules are added criteria of integration between the central-city county and outlying counties, based on percentage of commuting (e.g. 15 per cent of workers in the outlying county must work in the central-city county) and telephone communication (calls per month to central-city county at least four times that of the number of the subscribers in the outlying county).

Although even with these rules, exceptions had to be made (e.g. for New England, with its historically distinct 'town system'), this careful attempt by the United States Census Bureau has placed the problem of city definition on a new level. It has led directly to work such as that of the International Urban Research group at Berkeley which has produced the most complete tally of world cities on a comparable basis yet achieved. Their definition of a 'metropolitan area' runs to twelve closely argued pages (including two on 'hard cases') (International Urban Research, 1959, pp. 20–32).

Understandably, other and less complex solutions have been proposed. Grytzell (1963) has used a 'sliding-scale' of population density, illustrating his method of demarcation for five major cities (New York, London, Paris, Stockholm, and Copenhagen). He argues that fixed population densities obscure important regional variations in the density of urban areas, and that it is the relative density of the city which distinguishes it from surrounding areas.

While the definition problem has been discussed here with reference to urban areas, it extends to all geographical populations. Overlap of alternative definitions of a city has similarities to the farm boundary/parish boundary problem discussed by Coppock (1955) and illustrated for the Chiltern area of southern England. Here, as Fig. 7.1-D suggests, the outline of the areal unit for which agricultural statistics appear to be collected (i.e. the parish) and the areal unit to which they in fact relate (i.e. the land belonging to *farms located in that parish*) may show considerable divergence. As a result, a significant proportion of the farmland lies outside the boundaries for which it has been mapped (Fig. 7.1-E).

II. COVERAGE PROBLEMS

The coverage problem is simple and immediate. The earth's surface is so staggeringly large that, even if we caricature the problem, each of the geographical profession's 3,000 nominal practitioners (Meynen, 1960) might be assigned an area of some five thousand square miles for individual study. If we agree with Hartshorne, that the purpose of geography is '. . . to provide accurate, orderly, and rational description and interpretation of the variable character of the earth surface' (Hartshorne, 1959, p. 21) then this is a gross measure of the magnitude of the task we set ourselves.

This can hardly be regarded as a new problem. At least from the time of Eratosthenes the size of the problem has been apparent and it may well be that our predecessors were more keenly aware of its importance. Many a doubtful isopleth now strays self-importantly across areas that our more honest forbears might have filled with heraldic doodles labelled 'Terra Incognita'. There are broadly two ways in which the problem may be overcome: (i) indirectly by the employment of sampling methods, and (ii) directly by increasing the rate of data accumulation.

1. Indirect solution: sampling

Sample studies have long been used in both research and teaching in geography. Platt (1942, 1959) was acutely aware of the '. . . old and stubborn dilemma of trying to comprehend large regions while seeing at once only a small area' (1942, p. 3) and he skilfully used sample field studies to build up an outstandingly clear series of pictures of the regions of Latin America. Similarly Highsmith (Highsmith, Heintzelman, Jensen, Rudd, and Tschirley, 1961) has used a world-wide selection of sample studies as the basis for an extremely useful teaching manual in economic geography.

There is an important difference, however, between these attempts to use sampling to circumvent the coverage problem, and the way in which sampling is now being used in research. This essential difference is between *purposive* and *probability* sampling. In purposive or 'hunch' sampling, individuals are selected which are thought to be typical of the population as a whole; thus Platt (1942) chooses one *fazenda* as representative of the São Paulo coffee belt. The validity of the choice depends on the skill of the selector, and is usually open to debate. In probability sampling (Table 7.2) the samples are drawn on the basis of rigorous mathematical theory and, once the design is adopted, individuals are drawn from the population by established rules. Only samples of the wide range of sampling designs are described here; there are excellent general surveys by Cochran (1953), and Yates (1960), and an extremely valuable short review of sampling concepts by Cochran, Mosteller, and Tukey (1954).

a. Size of sample. The larger our sample, the more likely it is to give an accurate impression of the population from which it is drawn. Fig. 7.2 shows this relationship to be true for two random samples of the proportion of woodland in the English Midlands (Haggett, 1963, p. 112); as sample size increases (measured on the *x*-axis of the graph), so the cumulative sample mean (*y*-axis), after some initial fluctuation, settles around the population mean as bounded by the broken lines. The relationship is not, however, simple or linear; accuracy appears to increase sharply at

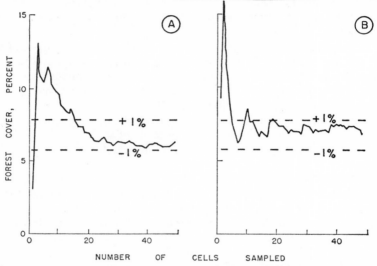

Fig. 7.2. Improvement in accuracy of stratified random samples with increase in the number of observations. Source: Haggett, 1963, p. 112.

first as sample size is increased, but then more slowly with subsequent increases, almost in the manner of a law of diminishing returns.

The form of the relationship between sample size and accuracy is in fact known for alternative sampling designs, implying that it is possible to estimate how large a sample we are likely to need from the information actually collected during the sample survey. This means that, given a limited budget, the probable accuracy of any sample survey can be estimated; or, vice versa, given a fixed limit of accuracy, the necessary time-cost estimates can be made. For random sampling there is a simple relationship, other things being equal, where the random sampling error is proportional to the square root of the number of observations. The importance of the *square-root* relationship indicates therefore that doubling the number of observations will not double the accuracy: if the accuracy of a given observation based on twenty-five observations is ten units, the accuracy based on fifty will not be five units.

Berry (1962) has reproduced a chart (Fig. 7.3) which shows this relationship very clearly. This chart plots the proportion of a sample with a given characteristic (on the *x*-axis) against the number of observations

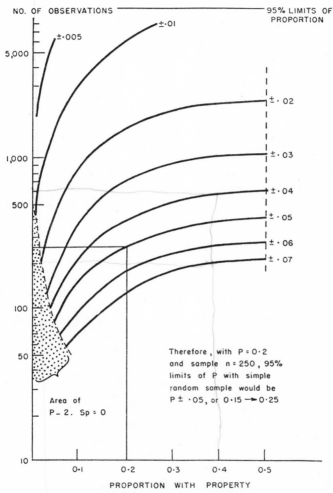

Fig. 7.3. Ninety-five per cent limits of proportions for simple random sample.
Source: Berry, 1962, p. 3.

in the sample (on the *y*-axis). Values on the *y*-axis are plotted logarithmically. Let us assume that a random sample of 200 observations of land use have been taken, and eighty of them are found to be of woodland. We can express the proportion of woodland as 80/200 or $P = 0.40$ on Fig. 7.3.

Superimposed on this graph are a set of curved lines. Each line represents a 95 per cent confidence limit of a proportion which runs from ±0·005 through to ±0·07. With the estimated 40 per cent woodland based on 200 random observations our two axes meet on the ±0·07 line. This means that the true value of the woodland has a 95 per cent chance of being between 0·33 and 0·47. There is also of course a small chance, 5 per cent, that it lies outside these limits.

By increasing the number of observations, those confidence limits will creep inwards. For example, with a sample of 600 observations, the limits are plus or minus 0·04, and with 2,000 observations plus or minus 0·02. This relationship is clearly shown on the graph by extending a line upwards over an increasing number of observations, and by noting its intersection with the curved confidence limits.

There is of course a danger in estimating proportions where either (i) the sample size is too small, or (ii) the estimated proportion is too small. In Fig. 7.3 the shaded area in the lower left section of the graph shows the danger area (again for the 95 per cent confidence limit) where the lower confidence limit drops *below* zero. Since this is an impossibility (i.e. we cannot conceive any area with less than zero woodland) the number of observations must be increased or a lower confidence level accepted. As Cochran (1953) has pointed out, the use of random sampling for determining the proportion of rare characteristics (for example, built-up areas in a land-use survey of a rural district) is like looking for a needle in a haystack. Here, other and more complex sampling procedures may be more appropriate.

b. Problems of sample design. The design of a sampling plan in locational research hangs largely on the type of distribution being investigated. A sample survey of traffic movements along a network of rural roads will demand a totally different plan from a sample survey of industrial plants being established in a large city. Thus, if we compare Birch (1950) on farm mapping in the Isle of Man, and King (1961) on settlement spacing in the United States, we find that though both used probability sampling methods their designs were quite different. Yates (1960, pp. 20–101) has a very full discussion of the practical considerations that affect sample design over a very wide range of geographical distributions.

Treatment here is restricted to a single but very important type of locational distribution, i.e. land use. This is a distribution which we can regard as continuous and which has tended to be studied in the past by direct and complete survey, rather than by sampling. Various types of sampling design have been evolved for this kind of distribution (Table 7.2): four of them—simple random sampling, stratified sampling, systematic sampling, and stratified systematic unaligned sampling—are discussed here. Two others—nested or multistage sampling and multifactor sampling —are discussed in later chapters (9.III(2a) and 10.II(4)). The treatment

Table 7.2. A model of sampling designs

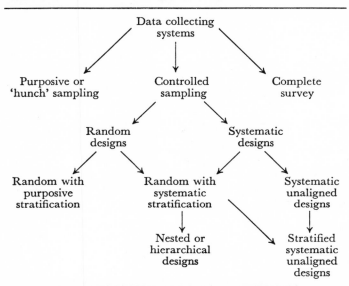

Source: Haggett. In Chorley and Haggett, 1965-A, p. 166.

here is based on that of Krumbein (1960), Berry (1962), and Quenouille (1949).

(i) In *simple random sampling* a sample of N individuals is drawn from the areal population at a series of random co-ordinates. The two axes of the area are numbered and a location is chosen by a pair of random co-ordinates. For example, the random numbers ninety-eight and twenty-six would give a location ninety-eight units north by twenty-six units east; or a grid reference of 9826 in terms of a standard reference system. Fig. 7.4 shows the location of twenty-four points drawn by simple random sampling for a hypothetical study area.

(ii) In *stratified sampling* the study area is divided into natural segments (such as cropland and woodland) and the individuals in the sample are drawn independently from each segment. Within each segment the location of the points is determined by the same randomization procedure as in simple random sampling. Fig. 7.4-B shows such a sample for twenty-four points. In this case the number of individuals has in each segment been made proportional to its area; sixteen points in the left-hand segment (two-thirds of the area) and eight points in the right-hand segment (one-third of the area). This method has been used frequently in geographical research, notably by Wood (1955) in a study of land use in eastern Wisconsin, United States.

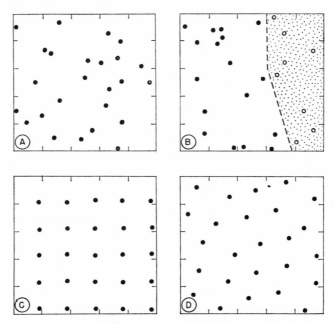

Fig. 7.4. Alternative sampling designs: random (*A*), stratified random (*B*), systematic (*C*), and stratified systematic unaligned sample (*D*). Sources: Krumbein, 1960, p. 361; Berry, 1962, p. 7.

(iii) In *systematic sampling* a grid of equally spaced locations is defined with one individual at each location. Fig. 7.4-c shows a simple case for twenty-five individuals. Here the grid is square and at right angles to the sides of the study area. The origin of the grid is decided by the randomization of the original grid point.

(iv) A *stratified systematic unaligned sample* (Fig. 7.4-d) is a composite design derived from the preceding sampling designs by Berry (1962, p. 7) with the theoretical advantages of (*a*) randomization, and (*b*) stratification, together with the useful aspects of (*c*) systematic samples. By avoiding alignment of the sample points, it also avoids the possibility of error caused by periodicities in the phenomena. Its construction is shown in Fig. 7.5 where the study area is systematically divided into a regular checkerboard of sub-areas. Beginning with the corner sub-area, a point, I, is determined by random numbers (Fig. 7.5-a), the *x*- and *y*-axes of the sub-area being numbered zero to nine so that a random number between zero and ninety-nine gives a co-ordinate position with respect to both axes. Fig. 7.5-b shows the completion of the lower row of the plan: the *x* co-ordinate being kept constant all along the row, but the *y* co-ordinate varied from a random-numbers table. As these numbers, 2, 9, 8 . . ., are drawn, the points move up and down with respect to the y-axis but remain in the same position with respect to the x-axis. Fig. 7.5-c shows the completion of the left-hand column where the same principle is followed, but here it is the y co-ordinate which remains fixed and the x co-ordinate which alters. When both the first row and column are completed, a new corner point must be generated, point II. As Fig. 7.5-D shows, its location is determined from the points drawn in the previous stage. The random x co-ordinate of point X_1 and the random y co-ordinate of point Y_1 are combined to locate point II. This point is then the starting point for a new row and a new column, which in their turn, are used to generate a new corner point, point III. This process continues until all columns and rows are full. Open circles in Fig. 7.5-D show the completed quadrangle.

Berry (1962, pp. 10–11) has carried out field testing of the alternative patterns to determine their relative efficiency in land-use sampling. For a ten square mile area (Coon Creek) he successively tested stratified systematic unaligned samples (randomly oriented with respect to each other), and stratified random samples against the expected variance of a simple

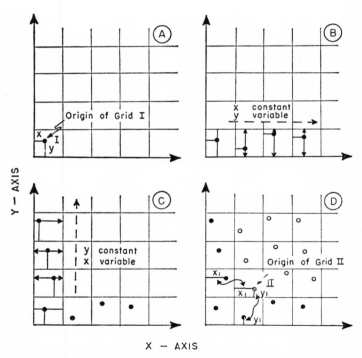

Fig. 7.5. Stages in the generation of a stratified systematic unaligned sample.
Source: Berry, 1962, p. 7.

random sample. The results (Table 7.3) show the high relative efficiency
of the stratified systematic sample. Its margin over the random sample is
21·5 and over the stratified random sample 5·6.

Table 7.3. Comparative efficiency of sampling designs

Field areas:	Coon Creek	Montfort
Characteristic of field areas:		
Area in square miles	10	46
Pattern under investigation	Woodland	Cultivated land
Proportion of total area	40·8%	55·4%
Number of sample points	660	184
Relative efficiency of sampling designs (variance):		
Simple random sample (expected)	3·66	13·4
Stratified random sample (observed)	0·96	11·3
Systematic sample (observed)	—	12·8
Stratified systematic unaligned (observed)	0·17	10·2

Source: Berry, 1962, pp. 10–11.

Comparative tests were extended to a second area of about forty-five
square miles (Montfort). Here the differences were less impressive but the
same order of efficiency was maintained: (i) stratified systematic unaligned, (ii) stratified random, (iii) simple random. Differences in the
magnitude of the results in the two areas may well be linked to the different
type of areal pattern analysed—woodland in large blocks in the Coon
Creek cases and cultivated land in small blocks in the Montfort case.
Haggett and Board (1964) have shown that the accuracy of sample-based
estimates of land-use areas varies with both the proportion of the area
covered by the phenomena under survey and its fragmentation, and this
factor might well have operated in Berry's case.

c. Alternative sampling units. In this discussion of alternative sampling
designs, a *point* sampling unit has been assumed. Two other geometrical
forms are equally applicable—the area sampling unit or *quadrat*, and the
linear sampling unit or *transect*. Both transects and quadrats have traditionally been used in qualitative geographic studies, notably by Platt
(1959), but their main development in field sampling has been in botany.
Quadrats, the most common form of sampling unit in botany, are usually
square in shape and vary in size from a few centimetres to several metres.
As Fig. 7.6 shows, this variation in quadrat size has had a notorious effect
on the results obtained (Kershaw, 1964, p. 30), but fluctuations in the
result may be harnessed to yield important information about the scale of
the pattern being investigated (Greig-Smith, 1964, pp. 54–93). Similar
techniques in the breakdown of geographical patterns into scale components are discussed in Chapter 9.III(1).

Haggett (1963) compared the efficiency of point, quadrat, and transect methods in determining the proportion of woodland cover from Ordnance Survey maps for the West Midlands. In this area of low woodland cover

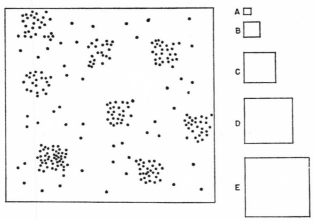

Fig. 7.6. Relations between sampling quadrats and pattern. Sampling with smaller quadrats (*A* and *B*) suggests slight clustering, with intermediate quadrat (*C*) strong clustering, and with large quadrats (*D* and *E*) regularity. Source: Kershaw, 1964, p. 104.

(about 5 per cent of the land area), the accuracy of the transect method (i.e. measuring the length of intercepts along traverse lines) was considerably higher than the other two. Further investigation of sampling from traverse lines on both maps and in the field seems justified.

2. Direct solution: extended coverage

More information is available about the earth's surface today than at any previous time. The trickle of maps and census reports available at the beginning of the century has now risen to a torrent which seems to be rising logarithmically with succeeding decades. Increases have not, however, been even so that regional contrasts in information are tending to become more acute. Indeed Berry (in Ginsburg, 1961, p. 110) has shown that a poor standard of data is one of the concomitants of under-development, so that there appears to be a direct relationship between economic development and information. Even for population density, the evidence for Brazil (Fig. 2.15) suggests that densely peopled areas have a fine mesh of subdivisions for which data is released compared to the broad mesh of the relatively empty areas.

Comparisons over time also run into difficulties. The very fact of improving information may make comparisons with earlier periods invalid. Fig. 2.13 shows the successive subdivision of an area of rapid population increase over successive thirty-year time periods. Although far more is known in detail about the area in the final period (1960) than in the initial period (1870), the degree of *comparable* detail is controlled by the largest areal denominator, i.e. the 1870 period. Dickinson (1963) has illustrated similar problems of subdivision and boundary change in England and Wales, while Hall (1962) has noted the problems in tracing the industrial growth of London from census data. For map coverage, Langbein and Hoyt (1959) have shown that even for the United States there are some curious lacunae in both coverage and age with the poorly mapped areas being revised rather less frequently; Fig. 7.7 shows the relative progress in mapping that country.

A vitally important supplement to such 'archival' data in maps and

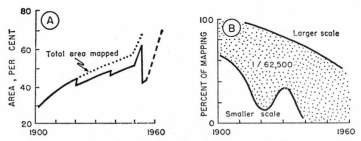

Fig. 7.7. Mapping progress in the United States, 1900–60, showing re-assessment of total area mapped on scale and age grounds (*A*) and changing scales of map production (*B*). Source: Langbein and Hoyt, 1952, p. 56.

censuses is the growth of air-photo coverage. Although this has a history going back to at least 1858, the effect of World War II and the 'cold war' that followed has been virtually to complete and/or revise the air-photo coverage of the whole earth's surface. Rapid improvements have been made in both lens and camera, in vehicles (through to U2's and satellites) (Colwell, 1960), in mapping with electronic plotters, and in interpretation with electronic scanners (Latham, 1963). More revolutionary changes are foreshadowed in 'completely automated terrain-sensing systems' in which information about the earth's surface may be recorded by satellite, relayed back to base, and made available on magnetic tape (Lopik, 1962). It seems possible that continuous recording of certain simple terrain information (e.g. ice distribution) may replace discontinuous mapping within the foreseeable future.

III. IRREGULAR COLLECTING AREAS

In Chapter 2.III(2) something was seen of the great variety in both size and shape of *territories*. Whether as states, counties, or parishes, these territories are the fundamental units for which most statistical data are collected and published, and they form the most common population we have to analyse in locational research (Fig. 7.8-A, B). It is true that some countries, notably Sweden, are investigating the possibilities of recording population data by *xy* grid co-ordinates (Hägerstrand, 1955), and that

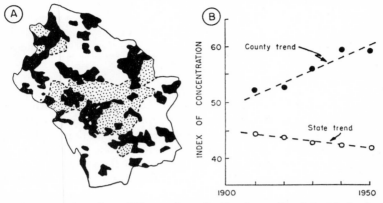

Fig. 7.8. Contrast based on different sizes of collecting units. *A* Arable land with over 50 per cent of farm area in the Amersham district, southern England (*G* = 6·6), as plotted by farms (*black*) and parishes (*stipple*). *B* Indices of population concentration for the United States by counties and states. Sources: Coppock, 1960, p. 321; Duncan, Cuzzort, and Duncan, 1961, p. 86.

more geographers are collecting their data by controlled sampling methods (as described in Chapter 7.II). Nevertheless, a very high proportion of essential locational data is likely to be available for territorial units only, at least for the next few decades. Therefore in this section we look at (1) the implications of these irregular collecting areas for locational analysis, and (2) the ways in which observations based on them may be standardized.

1. Distortion of locational measurements

a. Impact on regional comparison. The clearest illustration of the yoking of locational observations to the characteristics of the collecting area arises with measurements of density. Duncan studied an apparently simple question: what is the density of population in an area of downtown Chicago centred on 31st Street and Indiana Avenue? (Duncan *et al.*, 1961, p. 35). If the 'immediate vicinity' is defined by a census tract of 0·024 square miles, the answer is 91,300 people per square mile. However, by widening the term vicinity to include the local community area of about one and a half square miles the population density is halved. Clearly there is an inescapable indeterminacy about density ratios dependent on variable collecting units. For comparable densities, e.g. comparisons between cities, the situation becomes still more difficult. As Table 7.4 shows, Chicago may

Table 7.4. Urban population densities under alternative census boundaries

Areal definition	Chicago (C)* (inhab./sq. ml.)	Detroit (D)* (inhab./sq. ml.)	Ratio (D/C)
City	17,450	13,249	0·76
Urbanized area	7,713	6,734	0·86
Standard metropolitan area	1,519	1,535	1·01

Source: Duncan, Cuzzort, and Duncan, 1961, pp. 35–6.
* 1950.

be either more or less densely populated than Detroit depending on the areal definition used for the two cities. Still more striking contrasts are shown with comparisons over time where the population of the United States appears to be becoming more concentrated on the evidence of the counties, but more dispersed on the evidence of the states (Fig. 7.8-B).

Robinson (1956) makes clear the problem inherent in density comparisons with a simple hypothetical example. In Fig. 7.9 the regions are

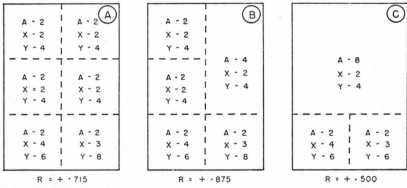

Fig. 7.9. Sample areas for correlation analysis showing impact of boundary changes on correlation coefficients (*R*). Source: Robinson, 1956, p. 234.

identical: they have the same area and the same distribution of variables *x* and *y*, and differ only in the extent to which they are subdivided; they range from six equal-sized divisions in the first case to three divisions of unequal size in the third case. Using the values for *x* and *y*, the coefficient of correlation, *r* (Kendall and Buckland, 1957, p. 67), is computed for each of the three regions giving values of +0·715 (Fig. 7.9-A), +0·875 (Fig. 7.9-B), and +0·500 (Fig. 7.9-C). Clearly the exact value of the coefficient varies with the extent of subdivision, notwithstanding the identical distribution of *x* and *y* in the three regions.

Similar difficulties arise with comparison of movements. For example Table 7.5 shows the striking differences between Belgium and the Nether-

---

Table 7.5. Apparent contrasts in commuting

Country:	Belgium (1947)	Netherlands (1947)
Commuters, percentage	40·0	15·2
Administrative unit, mean size in hectares*	1,880	6,670

Source: Chisholm, 1960, p. 187.
   * Weighted according to inhabitants in each administrative unit.

---

lands in the proportion of out-commuters in 1947 (Chisholm, 1960, p. 187). The difference is, at first sight, striking. But when (i) the subdivisions on which the figures are calculated and (ii) the census definition of a commuter are considered, the differences begin to look less conclusive. The Dutch basic unit for the calculations, the *Gemeente*, had an area on average three times as great as the Belgian unit, the *Commune*. Moreover, because of the census definition of a commuter (i.e. a worker moving outside the territorial unit in which he resides), the smaller the collecting unit the greater the apparent amount of commuting.

Unless great care is taken such 'mirage' effects are likely to become more common as more quantitative studies are made by geographers using secondary statistical sources. Indeed, one statistician, M. G. Kendall, has warned that with certain coefficients of geographical association (Chap. 8.II(1b)) we can get any coefficient we choose by juggling with the collecting boundaries (Florence, 1944, p. 113). It is an open question whether detailed medical maps (e.g. Murray, 1962) in which mortality indices are most carefully standardized for age and sex should not equally well be standardized for the size of the collecting areas for which they are computed. Certainly we need to be reassured that some of the apparently 'unhealthy' areas, representing small pockets of disease in Lancashire and Yorkshire, owe nothing to the fragmented system of local government areas.

b. Extent of the variation. The degree to which irregular collecting areas distort regional comparisons is directly related to their variability. McCarty (McCarty, Hook, and Knos, 1956, pp. 8–19) examined variations between the two main statistical areas in the continental United States (i.e. states and counties). The results are summarized in Table 7.6. For states, the range was from Texas with 71,289 square miles to Rhode Island with 289 square miles, with considerable bunching of the area values about the mean area of some 61,000 square miles. County values were obtained by (i) arranging states alphabetically, (ii) numbering all 3,074 counties

Table 7.6. Size and variability of administrative subdivisions*

Administrative subdivision:	Major (state)	Minor (county)
Number of subdivisions	48	100†
Area parameters in square miles:		
Arithmetic mean	60,757	1,356
Standard deviation	46,861	2,486
Coefficient of variation	67%	183%
Mean separation distance, miles	118	16

Source: McCarty, Hook, and Knos, 1956, pp. 13–15.
* United States, 1940.   † Random sample.

serially, and (iii) drawing one hundred counties by random numbers. Within this sample the variation between the largest and smallest was less extreme than in the case of states; San Bernardino county, California (20,160 square miles), is only about two hundred times the size of the smallest, Ohio county, West Virginia (109 square miles). The comparable ratio for states is nearer three hundred. On the other hand the counties are less strongly grouped around the mean value and the coefficient of variation is over twice as great.

By using the values for areal collecting units in correlation studies, *areas* may often be treated as *points*. Thus we may use county data for one variable, x (e.g. steel mills), and for a second variable, y (e.g. automobile plants), and relate them through a series of statistical tests (Chap. 10.II). It is relevant therefore to attempt to measure the degree of 'shrinkage' that is entailed in regarding areas as points.

A tentative measure of shrinkage was evolved by McCarty who assumed that all his areal units were square. From this assumption it is possible to prove that the average distance between all possible pairs of points within a square figure is given by the expression $d = 0.52\sqrt{A}$ where d is the average separation distance and A the area unit (McCarty, *et al.*, 1956, p. 14). In other words distance is 0.52 times one side of the square. Table 7.6 summarizes the findings derived from applying this formula to the United States. It suggests that we can regard states as points if we are prepared to accept the fact that our hypothetical steel mills and automobile plants will be about 120 miles apart on average and still be considered to be identical. For counties the degree of tolerance is less, around sixteen miles.

Chisholm (1960) has used an alternative type of separation index based for studies of movement to work in northwestern Europe. If the area of a subdivision is compared to a circle then its diameter, d, can be given as

$d = 2\sqrt{A/\pi}$ where A is the area of the subdivision. He shows for each of the seven *Länder* of West Germany that the mean diameter of their subdivisions (*Gemeinde*) varies from only 3·1 to 4·3 kilometres, but that this conceals more considerable variations. For one *Land*, Schleswig-Holstein, diameters of individual subdivisions varied from three to sixteen kilometres.

2. Standardization of collecting areas

a. Area-weighting solutions. Dangers in leaving the size of census areas out of account in correlation studies have led both Robinson (1956) and Thompson (1957) to suggest that observations should be weighted for the size of the area for which they are collected. Thus Robinson (1956, p. 236) would replace the conventional formula for the standard deviation, σ, by

$$\sigma = \sqrt{\{(\Sigma\, X^2)/N\} - (\Sigma\, X/N)^2}$$

with one in which the areas, A, are directly taken account, i.e.

$$\sigma_A = \sqrt{\{(\Sigma\, AX^2)/\Sigma A\} - (\Sigma\, AX/\Sigma A)^2}$$

To support this point cases are worked through to show that standard results may be obtained regardless of the subdivision structure. Using a weighted formula for the correlation coefficient, Robinson derived identical values for +0·715 for r in each of the three regions in Fig. 7.9.

On the face of it this would appear to be the ideal solution. Certainly when averages, ratios, or densities are being measured in each subdivision it provides reliable area-correction for the simple reason that it *removes* area from the values: patently if we take an index like population density per square mile and multiply it by an area-weighting factor (i.e. square miles) we are back where we started with population. However, as Duncan points out (Duncan *et al.*, 1961, p. 47), it is less clear how the area weights should be used when the measurements are not derived from area ratios.

b. Aggregation solutions. Where the collecting units are many and irregular, a fairly simple counter-measure is to group them into fewer but more regular areas. Such a technique was adopted by Coppock (1960) in a study of parish records in the Chilterns. Here not only were parishes irregular in shape and size and running orthogonally across the major geological boundaries, but the farms on which the data was collected themselves had land outside the parishes for which their acreages were recorded. Grouping parishes in this case allowed both more regular mapping units and reduced the farm overlap problem (Fig. 7.1-D) since, with larger units, the farm area outside the combined parish boundaries was proportionally much lower. There are some cases however (notably with the strip parishes of the Chilterns which run orthogonally across major physiographic zones) where bundling together yields very little advantage.

In each case the problem is to gain the maximum uniformity in collecting areas, while, at the same time, preserving as much of the original data as possible. Haggett (1964) has suggested that the coefficient of variation (Kendall and Buckland, 1957, p. 313) may be used as an indication of both loss of detail and of gains in uniformity, and that only when the latter exceeds the former is the loss of detail justified. The coefficient of variation is given by the standard deviation (s) of a distribution divided by the arithmetic mean ($\bar{x}$) and multiplied by 100. Table 7.7

Table 7.7. Aggregation of administrative units*

Areal unit:	County (municipio)	Super-county
Characteristics:		
Number of units	126	24
Mean area, sq. miles	133	699
Coefficient of variation	74·20%	7·91%

Source: Haggett, 1964, p. 373.
* Southeast Brazil, 1950.

shows a case in point in a regression analysis of county data in southeastern Brazil. Here the original 126 counties were grouped into twenty-four 'super-counties' but the 82 per cent loss in detail was less than the 89 per cent gain in uniformity as measured by comparisons in the coefficient of variation. Where units are in any case very regular, as with county units in the American Middle West (Weaver, 1956), the method is hardly ustified.

Aggregation and testing will be very much speeded up when computer programmes are developed for rapidly checking all possible number of ways in which contiguous units can be combined and recombined. In view of the enormously large number of possible combinations it is uncertain that the combinations used so far are the optimum ones in terms of uniformity of size.

c. Elimination solutions. Problems of the unevenness of areal statistical units might be remedied by eliminating the aberrant areas. As Table 7.8

Table 7.8. Elimination solution to irregular-areas problem*

Number of counties eliminated	0	1	4
Coefficient of variation of remaining counties	183	130	119

Source: McCarty, Hook, and Knos, 1956, p. 13.
* United States: sample of 100 counties.

demonstrates, the coefficient of variation for McCarty's 100-county sample (McCarty *et al.*, 1956, p. 13) was reduced by elimination of the largest county, San Bernardino county, California. When the four largest counties (all having areas of more than 500 square miles) were removed, the remaining 96-county sample showed a coefficient of variation of only 119. These results suggest that material improvements can be made by eliminating large aberrant areas; but that the trend (so far as McCarty's results go) is one of diminishing returns. In other words the gains to be made from this method fall off rather rapidly once outstanding values have

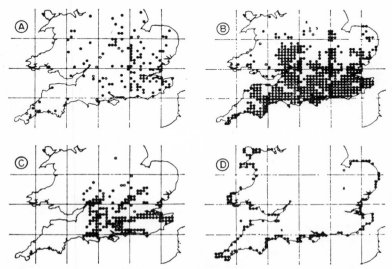

Fig. 7.10. Computer maps of distribution of four plant species by 10 × 10 kilometre quadrats in southern England (*G = 3·8*). Source: Perring and Walters, 1962.

been removed. How far the gains from standardization are matched by the losses of sample size is a matter for individual decision.

    d. Grid-type solutions. One difficulty in dealing with aggregated collecting areas is that they are themselves highly irregular in shape if not in size. Attempts have therefore been made to collect information not in areal units but in regular frames or grids.

    An outstanding example of this type of work is the *Atlas of the British Flora* (Perring and Walters, 1962), where field data on the occurrence of British vascular plants were collected for the 100 square kilometre grid-squares of the British National Grid System. This grid system was also used by Johnson (1958) in a study of the location of factory population in the West Midlands. Grid systems are extremely well adapted for mapping and the flora maps (Fig. 7.10) were all mechanically tabulated (Walters, 1957). This has very considerable merit in an era where more maps are being produced directly from punched-tape data (Tobler, 1959) and allows a very ready comparison between the original data and the distribution of controlling factors. It also allows micro-analysis by breaking down the original squares into smaller ones or macro-analysis by combining such squares into larger units on the lines of nested sampling discussed in Chapter 9.II(3).

In both examples cited, data were either collected on a regular grid pattern or were precisely located and could therefore be assigned to a grid. Where data only exist for irregular administrative areas the transfer to a grid is more complex. Robinson, Lindberg, and Brinkman (1961, p. 214) used a regular hexagonal grid in a study of population trends in the Great Plains of the United States (Fig. 7.11). County data were transferred to the grid by measuring how much of the area of each hexagon was contributed by any one county, and multiplying this share by the population

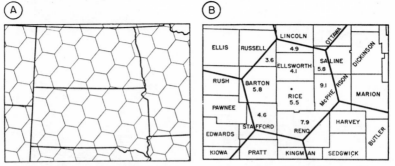

Fig. 7.11. A Hexagonal grid used in northern Great Plains, United States $(G = 2 \cdot 9)$. *B* Detail of the grid in central Kansas $(G = 4 \cdot 4)$ showing relation of the grid to county boundaries. Source: Robinson, Lindberg, and Brinkman, 1961, p. 214.

density of the county. The sum of all the county parts gave the average value for the hexagonal unit.

Fig. 7.11-B shows how the hexagon centred in Rice county, Kansas, includes the whole of that county and the adjoining Ellsworth county. It also includes parts of another seven adjacent counties. By assuming that the county averages for rural farm population (the figures shown on the map) exist uniformly throughout the county, this value could be multiplied by a proportion equal to the portion of the hexagon's area that the county contributed. For example McPherson county has a density of 9·1 per square mile and makes up 0·12 of the hexagon's area: its contribution to the resultant density is thus 9·1 × 0·12 or 1·09. The county products were summed to give a density for the whole hexagon of 5·94 (Table 7.9).

This principle was first used by Thiessen in 1911 for calculating the average rainfall over watersheds and its accuracy clearly hinges on two principles: (i) the degree to which population density (or any similar

Table 7.9. Computation of mean population density for hexagon*

Indices:	Rural farm population density (a)	Proportion of hexagon (b)	Product (ab)
County:			
Rice	5·5	0·17	0·93
Ellsworth	4·1	0·17	0·70
Reno	7·9	0·16	1·26
Barton	5·8	0·13	0·75
Stafford	4·6	0·12	0·55
McPherson	9·1	0·12	1·09
Saline	5·8	0·06	0·35
Lincoln	4·9	0·04	0·20
Russell	3·6	0·03	0·11
Total	—	1·00	5·94

Source: Robinson, Lindberg, and Brinkman, 1961, p. 214.
* Centre of hexagon in Rice county, central Kansas, United States, 1950.

measure) can logically be regarded as uniform over the county, and (ii) the number of counties which make up the regular hexagonal unit. Where each hexagon contains a number of undivided counties the assumptions under (i) become less limiting as the 'split' counties contribute less to the total value. Again the problem is one of optimizing, possibly through linear programming, both the reliability of each grid-unit (by increasing the hexagon size) and the number of such grid-units (by decreasing the hexagon size).

e. Grid-free solutions. Clearly the foregoing methods (aggregation, elimination, and grid-type solutions) must involve some loss in detail in that the revised units are fewer than the original. Attention has recently been directed to the problem of how generalized maps can be made which retain *all* the original control points. This problem first came to light through geophysical problems, e.g. through meteorology, where general weather patterns have to be mapped from irregular and often highly localized weather recording stations (Holloway, 1958), and through petroleum prospecting where basin and facies characteristics may have to be mapped from irregular well and bore records. Krumbein (1959) has illustrated how computers may be used to derive an algebraic formula which gives the average surface which 'fits' the irregular control points best. This 'best-fit' polynomial surface uses all the available records, and builds them into a generalized picture, and is of particular importance where there are gaps in the areal spread of records; e.g. it has been used by Whitten (1959) to fill in the 'ghost stratigraphy' of missing crystalline areas. Its potentialities for human geography are enormous (Chorley and Haggett, 1965-B), in that generalized surfaces of population density, etc., might be computed from a very irregular distribution of 'control points', i.e. the centres of gravity (*centroids*) of the irregular collecting areas. Applications of this type of analysis are illustrated in Chapter 9.II(4).

I. DESCRIPTION OF ABSOLUTE LOCATION: MAPPING SYSTEMS. 1. *Levels of measurement and mapping*. 2. *Single-component maps: isarithmic surfaces*. a. Number of contours. b. Spacing of contours. c. Arrangement of control points. 3. *Multicomponent maps*. a. Percentage data: facies mapping. b. Percentage data: combination mapping. c. Component standardization. d. Principal-component analysis. 4. *Problems of conventional map description*. a. Maps as data-storage systems. b. Alternative data-storage systems: machine mapping.

II. DESCRIPTION OF RELATIVE LOCATION: STATISTICAL INDICES. 1. *Contiguous areas*. a. Descriptions of shape. b. Descriptions of centrality and dispersion. 2. *Points and discontinuous areas*. a. Nearest-neighbour analysis. b. Indices of geographical association. 3. *Linear networks*. a. Dimensional analysis. b. Topological measures based on graph theory.

We consider in this chapter some of the methods that are used to describe accurately and briefly the locational patterns revealed by data collection. Consideration is first given to the traditional method of geographical description, mapping, in which the essential element of absolute location is retained. Alternatively absolute location may be relaxed so that statistical methods may be substituted and the emphasis changed to relative location, i.e. the relation of the individual parts of the pattern to the whole. Statistical analysis varies with the geometrical nature of the pattern —point, area, or line—and these are examined separately.

I. DESCRIPTION OF ABSOLUTE LOCATION: MAPPING SYSTEMS

One of the most convenient and commonly used methods for portraying the absolute location of data is through one of the conventional mapping systems. Indeed, maps and their study are so central to training in geography at school and university, that any attempt to compress their important role into part of a chapter must be presumptuous. There are, however, a number of excellent reviews of mapping systems: those by Robinson (1960) and by Schmid and MacCannell (1955) are recommended. Here we review some of the difficulties in using conventional maps to describe locational patterns, notably those which stem from the levels of measurement of the original data, from the number of items that are to be shown on the map, and from the familiar problems of scale and projection.

1. Levels of measurement and mapping

The types of maps that geographers can draw are directly controlled by the level of the measurements that they can collect. The notion of 'levels of measurement' is one that has fundamental applications in statistics (see Table 10.5), but its importance in mapping has been generally overlooked. Basically, the theory of measurement states that there are four scales—the nominal, ordinal, interval, and ratio scales—with radically different properties (Siegel, 1956, pp. 21–30).

Measurement is at its weakest at the *nominal* (or classificatory) level where numbers or symbols are used to identify an object. When we identify a piece of country as 'woodland', we are using a symbol to represent a type of land use. The only formal property of members of such a class is *equivalence* (=) and the range of cartographic operations we can perform is very limited; the nominal map is commonly only a mosaic of differently coloured or shaded areas in which each shade represents a definite class.

At the *ordinal* (or ranking) scale of measurement, numbers or symbols are used both to identify objects and to describe their relations to other objects. When we identify a 'Class B road' in Britain, we are using a symbol not only to identify a class of road, but we are putting it in some kind of relationship to other roads which are higher (e.g. 'Motorways' and 'Class A roads') or lower (e.g. minor roads) on our scale. The formal difference between the ordinal and the previous scale is that it not only has (i) equivalence (=) but also (ii) the relation 'greater than' or 'less than' (> or <). Ordinal scales are common in mapping conventions where we use symbols of different sizes to indicate settlements on a size scale (e.g. city–town–village–hamlet); or railways of different classes; or zones of varying agricultural productivity (e.g. Class I, Class II, . . . Class n).

The difference between the two highest scales, the *interval* scale and the *ratio* scale, is critically important in certain statistical operations (Table 10.1), but since most locational data are measured in ratio scales it has less direct significance for mapping. The fundamental difference between the two scales is that in the interval scale there are no absolute zeros whereas ratio scales have absolute zeros. If we compare two points on a time scale (e.g. A.D. 1900 and A.D. 1950) and on a distance scale (e.g. 1,900 and 1,950 miles from London) we can see that while the differences between the two are the same, fifty years and fifty miles, there is a fundamental difference in the ratios. For the measure of distance we can say that 1,950 miles is 1·02 times as great as 1,900 miles from London; however a similar statement is not possible about A.D. 1900 and A.D. 1950 since the base for the time scale is a quite arbitrary zero. On mathematical (though clearly not on theological) grounds the base might just as well be at A.D. 1800 which would make the second date 1·5 times as large as the first. Thus in the interval scale the ratio of any two points is dependent on the unit of measurement; in the ratio scale it is independent of the unit of measurement. In formal terms both scales have the property of (i) equivalence, of (ii) rank, and (iii) the known ratio of any two intervals (i.e. the ratio of A.D. 1850 to A.D. 1875 in relation to A.D. 1900 to A.D. 1950 is 1 : 2). Only the ratio scale has the additional property, (iv), the known ratio of any two scale values.

Most locational data are found to be measured on the highest (ratio)

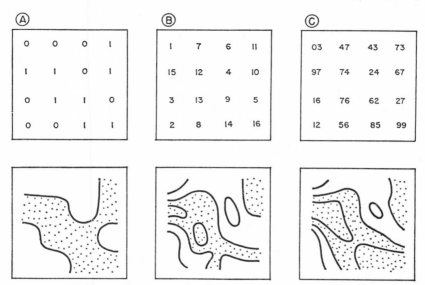

Fig. 8.1. Hypothetical relationships of nominal (*A*), rank (*B*), and ratio (*C*), scales of measurement to contour patterns on the map. Areas above the mean are shaded.

scale and are represented cartographically by isarithmic maps of features like population density; of flow maps of traffic volume; or of settlement maps in which the symbol is directly related to the population of the unit. The history of geographical exploration is also the history of improving levels of measurement, e.g. the substitution of exact height-contours for the hachured 'highs' and 'lows' (ordinal scale) of early maps.

A practical illustration of three of the measurement levels on cartographic method is shown in Fig. 8.1 in which the distribution of a type of land use (e.g. woodland) is shown over a sixteen-unit area. At the nominal scale the distribution of woodland is shown by one or zero denoting 'presence' and 'absence' (Fig. 8.1-A). In the ordinal and ratio scales this information is related to the sixteen sub-regions into which the area may

H

be divided. In the first, the sub-regions are ranked by the amount of woodland within their boundaries with contours drawn at ranks 4·5, 8·5, and 12·5 and areas over 8·5 shaded (Fig. 8.1-B). In the second, the percentage of woodland in each sub-region is measured at the ratio scale and contours drawn at 25, 50 and 75 per cent with areas over 50 per cent shaded (Fig. 8.1-C). As the level of measurement is raised so the corresponding isarithmic map increases in both complexity and accuracy; viewed the other way round (i.e. from right to left) the impact of falling levels of measurement and the error inherent in them can also be seen.

2. Single-component maps: isarithmic surfaces

Most locational data, whether it be originally linear, point, or areal in form, can be converted through density ratios into a continuous form, and plotted as an isarithmic map. Once in that form we may regard it, as does Robinson (1961-B), simply as a statistical surface in which height (e.g. rural population density) varies over area in much the same way as the terrain varies on topographic maps. Viewing the locational data in this way immediately suggests that much of morphometric analysis (co nven tionally restricted to topographic forms) may be applicable to the 'topography' of all isarithmic surfaces. Joint exploration by geomorphologists and human geographers of common techniques of surface analysis remains one of the most promising avenues of research for the coming decade.

Although such isarithmic maps are three-dimensional in the sense that a distribution (measured in the z-dimension) varies continuously over an area (measured in the xy-plane), we refer to it here as a *single-componen-* map in the sense that only one component is being 'mapped' on to the reference plane. In such maps the most common method of showing variations in the z-dimension is through the use of contours. Clearly such maps are based on the assumption that the distribution is a continuous variable, but as Warntz (1959) has shown, there are considerable theoretical and operational gains to be had by regarding such variations as continuous, even if, in practical terms, they appear discontinuous. Indeed, whether one regards population as discrete 'quanta' or as a continuous 'potential' is not a question of reality, but rather of scale and of the particular model being tested.

However we view the contoured isarithmic map, there are three immediate problems which affect construction, accuracy, and interpretation: i.e. (i) the number of contours, (ii) the spacing of contours, (iii) the relation of contours to the control-point system.

a. Number of contours. Although there is no definitive answer to the number of contours that might be used in plotting an isarithmic map, it seems logical that it should bear some systematic relation to the number of control points. A finely contoured map based on few control points gives an impression of accuracy unwarranted by the information on which it is based; conversely, it seems wasteful to use very few contours when in fact we know a great deal about rises and falls in the surface we investigate.

One rough guide may be suggested from comparison with a parallel problem in statistics. Here Brooks and Carruthers (1953, p. 13) have suggested that the number of classes in a histogram should not be more than five times the logarithm of the number of observations. In carto-graphic terms this would mean that a map based on, say, 500 control points should not be divided into more than thirteen classes. To show these thirteen classes we would clearly need twelve contours. As Brooks and Carruthers argue, there is nothing sacred about the relationship proposed; it merely gives a sensible relationship between accuracy and the available data, and so provides a rough rule-of-thumb which might be more widely used.

One logical outcome of this sort of rule, if adopted, is that the number of control points is determined by the contour interval. If then we need a ten-contour map we might argue, by the inverse rule, that we need at least 150 control points on which to base it.

b. Spacing of contours. In topographic maps, contours are normally plotted at equal height intervals, at least over the lower and intermediate altitudes. In statistical maps of locational data, equal-interval contours may be less useful. Jenks and Coulson (1963) have studied an area of central Kansas, where the range of rural population densities is from 1·6 to 103·4 persons per square mile and where the marked areal concentration of the high values make equal-step maps uninformative. On such a map with seven equal steps (intervals at 16·0, 30·6, 45·1, 59·7, 74·2, and 88·7 persons per square mile) only four classes were actually represented on the map while over 90 per cent of the map area was in one of the classes.

Problems of representing small pockets of high-value readings within great expanses of low-value readings are very common in human geo-graphy and have provoked considerable cartographic attention. Robinson (1960, pp. 190–4) has suggested that selection of appropriate contour intervals may be aided by cumulative frequency graphs in which the first component (area, xy) is plotted against the second component (values, z). To do this the collecting units (e.g. counties) are placed in order of their z-values (e.g. county population density), and their areas are progres-sively summed to give the cumulative frequency curve (Fig. 8.2-B). There are broadly three choices that can be made on the contour intervals: (i) to divide the z-values into equal divisions; (ii) to divide the xy-values (i.e. area) into equal divisions; or (iii) to divide the z-values into sections of uniform slope on the curve. The first method (Fig. 8.2-D) has the advantage of uniformity and ease of comparison with other areas; the second method (Fig. 8.2-C) has the advantage of a very even 'spread' of information over the map, but lacks comparability with other areas. The third method, using significant breaks in the cumulative frequency graph (Fig. 8.2-E)

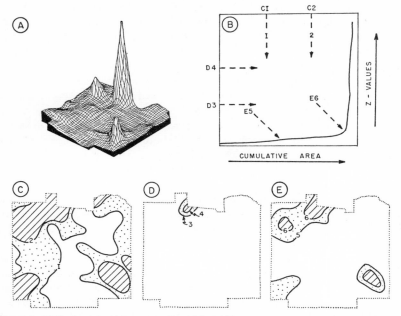

Fig. 8.2. A Smoothed statistical surface. *B* Graphic array of z-values against area. *C* Contour map with equal-area spacing. *D* Contour map with equal z-value spacing. *E* Contour map with spacing determined by critical breaks in the graph *B*.
Source: Jenks, 1963, pp. 16, 19.

gives the sharpest picture of local variations in detail, but lacks either the comparability or the evenness of the first two choices.

Perhaps the most useful approach to contour-interval decisions is to regard the mapped distribution as a statistical frequency distribution in which the locational concentration (i.e. skewness in statistical terms) may be met by an appropriate transformation. Transformed z-values may take the form of geometrical sequences (e.g. 2, 4, 8, 16 . . .) in cases of extreme locational concentrations of high values or an arc-sine sequence (e.g. 3, 12, 25, 42, 59, 75, 88, 97 per cent) where values are crowded at both lower and upper values of a sequence (Fisher and Yates, 1957, p. 70). In each case the transformation is appropriate to the form of the distribution and, since it gives a contour interval based on a known mathematical distribution, ready comparison with other cases is allowed.

c. Arrangement of control points. Accuracy of contour maps clearly depends on the original accuracy of the readings and the number of readings in any given area. Blumenstock (1953) discussed the problem at length for meteorological maps, and his analysis is of wider significance for all maps of geographical phenomena. There are, however, as Mackay (1953) has shown, problems in contour accuracy which spring not from the original data but from the locational pattern of the recording points or 'control' points. Fig. 8.3-A shows the original four values on a grid for which contour lines have to be interpolated. Unless other information is available it is assumed that the gradient between two points is linear and contour lines are geometrically interpolated. Geometrical interpolation is merely a matter of proportional allocation: if a 20 per cent contour is to be drawn between control points with values of 16 and 25 per cent respectively, then this contour would be placed four-ninths of the way along the line joining the lower and higher control point. The method is not, however, entirely foolproof. Fig. 8.3-B and Fig. 8.3-C show two alternative interpretations of the 20 per cent contour in which the areas above 20 per cent (shaded) are shown as a diagonal ridge across the map and then as two

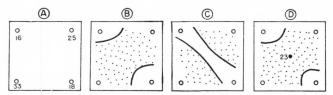

Fig. 8.3. Indeterminacy problems in contour interpolation between a regular grid of four control points. Source: Mackay, 1953.

ridges separated by a narrow col. Both interpretations are valid from the geometrical interpolation method.

Solution of this indeterminate case is possible if we assume a secondary control point at the centre of the square with a value equal to the mean of the four corner values, i.e. 23 per cent. Using this value the contours drawn in previous figures can be checked and the continuous 'ridge' confirmed (Fig. 8.3-D). It should be emphasized that such indeterminate cases spring from the use of *square* lattices for control-point location (the common National Grid type of reference frame) and where an alternative control-point arrangement can be chosen there is considerable value in adopting a *triangular* arrangement that eliminates this problem. Whether such a solution is worth the more complex arrangement of collecting areas,

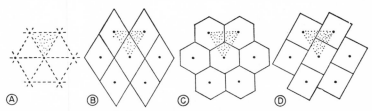

Fig. 8.4. Alternative collecting areas for triangular systems of control points. Source: Mackay, 1953.

i.e. the rhombic (Fig. 8.4-B), hexagonal (Fig. 8.4-C), or 'staggered-rectangle' (Fig. 8.4-D) forms, is a matter for debate. Certainly the hexagonal system has been used effectively in a recent study of population densities in the Great Plains of the United States (Robinson *et al.*, 1961) (Chap. 7.III(2d)).

3. Multicomponent maps

Where we have to deal with not one value varying regionally (the single-component map) but a whole series of such values, the cartographic problems become much more severe. There are certainly a number of ingenious ways in which simple contour maps may be superimposed—by the use of superimposed coloured contours or intervisible plastic overlays—but the point is quickly reached where the fall-off in comprehension outweighs any gains in completeness. Even the most successful of such maps, like those of Learmonth and Pal (1959) on disease in India, are rarely able to show more than two factors independently.

As a result, research has turned towards ways of breaking down the complexities of multidimensional systems *before* the mapping stage is reached. By doing this statistical complexities have been substituted for cartographic complexities, but the complications described above have been outflanked. Four of the more successful methods are described here.

a. Percentage data: facies mapping. Where the phenomena being mapped can be broken down into not more than three percentage components, we can make use of facies triangles or 'ternary' diagrams. Research on facies triangles developed in geology where the sedimentary rocks could be broken down into three components or 'end members' (sand, shale, and non-clastics) in terms of their percentage contribution to the total weight of the sample. A parallel problem in land-use studies would be the breakdown of an area into woodland, cropland, and other land-use types, in which each type was measured as a percentage of the total area.

Fig. 8.5-A shows a facies triangle in which the three vertices represent 100 per cent of each of the three components, *A*, *B*, and *C*, and points within the triangle represent combinations of these three. For example point *x* indicates a mixture of 60 per cent *A*, 20 per cent *B*, and 20 per cent *C*; and point *y* indicates a mixture of 10 per cent *A*, 30 per cent *B*, and 60 per cent *C*. Clearly the nearer the point lies to the middle of the triangle, the greater the mixing, and the nearer the point lies to one of the vertices of the triangle, the greater the dominance of a single component.

Facies triangles have been occasionally used in the non-geological literature to describe composition. Clark (1940) in the *Conditions of economic progress* suggested that the breakdown of a country's employment into primary, secondary, and tertiary industry might provide a sensitive index of economic growth, and that the changing composition of areas might be plotted on facies triangles. However, less use has been made of

the method than its potential suggests. Forgotson (1960) has reviewed a
number of uses of the method in geology which might be taken up in our
own compositional studies. One of the simplest uses of the facies triangle
was developed by Pelto (1954) in which a *classifying function* was used to
divide the triangle into seven classes: three single-component sectors (*A*,
B, and *C*), three two-component sectors (*AB*, *AC*, and *BC*), and one three-
component sector (*ABC*). Within each class the ratio lines are drawn to

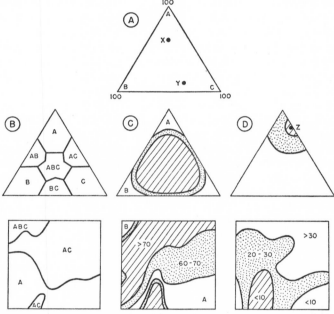

Fig. 8.5. Use of ternary diagrams in facies mapping of three-component systems.
B Classifying-function method. *C* Entropy-function method. *D* Facies-departure
method. The maps below each diagram show the application of the three methods
to the *same* facies data. Source: Forgotson, 1960, pp. 88–95.

indicate the relative strength of a component. In this system, point *x* falls
within class *A* and point *y* within class *BC* (Fig. 8.5-B). A second method,
also introduced by Pelto, attempts to establish quantitative facies
boundaries rather than classes through the concept of an *entropy function*.
Here 'entropy' refers simply to the degree of mixing of the components,
with high entropy values occurring near the centre of the triangle and low
values near the three end members. In Fig. 8.5-c contours for the 70 and 60
entropy ratios are plotted: both *x* and *y* have rather similar entropy functions
and Pelto suggests that in mapping these ratios, distinctive shading might
be superimposed on the contours to indicate the three end members.

Krumbein (1955) has suggested a simple *facies departure* method to map the relation of points on the triangle to a given control point. This control point might be either the average composition or optimum combination for the area; in Fig. 8.5-D it is point z, where A is 80 per cent, B is 0 per cent, and C is 20 per cent. Contours are drawn as concentric circles to show departures from the control point. The disadvantage of the method is that, although it shows the amount of regional departures, it does not show the direction of departure, and needs therefore to be compared to maps of classifying function. Sample maps of the three methods— the classifying function method, the entropy function method, and the facies departure method—are given below each facies triangle.

Little use has as yet been made in geography of this type of analysis. Board (Personal communication), however, has explored the use of a more complex derivative, the tetrahedron, to show four-component analyses of South African land use.

b. Percentage data: combination mapping. A typical problem in multi-component mapping is faced by the geographer working with zonal data. In agricultural zones he may have to investigate a range of a dozen or so crops which are grown in different rotational combinations in the different parts of his study area. How can such diversity be shown on a single map? One suggestion put forward by Weaver (1954) is the *crop-combination index* which sorts out the major crop combinations and thereby enables minor crops to be eliminated. Although Weaver worked on the crop distributions of the American Middle West and his method has been mainly used for crop studies in other areas (e.g. Thomas, 1963, on the agriculture of Wales during the Napoleonic Wars), the index is not intrinsically limited to agricultural studies: it can be applied to any distributional data expressed in terms of percentage components and is therefore described here simply as a *combination index.*

Calculation of the combination index is a simple procedure which is illustrated in Fig. 8.6. Here the sample problem is to determine the appropriate combination index for a Breconshire parish which in 1801 had six crops—wheat, oats, barley, peas, potatoes, and turnips—whose percentage contribution to the total cropland (100 per cent) was respectively 32·0, 31·5, 17·1, 11·7, 4·4, and 3·3 (Thomas, 1963, p. 81). The characteristic curve for the six crops in this parish is shown in Fig. 8.6 by a broken line.

The problem in mapping is to calculate how many of the six crops need to be included. Is this parish to be mapped as a one-crop unit (wheat) or as a four-crop unit (wheat–oats–barley–peas)? Weaver's answer to this problem is to suggest a series of model situations. He argued that in a model one-crop area, 100 per cent of the cropland would be in one crop and 0 per cent in the others; in a model two-crop area, 50·00 per cent of the cropland would be in each of two crops, and 0 per cent in

the others; in a model three-crop area, 33·3 per cent of the cropland would
be in each of the three crops, and 0 per cent in the others; and so on.
These ideal curves are shown in Fig. 8.6 by the heavy unbroken line.
Using these ideal curves as standards, Weaver then compared these with
his actual curves to find which of them it most closely resembled. To
measure this comparison he used the classic statistical methods of 'least
squares': that is the deviations (shown by the vertical lines in Fig. 8.6)
were measured (f), were then squared (f^2), and were finally summed
(Σf^2). The closest correspondence between the model and the actual

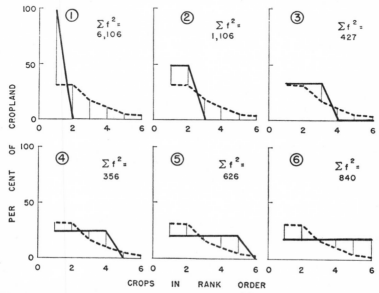

Fig. 8.6. Stages in the computation of combination indices. Source: Thomas,
1963, p. 81.

curves is given by the minimum least-squares value. In Thomas's case the
successive values for Σf^2 show a characteristic U-shaped curve with high
values for the one-crop and six-crop extremes. The lowest value,
$\Sigma f^2 = 356$, suggests that we can regard this parish as a four-crop unit and
disregard the two smallest crops.

   Combination indices may be mapped by shading the number of
activities, with the sequence 1, 2, 3, 4 . . . n indicating a combination
continuum from monoculture to diversity. In practice the crop components are coded by letters (e.g. W for wheat, O for oats, B for barley)
and the combination letters (e.g. WOB) overprinted on the shading, or
separate maps of leading combinations prepared.

   The role of the combination index is to reduce the confusion in multiple-component mapping, by sorting the dominant elements from the recessive. It is perhaps at its most useful where a few items are important, and least successful where a very even balance is found among a large group of items. Similar problems are met in plant ecology in the comparison and description of complex plant communities, and there would seem to be a number of worthwhile botanical indices, described by Greig-Smith (1964, pp. 1–19, 131–57), that might usefully be tested on comparable geographical problems.

c. Component standardization. If we are concerned with mapping a complex phenomenon like the 'development level' of a set of regions, we may have to use a number of measurements rather than any single one. Thus Ginsburg (1961) in his *Atlas of economic development* uses some ninety separate indices in an attempt to probe the elusive concept of development. Any method of reducing such measurements to a single index must overcome the problem of comparability: some measurements may range from 1 to 10^6, others may range from 0·98 to 1·02, and there is clearly some need to reduce these ranges to a single comparative level.

Ranking the regions in order from the highest to the lowest (rank 1, 2, 3 . . . *n*) on any given measure provides such a common yardstick; adding the ranks of regions on *all* measures provides an overall index. The problem with ranking, however, is that it throws away so much of the information gained in the measurement process: 10·7, 6·2, 6·1, and 0·004 become simply 1, 2, 3, and 4 despite the great differences in the original measurements. To retain the relative differences of regions along the measurements, Berry (1961-B) has suggested the use of standard scores or ω-values. Such values may be derived from the formula

$$\omega = (x_i - \bar{x})/s_x$$

where x_i is the value for the ith region, $\bar{x}$ is the arithmetic mean, and s_x the standard deviation of the measurement in question. Thus for any observation, the ω-score is expressed as a deviation from the mean value in units of the standard deviation.

One recent example of the use of rank-sums in building up a combined picture of regional variation has come from a study of the 'economic health' of New York state by Thompson, Sufrin, Gould, and Buck (1962, p. 5). Nine separate indicators of the economic activity of the state were taken, including items like *per capita* income and per cent unemployment, and the fifty-eight counties were ranked in order on each of the nine indicators. For each county its rank on each of the indicators was noted, the nine ranks summed, and the resulting totals re-ranked to give a combined index. As the authors point out, the method involves some curious additions: thus New York city has a high rank (4th) among the counties in economic *levels*, but a low rank (46th) in economic *trends*. Its overall position was given by this method as twenty-eighth. They concluded therefore that although the method gave reasonably accurate pictures of different levels of development within the state, they could find no basic mathematical logic in the method and went on to replace it by a more reliable method, factor analysis (Chap. 8.I(3d)).

   d. Principal-component analysis. Factor analysis provides one of the most powerful tools in the statistical analysis of multicomponent problems. It attacks the problem at the very point where standardization fails and recognizes that all measurements are not of equal weight but that many of them may overlap and tell us the same story about the ways in which a set of regions may vary. When several measurements show basically the same pattern of variation, we intuitively suspect that some are redundant and that a more basic pattern lies beneath: the principal component is an approximation of that 'basic pattern'.

   Although the details of factor analysis (outlined in Harman, 1960) are extremely complex and lie outside the scope of this book, we can see something of the power of the method from a study by Berry (1960). He carried out a world-scale study of ninety-five countries each characterized by forty-three indices of economic development. Using direct-factor analysis of the ranked measurements he was able to 'collapse' the forty-three indices into five basic patterns (Table 8.1) which together accounted

---

Table 8.1. Factor analysis of world economic development*

| Components | Variation explained | | Interpretation |
	Per cent	Cumulative per cent	
Factor I	84·2	84·2	Technological axis
Factor II	4·2	88·4	Demographic axis
Factor III	2·5	90·9	International trade axis
Factor IV	1·9	92·8	Size axis
Factor V	1·2	94·0	Error term (?)

Source: Berry, 1960, p. 82.
                     * Ninety-five countries.

---

for 94 per cent of the original variation between the countries. The most important axis, the technological scale, itself accounted for 84 per cent. Clearly Berry's analysis broke the back of his multiple-component mapping problem by providing a single index, the *principal component*, which may safely be substituted for the myriad indicators from which it was derived.

   To this extent principal-component analysis outflanks the difficult cartographic problem of mapping multiple indices by substituting more basic single values which can be simply presented as conventional isarithmic or choropleth maps. How reliable such maps are clearly depends on how much of the intercorrelation the principal axis embodies. In a New York study (Thompson *et al.*, 1962), the principal component (Factor I) accounted for only 50·1 of the intercorrelation between the nine indicators, but since this was more than three times the amount of any other component (Factor II = 15·7 per cent) it must be interpreted

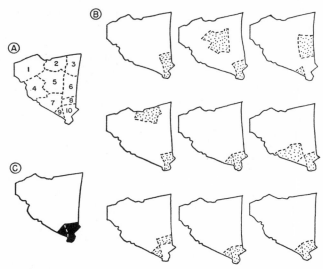

Fig. 8.7. Factor analysis applied to southern New York state, United States ($G = 4.5$). Source: Thompson, Sufrin, Buck, and Gould, 1962, pp. 6–17.

as the most basic single index so far constructed of the regional variations in economic development throughout the state.

As an illustration of the method Fig. 8.7 shows a ten-county fragment of the southern part of the state of New York with the leading two counties on each of the nine indicators stippled (Fig. 8.7-B) to show the variations in ranking between the indicators. The leading two counties in this area on the principal component (Factor I) are shown in Fig. 8.7-C; they are Rockland (9) and Westchester (10), lying immediately north of New York city, and were respectively 1st- and 3rd-ranking counties on the complete state survey of fifty-eight counties.

4. Problems of conventional map description

Although maps continue to be the most practical method of 'storing' locational information, there are signs that more and more data may be stored in alternative ways in the future. Here we look briefly at some of the problems both of map storage and of alternative co-ordinate systems.

a. Maps as data-storage systems. Two basic cartographic problems in map production, scale and projection, impose rather severe limitations on the use of maps for describing locational patterns. Robinson (1960, p. 226) suggests that at a viewing distance of eighteen inches, symbols less than 1/100th of an inch cannot be seen clearly.

In area terms this means that an area of one square kilometre cannot be shown to scale at scales smaller than about 1 : 1,000,000 (Amiran and Schick, 1961, p. 165): after this level, generalization of one kind or another must be used. Projections become of critical importance for areas too large to be regarded as plane surfaces; in practice, areas above about one hundred square miles. Paradoxically the problem is not so much the lack of projections as the range of alternatives. Except in national series and national atlases, maps of large parts of the earth's surface are unlikely to be on immediately comparable graticules although some progress on standardizing population data on the IMW 1/1,000 series has been made.

Nevertheless maps have a number of significant advantages. Locational patterns are plotted on a base-map which gives important secondary information, notably on orientation, reliability, and inference. Marginal co-ordinates, like the latitude and longitude of small-scale maps and the grid co-ordinates of large-scale maps, provide the most austere but most accurate form for such *orientation* data: this is commonly supplemented by showing the seacoast, state boundaries, rivers, or key towns within the area. Bunge (1962, pp. 44–8) has suggested that some of these conventional props might be replaced or re-examined, since rivers, for example, rarely have the locational significance that their frequent use on maps might imply. *Reliability data* consist of information indicating the source of error in the phenomena being mapped. For instance, Weaver (1956) plotted isarithms of crop patterns on maps showing the counties and townships from which the data were derived. *Inference data* consist of information not in the first two categories which helps to place a distributional map in some kind of perspective. For instance, Ginsburg (1961) in his *Atlas of economic development* plotted data for his indices of economic development on world base-maps of population density.

b. Alternative data-storage systems: machine mapping. One of the most significant developments for geography in the field of computer technology is that of machine mapping. By this system locational data are stored on punched cards, magnetic tape, etc., and can be 'translated' into a map of any desired characteristic by an automated plotter. The possibilities of such methods have been discussed by Tobler (1959). An outstanding example of machine mapping from coded geographical data is the *Atlas of the British Flora* (Perring and Walters, 1962). The basis of the atlas was a deck of punched-card records for each of the 2,000 British vascular species for every ten-kilometre square cell of the National Grid. Details of location, species (presence or absence), habitat, date, collector, and other relevant information was coded and the 1,500,000 pieces of information sorted mechanically. At a late stage in the analysis, data were fed into a mechanical tabulator which printed a dot (if the species is present) in the location indicated by the digits of the ten-kilometre reference system (Fig. 7.10).

In the case of the Perring and Walters atlas the problem of geographical co-ordinates was simply solved through the use of the existing xy co-ordinate system of the National Grid. Similar systems are available in a number of countries, notably Sweden where census data are being coded on a ten-metre grid on the 1 : 10,000 map series (Hägerstrand, 1955). For world-wide studies, the more complicated spheroidal reference systems of latitude and longitude must be substituted for rectangular co-ordinate systems. The complexities of automated computation of distances, areas, and directions on a spherical reference system are further complicated by the departure of the earth's form from that of a true sphere: lengths of a degree of a meridian range from 68·703 statute miles (at zero to one degree latitude) to 69·407 statute miles (at eighty-nine to ninety degrees latitude). Therefore, increasing use is being made of the Transverse Mercator projection to provide a conformal projection base for topographic maps series. The prime advantage of this projection is that scale departures are uniform along lines parallel to the standard great circle, allowing the build-up of an xy co-ordinate rectangular system in which '. . . a given x-value will have a uniform scale characteristic at any y-value' (Robinson, 1960, p. 91). It has been widely used by the United States in its UTM system (Universal Transverse Mercator) for building up a series of identical projections for mid-latitudes, each unit covering an area of six degrees of longitude by 800 kilometres.

Outside these standard systems, interesting use has been made of azimuthal projections. For example, in the migration studies reviewed in Chapter 2 (Fig. 2.4) information is stored in terms of *distance* (u) and *direction* (v) from the source of migration. Other systems with time and direction might prove useful in mapping traffic studies (Bunge, 1962, p. 55).

Coding of geographical locations for machine mapping poses further technical problems that lie largely outside this brief treatment. A simple illustration is the need in computer programming to substitute the mathematical convention of direction (i.e. the origin, zero degrees, at East with a counter-clockwise succession) for the geographical convention (i.e. the origin, zero degrees, at North with a clockwise succession). Like legal language, the translation of geographical realities into computer programmes may lead to cumbersome but precise definitions. Thus Nordbeck (1962) has been forced to use what at first sight appears a very long-winded system for describing areas. In a Swedish study, he approximates areas to polygons with the vertices numbered $P_1, P_2 \ldots P_n$, in an anticlockwise direction where P_n is equal to P_1. P_1 has the smallest y co-ordinate value and, if this is not unique, then the smallest x co-ordinate value. Areas of these polygons are then defined as the area situated to the left of all connecting lines between consecutive vertices!

II. DESCRIPTION OF RELATIVE LOCATION: STATISTICAL INDICES

1. Contiguous areas

a. Descriptions of shape. Some simple measures have been evolved in human geography to describe briefly the shapes of the phenomena studied, though by comparison with other disciplines considerably more work here is possible. Indeed, many of our basic concepts of shape have come from studies like sedimentary petrology where particle shape has

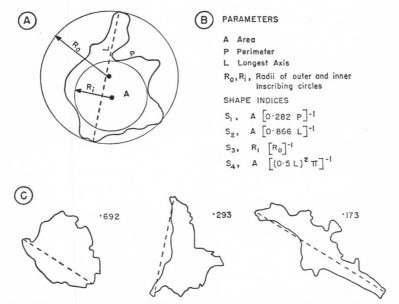

Fig. 8.8. Shape parameters applied to urban areas. Source: Gibbs, 1961, p. 101.

a vital dynamic significance. Here workers like Krumbein (1941) and Pettijohn (1957, pp. 54–68) have developed a series of powerful indices to describe briefly the three-dimensional shape characteristics of particles. Using a few basic parameters shown in Fig. 8.8 (area, perimeter, length of the longest axis, and the radii of the smallest circumscribing circle and the largest inscribing circle), it is possible to devise a series of shape ratios. Three simple ratios are given in Fig. 8.8-B in which pairs of measurements (area and perimeter, area and long-axis, and the radii of the two circles) are related. In each case the shape ratio is modified to allow ready comparison with a circle. Thus in the first shape index, S_1, the perimeter is multiplied by 0·282, and in the second shape index, S_2, the long-axis is multiplied by 0·866. A circle has a shape index of 1·00 on all three, and as the shapes become more elongated and irregular the indices drop towards zero.

Gibbs (1961, pp. 99–106) has made use of the S_4 index in describing the shapes of American cities. This index relates the area of the circle that would be generated by the longest axis $(0·5L)^2\pi$, to the actual area (A), so that values of 1·00 indicate a circular shape. Fig. 8·8-c shows the shapes of three American cities (Raleigh, Trenton, and Charleston) where Raleigh is relatively circular $(S_4 = 0·692)$ and Charleston $(S_4 = 0·173)$ is elongated. By comparing shape indices based on alternative definitions of the city, Gibbs was able to show that the administrative area of the city $(S_4 = 0·412)$ was rather consistently more circular than the urbanized area $(S_4 = 0·288)$.

Shape is one of the most difficult properties of a geographic pattern to measure. The problem is that in attempting to measure shape and shape only a number of unwanted properties, notably orientation, are also unwillingly measured. Subjective categories—'circular', 'shoestring', 'star-shaped'—are commonly used in descriptions of shape, but they are both limited in geometrical range and show strong operator-variance in assignment. Bunge (1962, pp. 73–8) has discussed these problems at length and suggested a method for overcoming them. This method is based on two theorems: (i) that any simply connected shape can be matched by a polygon of any number of sides, whose sides are of equal but variable length; (ii) that if the distances between all vertices of the polygon are summed in a standard manner there exists just one set of sums that uniquely describes the polygon shape.

Application of these two theorems is shown in Fig. 8.9. In this diagram the original shape (Fig. 8.9-A) is approximated by a six equal-sided polygon (Fig. 8.9-B). The vertices of this polygon are numbered, one to six. In Fig. 8.9-c lines are drawn between each vertex and the next vertex but one; i.e. the first is joined to the third vertex, the second to the fourth vertex, and so on. These lines are measured and summed to give the ratio, SS_1, and squared and summed to give the second ratio, SS_1^2.

Fig. 8.9-D shows the next stage of measurement, where lines are drawn between each vertex and the next lag-two vertex, i.e. the first is joined to the fourth, and so on. These lines are summed to give the third ratio, SS_2, and squared and summed to give the fourth ratio, SS_2^2. This process of lagging goes on until all previously determined sums reappear and therefore '. . . all unique sums have been determined' (Bunge, 1962, p. 77).

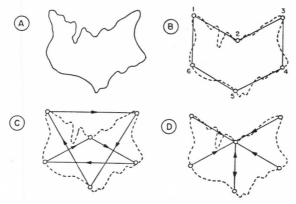

Fig. 8.9. Stages in the computation of Bunge shape sums.
Source: Bunge, 1962, p. 77.

For a six-sided polygon there are four such sums, $SS_1 \ldots SS_2{}^2$; with an eight-sided polygon there are six such sums, $SS_1 \ldots SS_3{}^2$.

By measuring all shapes in terms of the length of one side of the polygon which is taken as having a length of 1·00, different shapes can be readily compared both with each other and with standard geometrical figures. Fig. 8.10 shows the characteristic curves for the shape sums of two

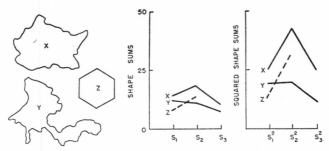

Fig. 8.10. Characteristic shapes and shape sums. Source: Bunge, 1962, pp. 79–86.

Mexican communities studied by Bunge, together with the appropriate curves for a common geometrical form, the hexagon. Bunge's interesting attempt to build up dimensionless ratios deserves more research into simplified comparative indices, and there is some evidence (e.g. Boyce and Clark, 1964) that it is being followed up.

b. Descriptions of centrality and dispersion. A second series of measures have been developed from formal statistical theory and are characterized by the extension of familiar statistical parameters (e.g. the arithmetic mean) into the two-dimensional plane. This idea is not of course a new one. As early as 1892, Johnson discussed the deviations of bullet marks around a target as a 'probability density surface' (Johnson, 1892) and by 1937 Sviatlovsky and Eells could publish an extensive review of geographical work, done largely in Russia, employing what came to be called 'centrographic methods'. The size of the literature on these methods, and their heavy dependence on formal statistical theory, precludes any extensive review here: Bachi (1963) has done this at length. Instead, we shall look here at some examples of the methods in use.

Warntz and Neft (1960) have shown how three familiar statistical measures of *central tendency*, the mean, median, and mode, may be transated into areal dimensions. The mean centre of a distribution they define as the point where

$$\int R^2 . G(dA)$$

is minimized; while the median centre is defined as the point where

$$\int R . G(dA)$$

is minimized. In both expressions G is the density of population over a very small part of area dA and R is the distance from each part to the mean

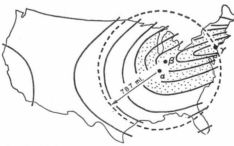

Fig. 8.11. Potentials of population in the United States ($G = 1 \cdot 8$) with the mean α), median (β), and mode (γ) of the distribution. Source: Warntz and Neft, 1960, p. 62.

or median point in question. In the same way the mode can be defined in terms of the position of the high point on the density surface.

Hart (1954) and Porter (1963) have described practical procedures for calculating points of minimum access. Hart's method consists of a series of trial-and-error approximations in which a transparent annular mesh is used to count the population at specified distances from the centre of the graph. Porter's method is more rapid but subject to considerable errors in the location of the point (Court and Porter, 1964).

Fig. 8.11 shows for the United States a smoothed density surface for its 1950 population potential with contours at intervals of fifty units and values above 300 units shaded. Here the mean centre (α) is located in southern Illinois, the median centre (β) is located in central Indiana, and the modal centre (γ) in New York city. The location of the three points shows the greater sensitivity of the mean centre to distant outlying centres of population, in this case on the Pacific coast of the United States.

Paralleling the measures of central tendency in statistical descriptions of frequency distribution are the measures of *range* or deviation. Stewart and Warntz (1958) have introduced a convenient measure of such dispersion which they term the 'dynamical radius' of a population. This they define by the expression

$$\sqrt{\{\Sigma\,(pd^2)\}/P}$$

where p equals the population of a small area, d is the distance from the mean centre (as defined above), and P is the total population. In 1950 the dynamical radius of the United States population of 150,700,000 was 790 miles, which is plotted as a circle about the Illinois centre in Fig. 8.11. About 69 per cent of the United States population lives within this circle, and Warntz and Neft (1960, p. 66) point out that the westward movement of the mean along the thirty-ninth parallel has been accompanied by a widening dynamical radius, so that, although the modal centre has remained at New York since 1840 and the gap between the mean and mode has been widening, the distribution has not become more skewed.

2. Points and discontinuous areas

Whether a given distribution is treated as a continuous surface, or as a conglomeration of separate points, is largely a matter of data and scale. Certainly the measures of central tendency can be rewritten to make them applicable to a cluster of points, and conversely some of the measures treated here could be generalized to analyse continuous distributions. Nevertheless, there are certain classes of locational data, such as settlements and their attributes, in which special problems are encountered and in which special measures have been developed. Two such groups of measures are discussed here.

a. Nearest-neighbour analysis. Despite a prolonged interest by European geographers in the quantitative study of rural settlement, briefly reviewed by Houston (1953, pp. 81–5), most attempts to introduce statistical and probability methods in this field have come rather recently. An important ecological study by Clark and Evans (1954) on *nearest-neighbour* analysis appears to be the starting point for much of the more recent work on settlement patterns. Their analysis is based on the measurement of the actual straight-line distance separating a point and its nearest-neighbour point, and comparison of these distances with that which might be expected if the point were distributed in a random manner within the same area. Comparison is measured by the nearest-neighbour statistic (R_n) given by the formula

$$R_n = \bar{D}_{\text{obs.}} / \{0 \cdot 50 \, (A/N)^{-\frac{1}{2}}\}$$

where $\bar{D}_{\text{obs.}}$ is the observed mean distance between points and their nearest neighbours, A is the area, and N is the number of points. The values of R_n range from zero (where all the points are clustered together at one place) through to $2 \cdot 15$ (where the points are as far as possible from each other and therefore form a regular hexagonal distribution). When R_n has a value of one the distribution of points is random.

Clark and Evans's method has been taken up by King (1962) in a study of urban settlements in the United States. Although the implications of his results for locational theory have already been discussed (Chap.

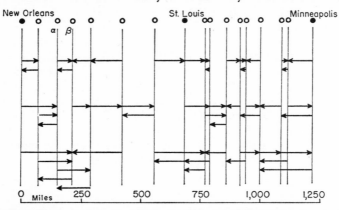

Fig. 8.12. Stages in nearest-neighbour analysis of Mississippi river towns, central United States. Source: Dacey, 1960, p. 60.

4.I(1b)), it is worth referring back to Fig. 4.2 which shows the range in the R_n statistic from 0·70 for the Duchesne area of Utah (clustered) to 1·38 for central Minnesota (regularly spaced). King is unwilling to place too much significance in the value of $R_n = 1 \cdot 00$ as a watershed between clustered and regular spacing, but he does stress the value of the measure in providing a continuous scale along which progressive changes in locational pattern may be located.

Dacey (1960) has analysed the spacing of river towns in the central lowlands of the United States using a form of nearest-neighbour analysis. His object was to test the qualitative generalization that the larger river towns '. . . reveal an interesting uniformity of spacing along the rivers' (Burghardt, 1959, p. 322) against the more rigorous statistical definition of uniform spacing. Clark (1954, p. 124) demonstrated that when points are spaced along a line (like the towns along the Mississippi river, in Fig. 8.12) we can distinguish 'reflexive pairs'. Reflexive pairs are pairs of points in which each has the other as its nearest neighbour. An example on Fig. 8.12 where arrows point in to the nearest neighbour for each town is Natchez (α) and Vicksburg (β). In the same way, we can distinguish reflexive pairs for 'second-nearest' neighbours (the second tier of arrows in Fig. 8.12), reflexive pairs for 'third-nearest' neighbours (the third tier of arrows in Fig. 8.12), and so on. In the case of the Mississippi river towns shown here, there are five reflexive pairs of first-nearest neighbours (i.e. ten reflexive points), three reflexive pairs of second-nearest neighbours (i.e. six reflexive points), and two reflexive pairs of third-nearest neighbours (i.e. four reflexive points).

Clark showed theoretically that when points are spaced randomly along a line, the proportion of points having nth-order reflexive-nearest-points is $(2/3)^n$. He distinguishes a *uniform* spacing of points when the proportion is greater than $(2/3)^n$ and a *grouped* spacing when the proportion is less than $(2/3)^n$: the greater the deviation from $(2/3)^n$ the more pronounced is the grouping or uniformity. In Table 8.2 the proportion of

Table 8.2. Nearest-neighbour analysis of town spacing*

Reflexive points:	*Number*	*Observed proportion*	*Expected proportion*	*Description*
Nearest-neighbour order:				
First	10	0·588	0·667	Grouped
Second	6	0·353	0·444	Grouped
Third	4	0·235	0·296	Grouped

Source: Dacey, 1960, pp. 60–1.
* 17 Mississippi river towns.

reflexive points for first-nearest points, 10/17 or 0·588, is shown to be less than the expected proportion in a random situation, $(2/3)^1$ or 0·667, and the pattern of Mississippi towns is described as 'grouped'. Similar lower-than-random proportions on the second- and third-nearest neighbours confirm the 'grouped' description rather than the 'uniform' description applied by Burghardt. However, before concluding that Dacey's mathematical analysis has reversed Burghardt's qualitative judgement, it is worth noting that while the former defined his seventeen large towns on population terms Burghardt did not closely define the sample he was describing. An amusing tailpiece to the Burghardt–Dacey discussion is provided by Porter (1960) in a paper entitled *Earnest and the Orephagians* in which he shows that there are certain possible (but unlikely) limiting conditions in which nearest-neighbour analysis completely inverts our intuitive concepts of clustering and uniformity.

b. Indices of geographical association. One of the descriptive indices most frequently encountered in geographical literature is the *coefficient of geographical association* (*G*). It has appeared under various guises as the 'coefficient of linkage' or the 'coefficient of similarity' since its first use in industrial location studies by Hoover (1936) some thirty years ago, and its great attraction would seem to spring from very easy computation. Basically it is a measure of the association between any two phenomena over a set of geographical regions.

A simple illustration of the use of the *G* coefficient is given in Fig. 8.13-A. Here the two distributions being compared are (i) the woollen

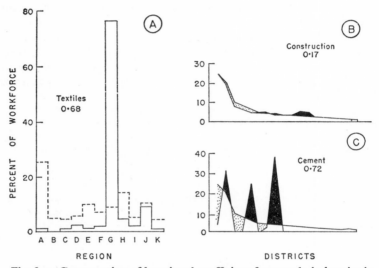

Fig. 8.13. Computation of locational coefficient for sample industries in England and Wales (*A*) and Portugal (*BC*).

industry and (ii) all industry, over the eleven 'standard regions' of Britain. In each case distribution is measured by the number of workers, and this is broken down into the percentages in each region. Thus the first region, *A*, on Fig. 8.13-A, has 0·90 per cent of Britain's woollen industry workforce and 25·20 per cent of all its industry, where the national total for both the woollen industry and all industry is 100 per cent. The percentage shares are plotted on Fig. 8.13-A with the heavy line showing the woollen industry and the broken line all industry. Gaps between the two lines indicate the difference (*f*) for each region.

The *G* coefficient is given by the formula

$$G = 1 - \left\{ \sum_{i=1}^{n} f_i \right\} \Big/ 100$$

where Σf is the sum of either the positive or the negative deviations. The sum of either sign may be used in the computation, as both are equal. In the case of Fig. 8.13-A there is only one region with a positive deviation, region G, the East and West Ridings of Yorkshire, in which the share of the woollen industry (76·5 per cent) exceeds the share of all industry (8·8 per cent) by 67·7 per cent. The value of the G coefficient is therefore 0·677. The coefficient has a range from zero to one with low values when the two distributions being compared are similar, and high values when the two distributions are very unlike. Fig. 8.13 also shows curves for two contrasting industries in Portugal: the building industry (Fig. 8.13-B) tends to be very dispersed, in the sense that it follows the general distribution of the industrial workforce, and has a G coefficient of only 0·17; conversely the cement industry (Fig. 8.13-C) is highly localized and has a G coefficient of 0·72. Clearly the index has considerable value in describing locational patterns along a continuous range, and workers like Chisholm (1962, p. 93) have used it with considerable success in agricultural studies. For England and Wales in 1956, Chisholm found that he could place the distribution of twenty-nine horticultural crops along a continuum ranging from 0·39 for lettuce, with its widespread distribution around urban peripheries, to 0·61 for celery, with its strong concentration on the deep, well-drained soils of the Fens and parts of Norfolk.

The prime drawback of the G coefficient lies in its critical dependence on the size and number of the collecting areas. With a few large areas, values of G are characteristically low; with many small areas, values are characteristically high (Chap. 7.III(1a)) so that direct comparisons with coefficients based on similar distributions in other countries are invalidated. This dependence stems from the fact that the G coefficient is not a true measure of association (like the Pearsonian correlation coefficient, r) but merely indicates '. . . that portion of one variable which would have to be moved across statistical unit boundaries in order to make its distribution identical with that of the second variable' (McCarty et al., 1956, p. 31). McCarty goes on to compare unfavourably the reliability of G and r. He finds that not only is G very dependent on the actual magnitude of the values being compared, but that it gives no indications of the existence of strong *inverse* association (i.e. when high values of one distribution are strongly associated with low values of another). In one case studied the G coefficient showed a value of 0·744 for two distributions which Pearson's r suggested were almost completely uncorrelated ($r = $ 0·006)!

Although modifications of the original index have been attempted (Thompson, 1957), there is a need to treat the ubiquitous G with considerable caution. It certainly provides a useful, if erratic, description of locational concentration *within* an area but provides little basis for comparison *between* different areas, or between the same areas in different times (save only in the case of unchanged internal boundaries). Similar strictures must be placed on the use of a less common by-product of the coefficient of geographical association, the *locational quotient* (L_Q). The locational quotient gives a region-by-region description of the situation shown in Fig. 8.12-A by comparing values of the two distributions. Thus region A, London and the southeast, with 0·9 per cent in the woollen industry but 25·2 per cent in all industry, has a locational quotient of 0·9/25·2 or $L_Q = 0.04$. Quotients above one indicate a regional 'surplus' of the industry with, for example, the East and West Ridings (G) showing a value of 8·64.

3. Linear networks

a. Dimensional analysis. The simplest description of linear features, like transport routes, is in terms of their dimensions. Thus we can measure the length of a railway system (L) and relate it to the area it serves (A) to give a simple ratio measure of density in terms of length per unit area (L/A). Ginsburg (1961, p. 60) has mapped world variations in railway density in this way, using as his index 'kilometres of railway per 100 square kilometres of area'. Western European countries were found to have high density ratios, with Great Britain at 12·7, while in the Americas the United States ratio was about one-third of this (4·47) and the Brazilian ratio only 0·43 (Chap. 3.II(3)).

A useful extension of the density ratio (L/A) is given by its reciprocal A/L, which represents the distance between adjacent lines. If we take one-half of this distance and write our formula for computational purposes in the form $(0.5A)/L$ we have an average measure of the *length of overland haul*. This ratio gives a useful measure of the distance of any part of an area from its transport lines. In the case of the railway examples given above, we can define the average length of overland haul for Great Britain as 7·84 kilometres, for the United States as 22·4 kilometres, and for Brazil as 232 kilometres. Such figures conceal of course the great regional contrasts in railway density, but provide, within the limitations of the data, a useful yardstick of comparison.

More sophisticated measures of the dimensions of transport networks are clearly possible and needed. Additional parameters in which lines are graded in terms of either potential capacity (e.g. width and metalling of a road system) or actual use (e.g. railway flow in ton-miles/mile) have been commonly used in national studies, like that of Ullman (1949) on United States railroads, although international comparisons are generally more difficult. Whatever the exact measurements may be, there is a strong case for geographers familiarizing themselves with parallel work in geomorphology where the study of stream channels has given rise to an impressive literature on the measurement and description of linear phenomena. The pioneer work on stream networks came from an engineer,

Robert Horton (1945), in a paper subtitled 'a hydrophysical approach to quantitative morphology' in which he introduced fundamental concepts of stream length, stream number, and stream order. Although some of these concepts have been modified by the last twenty years of research (see the review by Leopold, Wolman, and Miller, 1964, pp. 131–50), they represent a largely untapped source of ideas for the dimensional analysis of the vital channels of roads, railways, and related paths in the economic landscape.

  b. Topological measures based on graph theory. An alternative approach to transport networks has been suggested by Garrison (1960) and Kansky (1963) working towards the problem from the mathematical theory of graphs. Some fourteen measures of varying complexity are proposed by Kansky; we examine here only a few judged either to be fundamental in

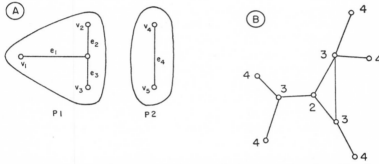

Fig. 8.14. A Fundamental measures of networks in terms of vertices (*v*), edges (*e*), and sub-graphs (*p*). *B* Measure of centrality of vertices by König numbers. Source: Kansky, 1963, pp. 11, 28.

illustrating the basis of graph theory, or alternatively suggested by empirical analysis to be rather closely associated with other aspects of regional development.

  Transportation networks may be reduced to rather abstract terms which enable basic properties to be recognized that might elude a 'head-on' study of the transport network as such. This process of simplification was touched on in Chapter 3.I(3), when the way in which the original railroad network of Sardinia could be reduced to a simple pattern of points connected by lines was illustrated (see Fig. 3.9).

  Fig. 8.14-A illustrates a simple case of such an abstract network. It consists of two isolated networks (*sub-graphs*), p_1 and p_2, which are each made up of a series of routes (*edges*), e_1, e_2 . . . e_n, and which connect a series of nodes (*vertices*), v_1, v_2 . . . v_n. We also know the distance along each route in miles (*edge distance*), d_e. These four measures, p, e, v, and d_e, form the basic elements which in various combinations form the more complex indices derived by Kansky. For convenience these measures are grouped here simply as (i) measures of centrality, (ii) measures of connectivity, and (iii) measures of shape.

(i) The first measure of *centrality* was developed by König in 1936 and is here termed the König number (Kansky, 1963, pp. 28–9). It describes the maximum number of edges by the shortest path from a vertex to any other vertex in the network. It is shown for each point in Fig. 8.14-B. It is then a measure of topological distance in terms of edges and suggests that vertices with low König numbers (e.g. the vertex with a number of 2 in Fig. 8.14-B) occupy a central place in the abstract transport system.

This measure becomes more meaningful if we realize that in many traffic movements (e.g. road transport) the nodes represent hold-ups and delays; and centres with low König numbers might be realistically 'near' the centre of the system. In any case, distance d_e can be reintroduced either as mileage or time into the calculations, and nodes with low König numbers re-examined in order to select the central location.

(ii) The simplest measure of the degree of *connectivity* of a transport network is given by the *Beta* index. This relates two of the four fundamental properties as e/v, where e is the number of edges and v the number of vertices (Kansky, 1963, pp. 16–18). In Fig. 8.15 the number of vertices remains constant at seven, while the number of connecting edges is progressively increased from six in Fig. 8.15-A to nine (Fig. 8.15-D). As the edges increase, the connectivity between the vertices rises and the Beta index changes progressively from 0·86 to 1·00, 1·14, and finally 1·28. Values for the index range between extremes of zero and three with values below one indicating trees and disconnected graphs, values of one indicating a network which has only one circuit (Fig. 8.15-B), and values between

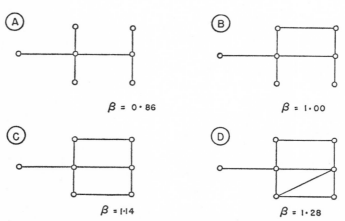

Fig. 8.15. Comparison of network connectivity through the *Beta*-index. Source: Kansky, 1963, p. 11.

one and three indicating a complex network. Practical examples of variations in the index for the railway networks in eighteen countries are given in Fig. 3.8.

(iii) The *shape* of a network is a more difficult concept to grasp. Here we begin with the concept of 'diameter' (itself a weak index for measuring transportation networks) and move on from this to the more complex but more useful measure of network shape. δ is an index measuring the topological length or extent of the graph by counting the number of edges in the shortest path between the most distant vertices. Thus in Fig. 8.16 the values of the diameter vary from two to four, rising as the 'extent' of the graph increases, but falling as improved connections are made between

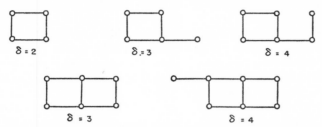

Fig. 8.16. Derivation of a measure of network diameter (δ). Source: Kansky, 1963, p. 13.

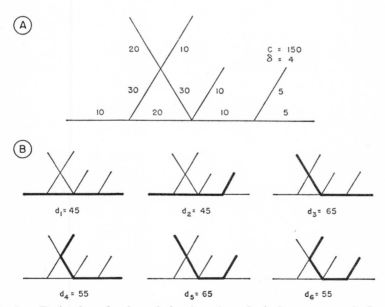

Fig. 8.17. Derivation of a shape index for a hypothetical route network. Source: Kansky, 1963, p. 23.

the vertices. Thus the third and fourth graphs in the series have different diameters even though their extent is the same.

Using this concept of diameter we can move on to relate this to the actual dimensions of the network, using an index π given by C/d, where C is the total mileage of the transportation network and d is the total mileage of the network's diameter (Kansky, 1963, pp. 21–3). In Fig. 8.17-A we have a network where the total mileage (C) is 150. Inspection of the graph's diameter in terms of the preceding diagram shows that the value of δ is four. There is, however, no unique diameter but six alternative paths that fulfil the minimum-diameter criterion: the location and length of these paths are shown in Fig. 8.17-B. The mean length of the six diameter paths is fifty-five miles; so that the shape index π is 150 divided by fifty-five, i.e. 2·73.

In practice shape indices vary considerably. Developed countries like France may have indices approaching thirty, while underdeveloped countries like Bolivia may have values of about one for their railway networks; there is considerable evidence that π is a sensitive index of the economic state of a transport network (Fig. 3.8).

Chapter nine   Region-building

I. REGIONS: THE IDENTIFICATION PROBLEM. 1. *Concept of a region*. a. Regions as a taxonomic problem. b. Regions and set-theory. 2. *Qualitative analysis: superimposed boundaries*. 3. *Quantitative analysis*. a. Thiessen polygons. b. Distance-minimization functions. c. Discriminant analysis. d. Graph-theory interpretation of regions.
II. REGIONS: THE ASSIGNMENT PROBLEM. 1. *General classification methods*. a. Distance analysis in *n*-dimensional space. b. Chi-squared analysis in classification. 2. *Assignment of areas to regional clusters*. a. Variance analysis. b. Correlation and regional 'bonds'.
III. REGIONAL GENERALIZATION AND SCALE. 1. *Nature of the scale problem*. 2. *Scale in regional hierarchies*. 3. *Scale-component analysis: sampling methods*. a. Nested sampling. b. Variance analysis of results. 4. *Scale-component analysis: mapping methods*. a. Filter mapping. b. Linear trend surfaces. c. Quadratic and higher-order surfaces. d. Choice of method.

Although regions are traditionally a central theme in geographical writing, geographers have always been curiously reticent about the ways in which regions could be built up. This reticence is particularly unfortunate in that it is in precisely this field that human geographers have much to offer both to other social sciences and to government and business. Already geographers have worked on improving the regional structure of both hospitals (Godlund, 1961) and schools (Yeates, 1963), as well as the more widely known cases of local government boundaries. This chapter sets out to bring together the explicit techniques that have been used in regional delimitation and in grouping, and touches on the related but more difficult problem of scale components in regional structure.

I. REGIONS: THE IDENTIFICATION PROBLEM

1. Concept of a region

Regions occupy a central position in geography and most of the 'classics' of geographical literature—Demangeon on Picardy, Sauer on the Ozarks, Bowman on the Andes—are regional monographs. Although regions have come under some heavy crossfire, notably from Kimble (in Stamp and Wooldridge, 1951, pp. 151–74), they continue to be one of the most logical and satisfactory ways of organizing geographical information.

Although some elaborate regional systems (e.g. Passarge, 1929) have been evolved, most can be broken down into the general categories developed by Whittlesey and shown in Table 9.1. This shows three broad

Table 9.1. Categories of regions

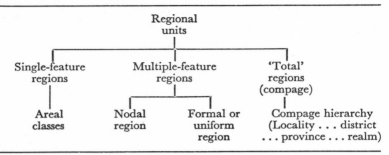

Source: Whittlesey. In James, Jones, and Wright, 1954, pp. 32–51.

categories of regions depending on the number of criteria that are used to delimit the region, although in practice both single-feature regions and 'total' regions are much less common than the middle category. Multiple-feature regions are broken down into two main categories: *formal* regions which are uniform throughout, and *nodal* regions which are organized with respect to some focus to which they are linked by lines of circulation. These categories, useful though they are, have had little positive impact on the organization of geographical writing; most geographers appear to use *ad hoc* divisions designed to meet specific teaching or research needs.

   a. Regions as a taxonomic problem. Much of the present dilemma in our regional thinking springs from what we have termed earlier the 'exceptionalist' viewpoint (Chap. 1.I(1)). Bunge (1962, pp. 14–26) attacks Whittlesey's scheme for treating regions as if they presented unique problems in classification, and insists that they are merely the areal aspects of a classification problem common to all sciences. To emphasize this point we may tabulate a number of terms common in geographical literature and range them against their general classification counterpart. A 'single-feature' region may be reduced to classification using a 'single category'; 'regional boundary' to 'class interval'; 'homogeneous region' to 'class with low areal variance'. Bunge argues that rather than depreciating regional geography, this approach places geography alongside the great natural sciences many of which either went through a *taxonomic* phase at some time in their evolution (e.g. chemistry) or have a strong continuing interest in this phase (e.g. botany). Conventions in geographical works, such as ignoring either the oceans or the land areas of the world in most non-climatic regional systems, may be seen as parallels to conventions in natural science. In biology, for example, the plant and animal 'kingdoms' are commonly regarded as separate even though they do jointly form part of total biology.

While we may agree with Bunge's attempt to put regions firmly in the group of general classification problems, there remains the difficult problem of absolute location. However they are classed, regions retain their locational uniqueness. Central Chile would certainly be placed in a *Mediterranean* areal class in a classification on climatic-agricultural lines; just as certainly it would have unique properties from its southern *South American* location.

b. Regions and set-theory. One unexplored avenue of regional study is through the link between regional classification and the mathematical study of sets (Fletcher, 1964, pp. 121–83). Some of the possibilities of the method can be shown by the Venn diagrams used in Figs. 9.1 to 9.3,

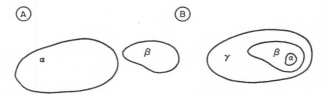

Fig. 9.1. Venn diagrams of two-set regional structure.

where we examine the countries of the American hemisphere. If we call this collection of countries a *set* and each separate country an *element* of the set, then we can illustrate two types of locational classification by the use of the Venn diagrams. Simple discrimination between two mutually exclusive groups, say North America and South America, is shown by regions α and β in Fig. 9.1-A; while a hierarchical type of regional classification, say Bolivia within South America, within the American hemisphere, is shown by regions α, β, and γ in Fig. 9.1-B. This simple classification illustrates the point that, for locational classification, the map is in fact a special type of Venn diagram.

A more complicated example comes when regions are not based wholly on locational criteria. For example, if we now take a set consisting of five tropical countries, together with a second set of eleven underdeveloped countries, how many elements are there? Fig. 9.2 shows through Venn diagrams that theoretically there are six possibilities ranging from Case 1 where the two sets are non-intersecting (Fig. 9.2-A), i.e. where no tropical countries are underdeveloped, through to Case 6 where all the underdeveloped countries are included within the tropical set (Fig. 9.2-F).

Much more complex relationships are of course possible. If we combine the previous two examples with three sets, American countries α, tropical countries β, and underdeveloped countries γ, then we can combine the three sets as in Fig. 9.3-A. Through intersection of the Venn diagrams we can see that there are seven categories into which countries may fall. Thus we may contrast the United States (1), which is part of the American set

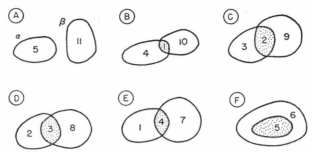

Fig. 9.2. Alternative intersection of α and β regional sets. Source: Fletcher, 1964, p. 125.

but is not part of the tropical or underdeveloped sets, with Colombia (2), which is part of the American, the tropical, and the underdeveloped sets. Countries like Uganda (3), China (4), Chile (5) suggest other sectors of

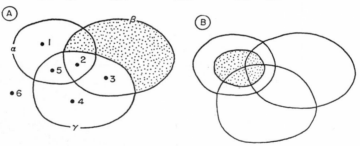

Fig. 9.3. Venn diagrams of three-set (*A*) and four-set (*B*) regions.

the diagram, while the United Kingdom (6) lies outside these sets (but forms part of the larger set made up of all the countries in the world). The two shaded areas represent empty parts of the sets, i.e. (i) tropical countries which are not underdeveloped, and (ii) American tropical countries which are not underdeveloped. The implications of this finding are largely supported by Berry (1960-B) in his study of the distribution of economically backward countries. Fig. 9.3-B suggests further possible elaboration of Venn diagrams by introducing Central America (shaded) as a separate sub-set within the American set, α.

These relationships are usually expressed in a shorthand form by symbols. Thus we can express Fig. 9.2-F as $\alpha \subset \beta$ which is read as 'is contained in'. While this shorthand type of logical statement is generally unfamiliar in geographical writing, it is beginning to be used (e.g. Kansky, 1963, pp. 122–7) in research literature, and may well be the appropriate formal language in which our regional and other theories should be couched. It has the merit that theories once written in this way can be tested for illogicalities (Chap. 10.III(3)).

2. Qualitative analysis: superimposed boundaries

Regions like the American 'South' or the 'Languedoc' of France may be recognized informally, almost intuitively. Even in the United States, sectionalism in social attitudes, political behaviour, and literature persists (Jensen, 1951) and these regions of social awareness have been used by Paterson (1960) as a basis for regional division in a textbook on North America. The prime difficulty with such instinctively appropriate regions is their mistiness; they remain distinct only when viewed from a distance— on close examination they dissolve into a new series of still smaller 'character areas'. As Wrigley demonstrates (in Chorley and Haggett, 1965-A,

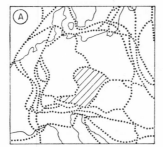 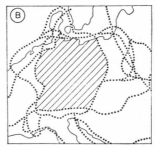

Fig. 9.4. Alternative definitions of Mitteleuropa ($G = 2·6$) in terms of human (*A*) and physical (*B*) criteria. Areas of common overlap shaded. Source: Sinnhuber, 1954, 19, 24.

Chap. 1), even the *pays* of France, the touchstones of regional identity, were seen by the ageing Vidal de la Blache with increasing scepticism.

Sinnhuber (1954) has illustrated the remarkable range of definitions that have been given to what is variously designated Central Europe, Mitteleuropa, or Europe Central. From some sixteen geographies, ranging from that of Schjerning in 1914 to Gottmann in 1951, Sinnhuber shows the remarkable variety in their regional definitions. Fig. 9.4-A shows these boundaries. Surprisingly, areas included within the term Middle Europe extend outside the limits of the map and Sinnhuber ruefully observes that the Iberian peninsula is the only part of Europe not included by at least one author. Conversely the area which all the authors agree belongs to Central Europe is remarkably small—no more than Austria and Bohemia–Moravia. This area is shaded in Fig. 9.4-A.

That this core is not by itself an adequate solution is shown by the companion map (Fig. 9.4-B) based on six concepts of Middle Europe as given by geographers writing over a comparable time period (1887 to 1937) but using physical criteria. This map shows a large core area with much less variation in the alternative definitions; one which includes within it the Austria–Bohemia–Moravia core area of the previous analysis.

Superimposition retains the great value of simplicity and demands little beyond the need to plot boundaries on a map. Green (1955) has extended superimposition in tackling the problem of boundary demarcation between the two major cities of the eastern seaboard of the United States (New York and Boston). Previous attempts by Park and Newcomb, based on newspaper circulation, and by the National Resources Committee had given widely different boundaries: the first placing the debated state

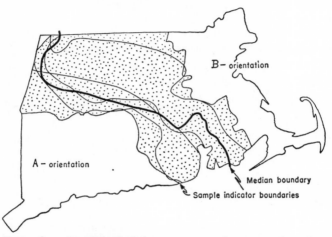

Fig. 9.5. Zone of overlap (stippled) in attempts to demarcate the urban fields of Boston and New York in southern New England ($G = 4 \cdot 1$). Source: Green, 1955, pp. 284–300.

of Connecticut into the field of Boston and the second placing it largely in the New York field.

Green's answer to this problem was to map separately seven indicators of transportation, communications, agriculture, recreation, manufacturing, and finance. Specifically the indices were (1) railroad ticket purchases, (2) estimate of truck freight movement, (3) metropolitan newspaper circulation, (4) long-distance telephone calls, (5) origin of vacationers, (6) addresses of directors of major industrial metropolitan firms, and (7) metropolitan correspondents for hinterland banks. These seven indicators form a series of curves plotted on Fig. 9.5.

As might have been expected, the curves did not coincide and Green synthesized the results of this trial plot by interpolating a median boundary (heavy line in Fig. 9.5) between these curves. Further, it was possible to isolate an area completely oriented to New York on all seven indices, α, and one similarly oriented to Boston, β. Green's study showed fairly con-clusively that Connecticut, traditionally a 'New England' state, is almost completely oriented to New York.

Superimposition of boundaries is clearly useful in the rapid determina-tion of core areas of regions, but there remains an element of uncertainty about the value of the method as a boundary marker. For example, in using a median line we assume that each of the individual boundary lines it describes is of equal validity as a regional determinant. Alternatively some boundaries are accepted, others rejected. Understandably, therefore, geographical research has been moving over the last decade towards evolving more reliable methods of regional identification.

3. Quantitative analysis

Although four quantitative methods—Thiessen polygons, distance-minimization functions, discriminant analysis, and graph-theory methods —are reviewed here, the pace of exploration is such that these can only be regarded as a sample of the potential range of identification techniques. The economic importance of regional delimitation for both government

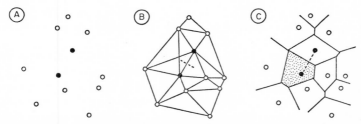

Fig. 9.6. Stages in the construction of Thiessen polygons around centres.
Source: Kopec, 1963, p. 25.

and private enterprise is sufficiently pressing to ensure further rapid development in this sector, particularly through the advent of operational research techniques and high-speed data processing (Kao, 1963).

a. Thiessen polygons. Bogue (1949, p. 17) makes use of a wholly geo-metrical procedure in delimiting the boundaries of his 67 metropolitan centres within the United States. This procedure is based on the method of 'Thiessen polygons' used by the U.S. Weather Bureau in generalizing the rainfall of a given water catchment from a network of meteorological recording stations. Fig. 9.6 illustrates the method of drawing the boun-daries: (i) lines are drawn joining a given centre to each adjacent centre; (ii) each of these inter-centre lines is bisected to give the midpoint of the line; (iii) from the midpoint of the line a boundary line is drawn at right angles to the original inter-centre line to give a series of polygons;

(iv) counties lying across the boundaries are included within the boundary of the centre within which the greater part of the county area lies.

The validity of the method lies in two assumptions. The first is that the area within the intersecting boundary lines of the polygon lies nearer to the enclosed centre than to any other centre. This is a simple geometric property of the Thiessen polygon. The second assumption is that a metropolis dominates all the area that lies geometrically nearest to it. This is clearly debatable and was used by Bogue as a working hypothesis only in the absence of other clear-cut criteria. Bogue, having defined his standard metropolis, gives it an equal weight in its drawing power over the hinterland. Whether this is true for cities as different as New York city and El Paso, Texas, seems less reasonable. Over the United States the use of straight lines to join cities is effectively to parallel an air-route definition, and studies by Taaffe suggest this is a valid element in the urban hierarchy.

In practice the drawing of Thiessen polygons is time-consuming, and there is usually some imprecision over the choice of diagonals to be used in drawing the boundaries of the polygon around a given centre. Kopec (1963) has reported an alternative method of construction in which arcs of circles of the same radius are drawn from adjacent points and the side of a polygon is located by drawing a line through the points of intersection on the arcs. The argument for this method is that it eliminates the need to draw diagonals and reduces the chance of error from using inappropriate ones in construction.

b. Distance-minimization functions. The effect of the high-speed computer on regional assignment problems is only now beginning to be felt. Yeates (1963) using an IBM 709 computer at Northwestern University, Chicago, has illustrated the way in which distance to a number of nodal centres may be optimized using a method from operations research designed for the solution of transportation problems. This solution consists, in economic terms, of minimizing the cost of shipping a product from a set of sources to a number of destinations, or vice versa.

Yeates has illustrated this approach to regional delimitation by a practical analysis of the problem of minimizing the cost of 'shipping' children to school; specifically, the cost of moving the 2,900 high school children of Grant county, Wisconsin, to the thirteen high schools in that county. The location of the schools and school districts for the central part of Yeates's study area is shown in Fig. 9.7-A.

To reduce the size of the computing problem both schools and pupils' homes were assumed to lie in the centre of the square-mile section in which they were located, and school boundaries were redrawn on this simplified basis (Fig. 9.7-B) by including the whole square-mile section within a school area, if the greater part was in that section. Since 754 sections were occupied by children from the thirteen schools the problem was reduced to a 754 × 13 matrix. With this data optimum boundaries were deter-

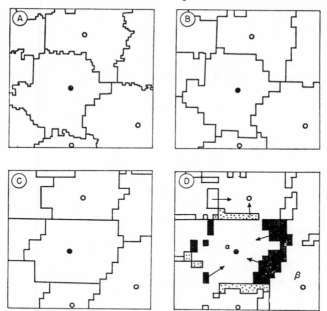

Fig. 9.7. Distance-minimization approach to the construction of optimum boundaries in a sample quadrat ($G = 5·5$) of Grant county, Wisconsin, United States. Source: Yeates, 1963, pp. 8, 9.

mined by computer such that: (i) total distance to schools was minimized; (ii) each school was filled to its capacity (in 1961). Subject to a number of restrictions the problem can be expressed algebraically as:

$$\sum_{i=1}^{n}\sum_{j=1}^{m} d_{ij}, x_{ij} = \text{minimum}$$

where d_{ij} is the distance from the ith section to any jth high school and x_{ij} is the number of schoolchildren in the ith section assigned to the jth high school.

The boundaries resulting from this minimum solution are shown in Fig. 9.7-C. Comparison with the boundaries of the formalized school districts shows that there is considerable change and overlap. The boundaries of the Lancaster high school, α, in Fig. 9.7-D, show losses to the north and south (stippled) but large gains (black) from the neighbouring Platteville high school, β, on the east.

How important are the changes shown in Yeates's reallocation? Analysis is made more difficult by two factors: the fact that the theoretical boundaries were based on children's distribution in a single year (1961) while the actual school districts must remain static over a longer time; and the difficulty of comparing the actual ground distance covered along roads by the children with the cross-country (direct) distance used in the theoretical analysis.

Table 9.2. Distances travelled with alternative district boundaries*

High school:	Boscobel	Platteville
Actual school districts:		
Mean road distance to school, miles	6·7	6·4
Mean overland distance to school, miles	5·5	5·6
Theoretical school districts:		
Mean overland distance to school, miles	5·1	5·3
Estimated saving on overland distance, miles	0·4	0·3

Source: Yeates, 1963, p. 9.
* Grant county, Wisconsin, United States, 1961.

Table 9.2 shows the results for a sample study of two high schools in the area, Boscobel and Platteville, where a comparison of the distances both by road and cross country suggests savings of the order of 0·4 to 0·3 miles. No figures on transport costs were available, but rough approximations suggest that if the revised boundaries were adopted, then this might save some $3,000–4,000 each year on school transport.

Support for the type of analysis used by Yeates comes from a number of sources (e.g. Claesen, 1964). Already one English county (Somerset) with acute problems of scattered rural students and few schools has applied this type of analysis to its school-bus problems with considerable success. In the field of industrial location Garrison (1959, pp. 471–82) has shown the applicability of the method to reducing distributing costs on products like petroleum.

c. Discriminant analysis. A further development in the drawing of boundary lines should be mentioned as it may well be used increasingly in the future. This is the method of *discriminant analysis*. Sebestyen (1962, pp. 69–71) has illustrated how this method may be used to set up classification criteria for complex geographical distributions. We begin with a distribution in two dimensions of phenomena ζ and η, arranged in a complex pattern of four clusters (Fig. 9.8-A). Sebestyen shows that successively more complex polynomial lines may be computed, which, when superimposed on the distribution, divide it into areas in which ζ and η are 'expected'. Simple first-order polynomials (Fig. 9.8-B) appear as a straight line; conversely a sixth-order polynomial (Fig. 9.8-D) appears as a complex line. The simple line misclassifies a third of the points whereas the complex line accurately classifies both ζ and η distributions. Between the two lie intermediate solutions of which the second-order polynomial (Fig. 9.8-c) appears particularly efficient in that it misclassifies only 9·0 per cent of the ζ and η distributions yet is a mathematically simple solution.

The advent of machine mapping (Tobler, 1959) suggests that this type of classification procedure, despite its computational complexity, may be applied to the type of boundary problems in which we need to predict the

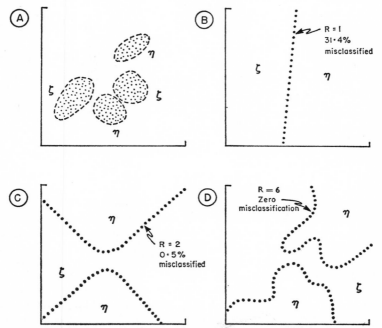

Fig. 9.8. Use of higher-order discriminant analysis to classify a mapped distribution (ζ and η) into discrete regions. Source: Sebestyen, 1962, pp. 69–71.

probable course of a boundary across areas where information is either absent or very sparse.

d. Graph-theory interpretation of regions. One of the most powerful of the newer analytical techniques that geographers have begun to use over the last decade is *graph theory* (Harary and Norman, 1953). Its relation to transport networks (Chap. 3.I(3)) and their quantitative description (Chap. 8.II(3)) has already been described. Nystuen and Dacey (1961) have shown how the same type of analysis may be used to define regional structure. Given a set of cities in an area and a measure of association between them, a regional hierarchy may be built up.

Table 9.3 shows a hypothetical matrix of cities ($a, b \ldots l$) for which the numbers in the matrix measure the flow (e.g. telephone calls) from one city to another. Thus the flow from city d to city a is nineteen units, and

Table 9.3. Matrix of flow between pairs of centres*

To centre:	a	b	c	d	e	f	g	h	i	j	k	l	Class
From centre:													
a	00	**75**	15	20	28	02	03	02	01	20	01	00	Satellite
b	**69**	00	45	50	58	12	20	03	06	35	04	02	Dominant
c	05	**51**	00	12	40	00	06	01	03	15	00	01	Satellite
d	19	**57**	14	00	30	07	06	02	11	18	05	01	Satellite
e	07	40	**48**	26	00	07	10	02	37	39	12	06	Dominant
f	01	06	01	01	10	00	**27**	01	03	04	02	00	Satellite
g	02	16	03	03	13	**31**	00	03	18	08	03	01	Dominant
h	00	04	00	01	03	03	06	00	12	**38**	04	00	Satellite
i	02	28	03	06	43	04	16	12	00	**98**	13	01	Satellite
j	07	40	10	08	40	05	17	34	**98**	00	35	12	Dominant
k	01	08	02	01	18	00	06	05	12	**30**	00	15	Satellite
l	00	02	00	00	07	00	01	00	01	06	**12**	00	Satellite
Total:	113	337	141	128	290	071	118	065	202	311	091	039	
Rank order:	8	1	5	6	3	10	7	11	4	2	9	12	

Source: Nystuen and Dacey, 1961, p. 35.

* Hypothetical data.

that from city k to city i is twelve units, and so on. The *order* of the city is measured by the total in-coming flow and is given by the column total, i.e. city b with a total of 337 units is the first city, j the second city, and so on. Hierarchic relations between cities are determined by the largest out-going flow to a higher-order city (*nodal flow*) shown in the matrix by heavier type. Thus the largest flow from a is to b (i.e. $a \rightarrow b$).

Examination of the matrix shows, however, that for four of the cities (b, e, g, and j) the largest flow is to a 'lower-order' city (where order is determined by the column totals). These cities form the *terminal points* of the graph. Beginning with these four terminal points (Fig. 9.9) the other eight cities can be plotted with vectors linking them directly or indirectly to the

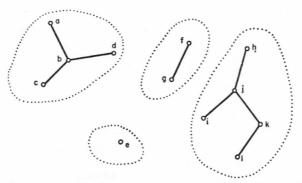

Fig. 9.9. Nodal structure of the matrix shown in Table 9.3 in terms of graph theory. Source: Nystuen and Dacey, 1961, p. 35.

terminals according to the nodal flow from each city. The resulting hierarchical structure describes the nodal structure of the region in terms of four distinct clusters (*sub-graphs*) of varying sizes.

Washington state was used by Nystuen and Dacey (1961, pp. 38–42) to illustrate the application of this matrix method to a specific region. Using forty cities in and adjacent to the state (Fig. 9.10-A), a 40 × 40 matrix was set up with flow data for long-distance telephone traffic. Certain cities north of Seattle were omitted for lack of data. Analysis of the matrix in terms of graph theory showed: (i) a large regional hierarchy centred on Seattle (α) with nested hierarchies around Yakima (β) and

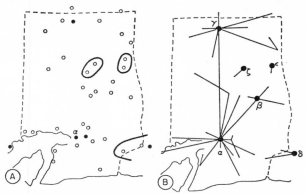

Fig. 9.10. Nodal structure of the state of Washington, northwestern United States ($G = 3\cdot5$), based on graph-theory analysis of flows between cities. Source: Nystuen and Dacey, 1961, p. 39.

Spokane (γ); (ii) a separate system centred on Portland (δ); and (iii) two small independent systems centred on Pasco (ε) and Moses Lake (ζ) (Fig. 9.10-B). The findings accord reasonably well with other empirical evidence on the regional organization of the state, but point up the unexpected independence of the two small interior systems.

Even with this fairly elementary application, the utility of graph theory is readily apparent. It allows decisions to be made on the relative strength of regional 'bonds' and, given appropriate empirical data, is likely to be useful in both administrative and business applications of region-building. Like 'basic pairs' analysis (Chap. 10.I(2)) it suffers from too great a dependence on dominant rather than the complete flows, but more sophisticated developments in graph theory are likely to correct this feature.

II. REGIONS: THE ASSIGNMENT PROBLEM

We have seen already how regions may be identified by successive demarcation of regional cores and boundaries. This method is of some special value in the study of nodal regions where the centre is well established and the problem is solely one of identifying its limits. More commonly, however, we are faced with unit areas (such as states or counties) whose limits are already established and here our problem is one of *assignment*, i.e. placing these units in a given regional class. This assignment process may be either (i) a simple classification procedure in which like units are grouped regardless of their location or alternatively, (ii) a more complex procedure in which both the location and contiguity of the areas have to be taken into account.

1. General classification methods

a. Distance analysis in n-dimensional space. In everyday life we intuitively group together things which are like or 'near' each other. Thus we talk of 'children' as a group which is composed of individuals near to one another in age. We use 'distance' in a non-geographical sense merely as distance along an age scale. Berry (1958) has examined a number of ways in which this concept of distance can be used in classifying geographical features.

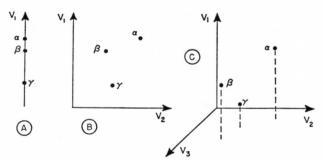

Fig. 9.11. Plotting of three values (α, β, and γ) in one-, two-, and three-dimensional space.

This concept of *n*-dimensional space is illustrated by the three points, α, β, and γ, in Fig. 9.11. In the simple case of one dimension represented by a single vector, V_1 (Fig. 9.11-A), α and β are close together. They remain close when a second dimension, vector V_2, is added (Fig. 9.11-B). When a third dimension is added, vector V_3, we can see the position is changed and β is now much nearer to γ (Fig. 9.11-C). Although we cannot show graphically a fourth dimension, vector V_4, there is no mathematical limit to adding this and further vectors to give a theoretical multidimensional space, i.e. n-dimensional space.

Distance between points in n-dimensional space follows from the well-known rule of the 'square of the hypotenuse'. It can be briefly written as

$$D = \sqrt{\sum_{i=1}^{n} (x_i - y_i)^2}$$

where $i = 1, 2 \ldots n$, where D is the distance (similarity) between points x and y, where x_i and y_i are the values of characteristic i and where vectors are orthogonal (Berry, 1958, p. 301). More complex measures of generalized distance have been derived by Mahalanobis and others (Mahalanobis, Rao, and Majumdar, 1949) where both the average value of a region and the dispersal of the units within it have to be taken into account.

The object of classification is simply then to place in one group areas which are near together (homogeneous) in n-dimensional space and to separate groups which are far apart (heterogeneous) in a similar space field.

Berry (1961-B) has illustrated this technique very clearly with reference to the service-industry characteristics of nine census divisions of the United States in 1954 (Fig. 9.12-B). Here he was concerned with six factors (derived from a series of measurements in the way outlined in Chapter 8.I(3d)) and measured the distance between points (D^2) in 6-dimensional space. This showed that of the nine census divisions, New England (α) and East North Central (β) had most in common (a D^2 value of only 0·69), while East South Central (θ), the heart of the 'South', and Pacific (ζ) were most dissimilar (with a D^2 value of nearly 35). By placing the two nearest divisions together the nine units were reduced to eight. Distances between the remaining eight regions were derived and the Middle Atlantic district added to the New England–East North Central region. By repeating this process the regions were progressively diminished till finally the whole of the United States formed a single region. These successive stages are shown in the nine maps of Fig. 9.12-A. We can then have nine different levels of regional breakdown of the United States, each one efficient at its particular level. Which of these is the most efficient?

Berry (1961-B, p. 273) has shown that in this breakdown process (in which we proceed from many to few regions) we are progressively gaining in generality and progressively losing in definition. Perfect detail is available only with all nine original regions; perfect generality is available only if we regard the whole United States as one unit. This loss of detail can be calibrated using the distance measured previously (within-group D^2) and ranges from zero with all nine divisions to 343·47 with only one region.

Fig. 9.13 plots this progressive loss of detail by the use of a 'linkage tree'

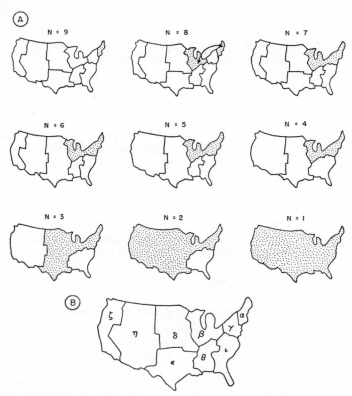

Fig. 9.12. Stages in the regional grouping of census divisions in the United States ($G = 1 \cdot 8$) by multivariate analysis. Source: Berry, 1961-B, p. 272.

which shows the progressive combination of regions as they were made, step by step, and mapped in Fig. 9.12-A. We should note in particular that the loss of detail (as measured by the within-group D^2) is plotted on a logarithmic scale, emphasizing the very small loss of detail in the first five grouping steps. Specifically only 3·5 per cent of the detail was lost in these steps. This means that we can learn almost as much by regarding the United States as four large regions as nine smaller census districts.

The implication of Berry's findings in Fig. 9.13 is that while we must choose the regional breakdown that serves our particular research purposes, we need to be aware of their relative efficiency. If it matters little whether we need two, three, or four service regions in the United States, then the loss of detail analysis suggests it is worth adopting four regions (only 3·5 per cent loss) or three regions (10 per cent loss) rather than two regions (40 per cent loss).

b. Chi-squared (χ^2) analysis in classification. Where data are available only

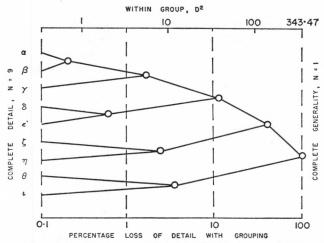

Fig. 9.13. Linkage tree of the grouping shown in Fig. 9.12 with percentage loss of detail. Symbols refer to the census regions. Source: Berry, 1961-B, pp. 272, 273.

on a nominal scale, some alternative to factor analysis may be employed. One such type of analysis was developed by two botanists working at Southampton University with a Pegasus computer (Williams and Lambert, 1959–62, and although the computer programme was originally designed to divide plant quadrat records into ecological regions it has since been used to classify towns in eastern England.

The chi-squared statistic is given by the formula

$$\chi^2 = \sum_{j=1}^{k} (n_j - v_j)^2 / v_j$$

where a set of n values is distributed over k classes so that the observed frequency in the jth class is n_j and the theoretical or expected frequency in that class is v_j (Kendall and Buckland, 1957, p. 41). Examples of its computation and application to geographical problems are given by Gregory (1963, pp. 153–66).

In this analysis we begin with a series of units (regions, settlements, etc.) for each of which we have a set of characteristics which are either present or absent. We can recast this first table, a matrix of regions and characteristics, into a second table in which characteristics occur along both axes of the table. Where the row for function A crosses the column for function B there is a value of χ^2 showing the extent to which they are associated. If it has a high value this is evidence that the two functions are not independent, and vice versa.

Williams found that by adding across the rows (or alternatively down the column) a sum for each species could be derived, and further that the species whose column sum was the largest provided the most efficient indicator for regional division. Thus quadrats could be broken into two groups, those with, and those without the indicator species (i.e. with the maximum χ^2 sum). From this stage the two groups could be further broken down using the species with the next highest sum, and so on. The general pattern of grouping is shown hypothetically in Fig. 9.14, where

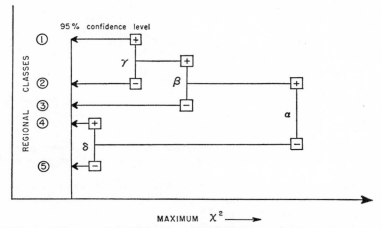

Fig. 9.14. Five-stage breakdown of a distribution into regional classes by χ^2 analysis. Source: Williams and Lambert, 1960, p. 692.

division into *five* regional classes is shown based on the presence ($+$) or absence ($-$) of four species, α, β, γ, and δ.

There are of course a large number of classificatory techniques which have not yet been adapted to regional demarcation. Kershaw (1964, pp. 130–70) and Greig-Smith (1964, pp. 158–209) have summarized the very wide range of classification techniques used in botany which have yet to be explored fully by human geographers.

2. Assignment of areas to regional clusters

We may argue that the methods outlined above are not specifically geographical, they merely classify geographical data. This is the view taken by Hagood and Price (1952, p. 542) when they argue, in the course of an agricultural classification of the United States, that '. . . California cannot be put into the same region as New Jersey because of geographical separation'. In the same way we find Bunge (1962, p. 16) arguing that it is the implicit inclusion of the category of location that makes for regional as against the purely classificatory approach to the earth's surface.

In seeking to build up contiguous regions we need then to carry on a sort of progressive comparison of any unit with its neighbours. In effect we are asking how nearly does a given area match its neighbours. Thus in the case of California we would be concerned to compare that state with its contiguous neighbours, Oregon, Nevada, and Arizona, but not (at least, not in the first rounds of analysis) with Missouri or Oklahoma.

Two of the techniques that have been used with some success in this comparing process are illustrated here: (i) variance analysis and (ii) correlation analysis.

a. Variance analysis. The total variation displayed by a set of observations can be measured by its *variance*, i.e. the sums of squares of deviations from the arithmetic mean. In certain circumstances it can be separated into components associated with specific sources of variation. Examples of this type of analysis, applied to geographical problems, with appropriate computational instructions are given in Gregory (1963, pp. 133–50).

Zobler (1958) used variance analysis to decide whether, in terms of its industrial population (number of workers in manufacturing and primary industries in 1950), the state of West Virginia should be grouped with one of three state regions: (1) Mid-Atlantic; (2) South Atlantic; (3) East South Central. The state regions are shown in Fig. 9.15-A with West Virginia shaded. Inspection of the figures for the states making up the three regions and for West Virginia give no decisive indication to which existing region the problem state should be added; and a more rigorous approach was adopted.

Zobler argued that when regions are being constructed from smaller units there are two sources of variation. There is variation among the states within a region (*within-region variation*) and variation among the regions (*between-region variation*). Variance analysis was used to measure this variation within and between regions under three conditions, with West Virginia assigned to each of the three regions in turn (Table 9.4).

Table 9.4. Regional assignment using variance analysis*

Variance ratios:	*Between-region variance* (a)	*Within-region variance* (b)	*Variance ratios* (a/b)
Alternative assignment of West Virginia:			
To Mid-Atlantic region	46·09	8·91	5·17†
To South Atlantic region	71·55	4·66	15·35‡
To East South Central region	72·13	4·57	15·78‡

Source: Zobler, 1958, p. 146.
  * Eastern United States, 1950.   † Significant at the 95 per cent confidence level.
  ‡ Significant at the 99·9 per cent confidence level.

The between-region variance, showing the variation of the regions around the mean of all the regions, was divided by the within-region variance,

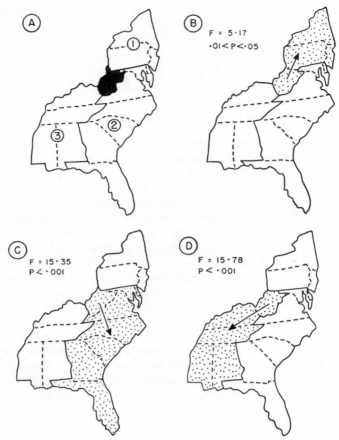

Fig. 9.15. Assignment of West Virginia to three alternative regional groups in the southeastern United States ($G = 2\cdot6$) with significance levels derived from variance analysis. Source: Zobler, 1958, p. 146.

showing the variation of the states around their respective regional means, to give the variance ratio or F-ratio. If the two variances are equal, the value of this ratio is one and the more F rises above one the greater the interregional differentials. In broad terms the variance ratio describes how successful the grouping procedure has been in keeping like states together and keeping unlike states apart.

Results in Table 9.4 show that although West Virginia could be assigned to any of the three regions the optimum allocation was to join it to Alabama, Mississippi, Kentucky, and Tennessee in the East South Central division (Fig. 9.15-D). Conversely, the worst classification on this analysis would be to place it with New Jersey, New York, and Pennsylvania in the Mid-Atlantic division (Fig. 9.15-B).

b. *Correlation and regional 'bonds'.* Correlation in a general sense denotes the association between quantitative or qualitative data. It is measured by correlation coefficients which vary between −1 and 1 with the intermediate value of zero indicating absence of correlation and the two extremes indicating complete negative or positive correlation. Kendall and Buckland (1957, p. 67) define a generalized correlation coefficient, Γ,

$$\Gamma = (\Sigma\ a_{ij}b_{ij})/\sqrt{(\Sigma\ a_{ij}{}^2\ \Sigma\ b_{ij}{}^2)}$$

where, in two sets of observations $x_1 \ldots x_n$ and $y_1 \ldots y_n$, a score is allotted to each pair of individuals a_{ij} and b_{ij} and Σ is a summation of all values of i and j from 1 to n. This general coefficient includes others such as Kendall's *tau*, Spearman's *rho*, and Pearson's *r*. Examples of the computation and application of correlation coefficients to geographical problems are given in Gregory (1963, pp. 167–84).

The problem studied by Hagood (Hagood, 1943; Hagood and Price, 1952, pp. 541–7) was to divide the United States into some six to a dozen contiguous groups of states with each group of states to be made as homogeneous as possible with respect to some 104 items taken from the 1940 Censuses of Population and Agriculture. These items were equally divided into two major groups, agriculture and population, and these were in turn divided into further sub-groups, fourteen in all. These groups varied in size from information on crops (twelve items) in the agriculture group, to information on race (five items) in the population group.

These items were used to draw up 'agriculture-population profiles' of each state. First, all the 104 items were standardized so that the mean value for the forty-eight states for each item was 50·0 and the standard deviation 10·0. Second, correlation coefficients (r) were calculated between the profiles of adjacent states.

The resulting coefficients varied from very high values between like states (e.g. Alabama and Georgia had a coefficient of +0·92) to very low values between unlike states (e.g. Ohio and its southern neighbour, Kentucky, had a coefficient of only +0·01, suggesting that the line between North and South remains strong in the United States). Part of Hagood's map is reproduced in Fig. 9.16. Here for an area of the northern United States the values of the coefficients have been replaced by lines of varying width. The result shows the scaffolding of 'regional bonds' between the thirteen states; it emphasizes the strong north–south links between Montana and Wyoming, between the two Dakotas, Nebraska and Kansas, and between Minnesota and Wisconsin. Likewise we see the rather weak links east–west across the grain of the country.

In practice, Hagood used these correlation bonds to supplement a single comparative index, the 'composite agriculture-population index'

Fig. 9.16. Pattern of interstate correlation bonds in the north-central United States
$(G = 2·5)$. Source: Hagood and Price, 1952, p. 545.

which she calculated by factor analysis, in much the same way as Thompson *et al.* (1962) calculated a single index of economic health for New York state (Chap. 8.I(3d)). Delineation began with the easily recognizable regional nuclei which formed the centres of homogeneous regions. Once these had been established, the marginal states were allocated to one of these nuclei on the basis of both its composite index and its intercorrelations with its neighbours.

This distinction between 'nuclear' and 'marginal' states is brought out clearly in Table 9.5. This shows that on average Alabama was nearly

Table 9.5. Coefficients of similarity for agriculture-population profiles*

State:	Nuclear type (Alabama)	Marginal type (Missouri)
Number of neighbouring states	4	8
Coefficients of similarity:		
Maximum similarity	0·92	0·45
Minimum similarity	0·44	0·08
Mean similarity	0·75	0·29

Source: Hagood and Price, 1952, p. 545.
* For states adjacent to Alabama and Missouri, 1950.

three times more like its adjoining neighbour states than was Missouri. Alabama clearly lies deep within the heart of the South with strong similarities to its neighbours, while Missouri lies on the border of four of the six major regions recognized by Hagood. As its highest link lay with the state of Illinois, Missouri was finally assigned to a Great Lakes region.

We find then that correlation bonds do not solve regional problems in the sense of creating homogeneity where none exists. What they appear to do is to help legislate in difficult cases and make the reasons for the choice, however marginal that choice may be, clear to the observer.

III. REGIONAL GENERALIZATION AND SCALE

1. Nature of the scale problem

The difficulties encountered in using data for units of different size has been described in Chapter 7.III(1). We found there that our basic dilemma is that generalizations made at one level do not necessarily hold at another level, and that conclusions we derived at one scale may be invalid at another. As McCarty argued: 'Every change in scale will bring about the statement of a new problem, and there is no basis for presuming that associations existing at one scale will also exist at another' (McCarty et al., 1956, p. 16). This difficult problem has also been discussed at length by Duncan (Duncan et al., 1961, pp. 26 ff.).

Practical examples of the scale problem come to light in industrial location. McLaughlin and Robock (1949) in their study of the 'migration' of industrial plants to the South of the United States found it necessary to divide their locational results into two stages: (i) reasons for the choice by companies of the South in general, or what they term *regional zoning*; and (ii) reasons for the choice of individual towns, *community screening*. Thus, although the market potential of the South is seen as a major factor at the regional level, it becomes very much less significant at the local level where factors like community amenities (e.g. education, hospitals, etc.) may play a more decisive part.

Scale problems in the locational analysis of a type of land use, residual forests, have been recorded by Haggett (1964). In a study of the distribution of timbered land in southeast Brazil, it was found that at the *regional* level (over an area about the size of West Virginia) the two dominant factors were forest-density and terrain ruggedness (Table 10.7). At the *local level* (over an area of about forty square miles) terrain and accessibility were the most important factors (Table 10.10). Not only were the results different at both levels but the type of analysis had to be altered: data available at one level were unobtainable at another, statistical techniques applicable at one level were inappropriate for another.

2. Scale in regional hierarchies

The fact that scale problems have long troubled geographers is rather plainly shown in the series of attempts that have been made to define regions in scale terms. With formal regions (Table 9.1) the early system applied by Fennemann (1916) to the landform divisions of the United States with his recognition of major divisions, provinces, and sections had a major effect on other writers (Table 9.6). Unstead (1933) in an interesting paper on 'systems of regions' put forward the scheme which filled in at the smaller levels the system Fennemann had begun at the larger.

Table 9.6. Comparative scales and terminology of regional hierarchies

Approximate size (ml.^{2})	Fennemann, 1916	Unstead, 1933	Linton, 1949	Whittlesey, 1954	Map scales for analysis*
10^0			Site		
10		Stow	Stow	Locality	1/10,000
10^2	District		Tract		
		Tract		District	1/50,000
10^3	Section		Section		
		Sub-region		Province	1/1,000,000
10^4	Province		Province		
		Minor region			
10^5	Major division		Major division	Realm	1/5,000,000
10^6		Major region	Continent		

Source: Haggett. In Chorley and Haggett, 1965-A.

* Whittlesey, 1954.

Linton (1948) integrated both preceding systems in a seven-stage scheme which ran through the whole range from the smallest unit, the site, to the largest, the continent. More recently Whittlesey (in James, Jones, and Wright, 1954, pp. 47–51) presented a 'hierarchy for compages' with details of the appropriate map scales for study and presentation, and followed this with a model study on Southern Rhodesia to illustrate his method (Whittlesey, 1956).

The decade since the Whittlesey scheme was put into operation and the call was made to '. . . fill this lacuna in geographic thinking' (in James et al., 1954, p. 47) has not seen any rush to adopt it. Of the few significant papers published in this field, only one, that by Bird (1956), subjected Whittlesey's scheme to field testing. Bird's two-scale comparison of the western peninsulas of Brittany and Cornwall suggested that while a general (or small-scale) approach showed the two areas to be similar, the intensive (or large-scale) study showed that the two peninsulas were quite dissimilar in most details. Bird's deft illustration of a fundamental and very common geographic problem passed scarcely without comment.

The second major move in the period since Whittlesey's papers came from Philbrick (1957) who published a very full scheme based on the concept of a sevenfold hierarchy of functions. Corresponding to each function is a nodal point with its functional region. Here scale is introduced through the geometrical concept of *nesting* with each order of the hierarchy fitting within the next highest order. Philbrick illustrates the hypothetical case where each central place of a given order is defined to include four central places of the next lower order. This gives a succession for a seventh-order region of four sixth-order places, sixteen fifth-order places, and so on down to the final level of 4,096 first-order places. His attempt to apply this scheme to the eastern United States, with New York and Chicago in the role of seventh- and sixth-order centres, was only partly successful, but the attempt to introduce a scale component into a system of nodal regions has given an important lead.

3. Scale-component analysis: sampling methods

Quantitative attempts to isolate and measure scale components have not been widely attempted in geographical analysis. In the sections which follow, two broad lines of attack are suggested: (i) nested sampling and variance analysis, (ii) filter mapping and a closely associated technique, trend-surface mapping. These are illustrated by work by the writer in central Portugal (Haggett, 1961-B) and by wider reference to work in other earth sciences, notably in geophysics (reviewed by Miller and Kahn, 1962, pp. 390–439; Chorley and Haggett, 1965-B).

a. *Nested sampling.* One approach to the problem of local and regional variation that cuts out the need for complete information on all the area considered is that of nested sampling (Olson and Potter, 1954; Krumbein, 1956). It is particularly valuable in exploratory studies where there is a need to cover as large a region as possible but at the same time pay attention to local variations.

The basic method of the nested approach (also termed the multilevel or hierarchical approach) is to divide the region into a few major areas of equal size. Several of these major regions are then chosen at random and broken down into a number of smaller sub-regions. Several of these sub-regions are chosen at random and broken down again, the process being continued until the smallest meaningful unit is reached, or data cease to be available. Fig. 9.17 illustrates this process by breaking down a 150 × 100 kilometre quadrangle into six 'regional units' each 50 × 50 kilometres,

Table 9.7. Nested sampling design for analysis of scale components*

Areal level:	Region I	Sub-region II	District III	Sub-district IV	Locality V
Area, km.²	2,500	625	156	39	10
Number of cells in population	6	24	96	384	1,536
Number of cells sampled	6	12	24	48	96
Sampling ratio	1	0·5	0·25	0·125	0·0625

Source: Haggett, 1961-B, pp. 9, 11.

* Tagus–Sado basin, Portugal.

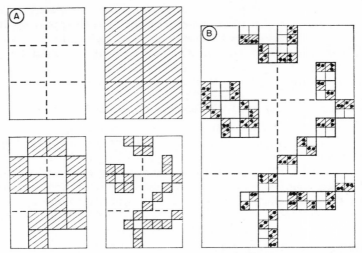

Fig. 9.17. Stages in the development of a five-level nested design in the Tagus–Sado basin, central Portugal ($G = 4\cdot5$). Source: Haggett, 1961-B, p. 7.

and then subdividing each square a further four times until the smallest units, squares $3\cdot125 \times 3\cdot125$ kilometres, are reached (Table 9.7). By selecting randomly at each level only two of the four available squares, only ninety-six of these smaller units are drawn for study from a possible total of over 1,500 units within the original area, i.e. a sampling fraction of $1/16$. Their location is shown in Fig. 9.17-B. Sampling on this hierarchical framework ensures not only that every part of the region is represented but that the fieldwork time in visiting each point is reduced well below that of a $1/16$ random sample.

b. Variance analysis of results. The main value of collecting data in this frame comes at the analysis stage. Here any 'local' value (X) can be regarded as being generated by the sum of independent deviations at each level of variability: i.e.

$X =$ Overall mean value (150 × 100 km.)
$+$ Region (50 × 50 km.) deviation from overall mean value
$+$ Sub-region (25 × 25 km.) deviation from regional mean
$+$ District (12·5 × 12·5 km.) deviation from sub-regional mean
$+$ Sub-district (6·25 × 6·25 km.) deviation from district mean
$+$ Locality (3·125 × 3·125 km.) deviation from sub-district mean

We assume that any single observation at a point on the earth's surface may be regarded as a deviation from the mean value of the district in which the point lies; we assume further that this district mean may be regarded as a deviation from the regional mean of the region in which the district lies. We can continue in like manner to regard each value as a deviation from the next highest level we care to postulate.

Krumbein and Slack (1956) carried out a geological study in south-west Illinois which illustrates this point. They identified a hierarchy of five levels, that of the coal outcrop regions of southwest Illinois (an area of about 150 × 25 miles), the supertownship (18 × 18 miles), the township (6 × 6 miles), the mine, and the sample. Fig. 9.18 shows these five levels in ascending size along the *y*-axis of the graph with the corresponding value of the characteristic under study along the *x*-axis of the same graph. The mean value for the single observation (1) can be seen either as a single value of 5·10, or alternatively, as a departure of +2·51 from the mine from which it was taken which has a value of 2·59 (2). This mine

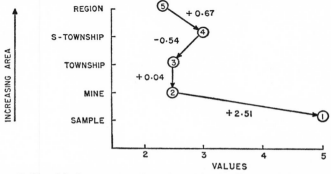

Fig. 9.18. Graphical representation of the hierarchical model of variance.
Source: Krumbein and Slack, 1956, p. 757.

value may also be regarded as a departure of +0·04 from the township (3) in which the mine lies with its mean value of 2·55. All values on this graph can be related to departures from the regional mean (5) for south-west Illinois of 2·42.

We can of course substitute for the graph and write the expression as:

$$5·10 = 2·42 + 0·67 + (−0·54) + 0·04 + 2·51$$

The value of this type of analysis is that it allows us to separate out the departures or 'kicks' at each of the regional levels in our hierarchy and furthermore to measure their strength. Fig. 9.19 shows the results of an analysis made by the writer into the pattern of variability shown by the forest distribution in central Portugal using this approach: the original pattern is shown in Fig. 6.1-A. The graph indicates the great contrast between the increment in variability at the third level, the district, com-pared to the negligible effect of the next higher level. In this case the basis for variance analysis was the nested sampling design shown in Fig. 9.17 and the regional levels identified (*I, II, . . . V*) are those described in

Table 9.7, i.e. the first level (*I*) refers to an area of 2,500 square kilometres while the fifth level (*V*) refers to an area of only ten square kilometres.

The first curve (Fig. 9.19-A) shows the great contrasts in variability between the five levels with major increments at the first, third, and fifth

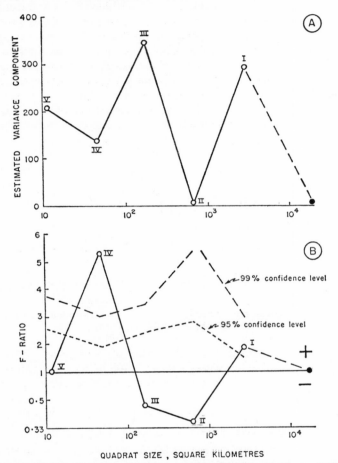

Fig. 9.19. A Scale components in the pattern of woodland in the Tagus–Sado basin, central Portugal. *B* Importance of the Mio-Pliocene outcrop on this distribution at each of the five scales. Source: Haggett, 1961-B.

levels. Inspection of the curves suggests that variability might be related to a series of controlling factors at different scales: e.g. broad climatic gradients within the area as opposed to sharp variations in soil-water conditions away from the alluvial floodplains. One of these hypotheses is examined in Fig. 9.19-B. Here the curve plots the *F*-ratio (Davies, 1958,

p. 66) for the variability between sample quadrats located 'on' or 'off' the Mio-Pliocene outcrop suggesting (i) that the effect of this factor is strongly significant at the fourth level, (ii) probably significant at the first level, and (iii) not significant at the other levels.

Use of this type of regional-local variance analysis has been successfully extended to problems in physical geography (Chorley, Stoddart, Haggett, and Slaymaker, in press) where 'hidden' periodicities in sand sheets at the 200-metre wavelength have been predicted statistically, and subsequently identified on oblique air photographs and in the field.

4. Scale-component analysis: mapping methods

The utilization of mapping methods for the separation of higher-scale (*regional*) from lower-scale (*local*) components has only recently been exploited. Despite its origin in geophysical prospecting and meteorological forecasting, this type of trend surface mapping has enormous possibilities within conventional geographical analysis; these possibilities have been examined at length by Chorley and Haggett (1965-B) and are not extended here. Instead we illustrate three methods of increasing complexity—the filter method, the linear trend-surface method, and the higher-order method—and discuss the problems of choosing between them.

a. Filter mapping. The basic ideas of filter mapping can be seen from a fairly simple example. Fig. 6.1 shows the stages by which a given distribution may be broken down into regional and local components beginning from the original forest distribution in a section of central Portugal (Fig. 6.1-A). For statistical purposes this pattern can either be expressed as a ratio (forested/non-forested area) or as a percentage, i.e. either 0·352 or 26·30. By covering the area with a rectangular grid these ratio values can be collected for small areas (in this case square cells of forty square kilometres) and contoured. The resulting map (Fig. 6.1-B) completely describes the area in two-dimensional form. Like contour values for terrain, it could be converted to a three-dimensional plaster model but in any case can be regarded conceptually as a three-dimensional trend surface.

This surface may be thought of statistically as a *response surface* (Box, 1954). That is the height (i.e. degree of forest cover) at any one point may be regarded as a response to the operation of that complex of '. . . geology, topography, climatic peculiarities, natural composition, economic disparities, and local and regional history' (Köstler, 1956, p. 82) which together determine forest distribution. Variations in the form of the surface may be regarded as responses to corresponding areal variations in the strength and balance of these hypothetical controlling factors.

These factors may be thought of as falling into two groups, regional and local. *Regional* factors might include such elements as growing seasons which are relatively widespread in operation and tend to change rather systematically and slowly across the area. Such regional factors may be considered to give rise to the broad larger-scale trends in the response surface. *Local* factors might include such items as soil composition which may be relatively restricted in operation. Such factors give rise to variations in the response surface which are unsystematic and spotty in distribution and do not give rise to recognizable secular trends across the map.

Fig. 6.1-c shows a *regional trend* map of the area. It was derived simply by constructing a circle around each cell with a radius of 28·20 kilometre so as to include a ground area of 2,500 square kilometres and then calculating the woodland fraction within this circular unit. Plotting this '2,500' surface caused local detail to be lost but the main lineaments of the pattern show up clearly. Nettleton (1954, p. 10) has likened the effect of such mapping to that of '. . . an electric filter which will pass components of certain frequencies and exclude others'. Certainly the detail has been lost in a predictable and controllable manner and comparison with other maps based on a similar 'grid' is made more reliable.

Separation of the local anomalies can be very rapidly derived from the regional map. For each cell the values of the original forty square kilometre cell are subtracted from those of the 2,500 square kilometre cell. Positive values (i.e. where local values exceed regional values) are shaded, and negative values (i.e. regional values exceed local values) are unshaded. Fig. 6.1-D therefore shows the operation of local factors as a pattern of positive and negative residuals.

Clearly an infinite number of trend-surface maps can be drawn and the nature of the resultant maps will vary with the grid interval chosen. To this extent the trend map is a quantitative expression of a qualitative choice. However, by including details of the generating grid with the map (in the same way that scale and orientation are conventionally included on a map), and by standardizing mapping around multiples of conventional levels—the 100 square kilometre unit would seem a useful basis for both aggregation and subdivision—this disadvantage can be nullified.

b. Linear trend surfaces. The problem of fitting planes to systems of points in space has long intrigued mathematicians (e.g. Pearson, 1901). Robinson and Caroe (in Garrison, *in press*) have developed a technique by which a best-fit surface may be fitted to a map which generalizes as a tilted plane or 'shed roof' the orientation and the dip of a distribution. This best-fit plane is merely a logical extension into a third dimension of the familiar two-dimensional regression line (Fig. 9.19) discussed in Chapter 10.II(3). Regression lines may be derived for an array of control-point values in two directions at right angles to each other and the resulting dip and strike of the surface derived from these two sloping regression lines after the manner of a geological map. Commonly the regression lines are derived from points arranged first in a north–south direction and then in an east–west direction.

Haggett (1964) has used a linear trend surface to separate regional and local components in a forest distribution in southeastern Brazil. The original distribution is shown in Fig. 9.20-A with contours at 10-unit intervals and areas below the mean value for the whole region shaded. The general trend shown by this forest distribution map is that the fitted plane (Fig. 9.20-B) falls off inland, dipping orthogonally to the coastline. Areas which rise above this plane, the positive anomalies (Fig. 9.20-C), include the heavily forested parts of the Serra do Mar and Serra da Mantiqueira escarpment. 'Lows' (Fig. 9.20-D) in the pattern occur in the dry Taubaté basin and in the northwestern part of the map.

Reduction of isarithmic maps to regional trend planes allows ready

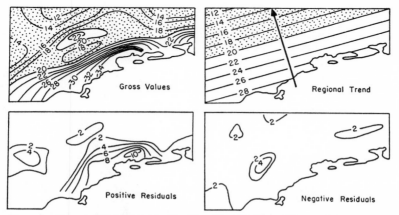

Fig. 9.20. Forest distribution in the Brazilian Sudeste ($G = 3.9$) in terms of simple regional trend and local anomalies. Source: Haggett, 1964, p. 372.

comparison in terms of dip and strike of geographical patterns. For the distribution shown in Fig. 6.1, application of *successive* planes is currently being investigated as a means of describing its patterns more completely (Fig. 9.21). Here the original surface (Fig. 9.21-A), the best-fit linear surface (Fig. 9.21-B), and the residual surface (Fig. 9.21-C) are derived in the conventional manner. Separate linear surfaces are then fitted to the residuals that fall within the *positive* part of the original linear surface and again on the *negative* part: the two sets of residuals are divided by the broken line in Fig. 9.21-C and the resulting surfaces are shown in Fig. 9.21-D. This process of fitting surfaces over successively smaller areas can be continued sequentially until the number of control points become too small to yield acceptable trends. At each stage the number of surfaces is doubled.

Although this analysis was carried out experimentally it seems clear that the method has certain further applications. It gives a simple means of describing a complex isarithmic map, like the first in Fig. 9.21, to a series of vectors in the fourth. Since each vector has a distinct *azimuth* (between 0 and 360 degrees) and a distinct *dip* (between 0 and 90 degrees), comparison of distributions, ordinarily a difficult and uncertain business, is likely to be made considerably easier.

   c. Quadratic and higher-order surfaces. Since it is clear that the linear surface represents only the first of a series of surfaces that may be fitted to any

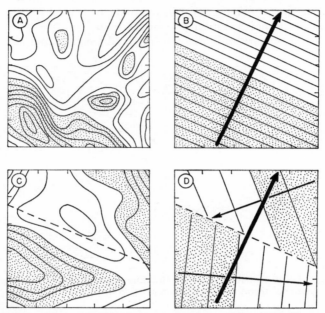

Fig. 9.21. Sequential linear-surface mapping of a sample quadrat ($G = 4.7$) in the woodland pattern of the Tagus–Sado basin, central Portugal. *A* Original isarithmic surface. *B* Best-fit linear surface. *C* Residuals from *B*-surface. *D* Best-fit linear surfaces for the positive and negative anomaly areas on the *C*-residuals.

given statistical distribution, the extension of the linear regression line to the linear surface may be matched with the extension of the curvilinear regression line to the curvilinear surface (Fig. 9.22). The addition of further terms allows the build-up of a series of polynomial surfaces, the quadratic surface, the cubic surface, the quartic surface, the quintic surface, and so on.

   In practice analysis of such higher-order surfaces rarely proceeds beyond the cubic phase. This is partly because of the computation involved which becomes considerable, even for high-speed computers, at the higher orders with large arrays of data. A further reason is the fact that with in-

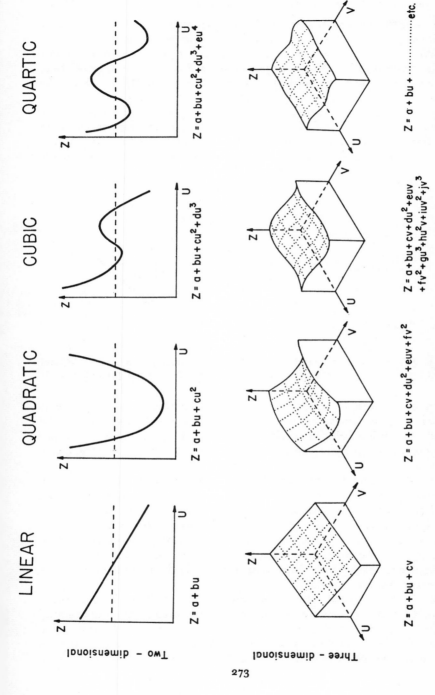

LINEAR

Two – dimensional

$Z = a + bu$

QUADRATIC

$Z = a + bu + cu^2$

CUBIC

$Z = a + bu + cu^2 + du^3$

QUARTIC

$Z = a + bu + cu^2 + du^3 + eu^4$

Three – dimensional

$Z = a + bu + cv$

$Z = a + bu + cv + du^2 + euv + fv^2$

$Z = a + bu + cv + du^2 + euv$
$+ fv^2 + gu^3 + hu^2v + iuv^2 + jv^3$

$Z = a + bu + \ldots\ldots\ldots$ etc.

Fig. 9.22. Relations between two-dimensional functions and their appropriate three-dimensional surfaces. Source: Chorley and Haggett, 1965-B; Krumbein, 1956.

273

creases in the number of terms used in computing, the computed surface rapidly approaches the complexities of the original surface.

We can see this effect graphically in Fig. 9.23 which reproduces part of a series of surfaces fitted to geological data in an area around Wichita, Kansas, by Krumbein (1959-B) using an IBM 650 computer. Here the original values are shown in Fig. 9.23-A, the fitted linear surface in Fig. 9.23-B, and the fitted quadratic surface in Fig. 9.23-C. It is clear that the polynomial surface approximates the original surface more closely than the linear but the increase becomes less marked as successively higher surfaces are fitted. If we regard the total variation of the original surface

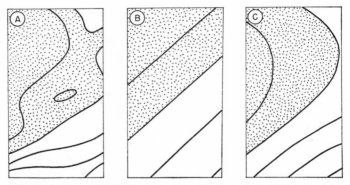

Fig. 9.23. Comparison of *original* surface (*A*) with first-degree *linear* surface (*B*) and second-degree *quadratic* surface (*C*). Source: Krumbein, 1959, pp. 828–31.

as having a variance of 100 per cent, then over three-quarters of this is explained by the linear surface (some 78·2 per cent). The addition of the quadratic surface brings the level of explanation up to 85·1 per cent, an addition of only around one-tenth to the amount explained by the linear surface.

A final reason for the popularity of lower-order surfaces lies in the purpose of the studies in which they are used. While they are sometimes used to 'reconstruct' surfaces from fragmentary data (as in the 'ghost stratigraphies' of Whitten (1959)) a more common use is in extracting regional trends and in examining the deviations from it. Krumbein (1956, p. 2193) has suggested that residuals from linear surfaces may be more useful in showing up local forms than either the original map or a higher-order trend-surface map.

d. Choice of method. The Tagus–Sado example (Figs. 6.1 and 9.21) showed the application of one method of trend-surface mapping bringing in the influence of nearby surrounding points. This does not, however, give a unique solution to the regional trend problem as a number of alternative methods exist—the linear and higher-order regression surfaces. These and other methods have been reviewed at length by Nettleton (1954), Chorley and Haggett (1965-B) and Krumbein (1956) and our purpose here is not to summarize these methods but to illustrate the range of results they produce.

A test case of the application of various trend-surface methods has been applied by Krumbein (1956, pp. 2167–77) to data in the West Brock area of Oklahoma. The original values for the area are shown in Fig. 9.24-A with contours at 10-unit intervals and the areas above 40 units stippled; these conventions are retained in the regional maps (Fig. 9.24-B, D, and F), but in the residual maps the contour interval remains at 10 units and the stippled area represents positive deviations (Fig. 9.24-C, E, and G).

Three alternative methods were used here to determine the regional trend: the *graphical-profile* method, the *regression* method, and the *'expected-value'* method. The first method was based on a series of thirteen profiles made along grid lines, six east–west and seven north–south. Smoothing

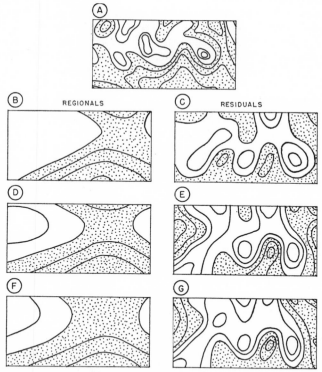

Fig. 9.24. Comparison of regional and residual maps made of distribution *A* by the *profile* method (*BC*), the *analytic* method (*DE*), and the *expected-value* method (*FG*). Source: Krumbein, 1956, pp. 2170–6.

was subjective but an attempt was made to keep the number of inflection points in the smooth lines to a minimum. The principles of the regression method have already been taken up in discussing the application of linear and higher-order surfaces to distributions: the regional surface shown in Fig. 9.23-D is a combination of the linear, quadratic, and cubic terms. The third method, the expected-value method, arranges the observed grid values in rows and columns. The values are summed west–east along the rows to give a row total and mean value, and summed north–south down the columns to give a column total and mean value. The expected value of any grid cell is given by adding the mean of the row in which it occurs to the mean of the column in which it occurs and subtracting from this sum the grand mean of all the observations for the area.

Comparison of the three regional trend maps shows that the three methods yield roughly similar maps, leading to roughly the same kind of interpretations. Although objective tests can be applied to select the optimum method, it remains true that the reliability of the finished product is about proportional to the amount of energy expended in computation. Where a detailed map is needed which may be carefully compared with similar results in other areas there is much to be said for using a high-speed computer and calculating a regression equation; where, however, the distribution is relatively simple, the short graphic method yields results which give a good approximation to the more carefully constructed analytical methods. It seems like a case of value for money.

The building, testing, and rebuilding of hypotheses is the slow path by which progress in human geography has been made. Testing, particularly testing in terms of probabilities, provides the appropriate check to the theoretical excesses of Part One of this book and a way in which new ideas may be thrown up. Indeed the best one can hope from existing theory is that it will provide the way to better things. The research cycle, like the nitrogen cycle, demands the death of old hypotheses and the building of new ones; indeed by the time these words are published, not a little of what has been put forward in this book will be being inevitably replaced: the sound of progress is perhaps the sound of plummeting hypotheses. Testing is of special importance to geography in that one of the essential roles it plays in relation to systematic social sciences is to subject 'general' theories to 'regional' tests.

This chapter tries to sketch out some of the rules under which simple tests may be made. Since it touches on statistical methods in a short space, it will be too complex for some, enragingly simplified for others. For those in the first category, Gregory (1963) provides a more gentle introduction, while for those in the second Miller and Kahn (1962) elaborate many of the specifically locational applications.

I. HYPOTHESES IN HUMAN GEOGRAPHY

The failure of the place–work–society chain of causation used by Vidal de la Blache (Chap. 1.II) or the material-orientation hypotheses of Weber (Chap. 5.IV) has been followed by a half-century of cautious fact-gathering in which our rate of data accumulation has far outrun our capacity to create models to explain its significance. Indeed, one of the sadder consequences of the retreat from environmental determinism in human geography has been an unwillingness to risk launching new hypotheses.

Collection of facts cannot, by itself, lead to understanding; indeed Karl Popper (1959, pp. 276–81) warned that such an approach is a reversal of the classic 'path of science' in which the formulation of theory plays the dominant role. Popper's opening quotation from Novalis: 'Theories are nets: only he who casts will catch' reflects the central role he gave to theory, believing that theory represented organized knowledge, facts disorganized knowledge. Although as we have seen in the first chapter (1.IV) theories cannot be proved to be either right or wrong in the absolute sense, they can be tested rigorously against the available facts using well-established experimental techniques.

1. Models of hypothesis testing

One of the simplest models for the testing of hypotheses in human geography has been evolved by McCarty (1956, p. 263). He argues for a *sequential* approach to geographical research in which (i) problems are defined, (ii) hypotheses are applied, (iii) their effectiveness evaluated, and (iv) new hypotheses evolved to explain the discrepancies. In specific terms we may frame McCarty's approach as a series of regression cycles (Chap. 10.II(4)), as those shown in Table 10.1. In the *first cycle* (C_1) the problem is defined, data are collected, statistically analysed, and plotted as an isopleth map: we may term this the problem distribution (Y). Analysis of the map of the Y-distribution leads to the formulation of a hypothesis (H_1) to account for geographical irregularities in its form. This initiates the *second cycle* (C_2) with the definition of an explanatory variable, X_1, for which data are collected, are statistically analysed, and related to the problem variable through regression analysis. Using the regression equation ($Y = fX_1$), the deviations of the actual distribution of Y from the predicted distribution Y_c can be measured. The map of these deviations or *residuals* represents the end of the second cycle. Analysis of the map of residuals may lead to a second hypothesis to account for the 'unexplained' distribution. This initiates the *third cycle* (C_3), beginning with the definition of the second explanatory variable, X_2. As Table 10.1 shows, this third cycle parallels the second cycle and may lead to further cycles (C_4 to C_n) until a satisfactory level of explanation is reached.

Thomas (1960) has drawn on an unpublished and somewhat whimsical study by McCarty to illustrate this method. In this paper, 'McCarty on McCarthy', McCarty tried to explain the pattern of voting in the American state of Wisconsin for one of its senators, Joseph McCarthy. In this case the problem pattern (Y) was the percentage vote cast for the senator by each of the voting areas within the state. McCarty began his study with the hypothesis (H_1) that the senator had been elected mainly on a farm vote. The independent variable was then measured as the per-

Table 10.1. Model of regression cycles in geographic research

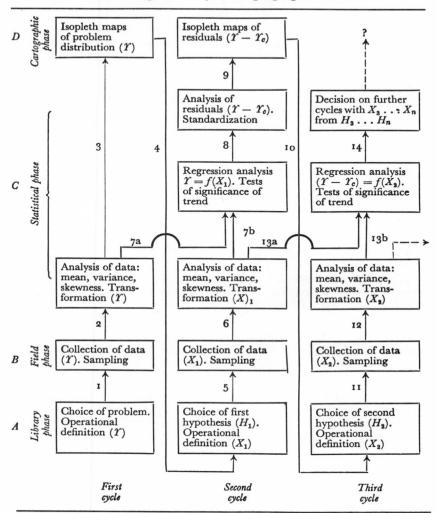

centage of rural population (X_1) in each voting area and a standard regression analysis $(Y = f(X_1))$ was carried out. The result was that about a third of the total variation in the McCarthy vote could be attributed to this factor. Plotting the residuals from this equation $(Y - Y_c)$ showed a high ridge in the north of the state and again in the central-eastern tract (Fig. 10.1-A). In both these areas the prediction based on H_1 had considerably under-estimated the true strength of the McCarthy vote. From this map McCarty suggested that a further factor which might explain part of the distribution of the vote might be given by the location of the senator's home town at Appleton, Wisconsin. Specifically this was reintroduced as a hypothesis (H_2) that the McCarthy vote increased with nearness to the senator's home town (α in Fig. 10.1). When this second factor (X_2) was introduced into the analysis the level of explanation rose from one-third to nearly one-half.

McCarty's argument follows one of the classic methods of logical

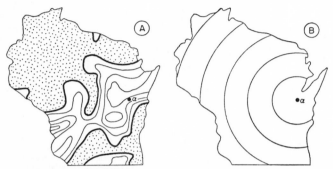

Fig. 10.1. A Positive residuals from regression analysis by H. H. McCarty on the McCarthy vote in Wisconsin ($G = 3.5$), United States. *B* Suggested second hypothesis based on distance from McCarthy home at α. Source: Thomas, 1960, p. 45.

reasoning. In his *System of logic*, J. S. Mill placed great emphasis on the *method of residues* which drew attention to the '. . . insufficiency of the obvious causes to account for the whole of the effect' (Mill, 1874, p. 285), and which he found the most fertile of his several methods of investigating the laws of nature. Residual maps provide the geographical equivalents of Mill's residues.

In practice, however, sequential analysis of geographical problems has been less common than *parallel* analysis. This has more in common with Chamberlin's method of 'multiple working hypotheses' (Chamberlin, 1897) in which various hypotheses are presented together, rather than in sequence, so as to allow a decision on their relative merits. This is the basis of the method, *multiple-regression analysis* (Chap. 10.II(3)), now very widely used in geographical analysis (e.g. King, 1961). Both sequential and parallel approaches embody the idea of multiple hypotheses. The advantages of the first lie in the simple clarity of the reasoning and in the step-by-step nature of the analysis, the advantages of the second in its greater inductive power and its stress on the multivariate nature of geographical problems.

2. Origins of hypotheses: the 'shotgun' or 'Pleiades' method

The foregoing discussion raises the question as to how hypotheses arise. Clearly some come from the lively imagination of individual workers: Mackinder's concept of the heartland (Mackinder, 1904), or Christaller's concept of the central-place hierarchy (Christaller, 1933), may fall into this class. Others may stem from the observation of repeating spatial patterns: Taaffe's model of transport development (Taaffe *et al.*, 1963) might fall into this 'quasi-inductive' class. Still others come from the transfer of ideas from more sophisticated but parallel disciplines. Bunge (1962), in his *Theoretical geography*, has shown how fields of study as unlike geography as crystallography, biometrics, or telecommunications may stimulate locational hypotheses. Indeed, in the broad view of the history of science, basic ideas in many applied fields (including geography) may be seen to derive from a small group of pure sciences which have mathematics and logic at their centre (Ackerman, 1963, p. 430).

While these sciences are likely to be fruitful in the long run, we are often faced with more immediate problems. Is it possible to 'stimulate' hypotheses within a particular field of locational research? Miller and Kahn (1962, pp. 315–24) suggest that it is. They put forward what they term the 'shotgun' or 'Pleiades' method for the analysis of large quantities of data in situations where there are no strong hypotheses or *a priori* expectations. In this method, all factors are intercorrelated and the matrix of relationships examined for significant patterns.

One example of the use of this method in human geography may be given from an unpublished study by the writer on the locational characteristics of Portuguese industry (Haggett, 1959). A series of eleven characteristics (variables A to K listed in Table 10.2) were measured for a sample of twenty-eight industries during the 1950–5 period. Each of the eleven characteristics was related to the others by the use of a rank correlation coefficient, Spearman's *rho*, R_s (Siegel, 1956, pp. 202–13). This coefficient makes no assumptions about the frequency distribution of the data which it relates, and is considerably easier to compute than the parametric coefficient of correlation, Pearson's r (Chap. 9.II(2b)).

Spearman's R_s is given by the formula

$$R_s = 1 - \left\{ \left(6 \sum_{i=1}^{N} f_i^2 \right) \Big/ (N^3 - N) \right\}$$

where N is the number of items (in this case, industries) and f_i is the difference between ranks for two indices for the ith item. Values of R_s vary from $+1$, indicating maximum agreement between two variables, to -1, indicating total disagreement. Values approaching zero suggest indeterminate relations between the two variables.

Table 10.2 shows a matrix of every possible combination of the eleven

Table 10.2. Matrix of correlation coefficients*

Locational characteristics:	A	B	C	D	E	F	G	H	I	J	K
Locational coefficient (A)	I	+0·72	−0·02	+0·19	+0·15	−0·09	+0·43	+0·13	−0·15	−0·19	−0·59
Location quotient (B)		I	−0·25	−0·08	−0·36	−0·18	+0·25	+0·46	−0·45	−0·25	−0·53
Plant spacing (C)			I	+0·52	+0·42	−0·40	+0·45	−0·14	−0·20	−0·19	−0·05
Plant size (D)				I	+0·79	+0·19	+0·25	−0·76	−0·02	+0·68	+0·04
Concentration (E)					I	+0·46	+0·28	−0·80	+0·40	+0·73	+0·34
Plant investment (F)						I	+0·34	−0·01	+0·27	+0·06	+0·56
Company size (G)							I	+0·33	−0·34	−0·57	−0·42
Material-cost ratio (H)								I	−0·32	−0·90	−0·22
Fuel-cost ratio (I)									I	+0·56	+0·55
Labour-cost ratio (J)										I	+0·38
Investment-cost ratio (K)											I

* Portuguese industry, 1950–5.

Source: Haggett, 1959, p. 19.

variables measured, taken two at a time. The numbers in each of the 'boxes' of the matrix are the correlation coefficients, R_s. However, since these numbers measure only statistical relations, it is essential to know how far the values obtained might be expected in terms of probability theory. Figures in heavy type in Table 10.2 show values of R which are significantly different from zero at the 95 per cent level (Chap. 10.II). This table may be analysed in terms of three basic concepts: (i) *basic pairs*, (ii) *p-clusters*, and (iii) *F-groups* (Olson and Miller, 1958).

(i) *Basic pairs* have the characteristic that each variable that is contained in them is more highly correlated with the other than with any other variable. They represent points of convergence of values and their primary role is that of 'set formers'. Scanning the R_s values in Table 10.2 it is clear that the highest value of mean labour-cost ratio (J) is with mean material-cost ratio (H), and vice versa. These two variables form a basic pair. Consideration of another variable, C, shows that its highest correlation is with D. In this case, however, plant size (D) is more highly correlated with yet another variable (E). Variables which do not form basic pairs are combined with the basic pair with which they show greatest correlation to form a set.

Basic pairs and the sets of which they form the nuclei are shown in Table 10.3. The three sets detected are as follows: *Set 1*, a 'cost ratio' set in

Table 10.3. Basic pairs at the 95 per cent confidence level*

Correlation set	Descriptive name
(1) $\boxed{H \longleftrightarrow J}\; \leftarrow G$	Cost-ratios set
(2) $\boxed{E \longleftrightarrow D}\; \leftarrow C$	Dimensional set
(3) $\boxed{B \longleftrightarrow A}\; \leftarrow K \leftarrow F$ $\nwarrow$ $\quad I$	Locational set

Source: Haggett, 1959, p. 17.
* Portuguese industry, 1950–5.

which material and labour costs variables are strongly but inversely related; *Set 2* is a 'dimensional' set in which plant size and concentration variables are positively connected; *Set 3* is a 'locational' set in which a larger group of variables is grouped around a locational coefficient-quotient axis.

(ii) While basic-pair analysis reduces the number of intersections and brings some order to the matrix, it has a disadvantage in not describing all the bonds shown. Table 10.2 shows, for example, that while A is part of the first set it is also bonded (though less strongly) to B, the third set. This criterion of *maximum* correlation as a set determinant used in basic-pair analysis may be replaced by the *p-cluster* concept at which all bonds at a given level of significance are shown (Fig. 10.2).

This diagram shows that the interrelationship of the structural variables

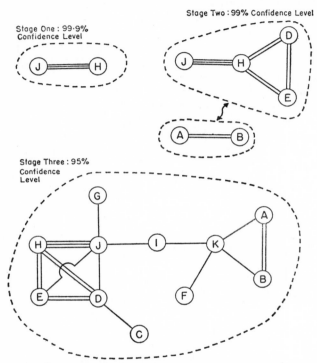

Fig. 10.2. Changes in bonding patterns between parameters of Portuguese industrial structure associated with a lowering confidence level. Source: Haggett, 1959, p. 20.

is a much more complex one than that revealed through basic-pair analysis. The three simple sets are replaced by two strongly bonded clusters, partly linked by a common fuel-cost variable (I). Clearly what has taken place is the combination of the first and second sets into one four-variable cluster (with three uncontained variables), while the third set has retained its independence as a three-variable cluster (with two un-contained variables).

(iii) An *F-group* is defined as any group of variables which are thought to be functionally related to each other. Analysis of correlation matrices in terms of *F-groups* distinguishes bonds between functionally related variables (e.g. those between the various locational parameters) from bonds with independent variables. In Fig. 10.3 the eleven variables have been separated on the diagram to form three separate clusters or *F-groups*. They are the locational group (*A*, *B*, *C*), the dimensional group (*D*, *E*, *F*, *G*), and the cost-ratio group (*H*, *I*, *J*, *K*). With the variables clustered on this

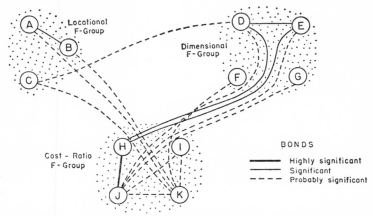

Fig. 10.3. F-group analysis of bonding patterns shown in Fig. 10.2. Source: Haggett, 1959, p. 21.

qualitative basis the separation of 'within-group' from 'between-group' bonds is apparent.

Analyses of the Portuguese industrial data by this method suggest two major hypotheses linking (i) the size of plant with cost ratios, and (ii) localization with investment. By highlighting the relationships of greatest importance (and eliminating those of lesser effect) it clears the way for conventional methods of hypothesis testing in the classic scientific tradition.

In criticism of the shotgun method, however, we must recall that relationships may exist between one variable and two or more other variables. These relations are not shown by the correlation matrix (Table 10.2) which measures relations only between pairs of variables. More sophisticated techniques are needed to handle this difficulty. Berry (1960-B) has shown how matrices may be inverted and *canonical* analysis applied to extract the 'latent structure' in such matrices. From a matrix of ninety-five countries and forty-three indices of economic development, the basic components shown in Table 8.1 were derived (see discussion in Chapter 8.I(3d)): these components point to a number of possible hypotheses linking economic development.

Although the imaginative hypothesis is likely to remain at a premium in geographical study, there are statistical techniques of varying complexity and efficiency which, by recognizing the organization which may be latent in our observations, is able to suggest certain working hypotheses.

II. TESTING VIA STATISTICAL METHODS

Few innovation waves have swept through geographical study more rapidly or more decisively than the vogue for statistical analysis. In 1955 the use of statistical methods in most geographical research papers was a curiosity (climatology perhaps stands apart from this generalization); by 1965 many American geographical journals, notably the *Annals of the Association of American Geographers*, carried many papers with a high statistical content and even the more conservative English journals were showing weak trends in this direction. Moreover, one statistical textbook specifically designed for geographical use (Gregory, 1963), one major study of areal statistics (Duncan *et al.*, 1961), one extensive bibliography of mathematical geography (Anderson, 1963), and one symposium on quantitative methods in geography (Garrison, *in press*) have been produced.

This is not the place to debate the role of statistics in geography. The case for their use has been strongly demonstrated by Burton (1963) who regards the 'quantitative revolution' as both inevitable and irreversible; the case against their use, or rather against their indiscriminate use, has been made by Spate (1960) in a plea for literary and qualitative analysis. Minor skirmishing over techniques have come from Reynolds (1956) and Garrison (1956) on the question of 'geographical' statistics, and from Zobler (1958) and Mackay (1958) on the utility of the χ^2-test in drawing regional boundaries. Much of the heat of the general debate is based on misinformation and misapprehension on both sides of the camp, and Robinson (1961-A), in a caricature of both extreme viewpoints ('perks' and 'pokes'), has shown how this dispute might be resolved profitably.

Such are the range and complexity of techniques within this field that a book of this length can only hint at the possibilities of the statistical approach. Attention is therefore restricted (i) to the initial problems in applying statistical tests to geographical populations; and (ii), to illustrating, through the use of five examples, some of the possibilities of the methods. A number of excellent statistical textbooks are available for those who wish to follow these methods further. Davies (1958) gives a very clear non-mathematical introduction to standard procedures and is excellent as a computational guide, while a summary of nonparametric statistical tests is given by Siegel (1956). Gregory (1963) has written an introduction to statistical methods applied to geographical data, and similar surveys are available for ecology (Greig-Smith, 1964;

Kershaw, 1964) and geology (Miller and Kahn, 1962). However, two of the most valuable short surveys were found by the author to be those of Strahler (1954) and Chorley (in Dury, 1965) on statistical applications in geomorphology, where both the morphological and areal problems in geographical analysis were stressed.

1. Difficulties in adopting statistical tests

Two of the fundamental difficulties encountered in trying to apply conventional statistical methods to the solution of geographical problems arise from the nature of geographical populations (Chap. 7.I). For when measurements of these populations—city sizes, slopes, network ratios—are made they commonly reveal (i) that the populations are not normally distributed, in the statistical sense, but strongly skewed or (ii) that the level of measurement, again in the statistical sense (Chap. 8.I(1)), is low. The effect of these drawbacks and the way in which they may be partly outflanked are discussed in this section.

a. Nature of geographical frequency-distributions. In most statistical tests one of the fundamental assumptions is that observations fall symmetrically around the mean value in the form of a *normal* distribution function—graphically represented as a bell-shaped curve (Davies, 1958, p. 15). While we know all too little about the statistical distribution of geographical populations, it is clear from the few studies already made that very little geographical data follows an exactly normal distribution. Almost all the indices plotted as cumulative curves in the Ginsburg Atlas (1961) are strongly skewed away from the normal curve.

When non-normal distributions are encountered there are two main ways around the difficulty:

(i) First, we may use the wide range of fairly simple statistical tests which are *non-parametric* or 'distribution-free', i.e. they do not demand a normal distribution of observations. Siegel (1956) has summarized many of these tests in his *Nonparametric statistics*. The problem with distribution-free tests is that we have to reduce our measurements to at least a rank-order scale and this may mean throwing away part of the information contained in the measurements we have made.

(ii) A second alternative is to analyse not the original data, but an appropriate *transformation* of it. Transformation stabilizes the variations and makes the distribution more nearly normal so that conventional parametric tests can be applied without difficulty. Table 10.4 summarizes some of the more important transformations and shows their main effects on the original data. Of these the *logarithmic* transformation is the most commonly used in geographical literature: King (1961) used it for the values of urban environments in a study of city-spacing in the United States, and Haggett (1964) for rural environments in a study of forest distribution in southeast Brazil. Thomas (1962, p. 17) used an extension of

Table 10.4. Transformations used to normalize or stabilize data

Distribution	Transformation	Remarks
Normal	None	—
Log-normal	Log X	Normalizes data
Binomial	Arc sine	Stabilizes variance
Poisson	$\sqrt{X}$	Stabilizes variance
Gamma	$\sqrt{X}$ or log X	Stabilizes variance (?)

Source: Krumbein, 1955, p. 8.

this transformation, the log-log transformation, by taking the logarithm of the logarithm of distance in a study of town-spacing in Iowa. In studies of land use the *arc-sine* transformation is of special value. The detailed arguments for its adoption in preference to either percentage data or ratio

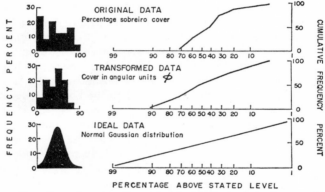

Fig. 10.4. Use of arc-sine transformation for land-use data. Source: Haggett, 1961-B.

data have been presented by Krumbein (1957). In broad terms its effect is to stabilize variance and allow the use of experimental designs that would otherwise be inappropriate. Fig. 10.4 shows the effect of converting percentage data on forest distribution in Portugal into *angular* units through the arc-sine transformation. Tables for this conversion are given in Fisher and Yates (1957, Table X, p. 20.)

With the angular transformation there is little difficulty in deciding that its use is appropriate: it is applied when percentage data is based on observations of less than 100 individuals, or when the percentages contain values less than 30 per cent or more than 70 per cent (Jeffers, 1959, p. 74). In many cases, however, there may be reasonable doubt which transformation is appropriate, or indeed if transformation is needed at all. Plotting alternative transformations on probability paper on which a normal distribution appears as a straight line is a useful trial-and-error method; Jeffers (1959, p. 75) has presented a short-cut method for determining the appropriate transformation by comparing the sample variance (see Chap. 9.II(2a)) and sample mean on double logarithmic paper. For most practical purposes many statistical tests are robust enough to accommodate small departures from normality and approximate transformations are therefore sufficient.

Thus transformation allows non-normal geographical populations to be studied using the full range of parametric statistics. Against this, transformation of the results of statistical analysis back into the original form may be extremely difficult, and individual workers must balance the theoretical gains against the practical losses for each problem. Krumbein (1957) has, however, reminded us that our concern for preserving certain forms of measurement (e.g. per cent scales in land-use measurement) is often based more on convention than on any unique or immutable qualities of this form as against others: we are, for example, prepared to accept the *pH* scale of acidity despite the fact that differences between points on it are logarithmic and not arithmetic.

b. Levels of measurement. We have already seen (Chap. 8.I(1)) how the notion of levels of measurement is related to the range of cartographic techniques appropriate to a given set of locational data. This relationship extends to that between levels of measurement and statistical operations. In Table 10.5 the four basic types of measurement scale, viz. classed data, ranked data, interval data, and ratio data, are related to the number of components in a study. In the *one-component case* we are concerned with a single set of characteristics (X_1): in practice, this might be the mean distance between settlements in a region. In the *two-component case* we relate two such sets of characteristics: thus we might relate distance between settlements (X_1) to a supposed controlling variable such as population density (X_2). We can see, however, that here the case becomes more difficult, for the second variable X_2 may itself be measured at one of three scales. We could relate our distance measurement (X_1), which is measured on the ratio scale, to an X_2 component like type of land use (measured on the nominal or class scale), or period of settlement (measured on the ordinal or rank scale), as well as to population density (measured on the ratio scale). There are clearly six possible combinations of the two components which are shown as a matrix in the second level of Table 10.5. In the *multiple-component case* we relate many sets of characteristics: thus we might relate distance between settlements (X_1) to both population density (X_2) and a range of other characteristics $(X_3 \ldots X_n)$.

In the body of the table some characteristic statistical tests are listed under the appropriate sections: details of the computation and their

Table 10.5. Levels of measurement and statistical operations*

Level of measurement of variable X_1		Ratio, interval, rank-order and nominal data	Ratio, interval and rank-order data	Ratio and interval data	Ratio data only
		One-component case			
—	—	Frequency Mode	Median Percentiles	Mean Variance	Geometric mean Harmonic mean Coefficient of variation
		Two-component case			
Second component (X_2)	Class data	Chi-square Contingency coefficient	Mann–Whitney U test	Means comparison (e.g. t test) Variance comparison (e.g. F test)	
	Rank-order data		Order-correlation (Spearman's R_s) (Kendall's τ)		
	Interval + ratio data			Correlation coefficient (e.g. Pearson's) Linear and non-linear regression	
		Multiple-component case			
Other components $(X_3 \ldots X_n)$	Interval + ratio data	Multiple-variance analysis Co-variance analysis		Multiple correlation Multiple regression	

* Sample operations only.

application in the earth sciences are given by Gregory (1963) and by Miller and Kahn (1962). It is clear from the table that changes in both the level of measurement and in the number of components are systematically related to the range of appropriate statistical tests. In the first level of the table we see that we can compute only two parameters for data in classes but at least nine parameters for data at the ratio scale. Since range is also associated with the statistical power of the tests, the need to raise progressively the level at which we measure locational phenomena is self-evident.

2. Exploratory methods: simple comparative tests

Only two simple comparative tests are given here. Full discussions of alternative tests are given by Davies (1958, pp. 69–95) and Gregory (1963, pp. 115–66), while Chorley (in Dury, 1965, pp. 275–387) has brought together a number of examples of their field use.

Example I: Comparison of means. One of the simplest but most frequent problems in any research arises when data are classified in terms of only one of the variables but very accurately measured in terms of the other. Such a case is shown in Fig. 10.5 where data on town-spacing is at two levels: *nominal* for the independent variable (i.e. a simple classification into two geographical areas: Iowa–Missouri and the Texas Black Belt); *ratio* for the dependent, where the exact distances between towns in the two areas are known in kilometres.

When the two means ($\bar{X}_1$ and $\bar{X}_2$) are compared, we can see that the distance separating small towns in the Texas region (20·5 kilometres) is greater than that separating towns of similar size in the Iowa–Missouri region (19·2 kilometres). However, when the two histograms are compared

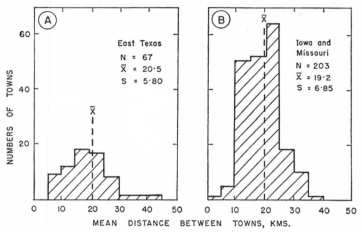

Fig. *10.5*. Histograms of spacing of towns in two sample areas of the central United States. Source: Lösch, 1954, p. 392.

a doubt enters our minds. For we see not only that the two distributions overlap considerably, but also that the number of towns on which the sample mean is based is nearly three times as great for the Iowa–Missouri region as for the Texas region. Is then the mean difference of real significance, or has it arisen through chance?

To test the difference between sample means a *null hypothesis* is set up which states that there is no real difference between the two means of the two areas. The null hypothesis may be tested by the statistic *t*, where

$$t = (\bar{X}_1 - \bar{X}_2)/\{S_p\sqrt{(1/N_1) + (1/N_2)}\}$$

where $\bar{X}_1, \bar{X}_2$, are the means of the first and second sample, N_1 and N_2 the size of the first and second samples respectively, and S_p is a statistic known as the *pooled estimate of variance*. This is an average value derived from the standard deviations (*S* in Fig. 10.5) and sample sizes (N_1, N_2) of the two classes.

In the case of town-spacing in the middle United States, t is computed as,

$$t = (20 \cdot 5 - 19 \cdot 2)/\{43 \cdot 4 \sqrt{(1/67) + (1/203)}\} = 0 \cdot 219$$

Consultation of the 't-table' (Fisher and Yates, 1957, p. 44) shows that with 268 degrees of freedom ($N_1 + N_2 - 2$), the value of t shows a probability lying between 0·8 and 0·9. This is vastly greater than our lowest acceptable significance level of 95 per cent ($P < 0 \cdot 05$), and the null hypothesis must therefore be retained. In other words, the difference in spacing of 1·3 kilometres between the Texas and Iowa–Missouri settlements might have arisen by chance and is statistically *not significant*.

Example II: Comparison of ranks. A number of measures have been evolved to meet the problem of measurements that fail to reach the parametric level. One of the most powerful tests of association, when X_1 is measured in classes and X_2 is ranked, is the Mann–Whitney U test. For large samples, $n_2 > 20$, the null hypothesis is tested by a statistic known as U where

$$U = N_1 N_2 + \{N_1(N_1 + 1)\}/2 - R_1$$

in which N_1 is the number of cases in the smaller of the two groups, and N_2 the number of cases in the larger. R_1 is the sum of the ranks assigned to the group whose sample size is N_1 (Siegel, 1956, pp. 116–27).

Table 10.6 shows an array of measurements from a sample of air photographs from the Fortaleza basin (São Paulo state, Brazil) in which

Table 10.6. Rank order of estimates of cultivated land*

Parameters:	Number of air photographs (N)	Rank order of estimates of cultivated land
Terrain classification:		
Valley-bottoms	10	1 2 3 6 8 10 14 16 18 33
Hillsides	30	4 5 7 9 11 12 13 15 17 19 20 21 22 23 24 25 26 27 28 29 30 31 32 34 35 36 37 38 39 4c

* Fortaleza basin, Taubaté county, southeast Brazil.

amount of cultivated land has been estimated for two terrain types (Haggett, 1961-A, p. 52). The estimates of cultivation are so arranged that a rank of *one* is assigned to the highest value, a rank of *forty* to the lowest value, and values from both groups are included in a common ranking.

The value of U in this illustrative case was computed as

$$U = 10(30) + \{10(10 + 1)\}/2 - 111 = 244$$

The methods for determining the significance of the observed value of U depend on the size of N_2. If N_2 is less than eight, or between nine and twenty, the significance of any observed value of U can be determined from Mann–Whitney tables reproduced in Siegel (1956, Table J, pp. 271–3; Table K, pp. 274–7). If, however, as in this case, the N_2 group is larger than twenty the probability must be determined by computing the statistic z, where

$$z = \{U - [(N_1 N_2)/2]\}/\sqrt{[N_1 N_2 (N_1 + N_2 + 1)]/12}$$

and testing this value of z in a probability table (Siegel, 1956, Table A, p. 247).

In the Brazilian case the value of z is computed as:

$$z = \{244 - [10(30)/2]\}/\sqrt{[10(30)(10 + 30 + 1)]/12} = 2 \cdot 94$$

By reference to a table of z-distributions we find that the probability, P, is 0·0026 (Siegel, 1956, Table A, p. 247). This is well within our confidence levels ($0·01 < P < 0·001$) and we can consider the relationship between the two types of terrain and the degree of cultivation as statistically *significant* at the 99 per cent confidence level.

The Mann–Whitney U test is one of a number of tests which are useful in testing the 'significance of the difference' between independent non-parametric samples. Among the other tests, the Kolmogorov–Smirnov test and the Wald–Wolfowitz test are valuable in determining whether or not the two samples are from statistical populations which differ in any respect at all, while the one illustrated here is of special sensitivity to differences in central tendency. To determine the exact test to be used in a given situation, the relative power of the tests as well as the sample size and strength of the measurement must be taken into account (Siegel, 1956, pp. 156–8).

3. Exploratory methods: trend comparisons

Where data are collected simultaneously over a wide number of locations, we may wish to investigate the *trends* in the relationships between the two or more sets of data. The conventional statistical method for handling this problem is through *regression* analysis. Here we briefly review the application of both simple and multiple-regression analysis to two characteristic geographical problems. Clear summaries of the main stages in regression analysis are given by Davies (1958, pp. 150–272) and Gregory (1963, pp. 185–208). A standard work on multiple-regression analysis is Ezekiel and Fox (1959), but geographers may find it more useful to follow Krumbein's extremely clear exposition of this method applied to the 'sorting out' of a group of factors controlling beach firmness (Krumbein, 1959-A). The problems in applying regression analysis to areal data have been discussed by Duncan (Duncan *et al.*, 1961, pp. 99–128), while Robinson (Robinson and Bryson, 1957; Robinson, 1962) has experimented with the difficult problem of the statistical comparison of isarithmic maps of trends.

Example III: Simple regression analysis. The first type of association between two fully calibrated variables is *linear regression*. It seeks to measure the nature of the function linking X and Y, $Y = f(X)$ where Y is considered to be an 'effect', X a 'cause', and f is the symbolic statement of 'function of'. In this type of research there must be strong logical grounds for assigning one variable, rather than the other, as the cause. For instance, low rainfall may be the cause of wheat failure, but wheat failure can hardly be the cause of low rainfall!

An example of regression analysis, in which a strong trend is evident, is shown in Fig. 10.6. Data for this graph were collected from Lösch's examination of the distances separating towns (with populations between 1,000 and 4,000) in an eighty-mile-wide belt running west from Chicago

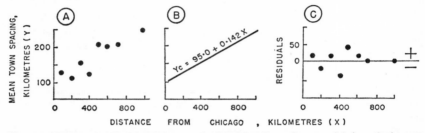

Fig. 10.6. Stages in the regression analysis of spacing of towns (y) in relation to distance from Chicago (x). *A* Scatter diagram. *B* Best-fit linear regression line. *C* Residuals from regression ($y - y_c$).

to the eastern boundary of Nebraska, i.e. for the first 1,000-kilometre tract out from Chicago. The data are plotted graphically in Fig. 10.6 with the independent variable ('cause') on the x-axis, and the dependent variable ('effect') on the y-axis. The points on the graph show some increase in spacing with increasing distance from Chicago, but the increase is not consistent and we may rightly feel that the situation is by no means a simple one. We want, therefore, to discover the exact form of the function linking X and Y, and to test whether the relationship is statistically significant.

To determine the function we find the best-fit regression line, i.e. the line which best fits the series of points plotted on the graph (Gregory, 1963, pp. 185–208). This line will be of the general form, $Y = a + bX$ in which a and b are two constants. Constant a determines the position of the regression line on the Y-axis, while constant b determines the slope of the line, and is termed the *regression coefficient*. While in Fig. 10.6 the relationship is direct, indicating that an increase in X is accompanied by an increase in Y, an equally common form is $Y = a - bX$. This is an inverse relationship in which the regression coefficient (b) has a minus sign, and the line slopes downwards to the right.

In Fig. 10.6 a regression line has been fitted to the Lösch data using the *method of least squares*. The form of the relationship of spacing (Y) to distance from Chicago (X) is $Y = 95 \cdot 0 + 0 \cdot 142X$.

This best-fit regression line approximates the trend of the points in Fig. 10.5, but it is evident that none of the points actually lies on the line and a number of values are some distance from it. There is therefore a need for some test to determine whether the relationship of Y to X is statistically significant, or whether the regression could be due to a chance occurrence of values. Inspection of the graph shows that three factors are of prime importance in determining the significance of the trend—(1) the number of points; (2) the slope of the line; and (3) the degree of scatter of the points about the line. If the number of points is very few, or the trend of the line has a very low slope (almost parallel to the X-axis), even a cursory examination of the graph would suggest a weak trend.

In this case, measurement of the number of points ($N = 10$) and the slope of the line ($b = 0 \cdot 142$) have already been obtained. A measurement of the degree of scatter is given by a statistic known as the *standard* error of estimate denoted by the symbol $S_{y.x}$, where

$$S_{y.x} = \sqrt{\{\Sigma \, (Y - Y_c)^2\}/(N - 2)}$$

where Y is the ordinate of the observed point, and Y_c the ordinate on the fitted regression, both Y values being for the same X value and measured parallel to the Y-axis. This term is illustrated in Fig. 10.5 by short vertical lines linking the points to the regression line. This statistic is analogous to the *standard deviation* inasmuch as it measures the dispersion of values about the regression line.

The value of $S_{y.x}$ in the settlement-spacing case was computed as 26·9 kilometres, meaning that roughly two-thirds of the Y-values would be expected to fall within approximately twenty-seven kilometres of the estimated value for any particular distance from Chicago.

With these three factors (number of points, slope, and scatter) known, we can return to the problem of the significance of the trend shown in Fig. 10.6. To test for significance we set up a *null hypothesis*, that is we adopt a conservative or sceptical viewpoint stating—'there is actually no real trend relating town-spacing and distance from Chicago', and we hold this hypothesis until grounds are presented for abandoning it. To test the null hypothesis, a statistic known as t is used. This is derived from the expression,

$$t = \{b\sqrt{\Sigma \, (X - \bar{X})^2}\}/S_{y.x}$$

In this expression $\sqrt{\Sigma \, (X - \bar{X})^2}$ is a measurement of the dispersion of all the X values about the mean ($\bar{X}$). In the illustrative case used here the value of t was computed as:

$$t = \{0 \cdot 142(905 \cdot 5)\}/26 \cdot 9 = 4 \cdot 78$$

With this value we refer to the table of *t*-distributions (Fisher and Yates, 1957, p. 44), and find that in the row eight *degrees of freedom* (two less than the number of pairs in the regression) our value lies between columns 0·01 and 0·001. There is therefore only a very remote chance (between 1/100 and 1/1,000) of this relationship being due to chance. The null hypothesis is thus rejected and we can consider the slope obtained to be statistically *significant* at the 99 per cent confidence level.

So far the regressions discussed have been of a simple or linear type, i.e. both *X*- and *Y*-axes are linear and the regression line is a straight line.

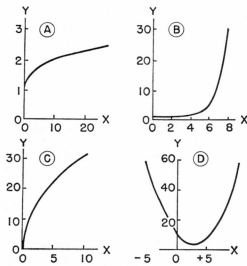

Fig. 10.7. Non-linear relationships. Source: Brooks and Carruthers, 1953, p. 301.

There are, however, a number of other functions which may give better fits to the plotted data. In Fig. 10.7 are examples of four other functions: a logarithmic function

$$Y = 1 + \log_{10}(X + 2)$$

(Fig. 10.7-A), an exponential function

$$Y = 1 - 0·01eX$$

(Fig. 10.7-B), a 'power' function

$$Y = 10X^{\frac{1}{2}}$$

(Fig. 10.7-C), and a polynomial function

$$Y = 10 - 5X + X^2$$

(Fig. 10.7-D). In each of these cases *X* and *Y* are related but not in a simple linear fashion. Some can, however, be 'transformed' by plotting one or both variables on a special scale but, as emphasized in Chapter 10.II(1a), these 'non-normal' distributions are important inasmuch as a number of known geographical distributions seem to be of this type.

Example IV: Multiple-regression analysis. When, as is frequently the case, an effect is not explicable in terms of one cause but in terms of a group of causes, there is a need for an expression in which an effect (Y) can be associated with a number of causes in combination ($X_1 X_2, \ldots X_n$). This problem is overcome by the use of *multiple-regression analysis,* where in mathematical terms, Y is given by

$$Y = a + bX + cX_2 \ldots + zX_n$$

where $a, b, \ldots z$ are constants. A typical illustration of the use of multiple-regression analysis for the analysis of geographical distribution is given by McCarty *et al.* (1956), who investigated the distribution of the machinery industry among the prefectures of Japan. The nature of the association found was described as,

$$Y = 0.68X_1 + 0.37X_2 + 0.42X_3 + 0.46X_4 - 44.56$$

where Y was the distribution of the machinery industry, X_1 was the printing industry, X_2 the chemical industry, X_3 the spinning industry, and X_4 the food industry. Through using this type of analysis McCarty was able to test the validity of a number of theories previously put forward to explain the geographical distribution of industry.

Haggett (1964) analysed the distribution of the forest cover (Y) in southeastern Brazil shown in Fig. 9.20 in terms of five alternative hypotheses ($X_{1, 2, 3, 4, 5}$). These are listed in Table 10.7. Each hypothesis was

Table 10.7. Factors used in multiple-regression analysis of forest cover*

	Transformation	Relationship	Variance reduction
Factors:			
Terrain index (X_1)	Logarithmic	Direct	38.4%
Settlement spacing index (X_2)	,,	,,	7.2%
Rural population density index (X_3)	,,	Inverse	19.4%
Forest density index (X_4)	,,	Direct	47.5%
Land values index (X_5)	,,	Inverse	13.2%

Source: Haggett, 1964, p. 374.
        * Southeast Brazil.

tested by using simple regression analysis and the relative success of each factor in 'explaining' the distribution of forest cover is shown in the column headed 'variance reduction'. If the total variation from place to place in the forest cover is reduced to an index of 100 per cent then we can similarly express as percentages the reduction in that variation that is achieved by introducing our five hypotheses.

It is clear that the forest density index (X_4) and the terrain index (X_1), with values of 47 and 38 per cent respectively, appear to be particularly important factors in determining the forest pattern.

One difficulty in interpreting the five separate equations is that they each suggest a simple relationship, whereas experience suggests that each factor works as part of a complex of environmental factors. Multiple-regression analysis allows the factors to be combined, either in pairs, threes, fours, or as five together. Two-factor combinations, shown diagram-

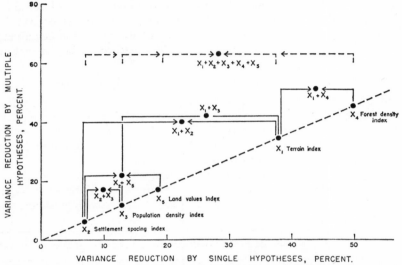

Fig. 10.8. Comparison of the results of simple- and multiple- regression analysis of the distribution of forest cover in the Brazilian Sudeste. Source: Haggett, 1964, p. 374.

matically in Fig. 10.8, illustrate the improved performance as more factors are built into the equation. With all five factors operating together about two-thirds of the regional variation in the forest pattern of the Sudeste is predictable.

An extremely interesting and perhaps more easily appreciated way of showing the results of regression analysis, is *residual mapping*. This has been discussed by Thomas (1960) and is illustrated in Fig. 10.9. Shaded areas show those areas which are above the value they would have had, were they to conform exactly to the regression hypotheses. Similarly shaded areas show negative anomalies. Hypotheses which provide a better prediction of the forest areas are shown by rather small 'highs' and 'lows' while conversely rather poor fits are indicated by more extensive anomaly zones. Examination of the *positive* residuals shows that for all six equations the positive residuals are located in a strip within thirty miles of the coast. Within this coastal strip certain hard-core areas appear and reappear on

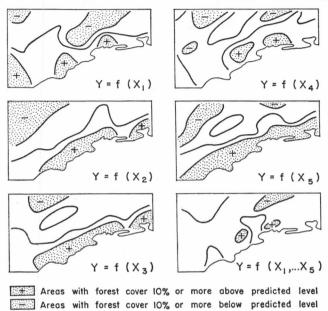

┌─────┐ Areas with forest cover 10% or more above predicted level
└─────┘ Areas with forest cover 10% or more below predicted level

Fig. 10.9. Residual maps of Brazilian Sudeste $(G = 3.9)$ showing 'unexplained' areas after simple- and multiple-regression analysis. Source: Haggett, 1964, p. 375.

successive residual maps, but when all five factors are combined, the area of positive residuals shrinks to two small elliptical 'highs', each about twenty miles by ten miles along their major and minor axes respectively. The *negative* residuals show a similar pattern of concentration, but in this case the location is shifted to the inner margins of the area with two important areas of recurring concentration standing out. The negative areas are broken (by the high ground of the Serra da Mantiqueira escarpment) and less stable in both location and extent than the positive residuals. The five-factor analysis left only one residual 'low' in the second of the two areas as a wedge, forty miles deep, thrusting towards the southwest. Both the positive and negative residual areas are probably zones where other factors not included in this analysis are operating. They are clearly just those areas which would repay a close-up, 'case history', type of analysis.

4. Experimental designs

The tests illustrated in the two preceding sections (Examples I to IV) dealt mainly with statistical methods useful in extracting information from pre-existing locational data. This section deals with the rational design of locational experiments in which (i) questions are first formulated, (ii) statistical tests are chosen, and only then (iii) field observations are collected. In experimental design the collection of data in the field comes at a very late stage in the research process. A useful review of experimental designs used in the earth sciences is given by Krumbein (1955–B), while Davies (1956) in his *Design and analysis of industrial experiments* has provided a mine of ideas and methods that might prove widely applicable to geographical study in the future. For a working example of one experimental design applied to a field situation, Melton's (1960) study of slopes in relation to local environmental factors is particularly helpful.

Example V: Factorial experiments. One elementary type of experimental design, *factorial* design, was used by Haggett (1964) in a study of forested areas within a small 100 square kilometre tract in southeastern Brazil (the Fortaleza basin). Preliminary study of the area suggested four factors —terrain (A), soils (B), farm-size (C), and farm accessibility (D)—might be important environmental factors. Each of the factors was tested at two levels. For example, the first factor, terrain, was defined by angle of slope and a critical division made at an angle of five degrees: i.e. slopes of less than five degrees (1) were distinguished from those above (a). Fig. 10.10 shows the division for both a theoretical area and for the Brazilian example. The second factor, soils, was divided into two classes—mica schist soils (b) and other soils (1); the addition of the second factor giving four possible

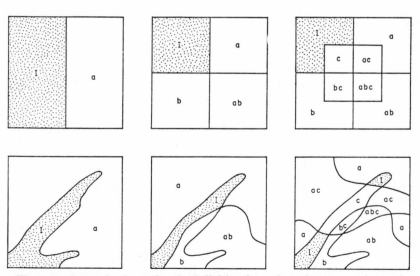

Fig. 10.10. Stages in the regional subdivision for a three-factor experimental design.

combinations, 1, *a*, *b*, and *ab*, which are plotted on Fig. 10.10. Addition of the other two factors at two levels raises the number of factor combinations to sixteen as shown in Table 10.8. They run from 1 in which no

Table 10.8. Derivation of factor combinations*

	Factor A: Terrain	Factor B: Soils	Factor C: Farm size	Factor D: Farm accessibility
Fortaleza basin	*a* Slopes above 5°	*ab* Mica schist	*abc* Medium	*abcd* Within 2 km. *abc* Beyond 2 km.
			ab Large	*abd* Within 2 km. *ab* Beyond 2 km.
		a Others	*ac* Medium	*acd* Within 2 km. *ac* Beyond 2 km.
			a Large	*ad* Within 2 km. *a* Beyond 2 km.
	I Slopes below 5°	*b* Mica schist	*bc* Medium	*bcd* Within 2 km. *bc* Beyond 2 km.
			b Large	*bd* Within 2 km. *b* Beyond 2 km.
		I Others	*c* Medium	*cd* Within 2 km. *c* Beyond 2 km.
			I Large	*d* Within 2 km. I Beyond 2 km.

Source: Haggett, 1964, p. 369.
* Fortaleza basin, Taubaté county, Brazil.

factor is expected to exert a positive effect on the forest cover to *abcd* in which all four factors are working together. Boundaries for each of the four levels were plotted on a 1/10,000 base map of the Fortaleza basin. The crossing and recrossing of the boundaries gave over one hundred sectors, each of which was classified into one of the sixteen factor-types. For each type, sixteen sample plots were located on the map by random co-ordinates (Chap. 7.II(1b)), to give a total of 256 sample plots (i.e. sixteen plots for each of the sixteen factor-combination types of land). Their location in relation to the factor-combination regions is shown in Fig. 10.11. These plots were then marked on 1/25,000 air photographs as circles equivalent to 2·50 acres in area and the proportion of forest within the circle calculated under an enlarged graticule.

The results of this analysis are set out in a standard summary form in Table 10.9. In examining the table it should be noticed that the proportion of forested area in each factor-combination type is not given in a

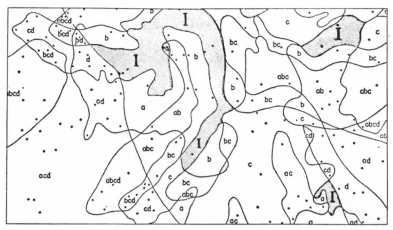

Fig. 10.11. Location of sampling points within factor-combination regions in the Fortaleza basin ($G = 6·9$) Taubaté county, Brazil. Source: Haggett, 1964, p. 368.

Table 10.9. Forest cover variation under a four-factor classification*

		Farm access (D)			
		Poor (I)		Good (d)	
Terrain (A)	Soils (B)	Farm size (C)		Farm size (C)	
		Large (I)	Medium (c)	Large (I)	Medium (c)
Lower slopes (I)	Others (I)	12·9 (I)	23·6 (c)	19·4 (d)	10·0 (cd)
	Mica schist (b)	8·1 (b)	22·1 (bc)	30·1 (bd)	22·0 (bcd)
Upper slopes (a)	Others (I)	24·4 (a)	30·0 (ac)	31·3 (ad)	17·5 (acd)
	Mica schist (b)	8·2 (ab)	23·6 (abc)	37·5 (abd)	54·9 (abcd)

Source: Haggett, 1964, p. 369.
* Fortaleza basin, Taubaté county, Brazil.

conventional form, as percentage of the total area, but in angular units. Percentage data are notoriously difficult to accommodate in statistical analysis and particularly difficult when, as in this case, the percentage values are largely drawn from the lower extremes of the percentage range, i.e. from 0 to 30 per cent. It was necessary therefore to convert the original percentage values into a more stable form by transforming them into angular values of between zero and ninety degrees. The case for this conversion has been discussed in § II(1).

Analysis of the results of Table 10.9 were carried out using a standard

Yates 2^n procedure (Davies, 1956, p. 283) and the findings are shown in
Table 10.10. In the first part of the table the effect of each individual

Table 10.10. Sources of variation in forest cover*

Nature of the effect	Source	Amount of the effect (angular units)	F-ratio	Conventional significance level
Main factors:				
	Terrain (A)	+9·8	9·3	Probably significant†
	Soils (B)	+4·7	1·6	Not significant
	Farm size (C)	+4·0	1·2	Not significant
	Farm access (D)	+8·7	8·2	Probably significant†
Interactions:				
	BD (soils × farm size)		10·7	Probably significant†
	Other interactions between pairs		1·8	Not significant
	Higher-order interactions (ABC, ABD, ABCD)		—	—

Source: Haggett, 1964, p. 370.
    * Fortaleza basin, Taubaté county, Brazil.   † 95 per cent confidence level.

factor is assessed and shown as a positive value in degrees. It is worth
noting that, while each factor has an effect, only two factors (terrain and
farm accessibility) are shown to be statistically significant at the 95 per
cent confidence level. One interesting point from the second part of the
table is the strong interaction between soils and farm accessibility (BD).
It suggests that the accessible farms tend to be located on areas of soils
derived from mica schist; thus there may be a 'hidden' soil factor included in the strong effect of accessibility on forest cover.

Factorial analysis is only one of the many methods of experimental
design possible in geography. *Nested* designs have been used in the analysis
of scale components (and were discussed in Chapter 9), while *latin-square*
designs have been used in other earth sciences (Krumbein, 1953). A less
efficient experimental design, *paired comparisons*, was used by Haggett
(1961) in a study of small watersheds in Brazil; watersheds were 'paired'
so that they matched each other in terms of climate, bedrock, slope, area,
and morphometry, but were totally unlike in one respect—one of the pair
was forest-covered, the other having been cleared. David (1963) in his
Method of paired comparisons has shown how this 'elimination' method can
be used, under favourable conditions, to test the significance of the remaining unlike factors.

III. TESTING VIA ANALOGUES

We have seen in an earlier consideration of model building (Chap. 1.III(2)) that the mathematical-statistical approach to research is paralleled by approaches in which experiments and natural analogies are used to corroborate theories. Although these latter methods have not been widely employed in geography as a whole, still less in human geography, there are signs that this situation is changing. In this final section we look at some of the more exciting ways in which *simulation* methods are being explored. Chorley (1964) has provided a useful review of the application of some of these methods to geography.

1. Simulation by physical analogues

Even in the physical branches of geography, direct physical experiments pose severe dimensional problems: in human geography, it is still more difficult to see their relevance. None the less Bunge (1962, pp. 109–19) has shown how useful such experiments may be in examining the more abstract spatial theories concerning movement and regional organization. He shows how Enke (1951) was able to solve problems in spatial equilibrium using an electric circuit analogue, and how Hotelling (1921) could present a theory of human migration in terms of heat, flowing through a copper sheet. Other examples suggest the relevance of flow dynamics—both the fluid theory of hydrodynamics and the kinetic theory of gas—to the solution of movement problems within human geography.

One extremely simple physical experiment is described (Bunge, 1964, pp. 33–5) in which the Christaller–Lösch central-place model was simulated by floating bar magnets. Bar magnets were embedded into corks with their positive poles towards the top of the cork and the bottom weighted with lead to ensure a uniform floating position. It was argued that since the positive poles would repel each other, floating magnets would tend to arrange themselves in such a way as to maximize the distance between each of them. Twenty such magnets were dumped simultaneously into a circular tank partly filled with water and the final resting or equilibrium position of the corks recorded. This random dumping was repeated one hundred times.

The interesting results of this apparently 'Heath-Robinson' type of experiment are shown in Table 10.11. Here the patterns have been assigned to the geometrical class they most nearly represented; and polygons both with and without central points have been recorded. The dominance of the hexagonal form is outstanding in these results; nearly half the trials gave a 'true' Christaller–Lösch form with a central point, another quarter formed a hexagonal ring without a centre. Altogether hexagons and adjacent pentagons made up 94 per cent of all the trials.

Table 10.11. Simulation of central-place patterns by floating magnets

Arrangement:	Square	Pentagonal	Hexagonal	Heptagonal	Others
Proportion of trials:					
With central point	1%	22%	43%	2%	—
Without central point	1%	4%	25%	—	2%
Total	2%	26%	68%	2%	2%

Source: Bunge, 1964, p. 35.

Improvements on this type of model are clearly possible. Flemming (1964: Personal communication) has suggested that positively charged pith-balls might be substituted for the magnets and that, by varying the electrical charge, differences in magnitude and spacing might be introduced into the model. By modifying the slope and form of the dry surface over which the balls move, the concept of local environmental 'resistances' might also be explored.

2. Monte Carlo simulation

We have already seen, from Neyman and Scott's model of diffusion waves (Chap. 2.IV(26)) and from Hägerstrand's ideas on the evolution of settlement patterns (Chap. 4.I(3a)), how we can make use of random or stochastic processes to simulate geographical patterns. Garrison (1962, pp. 91–108) has provided a useful review of the possibilities of these methods in predicting urban growth, and Kansky (1963, pp. 128–47) has fused the ideas of random processes and graph theory (Chap. 8.II) in predicting (or as Kansky would term it, 'postdicting') the 1908 railroad network of Sicily from (i) his general findings on network geometry and (ii) the population and income of the leading thirty Sicilian towns in that year. Comparison of Fig. 10.12-A, showing the predicted pattern, and Fig. 10.12-B, showing the actual pattern in 1908, show the encouraging results that are beginning to come from this type of predictive simulation model.

Perhaps the most ambitious use of stochastic models has come from

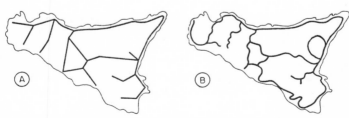

Fig. 10.12. Simulated (A) and actual (B) railway networks in Sicily $(G = 4\cdot3)$ in 1908. Source: Kansky, 1963, pp. 143, 146.

Morrill (1963) in a study of the growth of towns in the Värnamo area of southern Sweden. In this mostly forested area which has today a population of about a quarter of a million with a mean density of about fifty people to the square mile, industrial growth began around 1865 but was not significant until 1880. Morrill traces the growth of population in this area from 1860 onwards using the census records of some 155 local parishes. He then attempts to simulate this population growth and to predict its future distribution by using Monte Carlo methods (Hägerstrand, in Centre International d'Étude des Problèmes Humains, 1963, pp. 61–84).

Morrill's model runs in a series of twenty-year cycles from 1860 through to 1980. Each simulation cycle consists of six phases: (i) the benchmark distribution (the 1860 situation in the case of the first cycle) with a known pattern of population, routes, manufacturing, and so on; (ii) assignment of new transport routes; (iii) assignment of 'non-central-place activities' (i.e. manufacturing); (iv) assignment of central-place activities; (v) assignment of migrants between areas; (vi) end of the first cycle—this becomes the starting point for the next simulation cycle.

Each phase of the cycle is marked by the 'assignment' of routes, or activities, or population. An example of how this assignment is made in practice can be illustrated from the fifth phase—assignment of migrants. Morrill assumes that the propensity to migrate, that is the expected volume of migration from each source area, is a function of the size and characteristics of the population in the source area (its employment conditions, age structure, etc.). Probability of migration between two areas is viewed as a function of (*a*) the distance between two areas, (*b*) the difference in the attractiveness of the two areas, and (*c*) the history of previous migration contacts. Relative attractiveness is built into the model from the opportunities which are assumed to be created as a result of the assignment of activities carried out in the previous stages of simulation. The possibility of a given migrant following a particular path is assumed to be an inverse distance function with the relative strength of distance as a barrier, varying with the state of transport technology and with the urban–rural population composition.

Fig. 10.13 illustrates the migration process. First, the relative attractiveness of each of the twenty-three sub-areas of the region is weighted for its 'migration probability' potential. This ranges in value from twenty-four, for an accessible industrial centre, to one, for distant outlying areas (Fig. 10.13-B). These values are summed and converted to give a total of 100. Using these values, to each sub-area is assigned a series of numbers (these are of course effectively 'chances') between one and 100; these are shown in Fig. 10.13-C. The number of migrants from the field under consideration is chosen, in this case twenty migrants, and twenty random numbers are drawn from a random numbers table. Since each of these numbers represents also a value in one of the sub-areas, the destinations of the migrants are known. Lines connecting the source area with the destination are shown in Fig. 10.13-D.

By repeating this process for each area the net gain or loss in migrants can be determined and trends in the population changes inferred. By summing the results both of the activities which have been assigned, and these migration changes, the overall population changes in the area over a period of time can be inferred. This changed population distribution becomes the basis for a new simulation cycle in a subsequent time period, and so on.

The technique used by Morrill for simulating population change in an

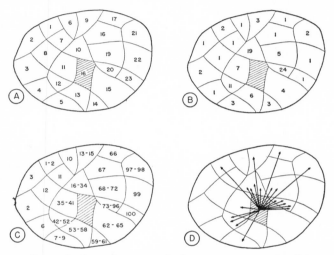

Fig. 10.13. Stages in the assignment of migrants to areas using Monte Carlo simulation processes. Source: Morrill, 1963, p. 13.

area has a number of advantages and disadvantages. Among the former are its great flexibility and its very simple mathematics. It is particularly useful, therefore, for attacking problems which have no unique solution (e.g. How far will migrants move from a home area?) but which have a range of possible answers. By assigning probabilities to various alternatives—we know for example that nearby locations have a greater chance of being selected than very distant ones—we can make the final choice by a sampling procedure using random numbers. Since the selection of any location depends ultimately on earlier decisions (shown in the weighting) the random event is linked into the total pattern of decisions over time.

One disadvantage of the method which is probably only a temporary check is the sheer size of the computations needed. In Morrill's study which used 155 areas, there are 155 × 155 or over twenty-four thousand possible migration paths and probabilities. These have to be completely recomputed for each time period of simulation cycle. The ultimate solution clearly lies in the programming of the entire simulation process by computer.

Leopold and Langbein (1962) have shown how random processes

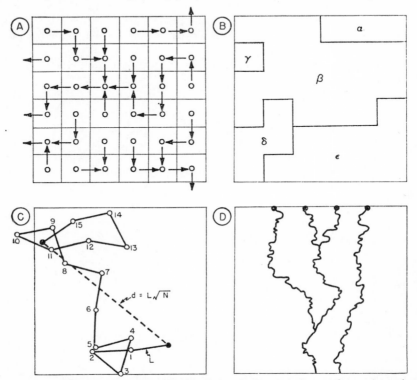

Fig. 10.14. AB Sample of cells showing linkage of centres by random orientation with resulting boundary divisions. *C* Random walk with sixteen steps of equal length. *D* Application of random-walk model to network evolution. Sources: Leopold and Langbein, 1962, pp. 16, 18; Krumbein, 1955, p. 10.

may lead to regular hierarchies of areal units of different sizes: thus random movements of water particles (Fig. 10.14-A) may lead to a regular hierarchy of catchments (Fig. 10.14-B). Although they were concerned with simulating river networks and catchments, it is clear that similar models might be evolved within the framework of human geography in relation to the trade-areas of settlements, administrative subdivision, and so on. In the same way, it might prove possible to adapt random-walk models (Fig. 10.14-C) to the development of communication paths around centres. With the introduction of a *gravity* component, Leopold and Langbein are able to produce tolerably good simulations of river patterns (Fig. 10.14-D); with the introduction of a *centrifugal* component similar simulation of route patterns developing around centres might be possible.

3. Logical simulation: semi-axiomatic systems

No attempt has yet been made to base any part of geography on a set of axioms from which everything else in that part can be logically derived: nor is such an attempt immediately likely. There are none the less periods in the history of all branches of thought when the desire to axiomatize is dominant: '. . . when an effort is made to co-ordinate and codify what is already known, to tidy up the loose ends and to discard what is unimportant or of dubious value' (Fletcher, 1964, p. 181). The second half of this century is likely to be such a period for geography, a period when accounts are squared, and our models are revised and extended.

Axiomatics is concerned with the strict deduction of a sequence of results from a few *minimum* assumptions. It is directly related both to logic and to mathematics through Boolean algebra and the algebra of sets, and we have already seen some aspects of its use in our discussions of the nature of geography (Chap. 1.II(2) (and of regional structure (Chap. 9.I(1b)). One simple working definition of axiomatics is 'the calculus of statements' and this summarizes the essential union of (i) statements derived from empirical evidence, and (ii) logical-mathematical manipulation of these statements. How far geography can meet the full requirements of an axiomatic system (as defined by logicians) is still at issue, but certainly we can work a great deal closer towards such a system.

Kansky (1963, pp. 122–7) has pioneered the path towards a semi-axiomatic system in human geography in his study of transport networks. His analysis consists of three phases: (i) rigorous definition of eight *terms* defining components in the system, (ii) statement of nine *axioms* proven in part by empirical evidence, and (iii) deduction of four locational *trends* from the axioms. Thus in the first phase the term *network* is defined as the '. . . union of all transportation routes E_i' and given by the algebraic symbols:

$$N = \text{df. } \mathbf{U}\ E_i$$

In the second stage, Kansky is able to condense his Seventh Axiom ('When the network N_i develops into the network N_j, then the metrical length of the edges of N_j (E_j) tends to be shorter than the metrical length of the N_i edges (E_i)') to the symbolic form

$$(N_i \tau N_j) \supset (E_i > E_j)$$

Langer (1953) in her *Introduction to symbolic logic* has shown that although

the reduction of language to symbolic form brings a stiffness and un-
familiarity it has, like legal language, compensating advantages in precision. Unlike legal language, the symbols can be written into equations
which may be treated mathematically to test for contradictions or to yield
further unsuspected relationships.

Although we may intuitively shy from a system which threatens to
reduce 'Ophelia loves Hamlet' to $H \leftarrow O$, the rigour of the axiomatic
method has a powerful attraction. At a time when more attention is being
paid to measurement and quantification in human geography, symbolic
logic offers opportunities for wedding this movement to traditional and
commonsense patterns of thought within the field. In the long run the
quality of geography in this century will be judged less by its sophisticated
techniques or its exhaustive detail, than by the strength of its logical
reasoning.

References

ABRAMSON, N. (1963). *Information theory and coding*. New York.
ACKERMAN, E. A. (1963). Where is a research frontier? *Annals of the Association of American Geographers*, **53**, 429–40.
ACKOFF, R. L., S. K. GUPTA, and J. S. MINAS (1962). *Scientific method: optimizing applied research decisions*. New York.
ALEXANDER, J. W. (1944). Freight rates as a geographic factor in Illinois. *Economic Geography*, **20**, 25–30.
ALEXANDER, J. W. (1963). *Economic Geography*. New York.
ALEXANDER, J. W., E. S. BROWN, and R. E. DAHLBERG (1958). Freight rates; selected aspects of uniform and nodal regions. *Economic Geography*, **34**, 1–18.
ALEXANDERSSON, G. (1956). *The industrial structure of American cities*. Lincoln, Nebr.
AMIRAN, D. H. K. and A. P. SCHICK (1961). *Geographical conversion tables*. Zurich.
ANDERSON, M. (1963). A working bibliography of mathematical geography. *Michigan Inter-University Community of Mathematical Geographers, Discussion Papers*, **2.**
ANDERSSON, T. (1897). *Den inre omflyttningen: Norrland*. Mälmo.
APPLEBAUM, W. and S. B. COHEN (1961). The dynamics of store trading areas and market equilibrium. *Annals of the Association of American Geographers*, **51**, 73–101.
AUERBACH, F. (1913). Das Gesetz der Bevölkerungskonzentration. *Petermann's Mitteilungen*, **59**, 74–6.
AZEVEDO, A. DE, Editor (1958). *A cidade de São Paulo: estudos de geografia urbana*. Four volumes. São Paulo.
BACHI, R. (1963). Standard distance measures and related methods for spatial analysis. *Regional Science Association, Papers and Proceedings*, **10**, 83–132.
BACKE, H. (1942). *Um die Nahrungsfreiheit Europas*. Leipzig.
BAILEY, N. T. J. (1957). *Mathematical theory of epidemics*. New York.
BAIN, J. S. (1954). Economies of scale, concentration, and the condition of entry in twenty manufacturing industries. *American Economic Review*, **44**, 15–39.
BAKER, O. E. (1921). Increasing importance of the physical conditions in determining the utilization of land for agriculture and forest production in the United States. *Annals of the Association of American Geographers*, **11**, 17–46.
BARFORD, B. (1938). *Local economic effects of a large-scale industrial undertaking*. Copenhagen.
BARROWS, H. H. (1923). Geography as human ecology. *Annals of the Association of American Geographers*, **13**, 1–14.
BARTHOLOMEW, H. (1955). *Land use in American cities*. Cambridge.
BASKIN, C. W. (1957). A critique and translation of W. Christaller's 'Die zentralen Orte in Süddeutschland'. *University of Virginia, Ph.D. Thesis*.
BECKERMAN, W. (1956). Distance and the pattern of intra-European trade. *Review of Economics and Statistics*, **38**, 31–40.
BECKMANN, M. J. (1952). A continuous model of transportation. *Econometrica*, **20**, 643–60.
BECKMANN, M. J. (1955). Some reflections on Lösch's theory of location. *Regional Science Association, Papers and Proceedings*, **1**, N1–N9.
BECKMANN, M. J. (1958). City hierarchies and the distribution of city size. *Economic Development and Cultural Change*, **6**, 243–8.

BEESLEY, M. (1955). The birth and death of industrial establishments: experience in the West Midlands conurbation. *Journal of Industrial Economics*, **4**, 45–61.

BERRY, B. J. L. (1958). A note concerning methods of classification. *Annals of the Association of American Geographers*, **48**, 300–3.

BERRY, B. J. L. (1960). An inductive approach to the regionalization of economic development. *University of Chicago, Department of Geography, Research Paper*, **62**, 78–107.

BERRY, B. J. L. (1961-A). City size distributions and economic development. *Economic Development and Cultural Change*, **9**, 573–88.

BERRY, B. J. L. (1961-B). A method for deriving multifactor uniform regions. *Przeglad Geograficzny*, **33**, 263–82.

BERRY, B. J. L. (1962). Sampling, coding, and storing flood plain data. *United States, Department of Agriculture, Farm Economics Division, Agriculture Handbook*, **237**.

BERRY, B. J. L. In press. Market centres and retail distribution. New York.

BERRY, B. J. L., H. G. BARNUM, and R. J. TENNANT (1962). Retail location and consumer behaviour. *Regional Science Association, Papers and Proceedings*, **9**, 65–106.

BERRY, B. J. L. and W. L. GARRISON (1958-A). A note on central place theory and the range of a good. *Economic Geography*, **34**, 304–11.

BERRY, B. J. L. and W. L. GARRISON (1958-B). Functional bases of the central place hierarchy. *Economic Geography*, **34**, 145–54.

BERRY, B. J. L. and W. L. GARRISON (1958-C). Alternate explanations of urban rank size relationships. *Annals of the Association of American Geographers*, **48**, 83–91.

BERRY, B. J. L. and A. PRED (1961). Central place studies: a bibliography of theory and applications. *Regional Science Research Institute, Bibliographic Series*, **1**.

BERRY, B. J. L., J. W. SIMMONS, and R. J. TENNANT (1963). Urban population densities: structure and change. *Geographical Review*, **53**, 389–405.

BERTALANFFY, L. VON (1951). An outline of general system theory. *British Journal of the Philosophy of Science*, **1**, 134–65.

BIRCH, J. W. (1960). A note on the sample-farm survey and its use as a basis for generalized mapping. *Economic Geography*, **36**, 254–9.

BIRD, J. (1956). Scale in regional study: illustrated by brief comparisons between the western peninsulas of England and France. *Geography*, **41**, 25–38.

BLUMENSTOCK, D. I. (1953). The reliability factor in the drawing of isarithms. *Annals of the Association of American Geographers*, **43**, 289–304.

BOARD, C. (1962). *The Border region: natural environment and land use in the eastern Cape*. Cape Town.

BOGUE, D. J. (1949). *The structure of the metropolitan community: a study of dominance and subdominance*. Ann Arbor.

BORCHERT, J. R. (1961). The twin cities urbanized area: past, present, and future. *Geographical Review*, **51**, 47–70.

BOUSTEDT, O. and H. RANZ (1957). *Regionale Struktur- und Wirtschaftsforschung*. Bremen.

BOWMAN, I. (1916). *The Andes of southern Peru: geographical reconnaissance along the seventy-third meridian*. New York.

BOWMAN, I. (1931). *The pioneer fringe*. New York.

BOX, G. E. P. (1954). The exploration and exploitation of response surfaces. *Biometrics*, **10**, 16–30.

BOYCE, R. B. and W. A. V. CLARK (1964). The concept of shape in geography. *Geographical Review*, **54**, 561–72.

BRACEY, H. E. (1952). *Social provision in rural Wiltshire*. London.

BRACEY, H. E. (1962). English central villages: identification, distribution and functions. *Lund Studies in Geography, Series B, Human Geography*, **24**, 169–90.

BRILLOUIN, L. (1964). *Scientific uncertainty and information*. New York.

BRITISH RAILWAYS BOARD (1963). *The reshaping of British railways.* London.

BROEK, J. O. M. (1932). *The Santa Clara valley, California: a study in landscape changes.* Utrecht.

BRONOWSKI, J. (1960). *The common sense of science.* London.

BROOKS, C. E. P. and N. CARRUTHERS (1953). *Handbook of statistical methods in meteorology.* London.

BRUNHES, J. (1925). *La géographie humaine.* Two volumes. Paris.

BRUSH, J. E. (1953). The hierarchy of central places in southwestern Wisconsin. *Geographical Review,* **43,** 380–402.

BRUSH, J. E. and H. E. BRACEY (1955). Rural service centres in southwestern Wisconsin and southern England. *Geographical Review,* **45,** 559–69.

BUCHÉLE, C., JR. (1958). *Atlas geográfico de Santa Catarina.* Florianopolis.

BUNGE, W. (1962). Theoretical geography. *Lund Studies in Geography, Series C, General and Mathematical Geography,* **1.**

BUNGE, W. (1964). Patterns of location. *Michigan Inter-University Community of Mathematical Geographers, Discussion Papers,* **3.**

BURGESS, E. W. (1927). The determination of gradients in the growth of the city. *American Sociological Society, Publications,* **21,** 178–84.

BURGHARDT, A. F. (1959). The location of river towns in the central lowland of the United States. *Annals of the Association of American Geographers,* **49,** 305–323.

BURTON, I. (1963-A). The quantitative revolution and theoretical geography. *Canadian Geographer,* **7,** 151–62.

BURTON, I. (1963-B). A restatement of the dispersed city hypothesis. *Annals of the Association of American Geographers,* **53,** 285–9.

BUTLER, J. B. (1960). *Profit and purpose in farming: a study of farms and small-holdings in part of the North Riding.* Leeds.

BYLUND, E. (1960). Theoretical considerations regarding the distribution of settlement in inner north Sweden. *Geografiska Annaler,* **42,** 225–31.

CAESAR, A. A. L. (1955). On the economic organization of eastern Europe. *Geographical Journal,* **121,** 451–69.

CAESAR, A. A. L. (1964). Planning and the geography of Great Britain. *Advancement of Science,* **21,** 230–40.

CAIN, S. A. (1944). *Foundations of plant geography.* New York.

CAPOT-REY, R. (1944). *Géographie de la circulation sur les continents.* Paris.

CARELESS, J. S. M. (1954). Frontierism, metropolitanism, and Canadian history. *Canadian Historical Review,* **35,** 1–21.

CARROTHERS, G. P. (1956). An historic review of the gravity and potential concepts of human interaction. *Journal of the American Institute of Planners,* **22,** 94–102.

CENTRE INTERNATIONAL D'ÉTUDE DES PROBLÈMES HUMAINS (1963). *Les déplacements humains: aspects méthodologique de leur mesure.* Monaco.

CHAMBERLIN, T. C. (1897). The method of multiple working hypotheses. *Journal of Geology,* **5,** 837–48.

CHAPIN, F. S., JR., and S. F. WEISS, Editors (1962). *Urban growth dynamics in a regional cluster of cities.* New York.

CHISHOLM, M. D. I. (1959). Economies of scale in road good transport ? Off-farm milk collection in England and Wales. *Oxford Economic Papers,* **11,** 282–90.

CHISHOLM, M. D. I. (1960). The geography of commuting. *Annals of the Association of American Geographers,* **50,** 187–8, 491–2.

CHISHOLM, M. D. I. (1962). *Rural settlement and land use: an essay in location.* London.

CHORLEY, R. J. (1962). Geomorphology and general systems theory. *United States, Geological Survey, Professional Paper,* **500-B.**

CHORLEY, R. J. (1964). Geography and analogue theory. *Annals of the Association of American Geographers,* **54,** 127–37.

CHORLEY, R. J. and P. HAGGETT, Editors (1965-A). *Frontiers in geographical teaching: the Madingley lectures for 1963.* London.

CHORLEY, R. J. and P. HAGGETT (1965-B). Trend-surface mapping in geographical research. *Institute of British Geographers, Publications,* **37.**

CHORLEY, R. J. and P. HAGGETT, Editors (1967). *Models in geography: the Madingley lectures for 1965.* London.

CHORLEY, R. J., D. R. STODDART, P. HAGGETT, and H. O. SLAYMAKER. *In press.* Regional and local components in the areal distribution of surface sand-facies in the Breckland, eastern England. *Journal of Sedimentary Petrology.*

CHRISTALLER, W. (1933). *Die zentralen Orte in Süddeutschland: Eine ökonomisch-geographische Untersuchung über die Gesetzmässigkeit der Verbreitung und Entwicklung der Siedlungen mit städtischen Funktionen.* Jena.

CHRISTALLER, W. (1937). *Die ländliche Siedlungsweise im Deutschen Reich und ihre Beziehungen zur Gemeindeorganisation.* Berlin.

CHRISTALLER, W. (1938). Rapports fonctionels entre les agglomérations urbaines et les campagnes. *Congrès International de Géographie, Comptes Rendus,* **2,** 123–138.

CHRISTALLER, W. (1950). Das Grundgerüst der räumlichen Ordnung in Europa: Die Systeme der europäischen zentralen Orte. *Frankfurter Geographische Hefte,* **11.**

CLAESEN, C-F. (1964). En korologisk publikanalys: framställning av demografiska gravitationsmodeller med tillämpning vid omlandsbestamning på koordinatkarta. *Geografiska Annaler,* **46** (4).

CLARK, C. (1940). *Conditions of economic progress.* London.

CLARK, C. (1951). Urban population densities. *Journal of the Royal Statistical Society, Series A,* **114,** 490–6.

CLARK, P. J. (1956). Grouping in spatial distributions. *Science,* **123,** 373–4.

CLARK, P. J. and F. C. EVANS (1954). Distance to nearest neighbour as a measure of spatial relationships in populations. *Ecology,* **35,** 445–53.

CLAWSON, M., R. B. HELD, and C. H. STODDARD (1960). *Land for the future.* Baltimore.

COCHRAN, W. G. (1953). *Sampling techniques.* New York.

COCHRAN, W. G., F. MOSTELLER, and J. W. TUKEY (1954). Principles of sampling. *Journal of the American Statistical Association,* **49,** 13–35.

COLWELL, R. L., Editor (1960). *Manual of photographic interpretation.* New York.

COOLEY, C. H. (1894). The theory of transportation. *American Economic Association, Publications,* **9** (3).

COPPOCK, J. T. (1955). The relationship of farm and parish boundaries: a study in the use of agricultural statistics. *Geographical Studies,* **2,** 12–26.

COPPOCK, J. T. (1960). The parish as a geographical-statistical unit. *Tijdschrift voor Economische en Sociale Geografie,* **51,** 317–26.

COTTERILL, C. H. (1950). *Industrial plant location: its application to zinc smelting.* Saint Louis.

COURT, A. and P. W. PORTER (1964). The elusive point of minimum travel. *Annals of the Association of American Geographers,* **54,** 400–6.

COXETER, H. S. M. (1961). *Introduction to geometry.* New York.

CROWE, P. R. (1938). On progress in geography. *Scottish Geographical Magazine,* **54,** 1–19.

CURRY, L. (1962). The geography of service centres within towns: the elements of an operational approach. *Lund Studies in Geography, Series B, Human Geography,* **24,** 31–54.

CURRY, L. (1964-A). The random spatial economy: an exploration in settlement theory. *Annals of the Association of American Geographers,* **54,** 138–46.

CURRY, L. (1964-B). Landscape as system. *Geographical Review,* **54,** 121–4.

DACEY, M. F. (1960). The spacing of river towns. *Annals of the Association of American Geographers,* **50,** 59–61.

DACEY, M. F. (1962). Analysis of central place and point patterns by a nearest neighbour method. *Lund Studies in Geography, Series B, Human Geography,* **24,** 55–75.

DACEY, M. F. (1964). Imperfections in the uniform plane. *Michigan Inter-University Community of Mathematical Geographers, Discussion Papers*, 4.

DÅHL, S. (1957). The contacts of Västerås with the rest of Sweden. *Lund Studies in Geography, Series B, Human Geography*, 13, 206–43.

DANTZIG, G., R. FULKERSON, and S. JOHNSON (1954). Solution of a large-scale travelling-salesman problem. *Operations Research*, 2, 215–21.

DAVID, H. A. (1963). *The method of paired comparisons*. London.

DAVIES, O. L., Editor (1956). *The design and analysis of industrial experiments*. Edinburgh.

DAVIES, O. L., Editor (1958). *Statistical methods in research and production*. Edinburgh.

DAVIS, D. H. (1926). Objectives in a geographic field study of a community. *Annals of the Association of American Geographers*, 16, 102–9.

DICKINSON, G. C. (1963). *Statistical mapping and the presentation of statistics*. London.

DICKINSON, R. E. (1964). *City and region: a geographical interpretation*. London.

DUERR, W. A. (1960). *Fundamentals of forestry economics*. New York.

DUNCAN, O. D., R. P. CUZZORT, and B. DUNCAN (1961). *Statistical geography: problems of analyzing areal data*. Glencoe.

DUNN, E. S. (1954). *The location of agricultural production*. Gainesville.

DUNN, E. S. (1956). The market potential concept and the analysis of location. *Regional Science Association, Papers and Proceedings*, 2, 183–94.

DURY, G., Editor (1965). *Essays in geomorphology*. London.

EDMONSON, M. S. (1961). Neolithic diffusion rates. *Current Anthropology*, 2, 71–102.

ENKE, S. (1951). Equilibrium among spatially separated markets: solution by electric analogue. *Econometrica*, 19, 40–7.

EZEKIEL, M. and K. A. FOX (1959). *Methods of correlation and regression analysis: linear and curvilinear*. New York.

FARMER, B. H. (1957). *Pioneer peasant colonization in Ceylon*. London.

FENNEMANN, N. M. (1916). Physiographic divisions of the United States. *Annals of the Association of American Geographers*, 6, 19–98.

FISHER, J. L. (1955). Concepts in regional economic development. *Regional Science Association, Papers*, 1, W1–W20.

FISHER, R. A. and F. YATES (1957). *Statistical tables for biological, agricultural, and medical research*. Edinburgh.

FLETCHER, T. J., Editor (1964). *Some lessons in mathematics: a handbook on the teaching of 'modern' mathematics*. Cambridge.

FLOOD, M. M. (1956). The travelling salesman problem. *Journal of the Operations Research Society of America*, 4, 61–75.

FLORENCE, P. S. (1944). The selection of industries suitable for dispersal into rural areas. *Journal of the Royal Statistical Society*, 107, 93–116.

FLORENCE, P. S. (1953). *The logic of British and American industry*. London.

FOGEL, R. W. (1964). *Railroads and American economic growth: essays in econometric history*. Baltimore.

FOLGER, J. (1953). Some aspects of migration in the Tennessee valley. *American Sociological Review*, 18, 253–60.

FORGOTSON, J. M. (1960). Review and classification of quantitative mapping techniques. *Bulletin of the American Association of Petroleum Geologists*, 44, 83–100.

FOX, J. W. (1956). Land-use survey: general principles and a New Zealand example. *Auckland University College, Bulletin*, 49.

FRIEDRICH, C. J. (1929). *Alfred Weber's theory of the location of industries*. Chicago.

GARRISON, W. L. (1956). Applicability of statistical inference to geographical research. *Geographical Review*, 46, 427–9.

GARRISON, W. L. (1959–60). Spatial structure of the economy. *Annals of the Association of American Geographers*, 49, 232–9, 471–82; 50, 357–73.

GARRISON, W. L. (1960). Connectivity of the interstate highway system. *Regional Science Association, Papers and Proceedings*, 6, 121–37.

GARRISON, W. L. (1962). Towards simulation models of urban growth and development. *Lund Studies in Geography, Series B, Human Geography*, 24, 92–108.

GARRISON, W. L., Editor. *In press. Quantitative geography*. Evanston.

GARRISON, W. L., B. J. L. BERRY, D. F. MARBLE, J. D. NYSTUEN, and R. L. MORRILL (1959). *Studies of highway development and geographic change*. Seattle.

GEER, S. DE (1923). On the definition, method and classification of geography. *Geografiska Annaler*, **5**, 1–37.

GETIS, A. (1963). The determination of the location of retail activities with the use of a map transformation. *Economic Geography*, **39**, 1–22.

GIBBS, J. P., Editor (1961). *Urban research methods*. New York.

GINSBURG, N. (1961). *Atlas of economic development*. Chicago.

GODLUND, S. (1956). Bus service in Sweden. *Lund Studies in Geography, Series B, Human Geography*, **17**.

GODLUND, S. (1961). Population, regional hospitals, transport facilities and regions: planning the location of regional hospitals in Sweden. *Lund Studies in Geography, Series B, Human Geography*, **21**.

GOLDTHWAIT, J. W. (1927). A town that has gone downhill. *Geographical Review*, **17**, 527–52.

GOODRICH, C. (1936). *Migration and economic opportunity*. Philadelphia.

GOTTMANN, J. (1961). *Megalopolis: the urbanized northeastern seaboard of the United States*. New York.

GOULD, P. R. (1960). The development of the transportation pattern in Ghana. *Northwestern University, Studies in Geography*, **5**.

GOULD, P. R. (1963). Man against his environment: a game-theoretic framework. *Annals of the Association of American Geographers*, **53**, 290–7.

GRADMANN, R. (1931). *Süddeutschland*. Stuttgart.

GREEN, F. H. W. (1950). Urban hinterlands in England and Wales: an analysis of bus services. *Geographical Journal*, **96**, 64–8f1.

GREEN, H. L. (1955). Hinterland boundaries of New York city and Boston in southern New England. *Economic Geography*, **31**, 283–300.

GREENHUT, M. L. (1956). *Plant location in theory and practice: the economics of space*. Chapel Hill.

GREGOR, H. F. (1962). Agricultural region and statistical region: a dilemma in California geography. *California Geographer*, **3**, 27–31.

GREGORY, S. (1963). *Statistical methods and the geographer*. London.

GREIG-SMITH, P. (1964). *Quantitative plant ecology*. London.

GROTEWALD, A. (1959). Von Thünen in retrospect. *Economic Geography*, **35**, 346–55.

GRYTZELL, K. G. (1963). The demarcation of comparable city areas by means of population density. *Lund Studies in Geography, Series B, Human Geography*, **25**.

GULLEY, J. L. M. (1959). The Turnerian frontier: a study in the migration of ideas. *Tijdschrift voor Economische en Sociale Geografie*, **50**, 65–72, 81–91.

GUNAWARDENA, K. A. (1964). Service centres in southern Ceylon. *University of Cambridge, Ph.D. Thesis*.

HÄGERSTRAND, T. (1952). The propagation of innovation waves. *Lund Studies in Geography, Series B, Human Geography*, **4**, 3–19.

HÄGERSTRAND, T. (1953). *Innovationsforloppet ur korologisk synpunkt*. Lund.

HÄGERSTRAND, T. (1955). Statistika primäruppgifter, flykartering och data processing maskiner. *Meddelanden Frans Lunds Geografiska Institut*, **344**, 233–55.

HÄGERSTRAND, T. (1957). Migration and area: survey of a sample of Swedish migration fields and hypothetical considerations on their genesis. *Lund Studies in Geography, Series B, Human Geography*, **13**, 27–158.

HAGGETT, P. (1959). Locational, dimensional and cost-ratio variables in Portuguese industry: a matrix analysis. Mimeographed.

HAGGETT, P. (1961-A). Land use and sediment yield in an old plantation tract of the Serra do Mar, Brazil. *Geographical Journal*, **127**, 50–62.

HAGGETT, P. (1961-B). Multilevel variance analysis of *sobreiro* distribution in the Tagus–Sado basin, central Portugal. Mimeographed.

HAGGETT, P. (1963). Regional and local components in land-use sampling: a case study from the Brazilian Triangulo. *Erdkunde*, **17**, 108–14.

HAGGETT, P. (1964). Regional and local components in the distribution of forested areas in southeast Brazil: a multivariate approach. *Geographical Journal*, **130**, 365–80.

HAGGETT, P. and C. BOARD (1964). Rotational and parallel traverses in the rapid integration of geographic areas. *Annals of the Association of American Geographers*, **54**, 406–10.

HAGGETT, P. and R. J. CHORLEY. *In preparation. Network models in geography: an integrated approach*. London.

HAGGETT, P., R. J. CHORLEY, and D. R. STODDART (1965). Scale standards in geographical research: a new measure of area magnitude. *Nature*, **205**, 844–7.

HAGGETT, P. and K. A. GUNAWARDENA (1964). Determination of population thresholds for settlement functions by the Reed–Muench method. *Professional Geographer*, **16**, 6–9.

HAGOOD, M. J. (1943). Statistical methods for delineation of regions applied to data on agriculture and population. *Social Forces*, **21**, 288–97.

HAGOOD, M. J. and D. O. PRICE (1952). *Statistics for sociologists*. New York.

HALL, A. D. and R. E. FAGEN (1956). Definition of system. *General Systems Year-book*, **1**, 18–28.

HALL, P. (1962). *The industries of London since 1861*. London.

HANNERBERG, D., T. HÄGERSTRAND, and B. ODEVING (1957). Migration in Sweden: a symposium. *Lund Studies in Geography, Series B, Human Geography*, **13**.

HANSON, N. R. (1958). *Patterns of discovery*. Cambridge.

HARARAY, F. and R. Z. NORMAN (1953). *Graph theory as a mathematical model in social science*. Ann Arbor.

HARDY, T. (1886). *The life and death of the mayor of Casterbridge*. London.

HARMAN, H. H. (1960). *Modern factor analysis*. Chicago.

HARRIS, C. D. (1954). The market as a factor in the localization of industry in the United States. *Annals of the Association of American Geographers*, **44**, 315–48.

HARRIS, C. D. and E. L. ULLMANN (1945). The nature of cities. *Annals of the American Academy of Political and Social Science*, **242**, 7–17.

HART, J. F. (1954). Central tendency in areal distributions. *Economic Geography*, **30**, 48–59.

HARTSHORNE, R. (1939). *The nature of geography: a critical survey of current thought in the light of the past*. Lancaster.

HARTSHORNE, R. (1959). *Perspective on the nature of geography*. London.

HAWLEY, A. H. (1950). *Human ecology*. New York.

HELVIG, M. (1964). Chicago's external truck movements: spatial interactions between the Chicago area and its hinterland. *University of Chicago, Department of Geography, Research Paper*, **90**.

HIDORE, J. J. (1963). The relations between cash-grain farming and landforms. *Economic Geography*, **39**, 84–9.

HIGHSMITH, R. M., O. H. HEINTZELMAN, J. G. JENSEN, R. D. RUDD, and P. R. TSCHIRLEY (1961). *Case studies in world geography*. New York.

HOLLOWAY, J. L., JR. (1958). Smoothing and filtering of time series and space fields. *Advances in Geophysics*, **4**, 351–89.

HOOVER, E. M. (1936). The measurement of industrial localization. *Review of Economics and Statistics*, **18**, 162–71.

HOOVER, E. M. (1948). *The location of economic activity*. New York.

HORTON, R. E. (1945). Erosional development of streams and their drainage basins: hydrophysical approach to quantitative morphology. *Geological Society of America, Bulletin*, **56**, 275–370.

HOSKINS, W. G. (1955). *The making of the English landscape*. London.

HOTELLING, H. (1921). A mathematical theory of migration. *University of Washington, M.A. Thesis*.

HOUSE, J. W. (1953). Medium sized towns in the urban pattern of two industrial societies: England and Wales—U.S.A. *Planning Outlook*, **3,** 52–79.

HOUSTON, J. M. (1953). *Social geography of Europe*. London.

HOWARD, E. (1920). *Territory in bird life*. London.

HOWE, G. M. (1963). *National atlas of disease mortality in the United Kingdom*. London.

HOYT, H. (1939). *The structure and growth of residential neighbourhoods in American cities*. Washington.

HUFF, D. L. (1960). A topographic model of consumer space preferences. *Regional Science Association, Papers and Proceedings*, **6,** 159–73.

INTERNATIONAL GEOGRAPHICAL UNION (1964). *Abstracts of papers 20th International Geographical Congress*, London.

INTERNATIONAL URBAN RESEARCH (1959). *The world's metropolitan areas*. Berkeley.

ISARD, W. (1956). *Location and space-economy: a general theory relating to industrial location, market areas, land use, trade and urban structure*. New York.

ISARD, W., D. F. BRAMHALL, G. A. P. CARROTHERS, J. H. CUMBERLAND, L. N. MOSES, D. O. PRICE, and E. W. SCHOOLER (1960). *Methods of regional analysis: an introduction to regional science*. New York.

ISARD, W. and R. E. KUENNE (1953). The impact of steel upon the Greater New York–Philadelphia industrial region: a study in agglomeration projection. *Review of Economics and Statistics*, **35,** 289–301.

ISARD, W. and E. W. SCHOOLER (1955). *Location factors in the petrochemical industry*. Washington.

ISBELL, E. C. (1944). Internal migration in Sweden and intervening opportunities. *American Sociological Review*, **9,** 627–39.

JAMES, P. E. (1959). *Latin America*. New York.

JAMES, P. E., C. F. JONES, and J. K. WRIGHT, Editors (1954). *American geography: inventory and prospect*. Syracuse.

JEFFERS, J. N. R. (1959). *Experimental design and analysis in forest research*. Stockholm.

JENKS, G. F. (1963). Generalization in statistical mapping. *Annals of the Association of American Geographers*, **53,** 15–26.

JENKS, G. F. and M. R. C. COULSON (1963). Class intervals for statistical maps. *International Yearbook of Cartography*, **3,** 119–134.

JENSEN, M., Editor (1951). *Regionalism in America*. Madison.

JOERG, W. L. G., Editor (1932). *Pioneer settlement*. New York.

JOHNSON, B. L. C. (1958). The distribution of factory population in the West Midlands conurbations. *Institute of British Geographers, Publications*, **25,** 209–223.

JOHNSON, H. B. (1941). The distribution of German pioneer population in Minnesota. *Rural Sociology*, **6,** 16–34.

JOHNSON, H. B. (1957). Rational and ecological aspects of the quarter section: an example from Minnesota. *Geographical Review*, **47,** 330–48.

JOHNSON, H. B. (1962). A note on Thünen's circles. *Annals of the Association of American Geographers*, **52,** 213–20.

JOHNSON, W. W. (1892). *The theory of errors and method of least squares*. New York.

JOHNSSON, O. H. (1952). En stads flyttnings- och födelseortsfält. *Svensk Geografiska Arsbok*, **28,** 115–22.

JONASSON, O. (1925). Agricultural regions of Europe. *Economic Geography*, **2.**

JONES, E. (1960). *A social geography of Belfast*. London.

JONES, E. (1964). *Human geography*. London.

KAIN, J. F. (1962). The journey-to-work as a determinant of residential location. *Regional Science Association, Papers and Proceedings*, **9,** 137–59.

KANSKY, K. J. (1963). Structure of transport networks: relationships between network geometry and regional characteristics. *University of Chicago, Department of Geography, Research Papers*, **84.**

KANT, E. (1946). Den inre omflyttningen i Estland i samband med de estniska städernas omland. *Svensk Geografiska Arsbok*, **22,** 83–124.

KAO, R. C. (1963). The use of computers in the processing and analysis of geographic information. *Geographical Review*, **53**, 530–47.

KARIEL, H. G. (1963). Selected factors areally associated with population growth due to net migration. *Annals of the Association of American Geographers*, **53**, 210–23.

KATES, R. W. (1962). Hazard and choice perception in flood plain management. *University of Chicago, Department of Geography, Research Papers*, **78**.

KENDALL, M. G. (1960). New prospects in economic analysis. *Stamp Memorial Lecture*, 1960.

KENDALL, M. G. and W. R. BUCKLAND (1957). *A dictionary of statistical terms*. Edinburgh.

KERSHAW, K. A. (1964). *Quantitative and dynamic ecology*. London.

KING, L. J. (1961). A multivariate analysis of the spacing of urban settlements in the United States. *Annals of the Association of American Geographers*, **51**, 222–33.

KING, L. J. (1962). A quantitative expression of the pattern of urban settlements in selected areas of the United States. *Tijdschrift voor Economische en Sociale Geografie*, **53**, 1–7.

KLAASEN, L. H., D. H. VAN D. TORMAN, and L. M. KOYCK (1949). *Hoodflinen van de sociaal-economische anfwikkeling der gemeente Amerstoort van 1900–1970*. Leiden.

KOLLMORGEN, W. M. and G. F. JENKS (1951). A geographic study of population and settlement changes in Sherman county, Kansas. *Kansas Academy of Sciences, Transactions*, **54**, 449–94.

KOLLMORGEN, W. M. and G. F. JENKS (1958). Suitcase farming in Sully county, South Dakota. *Annals of the Association of American Geographers*, **48**, 27–40.

KOPEC, R. J. (1963). An alternative method for the construction of Thiessen polygons. *Professional Geographer*, **15** (5), 24–6.

KÖSTLER, J. (1956). *Silviculture*. Edinburgh.

KRUMBEIN, W. C. (1941). Measurement and geologic significance of shape and roundness of sedimentary particles. *Journal of Sedimentary Petrology*, **11**, 64–72.

KRUMBEIN, W. C. (1953). Latin Square experiments in sedimentary petrology. *Journal of Sedimentary Petrology*, **23**, 280–3.

KRUMBEIN, W. C. (1955-A). Composite end-members in facies mapping. *Journal of Sedimentary Petrology*, **25**, 115–22.

KRUMBEIN, W. C. (1955-B). Experimental design in the earth sciences. *Transactions of the American Geophysical Union*, **36**, 1–11.

KRUMBEIN, W. C. (1956). Regional and local components in facies maps. *Bulletin of the American Association of Petroleum Geologists*, **40**, 2163–94.

KRUMBEIN, W. C. (1957). Comparison of percentage and ratio data in facies mapping. *Journal of Sedimentary Petrology*, **27**, 293–7.

KRUMBEIN, W. C. (1959-A). The 'sorting out' of geological variables illustrated by regression analysis of the factors controlling beach firmness. *Journal of Sedimentary Petrology*, **29**, 575–87.

KRUMBEIN, W. C. (1959-B). Trend surface analysis of contour-type maps with irregular control-point spacing. *Journal of Geophysical Research*, **64**, 823–34.

KRUMBEIN, W. C. (1960). The geological 'population' as a framework for analysing numerical data in geology. *Liverpool and Manchester Geological Journal*, **2**, 341–68.

KRUMBEIN, W. C. and H. A. SLACK (1956). Statistical analysis of low-level radioactivity of Pennsylvania black fissile shale in Illinois. *Bulletin of the Geological Society of America*, **67**, 739–62.

KULLDORFF, G. (1955). Migration probabilities. *Lund Studies in Geography, Series B, Human Geography*, **14**.

LALANNE, L. (1863). Essai d'une théorie des réseaux de chemin de fer, fondée sur l'observation des faits et sur les lois primordiales qui président au groupement des populations. *Comptes Rendus Hebdomadaires des Séances de l'Académie des Sciences*, **42**. 206–10.

LANGBEIN, W. B. and W. G. HOYT (1959). *Water facts for the nation's future: uses and benefits of hydrological data problems.* New York.

LANGER, S. K. (1953). *An introduction to symbolic logic.* New York.

LATHAM, J. P. (1962). Methodology for instrumented geographic analysis. *Office of Naval Research, Contract NONR 3004(01), Technical Report,* **2.**

LEARMONTH, A. T. A. and M. N. PAL (1959). A method of plotting two variables on the same map, using isopleths. *Erdkunde,* **13,** 145–50.

LEOPOLD, L. B. and W. B. LANGBEIN (1962). The concept of entropy in landscape evolution. *United States, Geological Survey, Professional Papers,* **500-A.**

LEOPOLD, L. B., M. G. WOLMAN, and J. P. MILLER (1964). *Fluvial processes in geomorphology.* San Francisco.

LINDBERGH, O. (1953). An economic geographic study of the Swedish paper industry. *Geografiska Annaler,* **35,** 28–40.

LINTON, D. L. (1949). The delimitation of morphological regions. *Institute of British Geographers. Publications,* **14,** 86–7.

LOPIK, J. R. VAN (1962). Optimum utilization of airborne sensors in military geography. *Photogrammetric Engineering,* **28,** 773–8.

LÖSCH, A. (1938). The nature of economic regions. *Southern Economic Journal,* **5,** 71–8.

LÖSCH, A. (1940). *Die räumliche Ordnung der Wirtschaft.* Jena.

LÖSCH, A. (1954). *The economics of location.* New Haven.

LUTTRELL, W. F. (1962). *Factory location and industrial movement.* London.

McCARTY, H. H. (1956). Use of certain statistical procedures in geographical-analysis. *Annals of the Association of American Geographers,* **46,** 263.

McCARTY, H. H., J. C. HOOK, and D. S. KNOS (1956). The measurement of association in industrial geography. *State University of Iowa, Department of Geography, Report,* **1.**

McCASKILL, M., Editor (1962). *Land and livelihood: geographical essays in honour of George Jobberns.* Christchurch.

MACH, E. (1942). *The science of mechanics.* La Salle, Ill.

MACKAY, J. R. (1953). The alternative choice in isopleth interpolation. *Professional Geographer,* **5,** 2–4.

MACKAY, J. R. (1958-A). The interactance hypothesis and boundaries in Canada. *Canadian Geographer,* **11,** 1–8.

MACKAY, J. R. (1958-B). Chi-square as a tool for regional studies. *Annals of the Association of American Geographers,* **48,** 164.

McKENZIE, R. D. (1933). *The metropolitan community.* New York.

MACKINDER, H. J. (1904). The geographical pivot of history. *Geographical Journal,* **23,** 421–37.

McLAUGHLIN, G. E. and S. ROBOCK (1949). *Why industry moves south.* Kingsport.

MAHALANOBIS, P. C., C. R. RAO, and D. M. MAJUMDAR (1949). Anthropometric survey of the United Provinces, 1941: a statistical study. *Sankhya,* **9,** 89–324.

MARCH, J. G. and H. A. SIMON (1958). *Organizations.* New York.

MARSH, G. P. (1864). *Man and nature; or physical geography as modified by human action.* New York.

MARTHE, F. (1878). Begriff, Ziel und Methode der Geographie. *Geographisches Jahrbuch,* **7,** 628.

MAYFIELD, R. C. (1962). Conformation of service and retail activities: an example in lower orders of an urban hierarchy, in a lesser developed area. *Lund Studies in Geography, Series B, Human Geography,* **24,** 77–90.

MEAD, W. R. (1953). *Farming in Finland.* London.

MEAD, W. R. and E. H. BROWN (1962). *The United States and Canada.* London.

MEINIG, D. W. (1962). A comparative historical geography of two railnets: Columbia basin and South Australia. *Annals of the Association of American Geographers,* **52,** 394–413.

MEITZEN, A. (1895). *Siedlung und Agrarwesen der Westgermanen und Ostgermanen des Kelten, Römer, Finen und Slawen.* Three volumes; one atlas. Berlin.

MELTON, M. A. (1960). Intravalley variation in slope angles related to micro-climate and erosional environment. *Bulletin of the Geological Society of America*, **71**, 133–44.

MEYER, J. (1963). Regional economics: a survey. *American Economic Review*, **53**, 19–54.

MEYNEN, E. (1960). *Orbis geographicus, 1960*. Wiesbaden.

MIEHLE, W. (1958). Link-length minimization in networks. *Operations Research*, **6**, 232–43.

MIKESELL, M. W. (1960). Comparative studies in frontier history. *Annals of the Association of American Geographers*, **50**, 62–74.

MILL, J. S. (1874). *A system of logic*. London.

MILLER, A. A. (1949). The dissection and analysis of maps. *Institute of British Geographers, Publications*, **14**, 1–13.

MILLER, R. L. and R. S. KAHN (1962). *Statistical analysis in the geological sciences*. New York.

MINISTRY OF TRANSPORT (1961). *Rural bus services: report of the committee*. London.

MINISTRY OF TRANSPORT (1953). *Traffic in towns: a study of the long term problems of traffic in urban areas*. London.

MITCHELL, J. B. (1954). *Historical geography*. London.

MOMBEIG, P. (1952). *Pionniers et planteurs de São Paulo*. Paris.

MORGENSTERN, O. (1963). *On the accuracy of economic observations*. Princeton.

MORRILL, R. L. (1962). Simulation of central place patterns over time. *Lund Studies in Geography, Series B, Human Geography*, **24**, 109–20.

MORRILL, R. L. (1963). The development and spatial distribution of towns in Sweden: an historical-predictive approach. *Annals of the Association of American Geographers*, **53**, 1–14.

MOSER, C. A. and W. SCOTT (1961). *British towns: a statistical study of their social and economic differences*. Edinburgh.

MURRAY, M. (1962). The geography of death in England and Wales. *Annals of the Association of American Geographers*, **52**, 130–49.

MUTH, R. F. (1961). Economic change and rural–urban land use conversions. *Econometrica*, **29**, 1–23.

MUTH, R. F. (1962). The spatial structure of the housing market. *Regional Science Association, Papers and Proceedings*, **7**, 207–20.

NETTLETON, L. L. (1954). Regionals, residuals, and structures. *Geophysics*, **19**, 1–22.

NEUMAN, J. VON and O. MORGENSTERN (1944). *Theory of games and economic behaviour*. Princeton.

NEYMAN, J. and E. L. SCOTT (1957). On a mathematical theory of population conceived as a conglomeration of clusters. *Cold Spring Harbor Symposia on Quantitative Biology*, **22**, 109–20.

NEYMAN, J., E. L. SCOTT, and C. D. SHANE (1956). Statistics of images of galaxies with particular reference to clustering. *Third Berkeley Symposium on Mathematical Statistics and Probability, Proceedings*, **3**, 75–111.

NORDBECK, S. (1962). Location of areal data for computer processing. *Lund Studies in Geography, Series C, General and Mathematical*, **2**.

NYSTUEN, J. D. and M. F. DACEY (1961). A graph theory interpretation of nodal regions. *Regional Science Association, Papers and Proceedings*, **7**, 29–42.

OFFICE OF STATISTICAL STANDARDS (1958). *Criteria for defining Standard Metropolitan Areas*. Washington.

OHLIN, B. (1933). *Interregional and international trade*. Cambridge, Mass.

OLSON, E. C. and R. L. MILLER (1958). *Morphological integration*. Chicago.

OLSON, J. S. and P. E. POTTER (1954). Variance components of cross-bedding direction in some basal Pennsylvanian sandstones of the Eastern Interior Basin: statistical methods. *Journal of Geology*, **62**, 26–49.

PARK, R. E. (1929). Urbanization as measured by newspaper circulation. *American Journal of Sociology*, **35**, 60–79.

PARSONS, J. J. (1949). Antioqueño colonization in western Colombia: an historical geography. *Ibero-Americana*, **32**, 1–225.

PASSARGE, S. (1929). *Beschreibende Landschaftskunde*. Hamburg.

PATERSON, J. H. (1960). *North America: a regional geography*. Oxford.

PATTISON, W. D. (1957). Beginnings of the American rectangular land survey system, 1784–1800. *University of Chicago, Department of Geography, Research Papers*, **50**.

PEARSON, K. (1901). On lines and planes of closest fit to systems of points in space. *Philosophical Magazine*, 6th Series, **2**, 559–72.

PELTO, C. R. (1954). Mapping of multicomponent systems. *Journal of Geology*, **62**, 501–11.

PERLOFF, H. S. (1957). *Regional studies at U.S. universities*. Washington.

PERRING, F. H. and S. M. WALTERS (1962). *Atlas of the British flora*. London.

PETTIJOHN, F. J. (1957). *Sedimentary rocks*. New York.

PHILBRICK, A. K. (1957). Principles of areal functional organization in regional human geography. *Economic Geography*, **33**, 299–336.

PLATT, R. S. (1942). *Latin America: countrysides and united regions*. New York.

PLATT, R. S. (1959). Field study in American geography: the development of theory and method exemplified by selections. *University of Chicago, Department of Geography, Research Papers*, **61**.

PONSARD, C. (1955). *Economie et éspace: essai d'intégration du facteur spatial dans l'analyse économique*. Paris.

POPPER, K. R. (1959). *The logic of scientific discovery*. London.

PORTER, P. W. (1960). Earnest and the Orephagians: a fable for the instruction of young geographers. *Annals of the Association of American Geographers*, **50**, 297–9.

PORTER, P. W. (1963). What is the point of minimum aggregate travel? *Annals of the Association of American Geographers*, **53**, 224–32.

POSTAN, M. (1948). The revulsion from thought. *Cambridge Journal*, **1**, 395–408.

POUNDS, N. J. G. (1959). *The geography of iron and steel*. London.

PRED, A. (1964). The intrametropolitan location of American manufacturing. *Annals of the Association of American Geographers*, **54**, 165–80.

QUANT, R. E. (1960). Models of transportation and optimal network construction. *Journal of Regional Science*, **2**, 27–45.

QUENOUILLE, M. H. (1949). Problems in plane sampling. *Annals of Mathematical Statistics*, **20**, 355–75.

RAVENSTEIN, E. G. (1885), (1889). The laws of migration. *Journal of the Royal Statistical Society*, **48**, 52.

REED, L. J. and H. MUENCH (1938). A simple method of estimating fifty per cent endpoints. *American Journal of Hygiene*, **27**, 493–7.

REILLY, W. J. (1929). Methods for the study of retail relationships. *University of Texas, Bulletin*, **2944**.

REYNOLDS, R. B. (1956). Statistical methods in geographical research. *Geographical Review*, **46**, 129–32.

ROBBINS, L. (1935). *An essay on the nature and significance of economic science*. London.

ROBINSON, A. H. (1956). The necessity of weighting values in correlation of areal data. *Annals of the Association of American Geographers*, **46**, 233–6.

ROBINSON, A. H. (1960). *Elements of cartography*. New York.

ROBINSON, A. H. (1961-A). On perks and pokes. *Economic Geography*, **37**, 181–3.

ROBINSON, A. H. (1961-B). The cartographic representation of the statistical surface. *International Yearbook of Cartography*, **1**, 53–63.

ROBINSON, A. H. (1962). Mapping the correspondence of isarithmic maps. *Annals of the Association of American Geographers*, **52**, 414–25.

ROBINSON, A. H. and R. A. BRYSON (1957). A method for describing quantitatively the correspondence of geographical distributions. *Annals of the Association of American Geographers*, **47**, 379–91.

ROBINSON, A. H., J. B. LINDBERG, and L. W. BRINKMAN (1961). A correlation and regression analysis applied to rural farm population densities in the Great Plains. *Annals of the Association of American Geographers*, **51**, 211–21.

RODGERS, A. (1952). Industrial inertia: a major factor in the location of the steel industry in the United States. *Geographical Review*, **42**, 56–66.

ROGERS, E. M. (1962). *Diffusion of innovations*. New York.

ROSTOW, W. W. (1960). *The stages of economic growth*. Cambridge.

ROSTOW, W. W., Editor (1963). *The economics of take-off into sustained growth*. London.

SANDNER, G. (1961). Agrarkolonisation in Costa Rica: Siedlung, Wirtschaft und Sozialfüge an der Pioniergrenze. *Schriften des Geographischen Instituts der Universität Kiel*, **19**.

SAUER, C. O. (1920). *The geography of the Ozark highland of Missouri*. Chicago.

SAUER, C. O. (1925). The morphology of landscape. *University of California, Publications in Geography*, **2**, 19–53.

SAUER, C. O. (1952). Agricultural origins and dispersals. *American Geographical Society, Bowman Memorial Lectures*, **2**.

SCHAEFER, F. K. (1953). Exceptionalism in geography: a methodological examination. *Annals of the Association of American Geographers*, **43**, 226–49.

SCHEIDEGGER, A. E. (1961). *Theoretical geomorphology*. Berlin.

SCHMID, C. F. and E. H. MacCANNELL (1955). Basic problems, techniques, and theory of isopleth mapping. *Journal of the American Statistical Association*, **50**, 220–39.

SEARS, F. W. and M. W. ZEMANSKY (1964). *University physics*. Reading, Mass.

SEBESTYEN, G. S. (1962). *Decision-making processes in pattern recognition*. London.

SEMPLE, E. C. (1911). *Influences of geographic environment on the basis of Ratzel's system of anthropo-geography*. New York.

SIEGEL, S. (1956). *Nonparametric statistics for the behavioral sciences*. New York.

SILK, J. A. (1965). Road network of Monmouthshire. *University of Cambridge, Department of Geography, B.A. Dissertation*.

SIMON, H. A. (1955). On a class of skew distribution functions. *Biometrika*, **42**, 425–40.

SIMON, H. A. (1957). *Models of man*. New York.

SINNHUBER, K. A. (1954). Central Europe–Mitteleuropa–Europe Central: an analysis of a geographical term. *Institute of British Geographers, Publications*, **20**, 15–39.

SKILLING, H. (1964). An operational view. *American Scientist*, **52**, 388A–396A.

SMAILES, A. E. (1946). The urban mesh of England and Wales. *Institute of British Geographers, Publications*, **11**, 87–101.

SMITH, W. (1953). *An economic geography of Great Britain*. London.

SMITH, W. (1955). The location of industry. *Institute of British Geographers, Publications*, **21**, 1–18.

SOCIETY FOR EXPERIMENTAL BIOLOGY (1960). *Models and analogues in biology*. Cambridge.

SORRE, M. (1947–52). *Les Fondements de la géographie humaine*. Three volumes. Paris.

SORRE, M. (1961). *L'homme sur la terre*. Paris.

SPATE, O. H. K. (1952). Toynbee and Huntington: a study in determinism. *Geographical Journal*, **118**, 406–24.

SPATE, O. H. K. (1960). Quantity and quality in geography. *Annals of the Association of American Geographers*, **50**, 377–94.

SPECHT, R. E. (1959). *A functional analysis of the Green Bay and Western Railroad*. Stevens Point.

SPENCER, J. E. and R. J. HORVATH (1963). How does an agricultural region originate? *Annals of the Association of American Geographers*, **53**, 74–92.

STAFFORD, H. A., JR. (1963). The functional bases of small towns. *Economic Geography*, **39**, 165–75.

STAMP, L. D. and S. W. WOOLDRIDGE, Editors (1951). *London essays in Geography*. London.

STANISLAWSKI, D. (1946). The origin and spread of the grid-pattern town. *Geographical Review*, **36**, 105–20.

STEIN, S. J. (1957). *Vassouras: a Brazilian coffee county, 1850–1900*. Cambridge, Mass.

STEVENS, B. H. (1961). An application of game theory to a problem in locational strategy. *Regional Science Association, Papers and Proceedings*, **7**, 143–57.

STEWART, C. T., JR. (1958). The size and spacing of cities. *Geographical Review*, **48**, 222–45.

STEWART, J. Q. (1950). The development of social physics. *American Journal of Physics*, **18**, 239–53.

STEWART, J. Q. and W. WARNTZ (1958). Macrogeography and social science. *Geographical Review*, **48**, 167–84.

STODDART, D. R. (1965). Geography and the ecological approach: the ecosystem as a geographic principle and method. *Geography*, **50.**

STOUFFER, S. A. (1940). Intervening opportunities: a theory relating mobility and distance. *American Sociological Review*, **5**, 845–67.

STOUFFER. S. A. (1962). *Social research to test ideas*. New York.

STRAHLER, A. N. (1954). Statistical analysis in geomorphic research. *Journal of Geology*, **62**, 1–25.

SVIATLOVSKY, E. E. and W. C. EELLS (1937). The centrographic method and regional analysis. *Geographical Review*, **27**, 240–54.

TAAFFE, E. J., R. L. MORRILL, and P. R. GOULD (1963). Transport expansion in underdeveloped countries: a comparative analysis. *Geographical Review*, **53**, 503–29.

THATCHER, W. S. (1949). *Economic geography*. London.

THEODORSON, G. A., Editor (1961). *Studies in human ecology*. Evanston.

THOMAS, D. (1963). *Agriculture in Wales during the Napoleonic Wars: a study in the geographical interpretation of historical sources*. Cardiff.

THOMAS, E. N. (1960). Maps of residuals from regressions: their characteristics and uses in geographic research. *State University of Iowa, Department of Geography, Report*, **2.**

THOMAS, E. N. (1961). Towards an expanded central place model. *Geographical Review*, **51**, 400–11.

THOMAS, E. N. (1962). The stability of distance–population size relationships for Iowa towns from 1900 to 1950. *Lund Studies in Geography, Series B, Human Geography*, **24**, 13–30.

THOMAS, F. H. (1960). The Denver and Rio Grande Western Railroad: a geographic analysis. *Northwestern University, Studies in Geography*, **4.**

THOMAS, W. L., JR., Editor (1956). *Man's role in changing the face of the earth*. Chicago.

THOMPSON, D'ARCY W. (1917; abrid. edit. 1961). *On growth and form*. Cambridge.

THOMPSON, J. H., S. C. SUFRIN, P. R. GOULD, and M. A. BUCK (1962). Toward a geography of economic health: the case of New York state. *Annals of the Association of American Geographers*, **52**, 1–20.

THOMPSON, W. R. (1957). The coefficient of localization: an appraisal. *Southern Economic Journal*, **23**, 320–5.

THÜNEN, J. H. VON (1875). *Der Isolierte Staat in Beziehung auf Landwirtschaft und Nationalökonomie*. Hamburg.

TOBLER, W. R. (1959). Automation and cartography. *Geographical Review*, **44**, 536–44.

TOBLER, W. R. (1963). Geographic area and map projections. *Geographical Review*, **53**, 59–78.

TOULMIN, S. (1953). *The philosophy of science*. London.

TROXEL, E. (1955). *Economics of transport*. New York.

TURNER, F. J. (1920). *The frontier in American history*. New York.

TWAIN, M. (1896). *Tom Sawyer abroad*. New York.

UKWU, U. I. (1965). Markets in Iboland, eastern Nigeria. *University of Cambridge, Ph.D. Thesis*.

ULLMAN, E. L. (1949). The railroad pattern of the United States. *Geographical Review*, **39**, 242–56.

ULLMAN, E. L. (1957). *American commodity flow: a geographic interpretation of rail and water traffic based on principles of spatial interchange*. Seattle.

ULLMAN, E. L. and M. F. DACEY (1962). The minimum requirements approach to the urban economic base. *Lund Studies in Geography, Series B, Human Geography*, **24**, 121–43.

UNSTEAD, J. F. (1933). A system of regional geography. *Geography*, 18, 175–87.

VAHL, M. and J. HUMLUM (1949). Vahl's climatic zones and biochores. *Acta Jutlandica, Aarsskrift for Aarhus Universitet*, **21** (N6).

VAJDA, S. (1961). *The theory of games and linear programming*. London.

VALKENBURG, S. VAN and C. C. HELD (1952). *Europe*. New York.

VALVANIS, S. (1955). Lösch on location. *American Economic Review*, **45**, 637–44.

VANCE, J. E., JR. (1960). Labor-shed, employment field, and dynamic analysis in urban geography. *Economic Geography*, **36**, 189–220.

VANCE, J. E., JR. (1961). The Oregon Trail and the Union Pacific Railroad: a contrast in purpose. *Annals of the Association of American Geographers*, **51**, 357–79.

VANCE, J. E., JR. (1962). Emerging patterns of commercial structure in American cities. *Lund Studies in Geography, Series B, Human Geography*, **24**, 485–518.

VIDAL DE LA BLACHE, P. (1917). *La France de l'est*. Paris.

VIDAL DE LA BLACHE, P. (1922). *Principes de géographie humaine* Paris.

VINING, R. (1953). Delimitation of economic areas: statistical conceptions in the study of the spatial structure of an economic system. *Journal of the American Statistical Association*, **18**, 44–64.

VINING, R. (1955). A description of certain spatial aspects of an economic system. *Economic Development and Cultural Change*, **3**, 147–95.

WAIBEL, L. (1958). *Capítulos de geografia tropical e do Brasil*. Rio de Janeiro.

WALTERS, S. M. (1957). Mapping the distribution of plants. *New Biology*, **24**, 93–108.

WARNTZ, W. (1959). *Toward a geography of price*. Philadelphia.

WARNTZ, W. (1961). Transatlantic flights and pressure patterns. *Geographical Review*, **51**, 187–212.

WARNTZ, W. and D. NEFT (1960). Contributions to a statistical methodology for areal distributions. *Journal of Regional Science*, 2, 47–66.

WATSON, J. W. (1955). Geography: a discipline in distance. *Scottish Geographical Magazine*, **71**, 1–13.

WEAVER, J. C. (1954). Crop combination regions in the Middle West. *Geographical Review*, **44**, 175–200.

WEAVER, J. C. (1956). The county as a spatial average in agricultural geography. *Geographical Review*, **46**, 536–65.

WEBB, W. P. (1927). *The Great Plains*. New York.

WEBER, A. (1909). *Über den Standort der Industrien*. Tübingen.

WELLINGTON, A. M. (1886). The American line from Vera Cruz to the city of Mexico, via Jalapa, with notes on the best methods of surmounting high elevations by rail. *American Society of Civil Engineers, Transactions*, **20**.

WELLINGTON, A. M. (1887). *The economic theory of the location of railways*. New York.

WHITTEN, E. H. T. (1959). Composition trends in a granite: modal variation and ghost stratigraphy in part of the Donegal granite. *Journal of Geophysical Research*, **64**, 835–48.

WHITTLESEY, D. (1956). Southern Rhodesia: an African compage. *Annals of the Association of American Geographers*, 46, 1–97.

WILLIAMS, W. T. and J. M. LAMBERT (1959–62). Multivariate methods in plant ecology. *Journal of Ecology*, **47**, 83–101; **48**, 689–710; **49**, 717–29; **50**, 775–802.

WINSBOROUGH, H. H. (1961). A comparative study of urban population densities. *University of Chicago, Ph.D. Thesis*.

WISE, M. J. (1949). On the evolution of the jewellery and gun quarters in Birmingham. *Institute of British Geographers, Publications,* **15,** 57–72.

WOLFE, R. I. (1961). Transportation and politics: the example of Canada. *Annals of the Association of American Geographers,* **52,** 176–90.

WOLFE, R. I. (1963). *Transportation and politics.* Princeton.

WOLPERT, J. (1964). The decision process in spatial context. *Annals of the Association of American Geographers,* **54,** 537–58.

WOOD, W. F. (1955). Use of stratified random samples in land use study. *Annals of the Association of American Geographers,* **45,** 350–67.

WOODWARD, M. I. J. (1963). Geographical effects of building the Tamar road bridge. *University of Cambridge, Department of Geography, B.A. Dissertation.*

WOOLF, H., Editor (1961). *Quantification: a history of the meaning of measurement in the natural and social sciences.* Indianapolis.

WYNNE-EDWARDS, V. C. (1962). *Animal dispersion in relation to social behaviour.* Edinburgh.

YATES, F. (1960). *Sampling methods for censuses and surveys.* London.

YEATES, M. (1963). Hinterland delimitation: a distance minimizing approach. *Professional Geographer,* **15** (6), 7–10.

YUILL, R. S. (1965). A simulation study of barrier effects in spatial diffusion problems. *Michigan Inter-University Community of Mathematical Geographers, Discussion Papers,* **5.**

ZIPF, G. K. (1949). *Human behaviour and the principle of least effort.* Cambridge.

ZOBLER, L. (1957). Statistical testing of regional boundaries. *Annals of the Association of American Geographers,* **47,** 83–95.

ZOBLER, L. (1958). Decision making in regional construction. *Annals of the Association of American Geographers,* **48,** 140–8.

Further Reading

To add a section on further reading to an extended list of references (given on pages 311–326) may appear to be gilding the lily. None the less it is arguable that a list which derives from the reasonable need to document the many and varied sources from which the notes for this book were assembled is not likely to be very helpful to the student who is looking for some more limited or basic reading or wishes to keep up to date on current trends.

(a) *Basic reading.* If we may assume that the student is already familiar with the traditional literature of regional and human geography then very good starting points are provided by HOOVER (1948)* over the whole range of locational theory and by CHISHOLM (1962) and by ESTALL & BUCHANAN (*Industrial activity and economic geography*, 1961) over agricultural and industrial location respectively. BUNGE (1962) also provides a lively, stimulating and unusual approach to locational analysis from a strongly geometrical viewpoint. Students unfamiliar with more conventional geographical writing will find that HARTSHORNE (1959) gives a scholarly review of the aims, methods, and problems of the subject, while THOMAS (1956) and ALEXANDER (1963) are substantive studies of primary importance in human geography.

(b) *Advanced reading.* A number of the classic studies in locational theory—notably those of LÖSCH (1954) and Christaller (BASKIN, 1957)—are available in translation. Most of the early contributions have been summarized and greatly extended and developed by ISARD (1956) in what is probably the best advanced textbook in the field. For agricultural location ALONSO (*Location and land use,* 1964) is essential reading; GREENHUT (1956) is correspondingly useful for industrial location.

There is no single source for methods in locational analysis, although that by Isard (ISARD *et al.,* 1960) comes nearest. There are a variety of texts on statistical analysis of varying degrees of difficulty and relevance to areal analysis: they have been discussed in detail in the text (pp. 286–7). Standard cartographic procedures are well described in MONKHOUSE & WILKINSON (*Maps and diagrams,* 1964). Probably the most important reading here for student geographers is concerned with the whole strategy of scientific method rather than the tactics of individual tests: TOULMIN (1953) and HANSON (1958) provide excellent, uncomplicated introductions to this field, and POPPER (1959) a standard work of immense importance.

(c) *Current research.* The rapid rate of evolution of locational studies and the introduction of wholly new methods (e.g. Markov chains) means that journals are as important as textbooks if a student is to retain a reasonably contemporary view of the subject. Editorial policies are rapidly changing and even some of the more traditional geographical journals now carry occasional papers of locational importance. However the key journals, as judged on their content to 1964, are the ANNALS OF THE ASSOCIATION OF AMERICAN GEOGRAPHERS (Quarterly) followed in order of importance by the LUND STUDIES IN GEOGRAPHY—SERIES B & C (Occasional), the Regional Science Association's PAPERS AND PROCEEDINGS (Annual), and the GEOGRAPHICAL REVIEW (Quarterly). In addition to these formal periodicals a number of universities publish research theses (the Chicago Department of Geography has an outstanding series) and informal

* Full titles are given only where books have *not* been previously mentioned in the text.

discussion papers (like the intriguing series published by the Michigan Inter-University Community of Mathematical Geographers) which are important sources of ideas. Most difficult to keep track of are the Contract Reports of research done for government bodies (e.g. the Office of Naval Research in the United States) although these often emerge later as papers in the standard journals.

(*d*) *Research 'readers'*. One useful substitute for the student with access to a limited periodicals library is the research 'reader'—a collection of research papers on a specific topic drawn from a wide range of journals. Many items of locational interest are included in FRIEDMANN & ALONSO (*Regional development and planning: a reader*, 1964), MAYER & KOHN (*Readings in urban geography*, 1959), WAGNER & MIKESELL (*Readings in cultural geography*, 1962) and BURTON & KATES (*Readings in resource management and conservation*, 1965). Many of the methods of analysis described in the second part of this book are illustrated in BERRY & MARBLE (*Spatial analysis: readings in statistical geography*. In press).

Locational Index

References to places mentioned in the text are listed under their specific location. Countries or equivalent units are given in small capitals (e.g. UNITED STATES) and settlements, regardless of population size, are given in italics (e.g. *Rio de Janeiro*)

General Index

In view of the detailed lists of contents and the extensive use of cross-references the index to the subject matter of the text is abbreviated with major topics in small capitals (e.g. DIFFUSION MODELS). In the references to authors, these are given in italics (e.g. *N. Abramson*); the index lists both names in the case of work by two authors but only the first name where a work is by more than two authors.